380.5
B67

D1035055

WITHDRAWN

Introduction to Transportation

Introduction to

DONALD J. BOWERSOX
Michigan State University

PAT J. CALABRO
The University of Texas at Arlington

GEORGE D. WAGENHEIM
Michigan State University

Transportation

Macmillan Publishing Co., Inc.
New York
Collier Macmillan Publishers
London

Macmillan Publishing Co., Inc.
866 Third Avenue, New York, New York 10022

Collier Macmillan Canada, Ltd.

Library of Congress Cataloging in Publication Data
Bowersox, Donald J
    Introduction to transportation.

    Includes index.
    1. Transportation.   2. Transportation—United
States.   I. Calabro, Pat J., joint author.   II. Wagenheim, George D., joint author.   III. Title.
HE151.B755   1981   380.5   80-10582
ISBN 0-02-313030-X

Printing: 1 2 3 4 5 6 7 8   Year: 1 2 3 4 5 6 7

Photo Credits:

Title spread: American Trucking Associations, Inc.

Part I (p. 1): American Airlines

Part II (p. 45): Association of American Railroads

Part III (p. 143): American Airlines

Part IV (p. 217): The American Waterways Operators, Inc.

Part V (p. 339): Alyeska Pipeline Service Co. and American Petroleum Institute Photographic and Film Services

Preface

During the 1980s transportation will become more dynamic than in the past. Such change will have a direct effect on society's well-being because of new attitudes regarding how transportation is being viewed from a managerial and regulatory viewpoint. *Introduction to Transportation* has been written to provide a foundation for understanding the United States transportation system. The text material assumes no prior transportation education. The development initially provides the reader a background exposure of the role, scope, and history of transportation through a study of each major type of movement available to users. Next, attention is directed to the role of government. The treatment concludes with coverage of transportation management. In total, the reader is provided with an exploratory coverage of each type of transportation. It is expected that this approach will furnish a solid foundation for the understanding of commercial transportation.

Introduction to Transportation is the result of the efforts of many individuals and organizations too numerous to detail. The authors wish to acknowledge all who contributed to the text. Their patience and thoughtfulness have been invaluable. We wish to single out the contributions of Felicia Kramer, who served as coordinator of manuscript preparation. With so much available assistance, it is difficult to offer any excuse for the shortcomings that might follow. However, such faults are solely the responsibility of the authors. A final expression of gratitude is extended to our families, who offered encouragement and support necessary for the completion of this work.

D.J.B.

P.J.C.

G.D.W.

Contents

List of Tables

List of Figures

one

Transportation
Overview

The overall role of transportation in our society must be understood before individual parts of the transportation system can be studied. Transportation pervades all commercial activities and is integral to the high standard of living that United States citizens enjoy. Once its significance and pervasiveness are understood within a broad framework, transportation's importance to social, cultural, and economic development can be appreciated.

Chapter 1 examines the scope of transportation and introduces a framework for study that is followed throughout the text. The elements of transportation and the external forces that influence its operations are introduced.

Transportation's impact on the economy and its relationship to continued growth and development are explored in Chapter 2. A complete understanding of any topic requires an examination of its history. Chapter 3 reviews transportation's historical development in the United States by time periods from its early decades to the present. The significant historical accomplishments provide a foundation for studying the individual elements of the freight transportation system in Part II.

1

The Scope of Transportation

DEFINITION

DIVIDING THE TRANSPORTATION FUNCTION
Passenger Transportation
Freight Transportation

FRAMEWORK FOR STUDY

THE TRANSPORTATION SYSTEM
Freight Carriers
Management

EXTERNAL FORCES ON TRANSPORTATION
Legal and Regulatory Environments
Common Carriers
Contract Carriers
Private Carriers
Regulatory Environment
Transport Users
Government
Industry
Consumers

TRANSPORTATION SYSTEM ACHIEVEMENTS

SUMMARY

Transportation is fundamental to the development and operation of an industrial society. It permits the specialization of work effort necessary to achieve efficiency and productivity. Geographically distant resources become accessible with transportation. The economic growth of any society in any part of the world is directly related to the availability of transportation. Without question, a society without an advanced transportation system remains primitive.

In the United States, transportation has been integral to our social, political, and economic development. Without it, the United States would not have been settled, the revolution would not have been fought, and we would not have achieved the life-style we enjoy today. No matter where we turn, transportation is involved in our daily lives. The clothes we wear, the food we eat, the entertainment we seek, and the homes we live in are all available because of

3

transportation. Transportation contributes immeasurably to our personal well-being and to society in general. Given its importance to us, a thorough understanding of the transportation system and how it operates is essential for all potential business managers. The purpose of this book is to begin your development of such an understanding.

Transportation services are divided into two major categories: (1) the movement of materials and products (freight), and (2) the movement of people (passenger). The study of transportation necessarily involves an explanation of the transportation system, an understanding of the forces that shape it, and a discussion of what it accomplishes. A suitable starting point for developing an understanding of this diverse and complex field is a formal definition.

Definition

In a broad sense, transportation is defined as the movement of freight and passengers from one location to another. One of the many dictionary definitions for transportation calls it "a means of conveyance or travel from one place to another."[1] The important common element in any definition of transportation, however, is *movement:* changing the physical location of freight or passengers. Products must be moved to the locations where they are needed and wanted, such as groceries moved to a supermarket. You, in turn, must use some form of movement to get to the supermarket to buy the groceries you want and need.

Dividing the Transportation Function

This book focuses on the study of freight transportation. Before discussing the freight system, however, a few observations about passenger movement will provide a better overall appreciation of the field.

PASSENGER TRANSPORTATION

Passenger transportation includes private transportation such as automobiles or airplanes, and various forms of public transportation. Typical means of public transportation are buses, trains, airplanes, streetcars, and such waterway

[1] *Webster's New Collegiate Dictionary*, College Ed., (1976), s.v. "Transportation."

4

vessels as ferry boats, ocean liners, and cruise ships. Each form of private and public transportation has its own application and significance for passenger travel.

At the present time, a great deal of attention is being given to the problem of passenger mass transit in urban areas for a variety of social and energy conservation reasons. A steadily increasing population brings with it a desire for more and more private automobiles. The result has been increased congestion as greater numbers of automobiles vie for limited roads and parking spaces. Faced with this growing problem, local governments are trying to develop transportation alternatives to help alleviate urban congestion. Programs such as car pooling and fast-moving highway lanes for multiple-occupant automobiles are being developed. In addition, new public passenger transportation systems have been introduced in several major cities to reduce reliance on private transportation. A good example is San Francisco's Bay Area Rapid Transit (BART) system.

The field of passenger movement, a major component of the nation's transportation network, commands study and attention in its own right. College courses, textbooks, and government-funded studies are dedicated exclusively to passenger transportation. Urban study programs offer specialized training, concerned exclusively with passenger movement. This text, however, focuses on freight transportation.

FREIGHT TRANSPORTATION

This book in itself is an excellent example of how important freight transportation is to all social and business activities. A book is the result of many transportation movements. Large tree-cutting machinery had to be transported to timber locations to process raw materials. The cut trees required transportation to sawmills where paper pulp was produced. The pulp was then transported to paper producing locations. Finally, paper was moved to a printer. Ink and other supporting supplies also had to be transported to the printer, as well as huge printing presses, which were manufactured at a variety of locations from an assortment of raw materials. Once printing was completed, the loose pages of the text had to be moved to a bindery to be formed into books. Completed textbooks, produced in large quantities, required movement from the bindery to warehouses until bookstores ordered the text. Then, transportation was required to deliver the books to local stores so that individual purchases could be made. Following the initial sale, the books may be moved many more times as they pass through the used book market.

It is obvious from this one example that freight transportation is a large and complex field of study. In a formal sense, freight transportation is defined as *the economic movement of commodities and products and the effect of such movement on the development and advancement of business.* A framework for study is outlined in the following section.

5

Framework for Study

Figure 1–1 provides a framework of the freight transportation system. The center of the figure illustrates the overall freight transportation system, which consists of (1) carriers that perform the physical movement of goods, and (2) management that operates and controls the carriers. Essentially, the role of the transportation system is to satisfy the movement demand of the users, which is reflected by the achievements of the transportation system, illustrated at the bottom of Figure 1–1. The transportation system does not operate in isolation. Many external forces influence its operations and achievements. The major external forces, listed at the top of the illustration, are the legal and regulatory environments and user demands. Figure 1–1 could also be viewed as a circle: the transportation system achievements must satisfy the needs and wants of the environment and the users who, in turn, constitute the major external forces that influence the nature and operation of the system.

FIGURE 1–1. FRAMEWORK FOR STUDY OF THE TRANSPORTATION SYSTEM

EXTERNAL FORCES		
Legal	Regulatory	Users
Common Contract Private	Federal State	Government Industry Consumers

THE TRANSPORTATION SYSTEM	
Freight Carriers	Management
Rail Truck Water Pipeline Air Other	Carrier Management Traffic Management

ACHIEVEMENTS

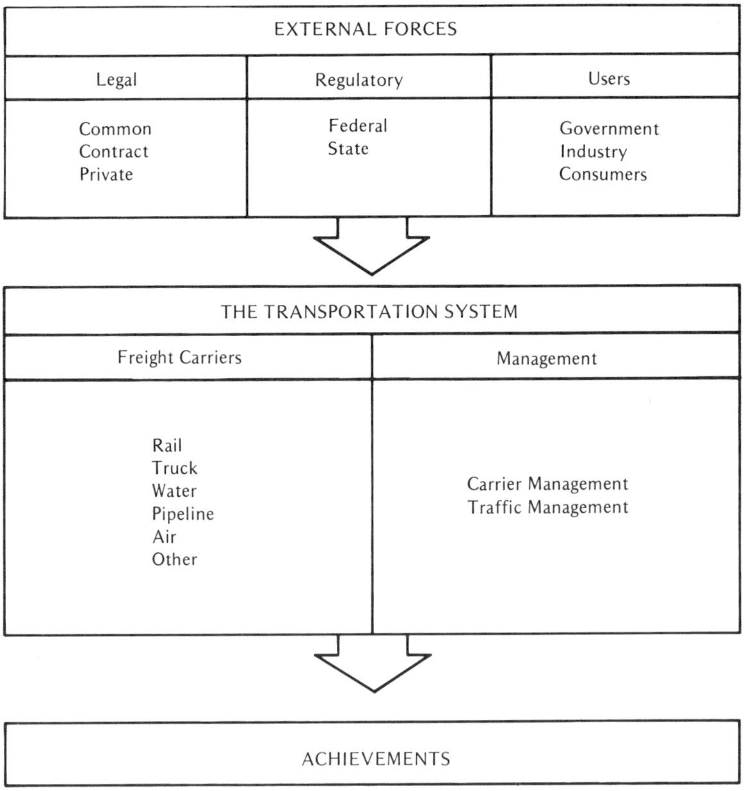

This framework provides an overview of the organization of this text. It is important that you keep this framework in mind as you study so as to maintain a clear understanding of how the chapters fit together. A brief discussion of each part of the framework follows.

The Transportation System

As previously stated, the transportation system consists of freight carriers and management.

FREIGHT CARRIERS

The freight system includes several distinct forms of transportation, called *modes*. The modes differ in terms of operating characteristics and capabilities, giving them comparative advantages and disadvantages. The five major modes are *water, rail, truck, pipeline,* and *air*. A sixth "others" group includes movement arrangements such as United Parcel Service, the United States Postal System, buses, and freight forwarders. The "other" category of transportation is not a mode in the strict sense of the term. In fact, the sixth category uses the other five modes to perform a special transportation service.

Each mode enjoys what might be called *natural product provinces*. For example, water transportation is usually used to move low-value, high-bulk products. Low value reduces the transportation urgency, and the high bulk, with little chance for breakage, is especially suited for the volume loading and unloading machinery used at dockside.

All the modes and their representative carriers play important roles in the overall transportation system. These roles will be examined in later chapters.

MANAGEMENT

Management of the transportation system falls into two general categories: (1) those who *sell* transportation services, and (2) those who *buy* transportation services. The sellers—carrier management—are responsible for operating the various transportation companies. Their major responsibilities are to obtain shipments for their firms, plan the time and method of movement, and arrive at prices to charge for services. These managers must be familiar with the rules and regulations, as well as the supporting documentation, that apply when performing the transportation movement. In addition to providing the actual transportation service for users, carrier management must also organize, administer, and control its internal operation.

The buyers—traffic management—are responsible for arranging transpor-

7

tation services when a firm wants to ship or receive freight. Depending on the freight moved, the mode, the cost, and a variety of other factors, the traffic management department can range in size from a single person to a large transportation group. The overall responsibility of a firm's traffic management is to secure the desired movement at the lowest total cost. Included with this responsibility are selecting the proper mode, obtaining the desired carrier, and identifying the best available combination of rates and services.

In summary, the freight transportation system consists of carriers and management. The overall responsibility of the transportation system is to provide services while responding to the demands of both its users and the external environment.

External Forces on Transportation

The transportation system is affected by external forces that are largely uncontrollable. Any activity that has such a significant impact on society cannot operate in a vacuum or remain oblivious to groups that affect and are affected by it. The major forces influencing the transportation system are the legal environment, the regulatory environment, and users of the transportation service.

LEGAL AND REGULATORY ENVIRONMENTS

Three types of carrier ownership are legal forms of transportation: (1) common carriers, (2) contract carriers, and (3) private carriers. Each type is distinct and has varying degrees of operating permissiveness and restriction as determined by governmental regulations.

COMMON CARRIERS
Common carriers are privately or publicly owned companies committed to performing a movement service of the same quality for all shippers on an equal basis and without discrimination. The scope and content of common carrier regulation have changed dramatically over the years. Recently, regulation of this form of transportation was modified. Less regulation was the general thrust of the regulation. The regulatory process, its history, and current direction of change are discussed in detail in Chapter 11.

CONTRACT CARRIERS
Individual contracts may be arranged between transportation users and carriers. With the formal agreement, the transportation company becomes a *contract carrier*. The contract usually covers a specific time period and includes a description of the products to be transported and the locations to be serviced. At

8

the present time, all contract arrangements must be approved by either a state or federal regulatory agency.

PRIVATE CARRIERS

The past decade has seen an increasing tendency among business firms to provide their own transportation capability and become *private carriers*. The primary mode of private transport is truck. Peculiarities in operations, desires for total distribution control, cost economies, and stringent service requirements are the major reasons for this trend. Private carriers are severely limited in the kinds of movements they can perform. At the present time, performance of the transportation service must not be the firm's predominant operation, and the firm must have legitimate ownership of the freight hauled.

REGULATORY ENVIRONMENT

The impact of the legal and regulatory environments on specific types of carriers is directly related to competition and public responsibility. In other words, common carriers (extensive competition) are subject to more legal control than are contract carriers (limited competition) and private carriers (no competition). Carriers are also subject to varying degrees of regulation, depending upon the mode and specific products transported.

The federal government's right to regulate transportation has often been questioned. But the government's power to do so was guaranteed by Article I, Section 8, of the Constitution of the United States, which gave the Congress the right ". . . to regulate commerce with foreign nations, and among the several states, and with the Indian tribes." The nature and scope of regulation have changed significantly over the years as the nation has expanded its commercial and industrial base. The responsibility for regulation of transport extends to all branches of the federal government. The general direction of the federal regulatory posture is the national transportation policy as articulated by the president and the Congress.

The legislative branch of the federal government implements executive policy by formulating transportation laws. Agencies created specifically by such legislation are responsible for enforcing the regulatory acts. The Interstate Commerce Commission (ICC), Civil Aeronautics Board (CAB), and Federal Maritime Commission (FMC) are examples of such federal agencies. Interpretation is often an issue with federal legislation. Therefore, the law allows issues to be "tried" by administrative processes within the regulatory system. Contested decisions of the agencies may be subjected to review by the judicial branch of government. Cases involving transportation have reached the United States Supreme Court on several occasions. In early 1978, the Supreme Court overruled a Wisconsin law that prohibited twin trailers on interstate highways within the state. The Court believed that the plaintiffs, Consolidated Freightways and Raymond Motor Freight, had been placed at a disadvantage by the regulatory ruling.

Transportation's significant role in the economy was further confirmed by the creation in 1967 of the Department of Transportation (DOT). The secretary of DOT is a member of the president's Cabinet. This aspect of transportation will be discussed in Chapter 12.

Federal policies apply to freight transportation between and among the states, known as *interstate* traffic. Freight movements within a single state are under the regulation of stage governments and are known as *intrastate* traffic. All states have regulatory policies with varying degrees of complexity and sophistication. The legal and regulatory structure of the combined federal and state governments was created to protect the interests of competition, the users, and the consuming public. As noted earlier, the posture of regulation is dynamic and is currently undergoing a great deal of examination and review.

TRANSPORT USERS

Many transportation users, representing a wide variety of interests, exist in our economy. Purchasers of freight transportation services are classified broadly as *government*, *industry*, and *consumers*.

GOVERNMENT

The largest buyer of direct freight transportation service is the federal government. It is difficult to pinpoint any commodity that is not purchased by the federal government. Purchases that must be transported range from logistical support of government facilities to food, weapons, and clothing for the military.

INDUSTRY

Support of industrial operations requires extensive transportation services. Transportation buyers in the industrial sector are classified as *producers* or *distributors*.

A significant volume of transportation is purchased by industrial producers, or business firms that use materials and products in manufacturing operations. Several examples illustrate this. A furniture manufacturer purchases lumber, plastics, and metals to produce office and household furniture. A steel producer purchases sand, limestone, and scrap metals as raw materials for steel. An automobile manufacturer purchases glass, tires, and upholstery as components for assembling automobiles. Finally, a college or university purchases large quantities of paper, typewriters, and other necessary supplies. In this sense, educational institutions are classified as *processors* because the products they purchase are used for the creation of a service: education.

A *distributor* is defined as a business enterprise that purchases and sells a product without changing its form substantially. The most dominant distributors are *wholesalers* and *retailers*. Wholesalers purchase large quantities of fin-

10

ished products and sell smaller quantities of the products to retailers. Although retailers purchase even smaller quantities than wholesalers, their quantities are still larger than those purchased by consumers. Transportation is a major expense for both wholesalers and retailers.

For example, a food wholesaler in Kansas City may purchase 1,000 cases of coffee from General Foods. The cases are transported to the wholesaler's warehouse in anticipation of orders from retail stores. Although individual supermarket outlets do not require large quantities, their total purchase within a geographical area over time will equal the 1,000 cases purchased by the wholesaler. The retail store places orders for, perhaps, ten cases at a time. The wholesaler performs what is called a *break-bulk function* by shipping the required cases to each retailer as purchase orders are received. The break-bulk function, simply stated, creates smaller shipments from a larger quantity. As will be examined later, performance of the break-bulk function by wholesalers reduces total transportation costs.

CONSUMERS

In the final analysis, you can see that society as a whole becomes the largest buyer for transportation services. Consider that the federal government, the largest direct buyer of transportation, pays various carriers for transportation services. However, those payments come from taxes paid by consumers and businesses.

Wholesalers incur transportation expenses when they purchase from manufacturers and processors. That expense must be included in the wholesalers' price to retailers. Similarly, the retailers must include transportation cost in the price of all products. Thus, consumers pay for all transportation in an *indirect* way.

Consumers may also purchase transportation *directly*. One example is when an individual moves household furnishings from one city to another. Household moving companies perform this service and charge the individual directly. Some retailers charge for transporting a product to the consumer's home as well. Furniture retailers, such as Levitt's or Wickes, may sell all products at a cash-and-carry showroom price. Consumers can arrange to transport the furniture to their homes, or they can pay a delivery charge to have the retailer perform the service. Many retailers, such as Sears, Roebuck and Co., assess a shipping charge in addition to the purchase price listed in their mail order catalogues. Monthly record and book clubs add shipping charges to the price of the products they sell.

As has been illustrated, the external environment has a significant influence on the operation and achievements of the transportation system. Federal and state governments regulate the behavior of transportation carriers. Users, direct or indirect, demand services from the transportation system. To complete our framework, let us examine the achievements of the transportation system.

11

Transportation System Achievements

The achievements of the transportation system are the efficient movements of freight within the existing legal and regulatory environments. As discussed, the overall transportation system affects the performance of all activities within our society. To realize the desired level of achievement, therefore, the national transportation system must be as efficient and effective as possible. Users of the system play an important role by shaping the transportation system and enjoying its achievements at the same time.

Summary

Transportation is fundamental to the development and functioning of an industrial society. The transportation system is divided into two categories: (1) the movement of freight, and (2) the movement of people. This text focuses on the study of freight transportation: *the economic movement of commodities and products and the effects of such movement on the development and advancement of business.*

The freight transportation system consists of both freight carriers and management. The five major modes of transportation are water, rail, truck, pipeline, and air. The management system includes both carrier and traffic management. The major external influences on the transportation system are the legal and regulatory environments and the users of transportation services.

The purposes of this text are to provide a basic understanding of the transportation system and to increase your awareness of its importance to economic growth. Perhaps your increased appreciation may encourage you to undertake advanced studies and to seek a career within some area of the industry.

Questions for Chapter 1

1. Define transportation.
2. Discuss the possible freight transportation activities that must take place to make a common lead pencil available for sale in your bookstore.
3. In the transportation framework, how are external forces, the transportation system, and achievements related?
4. Name the five major modes and describe the "other" category of transportation.
5. Define carrier management and traffic management. Briefly discuss the responsibilities of each.

6. Define common, contract, and private carriers.
7. What role does government play in the freight transportation system of the United States?
8. Name three governmental agencies that are responsible for enforcing regulatory acts.
9. Discuss the various groups that use freight transportation. Can you think of any group or individual that is not dependent on freight transportation in any way?
10. Define interstate traffic and what it means regarding federal policies and regulation.
11. Discuss natural product provinces for the modes and give an example for each mode.
12. What is the difference between a producer and a distributor? Are both equally dependent on the freight transportation system?

2

The Role of
Transportation

TRANSPORTATION AND SURVIVAL

SPECIALIZATION
Production Economies
Geographic Specialization

REGIONAL DEVELOPMENT

COMPETITION

NATIONAL DEFENSE

STANDARD OF LIVING AND LIFE-STYLE

SUMMARY

Chapter 1 introduced a framework for studying the freight transportation system, its environment, and its achievements. This chapter examines in depth the role of the transportation system in an industrial economy.

In 1977, $172.2 billion was spent on freight movement in the United States. This amount represented 9.1 per cent of the gross national product.[1] The United States contains approximately 29.6 million trucks (about one for every eight people), 29,000 barges, 1.7 million freight train cars, 25,500 miles of waterway, 191,000 miles of railroad track, 228,000 miles of pipelines, and 690,000 miles of improved highways.[2] Approximately 2.53 trillion ton-miles of freight were carried in 1977.

Why does transportation command so much attention in the United States? Why are we willing to spend so much money and to allocate so many human, financial, and raw material resources for the movement of goods from one place to another? What do we as citizens and as a society receive for this enormous investment?

Simply stated, we need transportation to survive. We expend resources on

[1] *Transportation Facts and Trends*, 15th ed. (Washington, D.C.: Transportation Association of America, July 1979), p. 3.
[2] *Transportation Facts and Trends*, p. 30–31.

14

transportation in order to save other resources and to improve our standard of living. Transportation affects our personal well-being, our life-styles, and our economic, social, and political development. Furthermore, the efficiency of our transportation system is directly related to the efficiency of our nation.

How does transportation affect all of these areas? Can we justify the enormous human, financial, and raw material outlay? How will increases in transportation efficiency affect our society?

To answer these questions, one must first look at the most simple conditions for survival to show that life cannot be sustained without some form of transportation and that increases in transportation efficiency directly affect economic development. Second, recognition that society seeks more than mere survival and that efficient resource allocation is particularly important leads to the concept of specialization. The benefits of specialization result in production economies and geographic specialization that would not be possible without transportation. Third, the effects of transportation on regional development, competition, national defense, and standard of living and life-style are discussed.

Transportation and Survival

In its broadest sense, transportation has been defined as the movement of freight and passengers from one location to another. Transportation has also been described as an independent action that is performed by a variety of legal forms of carriers using different modes of movement.

To survive, a person must consume products. The steps necessary for consumption are outlined in Figure 2–1. First, raw materials must be located and available. Tools are needed to extract raw materials. The tools have to be produced. Therefore, raw materials must be located and available for tool production. Second, the raw materials require processing. Again, tools for processing and raw materials to create the tools are required. Finally, the product is ready for consumption. Once again, tools and raw materials are necessary to complete the act of consumption. Given that a person must perform some or all of these activities to survive, is there a situation in which these activities could be accomplished without transportation?

One example might be a person sitting on the edge of a lake. Raw materials (fish) are in the lake. The tools for extraction are the person's hands or, perhaps, a net made from vines. Production (cooking) may take place. The tools for production are wood and flint to make a fire. Thus, the steps necessary for consumption of a product all take place in one location and without transportation. That is an extreme example. In reality, nature imposes two conditions that force the use of some kind of transportation. First, a person needs more

15

FIGURE 2–1. STEPS NECESSARY FOR CONSUMPTION OF A PRODUCT

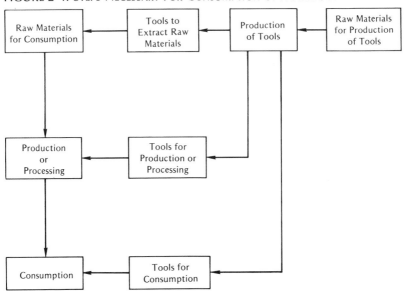

than fish to survive. Meats, grains, and vegetables are necessary for a balanced diet. Second, nature does not supply all of the needed raw materials in one location. Grains, vegetables, and animals require particular growing conditions found only in certain parts of the country. Thus, to perform all of the activities required for consumption, transportation becomes necessary. Either the individual must move to the raw materials (movement of people) or the raw materials must be moved to where the person is located (movement of goods), or a combination of the two activities must be performed. It is conceivable that each step in the consumption process shown in Figure 2–1 could take place at a different location.

The earliest form of transportation was the movement of people. As far as historians can determine, all peoples of the world were nomads until approximately 4000 B.C. People moved to the raw materials rather than moving the raw materials to themselves. As wild game, a source of food and clothing, migrated in search of food and a favorable climate, the nomads followed. For example, the American Indians migrated from Russia into North American through the Bering Straits and Alaska in search of game and a climate and soil favorable to the growth of grains and other crops. Gradually, the emphasis shifted from the movement of people to the movement of goods. Today, most of the world's population expects that the goods will be moved to them through some form of transportation.

However, the mere availability of tranportation may not be sufficient to survive. A distinction must be drawn between the availability of transportation and

16

the availability of *efficient* transportation. *Efficient* is defined as producing the desired effect or result with a minimum of effort, expense, or waste. Thus, efficient transportation would move goods or people more rapidly with the same or less effort, or it would move larger loads with the same or less effort.

Let us return to the example and add two conditions. First, because raw materials are found in a variety of locations, they may be close by or they may be at great distances. Also, the raw materials may be conducive to transportation, such as nonperishable, light raw materials, or they may not be. Second, the individual may need a greater variety of raw materials. Under these extended conditions, the person may find that no matter how many hours a day are devoted to work, the combination of the location and form of the raw materials plus the variety of needs is such that survival will be impossible. To overcome this situation, two alternatives must be explored: specialization, which will be discussed later, or an increase in the efficiency of transportation.

The application of animal power to transportation to increase speed or weight-bearing capacity is one means of increasing transportation efficiency. A horse, donkey, or other animal can be used for transportation of either the person or the goods. As the efficiency of transportation increases, the ability to move the necessary resources increases. Of course, other forms of natural power could also be employed to increase transportation efficiency. The important point is that as transportation efficiency increases, it has a direct and positive effect on the individual's ability to survive, even under very primitive conditions. Now that we have established some basic relationships between transportation and society, let us look at conditions that approximate the society in which we live today.

Specialization

Our society is more complex than the simple situation discussed in the previous example. People seek more than mere survival. They strive for a better life-style and standard of living with less time devoted to obtaining needs and wants. As previously noted, one means of accomplishing these goals is to specialize. *Specialization is defined as allowing human or physical resources to perform the tasks for which they are best suited.* For instance, if a person is particularly adept at farming, then society should allow that person to farm. If a certain geographic region is suitable for growing potatoes, then society should grow its potatotes in that area. Specialization has many benefits. Resources used in the best possible manner increase utilization. The overall efficiency of society is improved because fewer resources are employed to produce the desired output. The result is that less effort is expended to produce a particular product. Thus, specialization is a desired goal for society because it increases overall efficiency and directly improves our standard of living and life-style.

The benefits of specialization can be gained through either production economies or geographic specialization. Production economies are realized when a large volume of the same type of commodity is produced at one time in one location. Mass production of automobiles is one example. Geographic specialization involves using particular regions to produce specific products. Oranges grown in California and Florida are examples. If products are to be produced in suitable locations and people are to specialize in a task such as farming, then a movement of products among different locations must take place.

Thus, in order to be efficient, we must specialize. If we specialize, we must exchange. If we exchange, we must have transportation. Transportation, therefore, is directly interwoven with our ability to increase the overall efficiency of society.

The role of transportation in production economies and geographic specialization is complex, and the level of transportation efficiency directly affects the degree to which we can gain the benefits of specialization. To clarify this relationship, we now take a closer look and illustrate production economies and geographic specialization.

PRODUCTION ECONOMIES

Production economies are gained when many units are produced at a single location. The result is a lower cost per unit. There are many reasons that production economies are possible. Setup costs can be spread over more units, specialized equipment can be used, and tasks can be made routine. Thus, as more units are produced, the cost per unit goes down. Production economies are not endless. At some level the cost per unit stops going down and begins to increase as production is expanded beyond the most economical level.

Table 2–1 illustrates production economies for a product called X.

Production economies allow for efficient utilization of resources, which is a goal of all industrial societies. Thus, there is a desire to produce more units at one location. However, the demand for units at the producing location typically does not equal maximum production economies. For instance, the state

TABLE 2–1. Production Economies per Unit for Product X

Quantity Produced (Units)	Cost Per Unit (Dollars) (Including Profit But Not Transportation)
50	$20
100	17
150	15
200	14
250	15

18

of Michigan produces enough automobiles to satisfy several million customers; however, the demand for automobiles in the state is far less. Under these circumstances, one of two things could occur. Fewer automobiles could be produced, thus losing production economies, or the excess automobiles could be shipped to other states. Thus, if production economies are desired, transportation must be available. The mere availability of transportation, however, is insufficient to gain the full benefits from production economies.

The following example illustrates the relationship between production economies and transportation. Specifically, the example will show that

1. Without transportation, society could not take advantage of production economies.
2. The availability of transportation does not necessarily result in allowing production economies to be gained.
3. Inefficient transportation will deny the full benefits of production economies.
4. As transportation becomes more efficient, full production economies can be gained.
5. Further increases in transportation efficiency will result in additional benefits to society.

In our example, three production locations exist: A, B, and C. Each location has identical resources, identical production capabilities, demands the same product, and has the same level of demand. See Table 2–2.

First, without transportation, society cannot take advantage of production economies. With no transportation, each location must produce its own requirements of product X. The total cost to society to obtain product X is $3,600, and the unit cost is $12. See Table 2–3.

Second, the availability of transportation does not necessarily result in allowing production economies to be gained. Assume that transportation is available

TABLE 2–2. Demand, Production Capabilities, and Costs for Product X at Locations A, B, and C

Location A Demand = 100 Units		Location B Demand = 100 Units		Location C Demand = 100 Units	
PRODUCTION CAPABILITY		PRODUCTION CAPABILITY		PRODUCTION CAPABILITY	
UNITS	COST/UNIT*	UNITS	COST/UNIT*	UNITS	COST/UNIT*
100	$12	100	$12	100	$12
200	10	200	10	200	10
300	9	300	9	300	9
400	10	400	10	400	10

*Cost per unit includes profit but does not include outbound transportation.

TABLE 2–3. Total Cost of Product X Without Transportation

Each Location Demands 100 Units		
Location A produces 100 units @ $12/unit	=	$1,200
Location B produces 100 units @ $12/unit	=	1,200
Location C produces 100 units @ $12/unit	=	1,200
Total Cost of Product X	=	$3,600
Cost Per Unit	=	12

from Location A to Locations B and C. The cost to move one unit from A to B is $5, and the cost to move one unit from A to C is $7. All other conditions remain the same. When transportation is introduced, three alternatives become available. One, each location could produce for its own demand. Two, A could produce for its own demand and for that of B, while C produces for itself. Three, A could produce for itself and for B and C. This is illustrated in Table 2–4.

TABLE 2–4. Total Cost of Product X with Transportation at $5 and $7 per Unit

Alternative 1. Each Location Produces for Its Own Demand		
(See Table 2–3.) Total Cost of Product X	=	$3,600
Cost Per Unit	=	12

Alternative 2. A Produces for A and B C Produces for Itself		
A produces 200 units @ $10/unit	=	$2,000
A ships 100 units @ $5/unit to B	=	500
B produces 0		
C produces 100 units @ $12/unit for itself	=	1,200
Total Cost of Product X	=	$3,700
Cost Per Unit	=	12.34

Alternative 3. A Produces for A, B, and C		
A produces 300 units @ $9/unit	=	$2,700
A ships 100 units @ $5/unit to B	=	500
A ships 100 units @ $7/unit to C	=	700
B produces 0		
C produces 0		
Total Cost of Product X	=	$3,900
Cost Per Unit	=	13

Table 2–4 shows that even though transportation is available, no economies result. With each new alternative, the total cost to society and the cost per unit is greater than if each location produced its own products.

Third, inefficient transportation will deny the full benefits of production economies. All conditions remain the same except that the cost of transportation from A to B is now $3 per unit instead of $5 per unit. Again, the same three alternatives exist; each location produces for its own demand; A produces for A and B whereas C produces for itself; or A produces for all three. The results are illustrated in Table 2–5.

TABLE 2–5. Total Cost of Product X with Transportation at $3 and $7 per Unit

Alternative 1. Each Location Produces for Its Own Demand

(See Table 2–3.)	Total Cost of Product X	=	$3,600
	Cost Per Unit	=	12

Alternative 2. A Produces for A and B
C Produces for Itself

A produces 200 units @ $10/unit	=	$2,000
A ships 100 units @ $3/unit to B	=	300
B produces 0		
C produces 100 units @ $12/unit for itself	=	1,200
Total Cost of Product X =		$3,500
Cost Per Unit =		11.67

Alternative 3. A Produces for A, B, and C

A produces 300 units @ $9/unit	=	$2,700
A ships 100 units @ $3/unit to B	=	300
A ships 100 units @ $7/unit to C	=	700
B produces 0		
C produces 0		
Total Cost of Product X =		$3,700
Cost Per Unit =		12.34

The decision as to which location will produce the product and how much it will produce changes from the previous example. Alternative 2 in Table 2–5 is now the best condition. Allowing A to produce for A and B and allowing C to produce for its own demand results in a total cost of $3,500 ($11.67 per unit), rather than the total cost of $3,600 ($12 per unit) when each location produced for its own demand.

However, both total cost and unit costs exceed those of Alternative 1 when A produces for A, B, and C (Table 2–5, Alternative 3). Therefore, the cost of transportation is low enough to achieve some benefits of production economies, but the cost of transportation is too high to permit the full benefits of production economies. Table 2–5, Alternative 2, is the best alternative thus far. The cost of production is $3,200 (200 units @ $10/unit + 100 units @ $12/unit = $3,200). This is better than each location producing for its own demand (cost of production = $3,600), but it is still more costly than one location producing for all others (cost of production-$2,700).

Fourth, as transportation becomes more efficient, full production economies can be gained. Let us consider one more example in which all conditions (Table 2–2) remain exactly the same except that the cost to ship from A to B is $3 per unit and the cost to ship from A to C is $4 per unit. Once more, there are three alternatives as illustrated in Table 2–6.

In this example, we have realized the lowest point of production costs at $2,700, lowered the total costs including transportation to $3,400, and lowered the unit cost to $11.34. Thus, by increasing the efficiency of the transportation system, full production economies are realized and the overall benefits to society are increased.

TABLE 2–6. Total Cost of Product X with Transportation at $3 and $4 per Unit

Alternative 1. Each Location Produces for Its Own Demand

(See Table 2–3.)	Total Cost of Product X	=	$3,600
	Cost Per Unit	=	12

Alternative 2. A Produces for A and B
C Produces for Itself

A produces 200 units @ $10/unit		=	$2,000
A ships 100 units @ $3/unit to B		=	300
B produces 0			
C produces 100 units @ $12/unit for itself		=	1,200
	Total Cost of Product X	=	$3,500
	Cost Per Unit	=	11.67

Alternative 3. A Produces for A, B, and C

A produces 300 units @ $9/unit		=	$2,700
A ships 100 units @ $3/unit to B		=	300
A ships 100 units @ $4/unit to C		=	400
B produces 0			
C produces 0			
	Total Cost of Product X	=	$3,400
	Cost Per Unit	=	11.34

22

Fifth, further increases in transportation efficiency will result in additional benefits to society. In the previous example (Table 2–6), Alternative 3 achieved all available production economies. However, this does not mean that one cannot achieve further efficiencies. Additional reductions in transportation cost will lower total cost. For example, if the cost of transportation were lowered to $1 per unit for all movements, the total cost would be $2,900 ($9.67 per unit) instead of $3,400 ($11.34 per unit).

The foregoing discussion leads to the following conclusions:

1. The availability of transportation does not guarantee benefit from production economies (Table 2–4).
2. Increases in transportation efficiency improve production economies (Table 2–5, Alternative 2).
3. The level of transportation efficiency will determine if all possible production economies can be gained (Table 2–6, Alternatives 2 and 3).
4. Production economies coupled with transportation efficiencies increase overall efficiency and result in an increased standard of living through increased levels of satisfaction with the same resources (Table 2–3 versus Table 2–5, Alternative 2, and Table 2–6, Alternative 3).

GEOGRAPHIC SPECIALIZATION

Geographic specialization is similar in principle to production economies. *Geographic specialization* capitalizes on the fact that one region or one area has an advantage over other areas for some reason. The example used for production economies assumed that locations A, B, and C had the same resources and the same production economies. Given our heterogeneous society, this assumption may not be valid. One location could have a natural advantage over another location. For instance, A may be able to produce product X for $12 per unit, whereas B may be able to produce the same product for only $9 per unit. The reasons for the difference in cost are many and varied. One area may have more favorable climatic conditions, different natural resources, or better raw material availability. One location may also have more efficient human resources. Therefore, the area that is best situated should be the source of production. Again, the availability of efficient transportation is necessary to capitalize on these advantages. To explain this concept, consider the following example. Table 2–7 shows the production capabilities of A and B for products X and Y.

The demand in each location for each product is 50 units. Thus, without transportation, both would produce products X and Y, and the total cost would be as shown in Table 2–8.

If transportation is available, then each location can produce those products for which it is geographically suitable, and the total production cost would be as shown in Table 2–9.

TABLE 2–7. Locations A and B Capability to
Produce Products X and Y

Location A			
PRODUCT X		**PRODUCT Y**	
PRODUCTION	COST	PRODUCTION	COST
50	$12	50	$20
100	10	100	17
150	11	150	18

Location B			
PRODUCT X		**PRODUCT Y**	
PRODUCTION	COST	PRODUCTION	COST
50	$15	50	$18
100	13	100	16
150	14	150	17

TABLE 2–8. Total Production Cost
(Products X and Y Produced at A)
(Products X and Y Produced at B)

Location A		
50 Product X @ $12/unit	=	$ 600
50 Product Y @ $20/unit	=	1,000
Total Production Cost =		$1,600

Location B		
50 Product X @ $15/unit	=	$ 750
50 Product Y @ $18/unit	=	900
Total Production Cost =		$1,650
Total Production Cost, A and B =		$3,250

TABLE 2–9. Total Production Cost
(Product X Produced at A)
(Product Y Produced at B)

100 Product X (A) @ $10/unit	=	$1,000
100 Product Y (B) @ $16/unit	=	1,600
Total Production Cost =		$2,600

Thus, if the transportation system is capable of moving 50 units of X from A to B and 50 units of Y from B to A for a total cost of less than $650 ($3,250 − $2,600), then society is able to capitalize on not only production economies but also geographic specialization.

In summary, through specialization, specifically production economies and geographic specialization, a society can increase its overall efficiency. To enjoy the benefits of specialization, transportation must be available. The more efficient the transportation, the greater the benefits.

Regional Development

Nations are composed of heterogeneous regions with inherent natural and human resources. In the United States, the Northeast and North Central regions offer industrial skills, and the Central and Western regions offer agricultural products, forest products, and raw materials from mines. For a society to reach its full potential, regions must develop those resources for which they have a natural advantage. Regional development is a desired goal from both a regional and national perspective. People living in a particular area desire development that would improve their standard of living and life-style. As regions develop, so does society. And when the inherent advantages of an area are utilized, efficiencies from specialization are gained and a more efficient allocation of resources results.

Before 1800, the United States was composed of the territory from the Atlantic Ocean west to the Mississippi River and from the Great Lakes south to the Gulf of Mexico. Initial development took place on the seacoast, particularly between Boston and Philadelphia. The interior regions did not develop as rapidly, but it was soon apparent that those regions should be developed for their own good and for the good of the nation. As the interior regions grew, they were able to supply such raw materials as timber and coal, and the seacoast regions were able to enjoy better economies in production as a result of the demand from interior regions. Thus, both areas benefited and contributed to the overall economic development of the nation as well.

Of course, transportation plays an integral role in regional development. Efficient transportation facilities must be available for regional development. Goods must be moved from one area to another and that movement must be efficient to capitalize on the inherent advantages of each region. Some of the earliest transportation projects in the United States were undertaken to take advantage of regional differences. The Erie Canal linked New York with the Great Lakes, the National Turnpike linked the East Coast with the Midwest in Illinois, and the first transcontinental railroad linked the East and West Coasts. Without these and other projects, both regional development and overall national development would have been impeded.

Competition

In a free enterprise system, competition is desirable. Competition encourages technological innovation, lowers prices, and increases the efficiency of the economic system. If two producers are in the same location, transportation does not play a significant role. However, two or more producers in different locations can compete in one market only if efficient transportation is available. If the transportation system is inadequate or inefficient, the cost of transportation added to the cost of production will place a firm at a competitive disadvantage in areas beyond the local market.

The example of production economies showed how goods would not be shipped if total cost (production plus transportation) was more than the cost of manufacturing the same product at the other location. If a local producer does not have to compete with producers from other areas, the possibility of increased prices and inefficient allocation of resources exists. However, with transportation, the threat of geographic monopoly is lessened. One can logically extend this to conclude that the more efficient transportation becomes, the greater the degree of competition. First, the more efficient the transportation, the greater is the market area for a given producer. Assuming that it costs more to ship greater distances, if the cost of transportation is lowered, a producer can ship further and still remain price competitive. Thus, as transportation costs decrease, a producer can reach more markets and compete with more firms. Second, as transportation becomes more efficient, the number of firms competing in one market increases. The greater the number of competitors, the greater is the possibility of competition, which, in turn, increases the overall efficiency of society. Thus, the presence of efficient transportation facilitates competition and decreases the possibility of geographic monopolies that result in inefficient allocation of resources.

National Defense

A fundamental objective of all societies is defense from outside aggression. To guard against the possibility of physical invasion and to be able to repel such an attempt, several conditions must be present in regard to transportation. First, human and material resources must be able to reach the physical limits of the country. Access to all borders must be possible. Second, transportation facilities must exist to bring defenses from several areas across the country to a particular location. Third, a transportation network must be present to supply the defense effort during the conflict.

A transportation network that meets these criteria must exist for adequate national defense. Several transportation projects have been undertaken in the United States with this objective in mind. The intercoastal waterway on the East and Gulf Coasts was conceived to avoid the perils of the open sea, and the interstate highway system has national defense as one of its objectives. The logical assumption is that autonomous regions that lack the support and power of the whole will be more vulnerable than will a group of connected regions supporting one another.

Standard of Living and Life-style

It is difficult to define the concepts of *standard of living* and *life-style*. Generally, both reflect the manner in which individuals and societies are able to fulfill their needs and wants. One measure of standard of living and life-style is the amount and variety of goods people are able to acquire. A second measure is the amount of effort that must be put forth to satisfy needs and wants. A third measure is the level of comfort and ease with which basic needs and wants are fulfilled. Regardless of the measures used, one must admit that Americans are enjoying a higher standard of living and a better life-style today than their forefathers did in 1900 and that the life-style and standard of living was better in 1900 than it was in 1800. Many things have contributed to these improvements in our lives. Advanced technology, increases in machine efficiency, and improvements in management and labor have had an impact.

Transportation's role has been significant. Without transportation, we would not have been able to capitalize on production economies, geographic specialization, and competition to increase overall economic efficiency. Furthermore, as the efficiency of the transportation system increases, the ability to gain these advantages increases. A direct relationship exists between the availability of efficient transportation and the development of a culture. Thus, the standard of living and life-style of a society is tied directly to the availability of an efficient transportation system.

Summary

The availability of efficient transportation facilitates the survival, economic growth, and life-style of a society. Without transportation, survival in its simplest form would not be possible. Through an efficient transportation network, the benefits of specialization result in production economies and geographic

27

specialization. The more efficient the transportation system becomes—that is, the more inexpensively goods can be moved—the greater are the gains from production economies and geographic specialization. An efficient transportation system allows more goods to be produced at one time and in one location, thereby utilizing a specific geographic area's resources more efficiently.

Transportation also encourages regional development and competition. Successful regional development ensures utilization of all of the nation's resources. Competition fosters technological gains and efficient resource allocations. Collectively, the benefits of an efficient transportation system accrue in increases in our standard of living and life-style and form the foundation for our national defense.

Chapter 3 presents the history of transportation in the United States. By looking at the development of transportation over the last 300 years, one can see more directly the important role transportation has played in our nation's growth.

Questions for Chapter 2

1. Outline the possible steps a person must go through to procure food. Discuss this procedure in reference to transportation.
2. Define efficient transportation.
3. Discuss the relationship between efficient transportation and survival.
4. Before mechanical power was applied to transportation, how was efficiency increased?
5. Define specialization and discuss the relationship between specialization and transportation.
6. Discuss the two ways the benefits of specialization can be gained.
7. Give an example in which the full benefits of production economies cannot be gained because of inefficient transportation.
8. Discuss how increases in efficiency can be gained once full production economies have been achieved.
9. Describe geographic specialization.
10. Discuss the relationship between geographic specialization and regional development.
11. How does transportation affect competition?
12. Define standard of living and life-style. How are they affected by transportation?

3

History of Freight Transportation

To understand and appreciate freight transportation in the United States, one must look at its history, because history gives perspective. The present transportation system—its modes, policies, laws, and regulations—has developed over the last two centuries. Tracing this development provides the foundation and underscores the relevance of the transportation system of today. History also shows that economic development and transportation development are parallel and inseparable and that transportation is never developed fully because it constantly changes and adjusts to the needs of society. Furthermore, it is hoped that history will provide valuable inputs to solving transportation problems today and in the future. This chapter traces the development of the freight transportation system in the United States from before 1800 to the present.

A complete transportation history would require volumes. To cover the topic in one chapter, therefore, we must limit our discussion to modal development, relationship of the modes, interaction of public and private sectors, and increases in transportation efficiency. Modal development is concerned with when the modes were introduced, what precipitated their introduction, and how they grew into their present roles. The relationship of the modes looks at the relative importance and power of modes over time. Only since the 1920s has the United States truly had a five-mode transportation system. The interaction of public and private sectors examines the role each plays in transportation system development. Increases in efficiency illustrate the manner by which the transportation system ships freight faster and in greater quantities. As discussed in Chapter 2, increased efficiency is the transportation system's major contribution to society.

Basically, transportation efficiency can be improved by three methods. First, the vehicles used to move the goods can be improved. A better wagon can be designed that is lighter but stronger and rolls with less effort and less damage to the cargo. Or a hull can be designed that moves through the water with less resistance. Second, the path over which the vehicles move can be improved. Roads or turnpikes can be improved by replacing mud and potholes with a hard, smooth, all-weather surface. Canals can be built that reduce natural water currents and allow movements in both directions. Third, new modes that better fit the inherent characteristics of the goods can be created. An example is the pipeline. Liquids and gases can be moved by many modes, but the pipeline allows liquids and gases to be moved most efficiently. As you will see as you study the history of freight transportation in the United States, all of these methods for improving transportation efficiency have been used.

This chapter is organized by time, because the history of freight transportation in the United States can be divided roughly into four major eras. Each era is characterized by particular events and developments. The time division of these eras is somewhat arbitrary. No clear separation exists between them because transportation developed continuously. But this breakdown serves as a convenient guide to the history of transportation.

The first era, before 1800, lacked mechanical power in transportation. The only means of moving transportation vehicles was by natural power such as humans, animals, wind, and river currents. The second era from 1800 to 1860 saw the introduction of mechanical power, primarily steam. Of all the developments in transportation throughout history, the introduction of mechanical power was the most significant. Speed and load capacity increased dramatically, and natural barriers, such as topography and river currents, could be overcome.

The third period, from 1860 to 1920, could be called the era of the railroads. The railroads had a virtual transportation monopoly during that time. The period also witnessed the beginnings of government regulation. The fourth and final era is from 1920 to the present. This era is marked by the fact that all of the modes known today—water, rail, truck, pipe, and air—have been developed, and a new period of competition has resulted.

Before 1800

Transportation before 1800 was characterized by the lack of mechanical power and the lack of improvement in ways and vehicles. Transport of goods was slow, difficult, expensive, and often dangerous. Without mechanical power, the population had to rely on natural, human, or animal power as had its ancestors for many centuries. With little or no improvements in ways, the people had to rely on those provided by nature. Wagons, carts, or sleds pulled by animals, and boats propelled by humans, animals, or wind and river currents over natural ways were the major modes of transportation.

WATER TRANSPORTATION

Because nature provided the way, water transportation was the most efficient, least costly, and most widely used. Population settlements therefore occurred primarily on water routes, and those locations where rivers and oceans met were the most rapidly developed. Cities such as New York, Philadelphia, and New Orleans became focal points for shipping and receiving goods within the colonies and for trade with foreign countries. During this period, water transportation used three major methods: movement of goods across the ocean, movement of goods downstream, and movement of goods upstream. The dependence on water transport before 1800 was almost absolute.

> A long period elapsed, after most of the early settlements were made, before the natural watercourses, with avenues leading to the ocean, ceased to furnish the main reliance for all extensive movements of persons or property.[1]

Initially, the bulk of the traffic moved from the colonies to other parts of the world. However, as the year 1800 approached, there was a marked increase of freight traffic among the colonies. The vast majority of this was done by ocean-going vessels. Each of the thirteen original colonies had at least one seaport, and traffic moved up and down the Atlantic Coast from Boston to Savannah and into the Gulf of Mexico to New Orleans. The rivers of the East Coast and the Midwest provided access into the interior of the country. Downstream movement, though often dangerous, was relatively easy because of natural currents. Therefore, large amounts of goods, such as grains and firewood, were shipped to ocean ports. The Mississippi and Ohio rivers constituted the most

[1] J. L. Ringwalt, *Development of Transportation Systems in the United States* (New York: Johnson Reprint Corporation, 1888), p. 8.

extensive inland network in terms of miles. Flatboats were constructed in Pittsburgh, Cincinnati, and other points along the rivers and floated to New Orleans, a distance of more than 2,000 miles. Goods were sold along the way and in New Orleans. The boat was then sold for lumber, and the crew returned in any way possible. The trip took months and was often perilous. The crew faced natural dangers such as rapids, sandbars, and dead-end channels, and human dangers such as pirates who might kill to steal the cargo.

Even though descending the rivers was dangerous and slow, ascending the river was even more difficult. Boats had to be moved by sails, set poles, or animals. Consequently, the cost of moving goods upsteam was greater than the cost of moving downstream. One account reported as follows:

> from Louisville to New Orleans, a distance of 1,545 miles, the freight is $1.50 a barrel, but to come up from New Orleans to Louisville, it is $4.50 a hundredweight or $9.00 a barrel.[2]

Water transportation remained the dominant mode well past the turn of the century. Although it did not reach all parts of the country, the natural way provided the easiest and most efficient means of transportation.

LAND TRANSPORTATION

Unlike water transport, land offered no natural way. In fact, nature provided formidable obstacles such as rough terrain and impassable rivers. Therefore, the country's interior, particularly those areas accessible only by land, was slow to develop. Connecting existing settlements by land was extremely slow, especially for the movement of goods. Initially, horses and mules were used on paths used by the Indians. Just before 1800, carts and wagons, pulled by a variety of animals, were employed. The main drawback to land transportation of freight before 1800 was the lack of roads. Moving wagons with cargo of any weight under a variety of weather conditions and changes in terrain was virtually impossible.

TRANSPORTATION IMPROVEMENTS BEFORE 1800

For the most part, there were no significant improvements in transportation in the United States before 1800. New ocean craft were introduced and existing ones were made larger. New boats were designed, and rafts and arks were made larger. However, these minor improvements in water vessels did not alter the pattern of transportation drastically. There was some development of ways. Common roads were improved somewhat but remained in poor condition. Although provisions for development had been made through legislation as early as 1639, road improvement was extremely slow. Unable or unwilling to

---

[2] Ibid., p. 15.

improve the common roads of the day, some individuals turned their attention to turnpikes. Turnpikes were constructed by private companies and tolls were charged for their use. The first turnpike company was chartered by Pennsylvania in 1792, and the first turnpike was completed before 1800 from Philadelphia to Lancaster, a total of sixty-two miles. That was the beginning of turnpike construction that continued well into the nineteenth century. The economic significance of road improvements can be seen from the following:

> The strong pack-horses of Scotland usually carried three hundred pounds. With a cart, on inferior roads, one horse could haul five or six hundredweight. By material improvements in roads, it became practical to increase the load of a cart horse to eight or ten hundredweight. By making first-rate roads, the ordinary load of a cart-horse became sixteen hundredweight, and on some good roads a strong horse was able to carry more than a ton. This sevenfold increase in the power of the horse represents a corresponding increase in the areas over which bulky freight could be economically moved, in the incentives to production, and the development of national and individual wealth.[3]

Canals were also introduced just before 1800. The first canal was built in 1750, but it was just about the turn of the century when major canal construction took place. Canals, like roads, improved the way and made water transportation more efficient. In addition, canals could be constructed where waterways were not available. Even though roads and canals were built before 1800, their major construction and contribution belongs to the era between 1800 and 1860. The period from 1800 to 1860 is identified as the era of mechanical power, but the transition was slow. Many of the means of transportation that depended on natural power remained a significant part of the transportation system well into the 1800s. As an example, flatboats and rafts were still being constructed and used in 1885.

In 1800, few people realized the changes that would occur in transportation over the next fifty to 100 years. An era of transportation that was as old as humanity was about to end. A new era, in which levels of speed and load capacity never before possible would be reached, was about to begin.

1800 to 1860

The era from 1800 to 1860 was unique in several ways. First, it marked the beginning of mechanical power applied to both land and water transportation. Second, the waterways were expanded and improved by an ambitious program of canal building. Third, roads and turnpikes continued to improve, and fourth, railroads began their development.

Of any time in the history of transportation, this period had the most dra-

---

[3] Ibid., p. 27.

matic effect on the efficiency of moving freight. The development of mechanized transportation coupled with the industrial revolution led to increased economic development and set the stage for the rapid growth of the United States.

APPLICATION OF MECHANICAL POWER

If one had to pick an event in the history of transportation that was the most significant to the development of freight movement, the application of mechanical power would have to be chosen. Since the beginning of civilization, the only means of power were human, animal, or natural. Given those conditions, there were limits on how quickly a shipment could be made and how much of a load could be carried or pulled. With the application of the steam engine, goods could be moved more rapidly, larger loads could be carried, and natural barriers such as river currents and topography could be overcome more easily.

The major mode of transportation at the beginning of the nineteenth century was water; therefore, it was logical that the first application of mechanical power was an attempt to overcome river currents and improve upstream movements. The steam engine was developed and in operation for nontransportation applications before 1800. In addition, several people in separate attempts proved as early as 1785 that steam engines could successfully propel crafts against the current. However, because of a lack of foresight, financial backing could not be obtained, and it was more than two decades before a commercially successful steamboat was put into operation by Robert Fulton in 1807. As might be expected, development of the steamboat was slow. The first steamboat was on the Mississippi River in 1811; by 1817 only twelve steamboats were in operation. After that time, however, developments accelerated. By 1820, seventy-one steamers had been constructed on western rivers, and fifty-two had been constructed on the Atlantic Coast. By 1830, an additional 385 steamers, measuring 65,211 tons, had been constructed throughout the United States.[4] Thus, early in the nineteenth century a major step in transportation had been taken: the introduction of commercially successful, mechanically powered transportation vehicles.

CANALS

While a handful of farsighted investors and inventors were developing steam power for transportation, the country turned its attention to increasing the efficiency of the present transportation system by improving the ways for both land and water travel. The successful ventures in building turnpikes and canals that began slowly before 1800 were developed more fully between 1800 and 1860. The canals, which proved their usefulness by connecting navigable

[4] Ibid., p. 73.

34

rivers, increasing the reach of the water system, and reducing natural currents, experienced tremendous growth during the first half of the nineteenth century. The 1880 United States Census Report on agencies of transportation reported that 4,468 miles of canals had been built by that time. Most of this mileage was constructed between 1825 and 1840. Although some of these lines were financially successful, the majority were not, and by 1880, almost 2,000 miles had been abandoned and many others were losing money.

Many events contributed to the failure of canals during the last half of the nineteenth century. Mechanical problems plagued the canals. Repairs to breakage caused by water surges were very expensive. In addition, because of freezing, the canals were useful for only seven to nine months of the year. Most important, however, the introduction and growth of the railroads finally destroyed canal operations. Nevertheless, canals had proved to be essential to the increased efficiency of the transportation system. Capable of extending the water network and allowing extremely large loads to be moved less expensively than by any other mode, canals' contribution to the continued economic development of the United States and the opening of previously inaccessible areas cannot be underestimated. The most famous and probably the most commercially successful canal, the Erie Canal, connected the Hudson River in New York and the Great Lakes. It opened trade between the East and the Midwest and played a critical role in the growth of the United States during that time.

TURNPIKES AND ROADS

At the same time that attention was turned to improving the waterways, improvements were being made in roads. Because land transport had always been extremely difficult, attention had focused on water transportation. However, even with the canals, the water network could service only a fraction of the interior of the country. In 1800 the roads in the United States remained in poor condition, with the exception of one turnpike in Pennsylvania. During the early part of the 1800s, the construction of turnpikes increased significantly. By 1828, Pennsylvania had 3,110 miles of turnpike roads, and similar construction activity was taking place in the other states. Probably the most famous early turnpike in the United States was the national road that was initially constructed for 130 miles from Cumberland, Maryland, to Wheeling, West Virginia, and eventually extended to Vandalia, Illinois. The first 130 miles was completed in 1818; construction reached Vandalia in 1838. The impact of the turnpike on efficiency was significant. For instance, to travel from Baltimore to Wheeling before the turnpike was available required eight days. After the turnpike, the trip took three days. Even with turnpikes, land transport was still slow and difficult, primarily because of the lack of mechanical power. As with canal construction, many turnpikes were ill-conceived and were economic failures. With the coming of the railroad, the efficiency of land transport improved significantly and, during the last half of the 1800s, roads in general and turnpikes in particular were ignored. Roads fell into a general state of disrepair, and turnpike companies were dissolved. It was not until the turn of the century that roads once again became a focal point and were improved.

RAILROADS

During the period from 1800 to 1860 the railroad was born and came of age. Of all advances in transportation modes, none had the same impact on the development of the system and the well-being of the United States as did the railroad. The impact of the railroad must be viewed in perspective. In 1830, when the first railroad began, two modes were in operation: water transport with some mechanical power and land transport with no mechanical power. The major thrust in transportation development was on improving the way by building canals and turnpikes. With minor exceptions, such as improved vehicles, the only major development was the application of steam to water movement. The railroad represented advantages not previously possible. The way was a solid, smooth surface, the vehicle was mechanically powered, and the network was not geographically restricted. Collectively, these improvements increased loads and speed significantly and improved the efficiency of land transportation dramatically.

For the railroad to develop, two major conditions had to be present: the need to move large loads overland on a continuous basis and the availability of technology. Of the modes that have developed to date, with the possible exception of the airplane, none was developed without economic justification. During the mid-1800s, more trade was taking place within the boundaries of the United States, unlike the previous century when the majority of trade took place between the colonies and other nations. The interior of the country was rapidly developing and the existing means of connecting the Eastern Seaboard with the Midwest were insufficient. The advent of the industrial revolution created great volumes of traffic that required efficient land transport not dictated by the natural ways of water. However, economic necessity was not sufficient. Technology also had to be present.

The steam engine was developed in the 1700s and was in operation in the United States in the early 1800s for stationary applications. The locomotive, developed in Europe in the 1800s, was imported to the United States. The way was developed during the early 1800s and initially employed either animal power or stationary steam power. It was not until 1830, however, that all of these developments were put together to form the first railroad. Once again, development was slow, difficult, and disjointed. Initially, the railroads fed the water transportation system. Short lines radiated from ports as the spokes of a wheel. Eventually, lines were extended overland and joined to create the beginning of a railroad system.

The year 1830 is generally recognized as the beginning of the railroad era. During that year, 39.8 miles of rails were constructed by four different companies; the longest line extended fifteen miles, and the shortest, 3.8 miles. By 1840, there were 2,265 miles of track in the United States. Despite such obstacles to railroad development as lack of technology and capital and resistance from special interest groups including canal operators, railroad construction accelerated. By 1850, there were 8,590 miles of track, and by 1860, there were 30,794 miles of track.

Several occurrences between 1830 and 1860 formed the foundation of the railroad system as we know it today. The width of the tracks was standardized at four feet, eight inches so that movement could take place between connecting lines. Technological improvements were made that increased the power and reliability of locomotives. Steel "T" rails were introduced to replace the wooden rails. Roadbed construction improved dramatically to enable heavier locomotives and loads. The railroad was truly a new mode that would dominate transportation for nearly a century and be an integral part of the economic development of the United States.

THE ROLE OF GOVERNMENT

To facilitate the growth of the transportation system, government involvement was needed. Although the government had been involved with transportation before 1800, it was not until the nineteenth century that its role become more significant. The public sector became involved in transportation in two ways. It assisted in the development of transportation and it regulated transportation. Until 1860, the major role of government was assistance. For the most part, the transportation system was developed by private interests with the cooperation of the public sector, both as a source of funds and for other forms of assistance.

Provisions for roads are founded in British common law, with colonial law following and providing for the development of common roads. Governmental input initially came from three levels: the Commonwealth, the counties, and the townships. Laws were written to provide for the layout of roads, rights of eminent domain, repair, and maintenance. Waterways had always been considered a public good. Thus, government became involved in providing the way for both roads and water. For a variety of reasons, roads and rivers received little or no support from the government before 1800. Private companies that were granted charters by the states were responsible for initial way improvements in the form of turnpikes and canals. Governments invested in these ventures but did not subsidize their development.

Other than granting rights of operation, governments did not subsidize the development of way until the federal government became involved in the construction of the National Pike in 1818, and the state of New York built the Erie Canal in 1825. Since then, governments at the local, state, and federal levels have been involved in transportation development. Assistance is given in a variety of ways such as land grants, tax reduction programs, low-cost or no-cost guaranteed loans, and provisions for carrier facilities. The assistance is granted because of the anticipated economic impact on a region or the nation.

As the railroads started to prove their economic impact, governments rushed to give assistance that would speed development. Local governments provided station facilities, states granted land, and many local and state governments bought railroad bonds to support development. Probably the single most ambitious assistance program given to transportation was the federal grants of land to railroads, primarily west of the Mississippi. From 1850 to 1870, the federal government granted more than 131 million acres. In return, the railroads gave the government reduced rates on certain movements of goods. At all levels, assistance was given to the development of the transportation system, a practice that continues today.

The period from 1800 to 1860 saw unparalleled accomplishments in the development of the transportation system. Mechanical power was introduced to water transport, the railroads became successful, improvements in water and land way took place, and the government became involved in transportation development. Never before had the transportation of goods changed so radically.

1860 to 1920

The period from 1860 to 1920 can be characterized as the era of the railroad. The railroads dominated transportation as the network grew from coast to coast and border to border. The amount of freight carried increased dramatically during this time. Although the railroads were the focal point in transportation from 1860 to 1920, other significant developments took place. The government at all levels continued to be involved in transportation development and became involved further in transportation regulation. The pipeline, a completely new mode, was introduced. Water and road improvements that were virtually ignored during the last half of the nineteenth century re-emerged around the turn of the century, and motor and air transportation were introduced. As the country developed and changed rapidly, so did the transportation system.

RAILROADS AND REGULATIONS

During the last four decades of the nineteenth century and the first decade of the twentieth century, railroads developed at a rapid pace. In 1870 there were 52,922 miles of track. By 1890 there were 163,597 miles, and in 1916 railroads reached a peak of 264,378 miles of track. The railroads were the only mode of land transport and dominated all movement. They had successfully displayed their abilities and economic inputs between 1830 and 1860 and had been accepted by all. The railroads expanded to all parts of the country until very few towns were without rail service. Such tremendous growth was spurred by the anticipated economic consequences of railroad transportation. Larger loads could be carried faster and to locations never before possible. Towns could see the economic impact of railroads and pursued rail development vigorously. Many local and state governments, along with farmers and other businesses, made substantial investments. Lured by the possibility of large financial returns, individuals and groups not directly involved with the railroads also invested heavily. The availability of capital and the support of governments pushed railroad development ahead at an extremely rapid rate.

With such excesses and the virtual monopoly of the railroads, problems had to occur. These problems evolved during the decades of the 1860s and 1870s. Too many railroads and too much track were created. The duplication of lines caused ruinous competition. Single lines serving particular communities charged excessive rates, refused to carry some goods, and refused to service some customers. The railroads were dealing from a favorable position of strength. In desperation, shippers, particularly farmers from the Midwest, turned to their state governments for help. The state governments initially became involved, but when it was declared illegal for states to regulate interstate transportation, the federal government became involved.

In 1887, after a long period of abuses, the Act to Regulate Commerce became law. Although its intentions were noble, the actual capabilities of the law were weak. As a result, abuses continued, and new legislation appeared in the form of several laws designed to strengthen both the initial legislation and the Interstate Commerce Commission that had been established by the original act in 1887. Thus, during the period from 1860 to 1920, the federal government became increasingly involved in the regulation of the railroads. These origins set the foundation for government involvement in other modes and created the base for the transportation regulation that we have today.

The operation and development of the transportation system in the United States cannot be understood without knowing the role of the government. Its role and its effects on the transportation system and on society as a whole will be developed fully in Chapters 10 through 12, which discuss transportation policy, law, and regulation.

PIPELINES

The first pipeline was constructed in Pennsylvania in 1865. A few years earlier, oil had been discovered in Titusville, Pennsylvania. In an effort to move the oil to the railroad line six miles away, a two-inch pipeline was constructed. Unlike the railroads, the pipeline does not have a spectacular and romantic history. Nevertheless, its contributions are significant and it plays an extremely important role in our transportation system today. Whereas the railroad was viewed and used as a mode to transport all types of goods, the pipeline was designed to serve one type of product—oil. Like the railroads, however, it was initially constructed to combine movement with another mode. As the railroads were first constructed to coordinate with water movement, the pipeline was constructed to link with the railroad and water modes. It was not until several years later that the pipeline became an independent mode.

The growth of the pipeline is directly related to the demand for oil and related products such as kerosene and gasoline. Although the railroads attempted to stop development of the pipeline by not allowing construction through railroad property, the pipeline developed as a major mode. By 1900 there were 6,800 miles of pipeline, and by 1915 more than 40,000 miles of lines existed. Although a good portion of this mileage was feeder line that moved oil from the fields to water or railroads, a growing number of miles were trunk line through which oil was transported without involving other modes. Thus, the first real competition to the monopolistic railroads had emerged.

RE-EMERGENCE OF WATER

Water transportation was all but forgotten during the last half of the nineteenth century. Near the turn of the century, it re-emerged as a major mode. Several factors led to its redevelopment, including the recognition of water as a good natural resource, the growing power of the railroads, and the hope that water would be less expensive than other modes and would foster competition. Before 1920, several major events occurred to increase the use of water transportation. The old Erie Canal was improved in 1903; improvements began on the Ohio River to give it a nine-foot channel to the Mississippi; and a plan was proposed to improve the major routes from New Orleans to Chicago and from Pittsburgh to Kansas City. Thus, inland water transportation, which had been the backbone of the transportation system until 1850 but had fallen on difficult times, once again emerged as a major mode in freight transportation.

ROADS AND MOTOR TRANSPORTATION

With the development of railroads, natural barriers no longer existed to the location of cities and towns. In seeking alternative means of moving from town to town and developing feeders to the existing railroads, the nation turned its attention once again to road development. Like the canals, roads had been ignored for half a century because of the attention given to the railroads. Unlike the canals, however, road construction was not revitalized in response to railroad domination. Initially, road improvements took place in and around cities when the automobile was introduced. There were 8,000 autos registered in the United States in 1900, and the need for road improvement became evident. By 1914, a number of states had created highway departments, and in 1916, the Federal Aid Road Act was passed, allowing grants-in-aid for highway construction and repair. Freight transportation by truck also emerged at this time; however, major growth did not occur until after 1920, and motor transportation did not become a major competitor for rail movements until after World War II.

AIR TRANSPORTATION

The last of the modes known today developed with the invention of the airplane. From its meager beginnings in 1903 at Kitty Hawk, North Carolina, the airplane grew in use primarily for military reasons, and until this day it plays only a minor role in overall freight transportation.

In summary, although the period from 1860 to 1920 belonged primarily to the railroads, all of the modes that exist today were either reintroduced or were developing by this time. The period also marked the complete involvement of the government in the development and regulation of the transportation system. Just as the government became involved in railroad development before 1880, so it became involved in the development of water, road, and air transportation from 1860 to 1920. In addition, the regulatory role of the government increased during this period.

1920 to Present

The period from 1920 to the present is different in character from the previous periods. First, all modes that make up the transportation system today were either developed or developing by 1920, and railroads were losing their dominance. Second, new forms of competition arose, and a shift in the role of each mode occurred. Third, government became a full partner to transportation with continued promotion and regulation. Overall, the transportation system began to mature and become more stable after 150 years of vigorous, often chaotic, change that paralleled the growth and development of the United States.

A FIVE-MODE SYSTEM

In 1920, all of the modes used today were in existence. The railroads had matured, water was being revitalized, the pipelines had become a proven means of moving oil and related products, the foundation for motor transport had been created, and the worth and practicality of the airplanes had been proven in World War I. There was no longer a dominant mode; neither was transportation primarily a single-mode system. Before 1800, water had been

41

dominant. After 1800, canals and steamboats handled most freight movements, and in the mid-1800s, the railroads became the major mode. At the turn of the century, however, pipelines were growing, water and road transportation were re-emerging, and the airplane was introduced. By 1920, transportation was truly becoming a five-mode system, with each mode beginning to fill the economic niche for which it was best suited.

NEW FORMS OF COMPETITION

With all modes present, new forms of competition emerged. Because of the dominance of single modes in the past and the rapid development of the country, competition in transportation often did not occur. Since 1920, however, there have been shifts in the amounts of freight that each mode hauls and a gradual stability in the role that each mode plays. Generally, the railroads have declined, the motor carriers have increased dramatically, and water and pipelines have grown at a steady rate. The airplane still does not carry significant amounts of freight tonnage.

CONTINUED ROLE OF GOVERNMENT

The period from 1920 to the present is also marked by the continued involvement of the government in the transportation system, both from a developmental and a regulatory perspective. All levels of government continue to play an increasing role. *Promotion* of the system is defined as any assistance given to the system, such as direct subsidies, land grants, or special tax benefits. The initial involvement occurred with canal construction, although some canals were privately owned, and involvement continued with land grants to railroads, primarily west of the Mississippi during the nineteenth century. Since 1920, the government has been promoting transportation with large investments in road construction and maintenance, waterway improvement, maintenance of air lanes and safety equipment, guarantees of loans to railroads, and in many other ways.

The federal government's continued involvement in regulation of the railroads after 1920 also set the stage for its involvement in other modes. Before 1920, railroad regulation was primarily concerned with pricing. The Transportation Act, passed in 1920, covered such topics as jurisdiction over railroad revenues, securities of railroads, sleeping car companies, and other issues. Since that time, other regulatory acts have been passed. The most recent act of significance was the Railroad Revitalization and Regulatory Reform Act of 1976, which was aimed at partial deregulation as well as other issues. The pipeline industry became regulated in 1906 by passage of the Hepburn Act. The motor carrier industry became regulated with passage of the Motor Carrier Act in 1935. In 1938, the Civil Aeronautics Act was passed. Water transportation be-

42

came subject to regulation by passage of the Transportation Act of 1940. Thus, the period from 1920 to the present has been one of multimodal growth and competition, maturity and stability, and the continued involvement of the government, both in promotion and regulation of the transportation system.

Summary

The history of transportation provides a foundation and perspective for viewing the transportation system of today. Before 1800, human, animal, and natural power were the only means of propelling vehicles. As a result, the movement of goods was slow and difficult. Because nature provided the way, water transportation was dominant and shaped the geographical development of the nation. Freight movement on land was virtually impossible because of inadequate roads.

From 1800 to 1860, a transportation explosion was precipitated by the application of mechanical power. The steamboat became commercially successful, and the railroads, the first means of efficient land transportation, began to develop. In recognition of the need for an efficient transportation system, the government became involved directly and indirectly in transportation development.

Although the period can be called the era of the railroad, from 1860 to 1920, the pipeline emerged, attention toward roads and water was rekindled after fifty years of neglect, and motor vehicles and airplanes were invented. Nevertheless, the railroads dominated domestic transportation. Their growth was rapid. The railroads began to abuse their position and power, and the government became involved in a regulatory capacity with passage of the Act to Regulate Commerce in 1887. This was the beginning of a long history of transportation regulation that remains today. In a sense, since 1920, transportation has matured into a multimodal system.

Questions for Chapter 3

1. What is the value of looking at the history of transportation?
2. Discuss the three means by which transportation efficiency can be improved.
3. Discuss the nature of transportation before 1800.
4. How did transportation shape the development of the United States before 1800?
5. What was the major transportation improvement before 1800?
6. Why is the application of mechanical power described as the most significant event in the history of transportation?

7. Describe the impact that the advent of the railroad had on the transportation system.
8. Why did the railroad develop as rapidly as it did?
9. Why and when did the government become involved in transportation?
10. What caused the re-emergence of water transportation and road development?
11. How is the period from 1920 to the present best described?
12. Discuss the role of government in transportation from 1920 to the present.

two

The Transportation System

Systems consist of various elements. In Part I, the elements of freight transportation were introduced as they combine to form the existing network. Each element, called a mode, has its own characteristics and occupies a unique role in the transportation system. In Part II, these modes and their contributions to the total system are examined individually.

Each major transportation mode receives in-depth coverage. Separate chapters review water, railroad, truck, pipeline, and air freight transportation. A common format is followed to allow accurate comparisons between modes. The chapters systematically explore each mode's role, industry characteristics, performance characteristics, government assistance, and future projections. Chapter 9 examines special transportation arrangements that have evolved to satisfy necessary services not provided by individual modes.

4

Water Transportation

Water has played a varied role in the United States transportation system over the last 200 years. Until the mid-1800s, it was the major mode of freight movement. The availability of natural waterways and power coupled with extensive international trade encouraged water dominance. Water was the first mode of transportation to be mechanized and the first to attract large amounts of private and public capital for development. During the first half of the nineteenth century, an extensive network of canals was built and natural waterways were improved. From 1850 to 1900, however, water transportation lost its dominance. The Civil War and the development of the railroads significantly reduced its importance. Water has not recovered its original dominance and probably never will. However, because the railroads could not satisfy all transportation needs and water is a useful mode for certain industries and products, it re-emerged at the beginning of this century as an integral part of the domestic freight transportation system.

Water, as the other modes, has unique characteristics that make it suitable for shipping particular goods under certain conditions. Its major attributes are its low cost (the lowest of all general cargo carriers) and its capability to move large quantities at one time. For instance, a river tow (actually pushed) of twenty barges, with a carrying capacity of 40,000 tons, is the equivalent of almost 800 railroad cars. Water's major drawbacks are its slow speed (the slowest of all general cargo carriers) and its limited geographic reach. It has the fewest miles of network of all the modes.

The domestic water industry is composed of three systems: Great Lakes, domestic deep sea, and inland. The Great Lakes system includes the five Great Lakes and the St. Lawrence Seaway. Domestic deep sea includes any coastal movements on the ocean between United States ports. The inland system involves any waterways that are not part of the deep sea or Great Lakes systems. Thus, iron ore shipped from Duluth, Minnesota, to Detroit, Michigan, by way of Lake Superior and Lake Huron would be considered movement through the Great Lakes system. Traffic from New York City to Norfolk, New Orleans, Los Angeles, or Honolulu over the oceans would be a domestic deep sea movement. Freight from Pittsburgh to New Orleans via the Ohio and Mississippi rivers and on to Tampa, via the intercoastal waterways would be an inland movement.

Not only are these systems distinct for statistical purposes, but they also have different shipping conditions, vessels, competitive climates, and regulatory relationships. Therefore, a distinction will be noted whenever necessary.

This survey of the role of water in the transportation system will include an outline and description of the industry, an examination of its performance characteristics, and a discussion of the role of the government in water transportation. Finally, the future role of water transportation will be explored.

Role of Water

Water transportation grew in importance following its re-emergence at the turn of the century. It has stabilized since World War II and continues to play a significant role in the transportation system.

AMOUNT SHIPPED AND REVENUE

Water transportation accounts for nearly 23 per cent of the total ton-miles shipped in the United States.[1] (A *ton-mile* is one ton moved one mile and is generally accepted as the best comparative measure of freight movement.) Table 4–1 shows the domestic ton-miles shipped by water since 1945. Although water ton-miles have increased 120 per cent (271 billion ton-miles in 1945, compared to 595 billion ton-miles in 1978), the percentage of total transportation ton-miles it represents has decreased almost 1 per cent from 23.4 to 22.5 per cent. As a percentage of all ton-miles moved, water reached a peak of 31.1 per cent in 1955 and has declined since then.

TABLE 4–1. Domestic Water Transportation

Year	Great Lakes Ton-Miles (Billions)	Domestic Deep Sea Ton-Miles (Billions)	Inland Ton-Miles (Billions)	Total Ton-Miles (Billions)	Per cent of Total Transportation Ton-Miles
1945	113	128	30	271	23.4%
1950	112	221	52	385	30.0%
1955	119	261	98	478	31.1%
1960	99	256	121	476	30.3%
1965	110	227	152	489	26.2%
1970	114	276	205	595	26.9%
1975	99	223	243	565	24.7%
1976	106	218	267	591	24.4%
1977	95	212*	280	587	23.2%
1978	98	206*	291	595	22.5%

*Estimate.
Source: *Transportation Facts and Trends*, 15th ed. (Washington, D.C.: Transportation Association of America, July 1979), p. 8.

Great Lakes and domestic deep sea traffic has stagnated since World War II because of land competition from pipelines and railroads. Part of the domestic deep sea system has no land competition, such as a shipment from California to Hawaii, so the decline is significant. The inland system, on the other hand, has had the opposite experience. Its ton-miles have increased more than sixfold since 1945.

Water plays a significant role in the movement of freight in the United States transportation system. Although the amount of ton-miles is great, the money

---

[1] This figure includes domestic deep sea movements. When domestic deep sea is eliminated from the figures and a comparison of intercity freight movement is made, the share of total ton-miles for water becomes 16.0. Comparisons in the following modal chapters will not include domestic deep sea.

TABLE 4–2. Domestic Water Freight Revenue

Year	Domestic Water Freight Revenue (Millions of Dollars)	Per cent of Total Domestic Freight Revenue	Water Freight Revenue Including International (Millions of Dollars)	Per cent of Total Transportation Freight Revenue
1960	1,573	3.4%	3,338	7.1%
1965	1,677	2.7%	3,758	6.1%
1970	1,922	2.3%	5,109	6.1%
1975	2,960	2.4%	7,888	6.3%
1976	3,420	2.4%	8,860	6.1%
1977	3,788	2.3%	9,882	6.0%

Source: *Transportation Facts and Trends*, 15th ed. (Washington, D.C.: Transportation Association of America, July 1979), p. 4.

spent on domestic water shipments as a per cent of the total freight revenues is not significant. As Table 4–2 shows, the freight revenue expenditures for domestic water shipments has been below 3 per cent of the total since 1965.

NETWORK

The size of the water network increased 728 miles from 24,815 miles in 1945 to 25,543 miles in 1977. Figure 4–1 shows the water system in the United States. The inland system accounts for most of the mileage, with only 490 miles of improved waterways listed for the Great Lakes system. The Great Lakes constitute the largest freshwater body in the world and give the United States a fourth coastline. They are accessible to ocean vessels through the St. Lawrence River, which was expanded during the 1950s to accommodate larger ships. The Great Lakes are also accessible from the New York Barge Canal and from the Illinois Waterway. This extensive system allows water transportation penetration into the United States as far west as Duluth, Minnesota.

The inland system shown in Figure 4–1 includes shipping along each of the three coasts, which are made up of coastal rivers, bays, inlets, canals, and protected channels, and the interior river and canal system, the largest of which is the Mississippi River system. The Mississippi River system represents 35.1 per cent of the waterway mileage. It reaches north from New Orleans to Minneapolis-St. Paul, east to Pittsburgh, and west to Sioux City. Given the topography of the United States, the vast majority of the waterway system lies east of the Mississippi River.

Of total water mileage, 15,675 miles, or 61.4 per cent, has standard depth channels of nine feet or more. Although the network appears limited, water's reach is quite extensive.

FIGURE 4-1. WATERWAYS OF THE UNITED STATES
Source: *Big Load Afloat* (Washington, D.C.: American Waterways Operators, Inc., 1973).

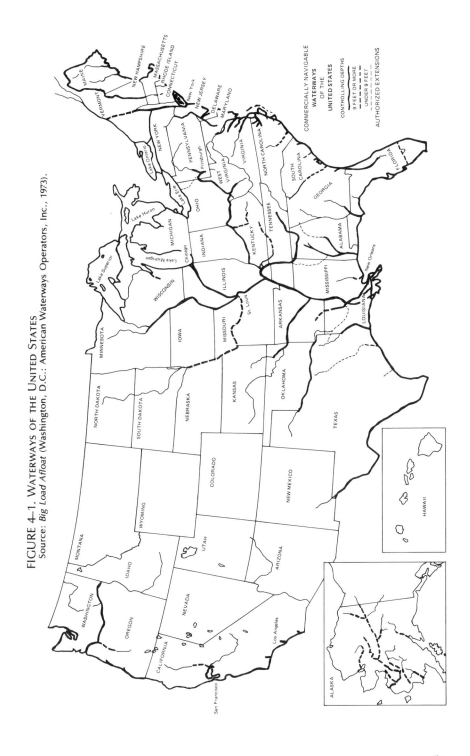

Thirty-eight of the 50 states with almost 95 per cent of the population have commercial transportation services provided by vessels operating on rivers, canals, bays, sounds, or lakes. One hundred thirty-one of the 150 cities having a population of 100,000 or more are located on commercial navigation channels.[2]

FREIGHT SHIPPED

Most of the freight moved in the water system is raw material. On the Mississippi River, 75 per cent of the total inland traffic is made up of petroleum and petroleum products, grain and grain products, bituminous coal and lignite, sand, gravel, crushed rock, and iron and steel products.[3] In the Great Lakes system, the situation is almost the same. Most of the movements are iron ore, grain, coal, and industrial bulk products. More than two thirds of domestic deep sea shipments are petroleum and petroleum products.

Thus, although water played a greater role 200 years ago, it still moves a large percentage of the freight in the United States at extremely low cost. Water has the fewest miles of network, but it reaches a large part of the nation's population and represents the transportation backbone for a variety of large-volume, low-value raw materials.

Water Industry Characteristics

Efforts to describe the economic characteristics of the water industry are complicated by the diversity of the systems, the lack of regulation, and the large proportion of private ownership. Furthermore, in the for-hire portion of the industry, the variety of contractual arrangements makes generalizations difficult. This section examines the economic characteristics of the water industry, including the number of firms, types of ownership, competition, and cost structure.

FLEET SIZE AND OWNERSHIP

In 1978, there were "1,800 companies operating 24,037 dry cargo barges and scows with a total cargo capacity in excess of 29,800,000 tons; 3,946 tank barges with a total cargo capacity of approximately 9,467,565 tons; and 4,380 towboats and tugs with a total aggregate power in excess of 6,300,000 horsepower in operation in the inland system."[4] In 1973, there were 196 ships in

---

[2]*Big Load Afloat* (Washington, D.C.: The American Waterways Operators, Inc., 1973), foreword.

[3]Ibid., p. 121.

[4]Correspondence with Neil D. Schuster, vice-president—Research (Washington, D.C.: The American Waterways Operators, Inc.)

the deep sea domestic trades with a total carrying capacity of 4,725,000 dead-weight tons.[5] In 1974, there were twenty-nine companies operating 193 vessels with 2,698,123 gross tons of capacity in the Great Lakes.[6]

The size of the inland fleet has grown steadily over the last three decades. There were 1,350 barge companies in 1943,[7] 1,700 in 1963,[8] and 1,849 in 1973.[9] The Great Lakes fleet has declined from its peak during the Korean War of 403 cargo ships with a capacity of 3,540,000 gross tons.[10] The overall domestic deep sea fleet has declined since 1973. However, the size of the fleet moving freight between the forty-eight contiguous states and the other states and possessions has stabilized over the last two decades.

Of the 1,849 companies that make up the inland fleet, 400 are engaged in private transportation and 216 are under ICC regulations as either common or contract carriers. The rest of the companies are engaged in for-hire service but are exempt from ICC regulation. The ICC exempts for-hire carriers when they are hauling no more than three dry bulk commodities in one tow or when they are hauling liquid commodities in bulk. Dry bulk commodities are nonliquid, nonpackaged products such as sand, gravel, and potash. As a result, it is esti-mated that only 16.3 per cent of the total ton-miles moved in the inland water system in 1976 was federally regulated.[11]

In the Great Lakes system, the largest carriers are either owned privately or by independent companies that charter their ships to industry clients. A few carriers are subject to ICC regulations. In total, they represent thirty-five of 193 vessels with a carrying capacity of 320,000 deadweight tons of the total fleet ca-pacity of 2,698,123 deadweight tons, or about 15 per cent of capacity.[12] In 1976, it was estimated that only 0.2 per cent of the ton-miles shipped on the Great Lakes was federally regulated.[13] As with the inland system, exceptions exist for not more than three dry bulk and liquid commodities.

The domestic deep sea fleet is owned primarily by private industries or is chartered. Of the 196 ships in service, 135 are tankers owned mostly by oil companies. Of the total ton-miles moved in 1976, only 3.7 per cent were under federal regulations.[14]

---

[5] U.S. Department of Commerce, Maritime Administration, *Employment Report of the U.S. Flag Oceangoing Merchant Fleet, June 30, 1973* (1974), p. 68.

[6] *Lake Carriers Association Annual Report, 1974* (Cleveland, Ohio: Lake Carriers Association, 1975), p. 37.

[7] John L. Hazard, *Transportation: Management—Economics—Policy* (Cambridge, Maryland: Cornell Maritime Press, 1977), p. 343.

[8] Ibid.

[9] *Big Load Afloat*, op. cit., p. 3.

[10] *Lake Carriers Association*, op. cit., p. 37.

[11] *Transportation Facts and Trends*, 15th ed. (Washington, D.C.: Transportation Association of America, July 1979), p. 9.

[12] U.S. Interstate Commerce Commission, *Transport Statistics in the United States—Part 5, Carriers by Water* (1972).

[13] *Transportation Facts and Trends*, op. cit., p. 9.

[14] Ibid., p. 9.

COST CHARACTERISTICS

For the most part, water is not a capital-intensive industry. Unlike railroads and pipelines, most costs are variable. Low fixed costs result from networks and terminals being provided from outside the industry. Therefore, major costs are incurred in equipment purchases, maintenance, fuel, and labor for operations and support.

The federal government has maintained the natural waterways and has improved their navigability by dredging, straightening, building locks, and providing navigation equipment. This government role of maintenance, improvement, and navigation aids is true for inland water, the Great Lakes, and domestic deep sea systems. No tolls or fees are charged for use except for the St. Lawrence Seaway, the Panama Canal, and a diesel fuel tax on barge tows.

Terminals, the interface points between water and land, are provided from outside the industry except for some private terminals. Public terminals on all domestic waterways are usually provided by local governments. However, unlike the waterways, fees are charged for services provided. At ocean ports, such charges might include dockage, harbor master fees, and mooring. In addition, water carriers also pay for loading and unloading while at the terminal.

Because networks and terminals are provided, the major investment is in equipment. Although the cost of tugs, barges, lake freighters, and ocean vessels has increased rapidly, water is not considered a capital-intensive industry. Capital turnover is a measure to describe the amount of capital needed in an industry. It is computed by dividing revenue by the required capital investment. For instance, if an industry has revenue of $100 million and a capital investment of $25 million, the capital turnover would be four. The lower the number, the greater the capital intensity of the industry. Capital turnover in the water industry ranges from 0.5 to one. Capital turnover in the pipeline industry is less (0.25), but turnover in the trucking industry is much higher (four). Line-haul costs are extremely low and, depending on the type of equipment, will range from one to two mills per ton-mile, with large Great Lakes vessels on the low end, and small barge tows on the high end.

Thus, the cost characteristics of water can be generally described as low fixed costs and high variable costs, with the majority of investment in equipment, and a capital turnover that makes water less capital-intensive than railroads or pipelines. Line-haul costs are very low, resulting in low costs to shippers.

COMPETITION

An analysis of competitive characteristics is hindered by the many different conditions found in the industry and the general lack of information. However, with the information available, some generalizations can be made about the competition within the water mode and between water and other modes.

Even though the cost of equipment is rising steadily and ship construction

54

may take as long as two years, entry into the industry is not difficult. From a shipper's perspective, a variety of water transportation alternatives is available, including private ownership, leasing, contract arrangements, and common carriage. The Great Lakes fleet has only twenty-nine companies, and a few of those control most of the shipments. Private carriage is a workable alternative. The domestic deep sea fleet is also small and controlled by a few firms. The inland fleet, however, includes a large number of firms, none of which has a large percentage of the total movement. These characteristics lead to the conclusion that the water industry is more competitive than it is monopolistic. The industry structure, size of firms, ease of entry, and the alternatives open to shippers imply a competitive structure.

Competition between water and the other modes is also evident. Over the last forty years, except for the inland tug/barge system, the water industry has declined rather than grown. Domestic deep sea shipping, particularly between ports in the contiguous United States, has dropped considerably. More than two thirds of the movements are petroleum and petroleum products moved in private vessels. Even though it is low-cost, terminal delays and the limited availability of ports have made this type of water movement vulnerable to railroad and pipeline competition. Movement on the Great Lakes has stabilized since the Korean War but, again, competition from railroads and pipelines is significant. Inland water movements, on the other hand, have grown and apparently are meeting pipe and rail competition successfully. Some of this success is artificial in the sense that regulation of the railroads has somewhat protected water movements, whereas the pipeline's ability to move only liquids and gases has limited its competitive impact.

From a national perspective, the water network is hauling the types of freight for which it is best suited, and it is hauling this freight at competitive prices. The water industry does not dominate other modes of the transportation system; neither does there appear to be an excessive concentration within the industry. Thus, a structure inclined to competition, rather than monopoly, exists.

Performance Characteristics

Of the five major modes in operation today, each offers unique performance characteristics that make it most suitable for shipping particular products under certain conditions. When selecting a mode, a shipper looks at several characteristics of the mode along with the cost to ship a product. The shipper does not evaluate the mode in a vacuum but compares one to the other modes available for shipping the same product. Depending upon the performance of a particular mode, the objectives of the shipper, the type and amount of product, and the cost, one mode will be selected.

This section considers water transportation from the viewpoint of shippers as to the performance characteristics the mode offers in comparison to other modes. First, the characteristics that are common to all modes and used for comparative purposes will be presented. These characteristics are used to review other modes in following chapters. Given this framework, the characteristics of water transportation are then discussed.

CLASSIFICATION OF PERFORMANCE CHARACTERISTICS

Shippers are concerned with six characteristics when evaluating a transportation mode. These characteristics are not independent of each other. Overlap and interdependence are the rule rather than the exception.

SPEED

Speed is a measure of the elapsed time from when a product is given to a transport mode until the movement is completed. As you will recall, transportation is a service. It is a means to move freight to production or from production to consumption. If a manufacturer is shipping to a retail store, the retailer is interested in when the product will be available for sale. Thus, the speed of air freight movement is not 600 miles per hour but, rather, the time it takes to move freight to a terminal, load the airplane, fly it to another terminal, and complete delivery.

COMPLETENESS

The degree of *completeness* refers to the extent of the modal network and the amount of required involvement of other modes. For example, airports do not exist at all possible shipment locations. The shipper must move the freight to the airport for shipment and from the airport after arrival. Therefore, air transport is less complete than motor transport.

DEPENDABILITY

Dependability is a measure of the mode's ability to perform as anticipated over time. From a shipper's and receiver's perspective, it is important to know when a product will arrive or if it will be shipped on schedule. Uncontrollable natural calamities, of course, may disrupt any mode and make it less dependable. However, other factors such as congestion, loading and unloading delays, and in-transit load-breaking affect the dependability of the mode.

CAPABILITY

Capability is a measure of a mode's ability to handle particular transportation requirements. This would include the type of freight (solid, liquid, bulk, packaged), the size of the individual product, the weight, and the load size required. For instance, pipelines would be considered the least capable because they are restricted to liquid and gaseous products.

FREQUENCY

Frequency is a measure of the number of times a mode can pick up and deliver during a particular period. For instance, shipments made only once a week are less frequent, and possibly less desirable, than shipments made twice a week.

COST

Cost is a measure of the amount of money a shipper or receiver must pay for freight movement. The most visible cost is the rate a person pays to each mode. However, other costs must be considered. These would include costs to load and unload if not provided by the mode, costs of extra insurance depending on the liability of the carrier and the probability of damage, and the cost to the shipper or receiver for inventory of the product while in transit.

Thus, each mode has particular advantages and disadvantages for certain types of products and shippers. Modal selection is made only after all of these characteristics have been considered together.

PERFORMANCE CHARACTERISTICS OF WATER

The modal characteristics just described will now be used to evaluate the attributes and limitations of water transportation.

SPEED

For line-haul services (once the mode is in movement), the speed of water ranges from a low of three to four miles per hour to a high of twenty-two to thirty-five miles per hour. Barges under tow will move at three to four miles per hour upstream and seven to eight miles per hour downstream. This speed can vary, depending upon the type of tow and the locks through which the barges must pass. Great Lakes and deep sea vessels are somewhat faster, and ocean container ships are the fastest. Loading and unloading time varies, depending on the type of product and the port facilities. Generally, bulk freight can be unloaded faster than general cargo. For most shippers and cargo, the slow speed of water transportation is a limitation. Some shippers use the slow speed to their advantage by using the time in transit for inventory storage.

COMPLETENESS

Because of its limited miles of network and dependence upon topography, water is considered incomplete compared to other modes. If shippers wish to move freight by water only, they must confine themselves to the relatively limited network and the availability of ports and terminals. However, because of the extremely low cost of water transport, shippers have adapted by moving plants to water sites or by bringing water to major metropolitan centers. Even with these adjustments, completeness cannot be considered a strong characteristic of water transportation.

DEPENDABILITY

For water, dependability can be measured on two levels. Under normal operating conditions, water is very dependable. Although little information is published on variances in arrival time, there is no reason to believe that line-hauls would be severely interrupted as a result of unforeseen conditions. Some complications are possible, of course, from lock and port congestion. The other factor affecting dependability is seasonality. Because of freezing, some waterways are operable only nine months out of the year. The New York Barge Canal and other inland waters close during the winter. The Great Lakes system is closed to the ocean, but attempts are being made to keep the lakes and their locks and channels open all year. Generally, water can be considered dependable. In comparison to other modes, it is less dependable than pipelines or motor transportation and on the same level as railroads and air transportation.

CAPABILITY

Given the physical characteristics of water equipment, water transport must be considered the most capable mode. Almost anything a shipper might want to ship could be handled by water. This is especially true when the freight volume to be moved is considered. In a single tow, the equivalent of 800 to 1,000 railcars can be transported. This characteristic makes water most desirable for certain freight.

FREQUENCY

Because of the large amounts of freight moved and the slow speed, the frequency of movement is low. Although this is not an asset, it is not necessarily considered a liability, considering the water movement circumstances.

COST

Measured on freight rate per ton-mile, water is generally comparable to pipelines but much lower than all other modes. Depending upon particular conditions such as the size of equipment, the amount of labor, and the product, the cost to ship by water ranges from 1.0 to 2.0 mills per ton-mile. Depending on size, pipeline costs will range from 0.6 to 1.5 mills per ton-mile. By far, low cost is water's major asset. For some types of movements, the other less desirable service characteristics are overcome by the low cost.

In summary, when compared to other modes, water is slow, incomplete, somewhat dependable, able to carry all types of freight, infrequent, and low cost. Consequently, water is best suited for large-volume, low-value, bulk raw materials.

The Role of Government

The development and operation of domestic freight transportation has been and continues to be primarily an undertaking of private enterprise. However, because of some unique characteristics of the freight transportation industry and its overall importance to the development of the nation, various levels of government have been involved in transportation. The government's involvement is in two major areas: promotion/provision and regulation. *Promotion/provision* is broadly defined as some form of assistance to a mode or modes, such as low-cost or guaranteed loans, provision of network or facilities, land grants for network, tax advantages not offered to other businesses, and government-sponsored research that aids in the development and operation of the transportation system. *Regulation* is defined as some degree of control over a transportation mode. It includes control over the prices charged for a service and the mode's operations in relation to safety, labor, or the environment. Government promotion of the modes will be discussed here and in the following modal chapters. Regulation is discussed in Chapters 10 through 12.

The government's promotion of the water system has been occurring for more than 200 years, but the type and amount of assistance has varied widely. Before 1800, government promotion was limited to granting rights of eminent domain, which requires the sale of private property at fair value for transportation purposes, and small grants of federal aid for harbor improvement. With the increased emphasis on water transportation, however, the level of government assistance increased substantially after 1800. The first major project was the Erie Canal, which was built by the state of New York. The success of that venture led to a massive campaign during the early 1800s of canal building, which then declined during the 1837 recession, and ended completely twenty to twenty-five years later.

Government involvement began primarily at the state level. The states granted land, gave or guaranteed loans, invested in canal companies, and sometimes built the canals. As the interest in canals grew, other forms of water transportation drew attention. In 1823, the Congress passed the first Rivers and Harbors Act, which provided for improvement and maintenance of the nation's water system. Although various governments provided assistance, no cohesive plan for the development of the water system emerged. Before such a plan could be designed, the railroads achieved prominence and water transportation was forgotten. Although the Congress continued to make regular appropriations to improve and maintain water transportation, it was not until the early part of this century that a conscientious program was developed and promotion/provision was increased.

Between 1900 and 1920, several pieces of legislation were passed that laid the foundation for federal promotion of the water industry. Today, the focus of government promotion is on the creation, improvement, and maintenance of ways, as well as provision of navigation facilities. This assistance is provided by the Congress through the Army Corps of Engineers. In addition to benefiting the water industry, the projects completed by the Corps serve many purposes including flood control, power generation, irrigation, and recreation. The Corps builds, maintains, and operates locks and dams on all water systems, operates and maintains the navigation system, and straightens and dredges channels. States and local transportation authorities also provide assistance to the water industry. Their involvement is primarily in the creation, maintenance, and operation of port facilities.

Thus, although the government has rarely become directly involved in water transportation (from 1924 to 1953, it owned a barge line to promote the feasibility of water transportation and has taken over facilities in times of national emergency), private operators have had the ways provided by nature. And the government has improved, maintained, and made those networks navigable.

Future

The future role that water will play in the United States transportation system depends on many factors both within and outside the control of the industry. These factors include future demand for movement of freight that best fits the water mode, technology, government, competition from other modes, and energy and ecology considerations. These factors will be discussed briefly, and their impact on the industry will be examined.

The demand to move products best suited for water has been forecasted to increase through the year 2000. These products are primarily basic raw materials such as grains, sand, gravel, coal, ore, and basic chemicals. Movement of petroleum, which is also shipped by water, may decline because of the supply shortage. However, the impact is not anticipated to be significant in the near future.

The demand for products that are best suited for water movement is expected to increase in the future. However, this does not necessarily mean that the water industry will grow accordingly. It simply means that the potential is there. To capture some or all of this increased potential, technology in its broadest sense must improve. The size of the water network will not increase substantially. Therefore, increases in productivity are necessary. Larger and more maneuverable tugs, some of which are already in operation, must continue to be introduced to enable the industry to handle larger tows. Further gains in productivity must be realized through advances in communication and navigation to alleviate congestion and allow all-weather operation. In the Great Lakes system, for example, efforts are being made to keep the upper four lakes open twelve months of the year. If these efforts are successful, the result will be an economic boost and an ability to satisfy the increased demand for the system.

The government, particularly through its promotion of the mode, will affect the future of water. Network locks must be improved to keep pace with the increased size of tows and ships. At the present time, the larger tows must be separated to move through certain locks. It has been proposed that the present lock system be replaced with fewer and larger locks. At best, this program will proceed slowly because of the large investment required. Although some work is being done, a massive investment in the locks is not anticipated.

Another way government can influence the future of water is with usage fees, such as tolls and taxes. For the most part, the water industry does not pay directly for government assistance. The government has been pressured for many years, particularly by the pipeline and rail industries, to levy water user charges. The other modes see themselves at a competitive disadvantage because of the government's assistance to water. In 1978, legislation was passed that imposes a tax on diesel fuel. The tax, which started in 1980 at four cents per gallon, will be increased gradually to ten cents per gallon by 1985. Although its full impact is not yet known, this tax will influence the competitive position of water in relation to other modes. Another form of direct payment by water carriers is the toll charges paid to pass certain canals and locks.

Water's future will also be directly affected by competition from other modes, particularly pipe and rail. The pipeline industry has consistently fought the water industry for petroleum traffic. This competition will not abate and will likely increase, because large-diameter pipelines cost significantly less than water transportation. Furthermore, the technology for slurry pipelines has been developed and is being put into operation. These pipelines take a solid, such as coal or sand, and suspend it in a fluid that allows it to be transported by pipeline. The growth of this type of movement would put water at a competitive disadvantage.

The railroads have consistently sought to compete with water. They have achieved rates that are competitive with water on parallel routes and, if deregulation continues, the rails will offer very serious competition. Railroad technology has also developed. "Big John" cars, which move 100 tons of grain at a time, and unit trains, which move without interruption to add or remove cars, pose a serious competitive threat to water transportation.

In addition to demand, technology, government, and competition, two additional factors must be considered: the availability of energy and the nation's growing concern with ecology. Water transportation is energy-efficient, but so are the pipelines and railroads. To move one ton one mile by pipe requires approximately 0.2 horsepower; water requires 0.2; rail 2.64; truck 7.0; and air, 500. Even though water and pipe require about the same horsepower to move one ton one mile, the directness of pipelines versus the winding water network makes water transportation somewhat less energy-efficient. If energy conservation becomes crucial, which appears likely, pipe, water, and rail will be favored to increase their roles in the transportation system.

As the nation places more emphasis on ecology, replacement of small locks and the extension of the water network may be slowed. Ecological considerations have already had an impact. New projects have been stalled because of ecological pressures and at least one project, the Florida Barge Canal, has been stopped completely.

The future of water transportation cannot be predicted accurately because it depends on many variables whose direction and impact are not known. However, the general agreement is that the future of water transportation is neither bleak nor bright and, to a great extent, it is beyond the control of the water industry. The best estimate of water's future is that it will grow in absolute terms but will remain steady as a percentage of the total ton-miles moved. If that is so, water will continue to be an important and integral part of our domestic freight transportation system.

Summary

Water, the oldest mechanized mode in our transportation system, plays a vital role in the domestic movement of freight. Almost 23 per cent of all ton-miles shipped are moved on water. The water network in the United States is composed of three elements: domestic deep sea, movements among United States ports on the high seas; the Great Lakes system, composed of the five Great Lakes and the St. Lawrence Seaway; and the inland system, the rivers, canals, and the intercoastal waterway. The water network has approximately 25,000 miles, the least of all modes, but it still allows access to a majority of the industrial and commercial centers in the United States.

Although individual elements of the water system are unique, water is categorized as competitive and not capital-intensive. Water's greatest asset is extremely low cost. Its slow speed and restricted network are liabilities. However, water's low cost and the ability to move large amounts of freight at one time make it the ideal mode for bulk materials.

The government has been assisting water transportation for nearly 200 years, but it was not until the beginning of this century that a comprehensive program was developed. The main assistance comes from the Congress through the Army Corps of Engineers, which creates, maintains, and operates the waterways.

The future of water's role in the domestic freight transportation system depends on many variables that are difficult to forecast. However, water should continue to play a major role in the domestic freight transportation system.

Performance characteristics common to all modes were presented and defined in this chapter. This performance characteristic framework is used in Chapters 4 through 9 to provide a basis for modal comparison.

Questions for Chapter 4

1. Discuss the role that water transportation has played in the transportation system over the last 200 years.
2. Discuss the role of water transportation today.
3. Describe the characteristics of the freight generally carried by water.
4. Each segment of the water industry has had different growth patterns. Discuss each and the possible reasons for the differences.
5. Describe the cost characteristics of water transportation.
6. What type of competition best describes water transportation?
7. Of all performance characteristics, which two give water transportation its greatest competitive advantage?
8. From an energy consumption perspective, which mode would be most efficient when making a shipment from New Orleans to Pittsburgh?
9. Name three different types of promotion/provision assistance given to water transportation by the government.
10. What effect will intermodal competition have on water transportation in the future?
11. In your opinion, what will be government's role in the future of water transportation?
12. In your opinion, what role will water transportation play in the United States transportation system in the year 2000?

5

Railroad Transportation

Since the beginning of time, moving large, heavy loads over land has been difficult. Nature provided ways for water transportation, but did not do the same for land movements. Barriers such as rivers, mountains, and forests, as well as the lack of motive power, inhibited efficient land transportation. Wagons pulled by animals or humans remained the major means of land transportation until 150 years ago.

Given these conditions and the increasing demand for land transportation, the significant impact the railroads had on the development of the United States is understandable. Trains could carry very large loads with relative speed at low cost. With the aid of the steam engine, trips that had taken days could be completed in hours. Because of its many advantages over water, railroad transportation became the dominant mode and held that position for nearly a century. The railroads were a prime contributor to the country's rapid economic growth. They provided the link between the East and West Coasts that allowed development of the United States west of the Mississippi River.

Eventually, as other modes such as pipelines and trucks developed and water re-emerged, the railroad industry's dominance waned. Although they no longer play the major role they once did and are now plagued with problems, the railroads remain an extremely important and irreplaceable mode in the domestic transportation system.

In comparison to the other four major modes, railroads are in the middle in relation to performance characteristics. Trains are not as slow as water but not as fast as trucks, their rates are not as low as those of water, but not as high as those of trucks. The loads they can carry are not as large as the load capacity by water, but far larger than that of trucks.

One performance characteristic unique to railroads is that they are operationally the only fully integrated mode. For example, even though railroads are privately owned, the equipment is standardized and cars owned by one company can move over other companies' lines. No one railroad network crosses the entire country, but a shipment can be routed over several railroads to move a product from coast to coast. The product never leaves the car until it reaches its destination, and the shipper receives only one bill for the shipment.

Although the railroads had been losing relative market share steadily since the early 1900s, it was not until the 1960s that they faced severe economic problems. Several railroads, particularly in the northeast portion of the United States, declared bankruptcy. The federal government has since become more involved with the railroad industry in an effort to stabilize it, but its future remains uncertain.

This chapter will look at the role of the railroads in the transportation system, the industry's structure, and railroad service characteristics from a shipper's perspective. The role of the government and the future of the mode will be discussed.

Role of Railroads

The railroads have steadily declined in importance since the turn of the century. During the past decade, even though the decline in relative ton-miles and revenues has slowed, the system continues to erode. Nevertheless, the railroads still carry more ton-miles than any other mode and continue to play a major role in the overall transportation system.

AMOUNT SHIPPED AND REVENUE

In 1978, the railroads shipped 35.8 per cent of all ton-miles moved in the United States. Table 5–1 shows the railroad ton-miles shipped since 1940. Although the percentage of total ton-miles declined from a high of 67.2 per cent

65

TABLE 5–1. Railroad Transportation

Year	Total Ton-Miles (Billions)	Per cent of Total Transportation Ton-Miles
1940	379	61.3%
1945	691	67.2%
1950	597	56.2%
1955	631	49.5%
1960	579	44.1%
1965	709	43.3%
1970	771	37.7%
1975	759	36.7%
1977	832	36.0%
1978	873	35.8%

Source: *Transportation Facts and Trends*, 15th ed. (Washington, D.C.: Transportation Association of America, July 1979), p. 8.

in 1945 to a low of 35.8 percent in 1978, the ton-miles moved increased from a low of 379 billion in 1940 to a high of 873 billion in 1978. From 1940 to 1978, railroad ton-miles have increased 130 per cent. During the same period, total ton-miles for all freight increased 310 per cent, from 618 billion to 2,531 billion. Total ton-miles shipped increased dramatically in the early 1940s to support the war effort. Since then, the overall trend has continued upward, but very erratically. The percentage of total ton-miles also increased from 1940 to 1945 but has been declining steadily since then. The decline has slowed somewhat during the last decade. From 1960 to 1970, the percentage of total ton-miles dropped 6.4 per cent, and from 1970 to 1978, it dropped only 1.9 per cent.

TABLE 5–2. Railroad Revenue

Year	Railroad Freight Revenue (Millions of Dollars)	Total Freight Revenue * (Millions of Dollars)	Per cent of Total Transportation Freight Revenue
1960	9,028	45,062	20.0%
1965	9,923	59,046	16.8%
1970	11,869	80,643	14.7%
1975	16,509	120,953	13.7%
1976	18,648	140,075	13.3%
1977	19,581	166,057	11.8%

*Does not include international water.
Source: *Transportation Facts and Trends*, 15th ed. (Washington, D.C.: Transportation Association of America, 1979), p. 4.

As would be expected, railroad revenues have also declined. Table 5–2 shows both the railroad revenues and percentages for selected years. Railroad revenue has increased from $9,028 million in 1960 to $19,581 million in 1977, whereas the percentage of the total has declined from 20 per cent in 1960 to 11.8 per cent in 1977. Although railroad revenues increased 117 per cent from 1960 to 1977, total transportation revenue increased 269 per cent during the same time.

These figures highlight the railroads' declining share of the total transportation system. Although they continue to move more goods and to increase revenues, the railroads are growing at a much slower rate than the transportation industry as a whole.

NETWORK

An estimated 191,205 miles [1] of railroad line [2] were in place in the United States in 1977. Railroad line mileage reached a peak of approximately 254,000 miles in 1916 and has been declining since, with little expected change in this trend. Table 5–3 shows the railroad network's decline from 1940 to 1976.

The railroad network shown in Figure 5–1 was built primarily by private enterprises, aided by a variety of government assistance. Since the beginning in 1830 when railroads were built to feed the water network, no single master plan has been followed for railroad network development. During the last half of the

TABLE 5–3. Railroad Line Mileage

Year	Line Mileage
1940	233,670
1945	226,696
1950	223,779
1955	220,670
1960	217,552
1965	211,925
1970	206,265
1975	199,126
1976	192,396
1977	191,205

Source: *Transportation Facts and Trends*, 15th ed. (Washington, D.C.: Transportation Association of America, July 1979), p. 31.

[1] *Transportation Facts and Trends*, 15th ed. (Washington, D.C.: Transportation Association of America, July 1979), p. 31.

[2] Line mileage represents the length of the way for line-haul railroads. When mileage is added for yards, siding, and two, three, or more parallel tracks, the total number of miles of railroad track was 324,219 in 1975.

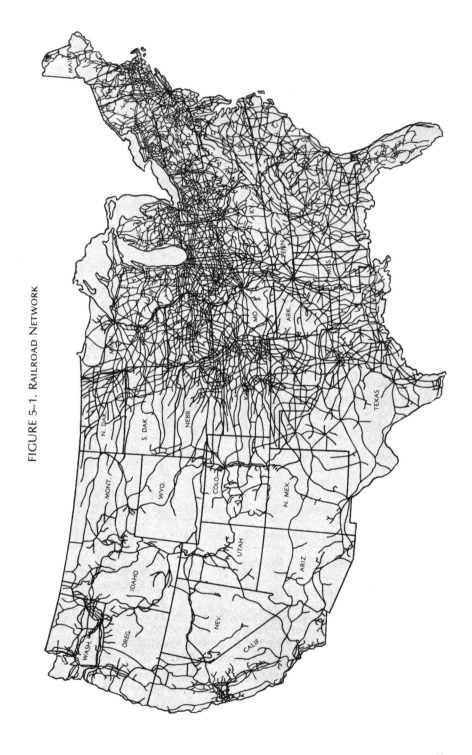

FIGURE 5–1. RAILROAD NETWORK

68

nineteenth century, the prospects for financial success and widespread optimism about the railroads' capabilities encouraged the greatest railroad construction boom in the history of the world. The result was overexpansion and many miles of unprofitable track. The combination of overexpansion and the declining role of the railroads during the twentieth century made track abandonment inevitable.

In spite of the decline of the railroads and the fact that the railroad network is smaller than that of pipe, truck, or air, the geographic reach and coverage of the railroads is extensive. As Figure 5–1 illustrates, the greatest concentration of track is in the Northeast and Midwest, which reflects the era of major railroad construction and the density of the population. All major commercial centers in the United States have rail service and most cities have access to the railroad network.

FREIGHT SHIPPED

When the railroads dominated, they shipped almost every type of product. As their role shifted, so did the composition of the freight moved. Today, the railroads most often ship large quantities of heavyweight, low-value products. On one end of a continuum, water moves large volumes of the lowest-value bulk products, such as basic raw materials. Trucks ship higher-value, finished products in relatively small, discrete volumes. The railroads stand in between, competing for both the products shipped by water such as petroleum, coal, and grain, and the general cargo shipped by trucks.

Table 5–4 lists seven product categories that had more than 1 million car loadings in 1979. Coal is by far the product shipped most often by rail. Of the remaining product categories, only fifth-ranked motor vehicles would not be considered basic raw materials. Thus, the composition of the traffic leans toward raw materials rather than finished goods.

TABLE 5–4. Products with More Than 1 Million Car Loadings, 1979

Product	Number of Car Loadings (000)	Per cent of Total Car Loadings
Coal	5,254	22.0%
Metallic Ores	1,765	7.4%
Chemical and Allied Products	1,488	6.2%
Grain	1,428	6.0%
Motor Vehicles and Equipment	1,122	4.7%
Pulp, Paper and Allied Products	1,097	4.6%
Primary Forest Products	1,055	4.4%

Source: *Yearbook of Railroad Facts* (Washington, D.C.: Association of American Railroads, 1980), p. 26.

Although the railroad industry has declined in overall importance to the transportation system, it remains the largest mode in ton-miles shipped, it is accessible to most of the country, and it is the ideal mode for certain types of products.

Railroad Industry Characteristics

This section will examine the economic characteristics of the railroad industry, including the number of firms, types of ownership, competition, and cost structure.

FLEET SIZE AND OWNERSHIP

Nearly 500 companies provide complete railroad services, including linehaul, switching, and terminal operations. Of these, forty-one have operating revenues in excess of $50 million and are thus designated as Class I railroads for statistical purposes.[3] In 1977, the Class I railroads handled 99 per cent of the traffic, owned and operated 96 per cent of the rail trackage, and employed 91 per cent of all railroad workers. Thus, an average Class I railroad has an investment in excess of $650 million, operates almost 5,000 miles of track, and employs about 12,000 people. The use of average figures, however, can be misleading because there is a wide variance in the size of the Class I railroads. For instance, in 1976, ConRail had freight revenues of $2.572 billion, 14.8 per cent of the Class I revenues. The six largest railroads are ConRail, Burlington Northern, Southern Pacific, Family Lines (consisting of the Clinchfield Railroad, the Louisville and Nashville Railroad, and the Seaboard Coast Line Railroad), Chessie System, and Norfolk and Western. In 1976, these railroads accounted for $9.5 billion of freight revenue, almost 55.5 per cent of all Class I revenues and 55.2 per cent of the total ton-miles.[4]

During this century and particularly during the last two decades, the number of railroads has declined and the size of the remaining railroads has increased correspondingly. The number of railroad mergers has increased dramatically as a partial response to the declining share of market and profits.

All railroads are common carriers subject to government regulation and are for the most part private enterprises. A few small railroads are owned by states and leased to private companies. The federal government owns the Alaskan and Panama Railroads and is ConRail's major stockholder. The relationship between ConRail and the government will be discussed later in this chapter.

[3] *Yearbook of Railroad Facts* (Washington, D.C.: Association of American Railroads, 1979), p. 2.
[4] U.S. Department of Transportation, *A Prospectus For Change in the Freight Railroad Industry* (October 1978), p. 15.

TABLE 5–5. Number of Freight Cars and Capacity

Year	Number of Freight Cars	Average Freight Car Capacity (Tons)	Total Capacity (Tons)
1944	2,067,948	50.8	105,051,750
1955	1,996,443	53.7	107,208,980
1967	1,822,381	63.4	115,538,950
1972	1,716,937	69.6	119,498,810
1977	1,666,533	75.5	125,823,240
1979	1,700,310	78.8	133,984,323

Source: *Yearbook of Railroad Facts* (Washington, D.C.: Association of American Railroads, 1980), pp. 49, 51.

In 1979, 1,700,310 freight cars and 28,402 locomotives were in service. The number of freight cars decreased slowly until 1979 and the size and carrying capacity of freight cars has increased. Table 5–5 shows this relationship for some representative years since 1944.

Over the last twenty years, the number of locomotives has remained almost constant. However, during the same period, overall horsepower has increased significantly. For example, in 1970, 27,086 locomotives had a combined horsepower total of 52.6 million. By 1978, 27,457 locomotives had a combined capacity of 61.2 million horsepower.[5]

Thus, the railroad industry, composed of privately owned common carriers, is becoming more concentrated but growing in capacity and motive power.

COST CHARACTERISTICS

The railroads and pipelines are the only modes that must pay all the costs associated with transporting goods because of their ownership and maintenance of their rights of way. For the most part, networks for air, truck, and water are provided, and terminals are often provided for air and water. Even though user fees are charged for some terminals and networks, the fact that railroads own and maintain their own networks and terminals has a significant impact on the cost characteristics of the industry.

Generally, the railroads can be described as highly capital-intensive, with slow capital turnover, high fixed costs, and low cost per ton-mile. Overall, they remain in a middle position in comparison to other modes.

In 1978 it was estimated that the Class I railroads had a net investment of $29.2 billion.[6] This included the track, real estate, terminals, cash, equipment, materials, and supplies. Operating revenues for 1977 were $20.1 billion. This is a capital turnover of 0.7, which is about the same as for water, better

[5] *Yearbook of Railroad Facts*, op. cit., p. 48.
[6] Ibid., p. 55.

than pipelines (0.25), but less than truck (4). Some controversy exists over the degree of fixed versus variable costs. However, most agree that next to pipelines the railroads have the largest proportion of fixed to variable costs. Therefore, regardless of the amount of freight moved, many costs remain constant, such as the investment in rails, maintenance necessary because of time rather than usage, taxes, and upkeep of terminals and yards.

One serious implication of this fixed cost situation is that railroads find it difficult to respond to changes in demand. If demand increases, a railroad that is close to full utilization cannot respond to the demand because of the capital required and because improvements cannot be made in small increments. For instance, if one track is at capacity and demand increases, the addition of another track will double the capacity even though only a fraction of the track might be required.

When market demand drops, the railroad faces more serious problems. Again, because of high fixed costs and an inability to shift resources, it is difficult for railroads to respond to small incremental declines in demand. Revenues decline but fixed costs continue, creating either a profit squeeze or a loss. This situation, coupled with the slow capital turnover and low rate of return on investment (1.26 per cent in 1977),[7] results in an industry inability to attract new equity capital.

The cost to the shipper to move goods by rail is relatively low. In 1977, the average revenue per ton-mile was 2.29 cents.[8] Although this is higher than pipe and water, it is lower than truck or air.

COMPETITION

Railroad competition exists at two levels, among the railroads and between the railroads and other modes. The railroad industry is more monopolistic than it is competitive. Entry is difficult because a large capital outlay is required, the physical plant cannot be moved easily to satisfy shifting geographic demand, and only one or two railroads usually service particular locations. Thus, railroads are in a position to control prices. During the growth era when the railroads often were the only mode of transportation available, it was this situation that forced the states and then the federal government to impose economic regulations.

Today, the basic structure of the railroad remains the same: entry is very difficult, forty-one firms control 99 per cent of the traffic, and few geographic locations are serviced by more than one or two railroads. However, government regulations, the need to cover high fixed costs, and the growth of other modes have caused the railroads to become more competitive. The method of setting rail rates (discussed in Chapter 13) allows shippers and competing railroads to

[7] Ibid., p. 20.
[8] Ibid., p. 33.

participate in establishing rates, with final approval given by the government. Therefore, rates tend to be uniform, one characteristic of an oligopoly. But because of the railroads' desire to cover fixed costs and to compete with other modes, rates are often below those that would recover full costs, bringing them closer to rates that would result from normal competitive actions rather than from a monopoly.

The emergence of other modes, particularly truck, water, and pipe, has had a significant impact on the railroads' competitive behavior. Trucks offer better service for which shippers are willing to pay a premium rate, the pipe and water offer comparable services at lower rates. Because the railroads were either unable or unwilling to meet competition, their share of market initially declined dramatically. Faced with extinction, however, the railroads have begun to meet competition with new technology and more aggressive management.

Thus, although it remains difficult to classify the railroads as competitive, oligopolistic, or monopolistic, it is obvious that competitive forces have shaped the railroad industry's behavior. Even though shippers may not have many alternatives as to which railroad to use, the influence of the government and the other modes has made the railroads more competitive than their basic structure would indicate.

Performance Characteristics

In this section, the performance characteristics of the railroad will be examined from the viewpoint of the shipper. When selecting a mode, shippers must consider several factors: their own objectives, the type and amount of products, and the characteristics of the mode. The performance characteristics defined in Chapter 4 are now used to evaluate the railroad industry.

SPEED

Speed was defined as the elapsed time from when a product is given to a transport mode until the movement is completed. For the railroads, this includes the time from when a car is loaded and ready to move until the car is delivered and ready for unloading. In 1977, the average freight train speed was 19.7 miles per hour, and the average car moved 58.0 miles per day.[9] Again, this places the railroads in the middle of the other modes, because pipe and water are slower and truck and air are faster.

No one factor is responsible for this relatively slow speed of trains, but a significant factor is the manner in which a railroad car moves. Once a car is

[9] Ibid., p. 43.

picked up by a railroad, it is put into a train moving in the appropriate direction. Some time may be lost if the railroad has to wait to collect a sufficient number of cars to make up a train. Once the train is made up, the car begins its move. Depending upon the length of haul, origin and destination points, and the number of railroads over which the car will move, the car may be regrouped into several trains. For instance, a car moving from Cleveland to Denver may leave Cleveland in a train with cars going to Chicago and other points west. Once in Chicago, the car is put in another train heading for perhaps Omaha, where it is placed in another train for Denver. Time is lost each time the car is regrouped.

In an attempt to overcome this service deficiency, the railroads have instituted unit trains that move from one location to another without stopping. The speed of the unit train is significantly above the average. However, the shipper must have large volumes of products for unit movement. The best application for unit trains is in shipment of coal, grain, and other bulk raw materials.

COMPLETENESS

Completeness was defined as the extent of the modal network and the involvement required from other modes. If both the shipper and the receiver have railroad sidings, rail service is complete. If sidings are not available, then other modes are required to complete the movement. Of all modes, trucks are the most complete because every shipper and receiver is located on a road. This is not so for the railroads. Once again, the railroads are in the middle in comparison to the completeness of other modes. The water network, about 25,000 miles and confined to the natural ways, is less complete. Air relies on airports, and even fewer shippers and receivers are serviced directly by airports than by railroads. Pipeline movement from well to refinery to local distribution is very complete. However, the move from pipelines to the final point of consumption, such as a manufacturer or a service station, must rely on other modes.

If the railroad network continues to shrink and industrial complexes continue to move geographically from cities to outlying areas, it will become even less complete. Its level of speed and completeness denies the railroad industry many types of products and moves, particularly high-value products and short hauls.

DEPENDABILITY

Dependability was defined as the ability of a mode to perform as anticipated over time. The railroads, theoretically, should be dependable. The rail network should not suffer from congestion; neither should it be severely affected by the weather. But, during the last several years, overall deterioration of track and a host of managerial problems have greatly reduced rail's dependability. For example, derailments have recently attracted public attention. For purposes of comparison of performance characteristics, it is necessary to discuss what "should and could be" rather than what the practical operating performance is of some or all carriers within a mode. In this sense, the railroad is viewed as a dependable mode. When classified comparatively, railroads are second only to pipelines in dependability.

CAPABILITY

Capability was defined as a mode's ability to handle particular transportation requirements. Water is the only mode more capable than rail. Railroads can handle almost all products except for extremely large shipments, extremely large items, and very perishable products. Pipelines can handle only two types of products, liquid and gas, and air and trucks are limited by weight and volume.

FREQUENCY

Frequency was defined as the number of times a mode can pick up and deliver during a particular period. Once again, railroads are in the middle in comparison to other modes. The major factors that influence frequency are the size of the loads moved and the speed. Water is the least frequent, pipe and rail are comparable, and air and trucks are more frequent. With the use of unit trains and improved car utilization, railroads can increase frequency. Of all performance characteristics, however, frequency is probably of lowest overall concern to shippers. Other performance characteristics will make the mode favorable or unfavorable.

COST

Cost was defined as the amount of money paid to move freight. In addition to the rate paid to the mode, cost includes loading and unloading if not paid by the carrier, insurance in transit, the probability of damage, and the cost of inventory while held by the transportation mode. In comparison to other modes, the freight rate to move a ton-mile by rail is neither high nor low. Water and pipe cost less; air and trucks are more expensive. In 1977, the average revenue per ton-mile for rail was 2.29 cents. Pipe and water were less than 1 cent, truck was more than 8 cents, and air was more than 20 cents.

One disadvantage of rail is that shippers and receivers incur extra costs for loading and unloading. In addition, rail's relatively slow speed increases inventory-in-transit cost.

Being in the middle is both good and bad for the railroads. The railroads can satisfy many shipping requirements, but other modes are able to fit specific shipping needs better: air for speed, trucks for completeness, pipe for cost and dependability, and water for cost and capability. As a result, railroads have been attacked from both ends and are being squeezed out of certain movements. The industry has responded to these attacks, which will be discussed later in this chapter.

The Role of Government

This section will examine the promotional role the government has played in railroad development. The regulatory aspects are discussed in Chapter 11. Promotion/provision was defined in Chapter 4 as any assistance given to a mode by the government. The assistance can range from granting rights of eminent domain to direct subsidies. The railroads, as the other modes, have been developed and owned by private enterprises. Except for the Alaskan and Panama railroads and a few other rare cases, there has been no government ownership of railroads. However, the government has played a significant promotional role.

When the railroads were introduced in 1830, the federal government adopted a hands-off policy and gave no assistance to the railroads. State and local governments, on the other hand, envisioned the railroads as a means for economic development and encouraged their growth. Various governments assisted by granting low-cost and guaranteed loans, eminent domain, property, material, labor, relaxed incorporation laws, and tax concessions. This assistance, along with an optimistic forecast of the railroad's economic impact, created a railroad building boom.

The federal government became involved for the first time on a large scale by granting land. From 1850 to 1870, 131 million acres were given to the states who, in turn, gave the land to the railroads. In addition to the land given for building the railroads, other acreage was given with which the railroads could do as they wished. Some land was sold to finance the railroads and some is still held by the railroads today. Most of the land granted was located west of the Mississippi to encourage the development of the West and the eventual linking of the East and West Coasts. In return for the land, the railroads agreed to move mail and government property at reduced rates. The railroads were freed from this commitment in 1946.

During the last thirty years of the nineteenth century, overexpansion and railroad prosperity led to a reduction in government assistance. Some railroads eventually became state-owned through default and were later leased to private companies. Except for the federal government's managerial control of the railroads during World War I and some loan guarantees during the 1930s, government promotion from the late 1800s until after World War II was minimal.

The government's stance of minimum promotion and involvement changed dramatically during the 1970s, precipitated by the declining position of the railroads since World War II. During the 1950s and 1960s the decline of the railroads accelerated. Competition from other modes, the attitude of railroad management, and the changing demands of the marketplace resulted in the railroads shifting from being carriers of all freight to carriers of low-value products. Market share, revenues, and profit dropped along with morale and the ability to attract capital.

Geographically, the railroads in the Northeast were affected the most. Competition from trucks for short-hauls was strongest, the physical plant was the oldest, and excess trackage the greatest. The situation continued to deteriorate throughout the 1960s without positive or immediate response from the railroads or the government. In 1970, the Penn Central Railroad, the largest in the nation and accounting for 14 per cent of the nation's rail revenues, declared bankruptcy. Faced with the possibility that the assets of the Penn Central and other railroads on the verge of bankruptcy would be liquidated, the Congress took action. The Regional Rail Reorganization Act was passed in 1973. The major provisions of the act were as follows:

Creation of the United States Railway Association (USRA), a government agency responsible for planning and financing the bankrupt railroads' restructuring.

Creation of ConRail, a private for-profit corporation that would operate the restructured system.

Commitment of more than $2 billion, $1.5 billion for guaranteed loans and $558.5 million in direct grants.

The final restructuring plan developed by USRA went into effect in 1976 and was funded by the Railroad Revitalization and Regulatory Reform Act (the 4R Act) of 1976. In total, the 4R Act provided $6.4 billion in financial aid, including ConRail. Some of the monies were outright grants and others were given in anticipation of repayment.

Thus, the federal government became substantially and directly involved in promotion of the railroads. Although the government is involved in financing and planning, it is not involved in ownership or operation. At the present time, the government's involvement is seen as a temporary move. Although the government is the major stockholder in ConRail, the restructuring was designed so that the government could sell the stock as soon as the railroads became financially viable. Although much discussion centers on further government involvement ranging from promotion to ownership to nationalization, no further involvement is planned at this time.

Future

Of all the modes, the future of the railroads is probably the most uncertain. During the 1960s and 1970s the railroads have experienced more changes than at any time since their early development. Furthermore, the forces that will shape the railroads' future are themselves uncertain. These include the demand for rail services, competition, technology, government, energy, and the ecology.

The demand for transportation services is expected to increase dramatically during the next twenty to thirty years. In 1977, 2,331 billion ton-miles were shipped; the total is expected to increase to more than 4 billion ton-miles by 1990. The products shipped predominantly by rail should increase proportionately. Coal, which accounted for 20 per cent of all railcar loadings in 1977, should increase at a much faster rate because of oil shortages and the large reserves of coal in the United States. Even if estimates of future demand are overly optimistic, there is little reason to believe that demand will either remain constant or decrease. Therefore, the market potential for the railroads will be present in the future. Will the railroads be able to service the demand?

New technology will most certainly affect the railroads' future. One reason often given for the industry's decline was its inability or lack of motivation to innovate. Without technological gains that lead to increases in service and productivity, the industry will continue to decline. To some extent, the railroads have accepted and met the technological challenge during the 1960s and 1970s. Although innovation has been slow in coming, it is on its way. Examples of recent innovations include piggyback service, increased size and specialization of freight cars, unit trains, and improved control.

Piggyback service includes trailer-on-flatcar (TOFC) and container-on-flatcar (COFC). The concept, designed to increase service levels by reducing handling, allows the product to remain in the trailer or container from point of origin to destination. Trailers are pulled by tractor to the railroad terminal, loaded upon the flatcar, moved by rail, then unloaded and moved to the final destination. COFC differs only in that the container does not have wheels and must be placed on a flatbed truck. The TOFC and COFC concepts are more than fifty years old. However, only recently have significant gains been made in this area by the railroads. In 1957, there were 249,065 piggyback car loadings, compared to 1,840,588 in 1978, an increase of 739 per cent. Piggybacks represented 7.9 per cent of total car loadings in 1978, and more than $1 billion in revenue.[10]

Railroads have also increased the size of their cars and have introduced specialized equipment. Cars of 100-ton capacity are not uncommon, and cars

---

[10] Ibid., p. 27.

designed for specific products such as automobiles and lumber are being put into service. Unit trains, which are not stopped in transit, and computer-based information systems that keep track of car locations are typical of the broad technological innovations introduced by railroads. If the railroads wish to increase movements or halt their declining market share, continued innovations are mandatory. Two promising concepts that may be introduced soon are articulated cars with a 250-ton capacity and a truck/trailer/train combination that has two sets of wheels and can move directly from the highway to the tracks.

As railroads continue to innovate and strive for increased traffic, so will competition increase. As discussed earlier, the service characteristics of railroads are in the middle in relation to other modes. Although this allows the railroads to gain traffic from water or truck, the reverse is also true. The degree of competition between the modes can be approached from two perspectives: the railroads' ability to compete for other traffic, and the other modes' inability to compete for railroad traffic. The railroads' ability to compete depends on technology, management, and the government. If the railroads are able to move larger loads to increase efficiency and lower the cost per ton-mile, they will be successful in attracting traffic away from water. On the other hand, if they can move more discrete loads with better service that includes speed and completeness, then trucks may become competitively vulnerable. To a significant degree, the future of the railroads will depend upon their ability to realize their inherent dependability performance characteristic.

The attitude of management and the regulatory policies of government must also be considered. Railroad management generally has lacked the ability or desire to make a competitive thrust. Continued government regulation of rates, some of which are designed to protect other modes, would hinder competitive efforts. However, the same general conditions exist for competitors. Specifically, coal slurry pipelines have been denied the right of eminent domain by the Congress, and a tax on water carrier fuel has been put into effect recently. Reduced speed limits on highways, the inability to increase highway loads significantly, and energy shortages do not help the future of trucks. Thus, vigorous competition by the railroads, combined with a lack of competition from other modes, may forecast future growth for the railroads. However, the factors that will affect the degree of competition are uncertain and many are beyond the control of the railroads.

As stated previously, the government can affect the future of the railroads from a competitive perspective. In addition, considering the government's involvement in the railroad industry during the 1970s, its effect is bound to be significant in many ways. Trying to forecast the role the government will play, however, might require a crystal ball. If railroads are successful in increasing their market share, becoming more profitable, and sustaining their own operations, chances are very good that government involvement will recede, at least from a promotional perspective. If the railroads are not successful, possible government actions could range from continued promotional involvement to outright ownership and operation. As discussed in later chapters, the government has traditionally preferred that the transportation industry be founded on free enterprise and healthy competition. On the other hand, the government is also committed to the maintenance of an efficient transportation system. Perhaps both goals can be achieved simultaneously.

The energy problems the nation faces will not be solved during the foreseeable future. The railroads, however, are in a favorable position because they are energy-efficient, particularly in comparison to trucks. If the demand for coal increases as forecasted, the demand for rail traffic will increase. Ecologically, the railroads are once again in a favorable position. The network is established and the diesel locomotive is relatively clean.

Thus, the railroads could go in one of two directions. They could continue to decline and become a national albatross, or the decline could be stopped or reversed. Considering all factors, a reversal is probably most likely. Because of their severe difficulties during the 1970s, the railroads are receiving more attention and help, and a rebirth through progressive management and modernization may be possible. The potential demand exists, the technology is available, government regulations that will affect competition seem to be in favor of the railroads, the government has displayed a desire to help through promotion, continued energy concerns are favorable to the railroads, and ecology considerations are not significant. The railroads may have seen their worst times; a resurgence may lie in the future.

Summary

During the last half of the nineteenth century, railroads were the dominant mode of freight transportation in the United States. The railroads have declined in importance since the turn of the century, primarily because of competition from two new modes, trucks and air, and the resurgence of water. However, railroads still move more ton-miles of freight than any other mode.

The railroad network has declined for many years but still consists of almost 200,000 miles, and very few cities lack rail service. The products shipped by rail are primarily large-volume, heavyweight raw materials such as coal, grain, and chemical products. Railroads also ship automobiles, food, and other high-value products.

More than 500 companies supply rail services, but less than 20 per cent are Class I railroads that move 99 per cent of the traffic. From an economic perspective, railroads are capital-intensive and have a large proportion of fixed costs because they own and maintain their own way. Competition within the industry is oligopolistic; however, competition from outside the industry forces railroads to keep rates competitive.

The railroads are unique in that no one service characteristic gives them a competitive advantage. Overall, the service offered falls in between the other modes. Air and truck are faster, more complete, and more frequent. Water and pipe cost less. Pipe is a more dependable mode. Water is more capable. Although railroads have a great potential for dependability, current performance falls short of realizing this competitive advantage.

Except for state and local promotion during development and the federal land-grant program between 1850 and 1870, the railroads received little government assistance until recently. In 1970, the Penn Central Railroad, the largest in the country, declared bankruptcy. Federal assistance has increased significantly since then. The 4R Act of 1976 authorized more than $6 billion to be used to help the railroads.

Of all the modes, the future of railroads is probably the most uncertain because it depends on other factors such as technology, competition, and government actions. The best forecast, however, is that the railroads will continue to play a major role in the transportation system.

Questions for Chapter 5

1. Railroads are the only fully integrated mode. What does this mean?
2. Discuss the reasons that large quantities of coal are shipped by rail.
3. Describe the cost characteristics of the railroad industry.
4. What effect does a capital turnover of about 0.7 have on the railroads?
5. What economic characteristics prohibit the railroads from responding quickly to changes in demand?
6. Why is the railroad industry considered more monopolistic than competitive?
7. The railroads have declined in percentage of total ton-miles shipped and revenue. What factors have caused these declines?
8. Considering performance characteristics, describe the railroads in relation to other modes.
9. Describe the role that government has played in the development and perpetuation of the railroads.
10. Discuss ConRail. Why did it evolve and what is the role of the government?
11. Describe TOFC and COFC. Why would these types of operations help the railroad industry?
12. Generally, in your opinion, what will be the future—the next twenty-five years—of the railroad industry?

6

Truck Transportation

Movement of freight by truck did not become a significant part of the transportation system until the third decade of the twentieth century. Although roads were built in the United States as early as the 1600s and the gasoline combustion engine for automobiles was commercially successful early in the twentieth century, truck transportation grew slowly. The main reasons for this slow growth were the lack of improved roads and the dominance of the railroads. Just after World War I, about 1 million trucks existed in this country. By 1930, there were 3.5 million; by 1947, almost 7 million;[1] and by 1980, more than 30 million. Today, trucks handle more shipments and receive more revenue than any other mode. This rapid rise in truck movement of intercity freight has had a significant impact on the transportation system in general and has been a contributing factor to the decline of the railroads.

The growth of truck transportation is an easily explained phenomenon. The

---

[1] U.S. Department of Transportation, *National Transportation Trends and Choices to the Year 2000* (January 1977), p. 156.

primary reason for the mode's success is its unique performance characteristics. Because of the extensive road network, almost 4 million miles,[2] trucks can service almost every home and firm in the country. Seldom must trucks depend on other modes to begin or end movements. In fact, trucks often begin and end moves for other modes. The relatively small loads carried by trucks move quickly from origin to destination with few interruptions.

This chapter will look at the role of truck transportation, the industry and performance characteristics, the role of government, and the mode's future.

Role of Trucks

Freight movement by truck has grown dramatically during the past fifty years. Today it plays a major role in the overall transportation system. Let us examine the amount of freight shipped, the revenue, the size and reach of the network, and the types of freight moved.

AMOUNT SHIPPED AND REVENUE

Trucks carry almost 25 per cent of all ton-miles shipped in the United States, second only to railroads. However, trucks ship more tons than any other mode. This difference in totals is accounted for by the fact that railroads move freight longer distances than do trucks. The average length of haul, the distance that the average shipment moves, was 587 miles for railroads and 301 miles for trucks in 1978.[3] Thus, the ton-mile measurement would be greater for the railroads even though they loaded fewer tons than the truck mode. Tables 6–1 and 6–2 show the ton-miles and tons shipped by truck since 1945. The ton-miles shipped by truck have increased 799 per cent (from 67 billion to 602 billion) from 1945 to 1978. Except for air freight, which ships less than 0.2 per cent of all available ton-miles, trucks have experienced the greatest percentage increase in ton-miles among all modes. More significantly, however, trucks have increased their share of the market (percentage of total ton-miles) from 6.5 per cent in 1945 to 24.7 per cent in 1978, the largest share increase of any mode. Except for a brief slowdown during the 1960s, the truck mode has enjoyed steady growth.

As Table 6–2 shows, the total tons moved by truck has increased dramatically. From 1945 to 1978, the number of tons increased from 304 million to 2,260 million, an increase of 643 per cent. The percentage of total tons

---

[2] Ibid., p. 131.
[3] *Transportation Facts and Trends*, 15th ed. (Washington, D.C.: Transportation Association of America, July 1979), p. 14.

TABLE 6–1. Truck Transportation Ton-Miles

Year	Ton-Miles (Billions)	Percentage of Total Transportation Ton-Miles
1945	67	6.5%
1950	173	16.3%
1955	223	17.5%
1960	285	21.8%
1965	359	21.9%
1970	412	21.3%
1975	454	22.0%
1977	555	24.0%
1978	602	24.7%

Source: *Transportation Facts and Trends*, 15th ed. (Washington, D.C.: Transportation Association of America, July 1979), p. 8.

TABLE 6–2. Truck Transportation Tons

Year	Tons (Millions)	Percentage of Total Transportation Tons
1945	304	N/A
1950	794	26.1%
1955	1,063	29.8%
1960	1,181	32.7%
1965	1,641	37.0%
1970	1,828	36.2%
1975	1,744	35.2%
1977	2,143	38.9%
1978	2,260	N/A

Source: *Transportation Facts and Trends*, 15th ed. (Washington, D.C.: Transportation Association of America, July 1979), p. 10.

shipped increased from 26.1 per cent in 1950 to 38.9 per cent in 1977. The difference between the percentage increase in ton-miles (799 per cent) and the percentage increase in tons (643 per cent) is accounted for by the increased length of haul for trucks from 1945 to 1977. In 1947, the average length of haul for Class I common carriers (carriers with more than $3 million in annual revenues) was 200 miles. This increased to 301 miles by 1978.[4] Thus, not only have ton-miles, tons, and share of market increased, but also the distance moved per shipment has increased.

Truck revenues are the largest by far of all modes. Table 6–3 shows the truck

[4] Ibid., p. 14.

TABLE 6–3. Truck Revenue

Year	Truck Freight Revenue (Billions of Dollars)	Total Freight Revenue (Billions of Dollars)	Percentage of Total Transportation Freight Revenue
1960	31.5	45.1	69.8%
1965	43.8	59.1	74.1%
1970	62.4	80.6	77.3%
1975	95.2	121.1	78.6%
1976	110.8	140.1	79.1%
1977	134.8	166.1	81.2%

Source: *Transportation Facts and Trends*, 15th ed. (Washington, D.C.: Transportation Association of America, July 1979), p. 4.

revenue, which increased 428 per cent from $31.5 billion in 1960 to $134.8 billion in 1977. The nation's total freight revenue increased from $45.1 billion to $166.1 billion, or 269 per cent during the same period. Trucking's percentage of the total revenue increased from 69.8 per cent in 1960 to 81.2 per cent in 1977. Thus, out of every $100 spent on freight movement in the United States, slightly more than $82 is spent for truck shipments. The mode with the second largest revenues is rail.

NETWORK

A major factor contributing to the increased importance of trucks and their present dominant position has been the growth of the highway network. Roads in the United States have grown not only in total mileage but in capacity and quality. In 1977, there were 3,857,000 miles of roads and streets in the United States. Of this total, 3.17 million miles were soil, slag, gravel, or stone surfaces. Therefore, 686,329 miles[5] of primary and secondary roads carried almost 100 per cent of the traffic. Table 6–4 shows the growth of the highway network in this category since 1945. Mileage increased from 342,558 miles in 1945 to 686,329 miles in 1977, or 100 per cent. This growth reflects both network expansion and road improvements such as widening, grading, straightening, and surfacing. Regardless of how it is viewed or measured, the road system offers trucking the most extensive network of any mode. Furthermore, trucks of varying types and sizes can move freely over this network with very few restrictions.

The most visible improvement in the road network during the past thirty years has been the interstate highway system (Figure 6–1). Construction of this addition to the road network has significantly assisted the growth of truck shipments. During World War II, road construction stopped almost completely.

[5] Ibid., p. 31.

TABLE 6–4. Road Network *

Year	Total Miles
1945	342,558
1950	409,133
1955	486,750
1960	557,729
1965	617,114
1970	665,903
1975	685,052
1976	689,648
1977	686,329

*Does not include roads with soil, slag, gravel, or stone surfaces. Does not include Alaska or Hawaii.
Source: *Transportation Facts and Trends*, 15th ed. (Washington, D.C.: Transportation Association of America, July 1979), p. 31.

After the war, the quality and quantity of roads could not support traffic demands. The interstate system was proposed during the late 1940s and was designed to connect the major population centers in the United States. The system was to extend 42,500 miles and be completed in seventeen years. Construction began in the 1950s. As of June 1978, 91.9 per cent of the proposed system, or 39,064 miles, was completed and open to traffic. Although progress has slowed, costs are rising, and the network is not yet complete, the interstate highway system has been a complete success. Although it accounts for only 1.1 per cent of road mileage, it handles more than 19 per cent of the traffic and has increased the average speed of movement within and among cities.[6]

FREIGHT SHIPPED

In addition to making complete moves, the truck mode is used widely to begin and end moves for other modes. Trucks move freight to and from airports, from pipeline-fed distribution centers to gasoline stations, and to and from railroad and water terminals. As a result, almost every type of freight is moved by truck. In general, trucks most often move relatively high-value manufactured products, although they sometimes ship sand, gravel, chemicals, and other basic raw materials.

Overall, trucks move many different types of products. They move more than 70 per cent of all ton-miles of meat and dairy products, textile mill and leather products, apparel and related products, fabricated metal products, industrial machinery, and transportation equipment. They move more than half of the ton-miles of candy, beverage, and tobacco products; rubber and plastic

[6]*National Transportation Trends and Choices to the Year 2000*, op. cit., p. 137.

86

FIGURE 6–1. INTERSTATE HIGHWAY SYSTEM

products; furniture and fixtures; and communication products and parts.[7] In addition to manufactured products, trucks move almost 90 per cent of fresh fruits and vegetables,[8] and play a major role in the movement of other agricultural products, household goods, petroleum products, refrigerated products, motor vehicles, and building materials. No one product or type of freight moves exclusively by truck, unlike water and rail. Overall, the types of products generally shipped by truck are those that require relatively short hauls, discrete movements, and good speed.

Truck Industry Characteristics

This section examines the truck industry characteristics, including fleet size and ownership, cost structure, and competition.

FLEET SIZE AND OWNERSHIP

The trucking industry is composed of private carriers, common carriers, contract carriers, and exempt carriers. Private carriers are owned and operated by organizations whose primary business is not truck transportation. The vehicles are used to move goods that the organizations buy or sell. Private carriers are not subject to economic regulations, but they must meet the safety and operational regulations established by federal and state governments.

Common carriers are for-hire carriers that move the goods of all shippers. Common carriers are regulated by the Interstate Commerce Commission (ICC) unless they operate solely within one state, carry exempt products, or operate within defined commercial zones (a thirty-five-mile radius around urban centers). The ICC regulates rates, the type of freight carried, and industry entry, merger, and exit.

Before a carrier can offer for-hire service, a Certificate of Public Convenience and Necessity (CPCN) must be obtained from the ICC. (The requirements and problems of obtaining a certificate are discussed in Chapter 12). The CPCN specifies the type of for-hire operation permitted, including commodities to be carried, routes and geographic areas covered, and size of shipments and trucks. Generally, CPCNs can be classified as general freight or specialized freight, and regular route or irregular route carriers. Within general freight, a CPCN is granted for a range of specified products. A specialized freight carrier

[7] *Transportation Facts and Trends*, op. cit., p. 12.
[8] *Research Review* (Washington, D.C.: American Trucking Associations, Department of Economics, May 15, 1978, Number 198), p. 3.

can move only one type of freight, such as heavy machinery, liquid petroleum, or motor vehicles. A CPCN for a regular route carrier specifies the geographic points that can be served, and for an irregular route carrier, CPCN grants authority for a geographic region.

For statistical purposes, the ICC classifies common carriers by size. Class I carriers have annual revenues in excess of $3 million, Class II carriers have annual revenues between $500,000 and $3 million, and Class III carriers have revenues of less than $500,000.

Contract carriers are also for-hire carriers that contract with one or more shippers to move their freight for a specific length of time, such as one year. They are subject to many of the same regulations as common carriers. Exempt carriers are for-hire carriers that are not subject to ICC regulations because of the types of goods they move, such as unprocessed agricultural products, newspapers, and livestock, or the geographic area they service.

In 1976, an estimated 44 per cent of all intercity ton-miles was moved by ICC-regulated carriers.[9] The remainder was moved by private and exempt carriers. ICC-regulated carriers had revenues of approximately $31 billion in 1977,[10] which was about 23 per cent of the nation's trucking bill. Nonregulated interstate carriers accounted for 27 per cent, and intrastate trucking, which is not regulated by the ICC, accounted for 50 per cent.[11]

In 1978, the ICC regulated approximately 15,500 trucking firms. Of this total, about 2,850 firms were Class I and II carriers that generated almost 90 per cent of common carrier revenues. The remaining 12,500 were Class III carriers, companies whose annual revenues did not exceed $500,000.[12]

Table 6–5 shows the growth in number of trucks since 1950. By early 1978, an estimated 30 million trucks were in operation in the United States.[13] Of that total, almost 75 per cent were light trucks (under 10,000 pounds (lbs.) gross vehicle weight) and, of that 75 per cent, almost 60 per cent were personal use vehicles such as pickups, vans, and recreational vehicles. Trucks used primarily for intercity freight (26,000 lbs. or more) represented about 8 per cent of the total truck population. Other statistics that help to characterize the truck fleet are as follows: one out of five are used for agricultural products; one out of twenty are for-hire (the majority of which are large semi-trailers); and one out of ten are used for transporting freight for manufacturing, wholesaling, and retailing establishments. The truck fleet is forecasted to grow at an overall annual rate of about 7 per cent, with small personal use vehicles growing at a relatively faster rate.

[9]*Transportation Facts and Trends*, op. cit., p. 9.
[10]*Transportation Facts and Trends*, op. cit., p. 4.
[11]*Transportation Facts and Trends*, op. cit., p. 4.
[12]*Transport Topics*, Number 2265 (Washington, D.C.: American Trucking Associations, January 8, 1979), p. 1.
[13]*Transportation Facts and Trends*, op. cit., p. 30, and *Research Review*, op. cit., p. 5.

TABLE 6–5. Number of Privately and
Publicly Owned Trucks

Year	Number of Trucks (Millions)
1950	8.6
1955	10.3
1960	11.9
1965	14.8
1970	18.7
1975	25.8
1977	30.8 (est.)

Source: *Transportation Facts and Trends,* 14th ed.
(Washington, D.C.: Transportation Association of
America, July 1978), and *Research Review* (Washington,
D.C.: American Trucking Association, Department of
Economics, April 14, 1978), p. 5.

COST CHARACTERISTICS

Compared to other modes, the truck industry has low capital requirements
and high variable costs, estimated at about 90 per cent. The amount of capital
needed to put a truck on the road is relatively small. Even though some trucks
may cost more than $100,000, that is modest in comparison to barges, tow-
boats, ocean liners, railroad cars, or airplanes. Just as for the water and air
modes, the network is provided for trucks. All highways and streets are built
and maintained by federal, state, and local governments. The largest fixed cost
incurred by motor common carriers is for terminal facilities.

The capital turnover for trucks (4) is the highest for all commercial carriers.
Therefore, the industry can have high operating ratios (operating expenses over
operating revenues) of about 0.95 and still receive an excellent return on investment. The return on transportation investment for Class I and II common
carriers was about 24 per cent in 1977.[14]

COMPETITION

Competition exists on two levels: within the industry, and between trucking
and other modes. Within the industry, several factors indicate that the trucking
industry is very competitive. A large number of firms operate for-hire service
(approximately 15,500 in 1978), capital barriers to entry are low, and regulatory
barriers to entry are being reduced. Furthermore, from a shipper's perspective,
many options exist for truck transportation, including common, contract, and

[14]G. Barry Kohler, *1978 Financial Analysis of the Motor Carrier Industry* (New York: Bank of
America, 1978), p. 6.

private carriage. In addition, shippers can move with relative ease from one type of carriage to another, and a large number of common carriers are usually available to any one shipper.

Even though that part of the trucking industry that is regulated by the ICC is becoming concentrated, no one firm or small group of firms dominates the industry. For instance, in 1977, thirty motor carriers accounted for 45 per cent of the general freight Class I and Class II gross revenues. Industry structure is such that competition, rather than oligopoly or monopoly, is the rule.

Within the industry, another form of competition takes place between common carriers and private carriers. Several reports have shown that private carriage continues to grow at the expense of common carriers. The Regulated Common Carrier Conference of the American Trucking Association reached the conclusion that regular route carriers face their most significant and fastest growing competition from proprietary (private) trucking.[15] The private carriage option is open to all firms on a partial or total basis. Although the decision to use private carriage often results from specific industry needs such as special equipment or unique service characteristics, many firms adopt private carriage because it is less expensive and more reliable. This constant threat forces common carriers to attempt to remain competitive.

Other forms of competition that threaten the common carriers are backhauls by agricultural carriers and the possibility of awarding common and contract rights to private carriers. As indicated earlier, carriers moving certain agricultural products are exempt from ICC regulations. For the most part, agricultural shipments are one-way moves, with the return trip, or backhaul, empty. However, agricultural haulers are allowed by the ICC to backhaul nonagricultural products as long as the revenue from these operations does not exceed 30 per cent of their business. This activity is in direct competition with the common carriers.

The second threat is that recently some private carriers have been granted selected common or contract certification. This enables them to reduce their empty backhaul miles, conserve fuel, and earn a return on investment in equipment. Although the ramifications of these certifications are unknown at this time, it appears likely that they will become more prevalent in the future. The regulatory features of this threat are discussed in Chapter 12.

Competition between trucks and other modes is less vigorous than competition within the industry. From a service perspective, trucks are positioned between railroads and air. Air freight represents less than 1 per cent of total ton-miles and, although it is growing, it is not a significant threat. Railroads have been declining in importance and, except for some special cases, do not pose a significant competitive threat.

If the transportation system is viewed from an overall perspective, each mode should handle certain types of traffic that best suit its unique characteristics.

[15] Robert M. Butler, *Traffic World*, April 26, 1976.

Trucks are usually considered best suited for general cargo of limited size over relatively short hauls. However, in some cases, the trucking industry has overstepped these service boundaries and is trying to increase its load capacity and length of haul by handling bulk loads. The railroads are competitive for these shipments and could recover some of the freight now being shipped by trucks. In summary, competition is healthy within the industry and the potential exists for competition between trucks and other modes. The success of the trucking industry is the result, in large part, of its inherent performance characteristics, which are discussed in the next section.

Performance Characteristics

Each mode has particular characteristics that make it best suited for certain types of freight movements. When a shipper selects a mode, the service characteristics of speed, completeness, dependability, capability, and frequency are considered along with cost and objectives. Each of the characteristics and the cost of the trucking mode are examined here.

SPEED

Speed was defined as the elapsed time from when freight is given to a transport mode until the movement is completed. With the obvious exception of air, trucks are by far the fastest mode. Although trains and trucks can operate at comparable speeds once the vehicles are in motion, trucks have certain characteristics that increase the speed of the total movement. Railroads must wait to accumulate enough cars to complete a train. Trucks can move immediately after loading. Truck capacities often can be utilized by a single shipper, permitting door-to-door movement. In contrast, railroads require terminals and classification yards.

Because trucks can usually deliver without interruption, a shipment can leave the point of origin in the evening and arrive at a destination many miles away by the following morning. A short-haul truckload (TL) movement is the ideal shipment for the mode. Longer hauls and/or less-than-truckload (LTL) shipments cause delays in speed. On longer hauls, drivers must rest in transit. Also, freight may have to be transferred from one carrier to another if the destination is not within the area of authority of the originating carrier. For LTL shipments, freight must be picked up, consolidated at a local terminal, and placed on an over-the-road truck for shipment. The process then must be reversed at the destination point. This not only delays the shipment, but it increases costs significantly, because of the need for additional handling at terminal facilities. Thus, the mode's speed is excellent under ideal conditions but decreases significantly when longer hauls or LTL shipments are required.

COMPLETENESS

Completeness was defined as the extent of the modal network and the amount of involvement required from other modes. The road network is the largest of all the modes. Trucks seldom require another mode to begin or end a movement. In fact, trucks complete many movements for all other modes, such as to and from airports, water terminals, rail terminals, and from the end of the pipeline to the point of consumption. With few exceptions, trucks can pick up and deliver to any destination in the continental United States. This completeness, combined with speed, has been a prime contributor to the mode's success.

The completeness of the mode has some restrictions. All trucks cannot operate on all roads in the United States. Restrictions as to weight, length, width, height, number of axles, and axle weight are imposed by various levels of government. These restrictions are necessary because of the physical limits of roads and bridges, bridge deterioration, and highway safety. Figure 6–2 shows the restrictions imposed by each state on truck configuration (number of trailers), height, overall length, and gross vehicle weight. In addition, some states permit use on designated roads only, such as the interstate system, toll roads, and other limited access highways.

Imposition of these restrictions limits trucks in three ways. First, trucks cannot be built any larger or heavier than indicated, thus limiting their carrying capacity in terms of both weight and volume. Second, geographic reach is limited because the restrictions do not apply on all roads. Third, because there is no uniformity of restrictions among states, interstate freight must either be loaded to meet the requirements of the state having the highest restrictions or the shipment must be diverted around the state. For instance, New York State allows a double-bottom configuration (one tractor pulling two trailers), with a gross weight of 127,400 pounds (lbs.) and an overall length of 108 feet (ft.). Ohio allows a double-bottom configuration with a gross weight of 127,400 lbs. and an overall length of 98 ft. Pennsylvania does not allow double-bottoms, and the maximum weight allowed is 73,280 lbs., and overall length, 70 ft. Thus, truck traffic moving from the Midwest to New York and on to Massachusetts has several undesirable alternatives. It can move around the state of Pennsylvania. It can run illegally for the few miles across the northwest corner of Pennsylvania. It can drop one of the trailers in Ohio, move one trailer to New York, and then return for the other trailer. Or it can load the truck according to Pennsylvania specifications for what may be only a small part of the total move. Some of the present restrictions are temporary, and there is a movement toward making restrictions uniform.

93

FIGURE 6-2. TRUCK SIZE, WEIGHT, AND CONFIGURATION RESTRICTIONS

MAXIMUM STATE VEHICLE SIZE-WEIGHT LIMITS
(Height, Length, Weight on Designated Roads)

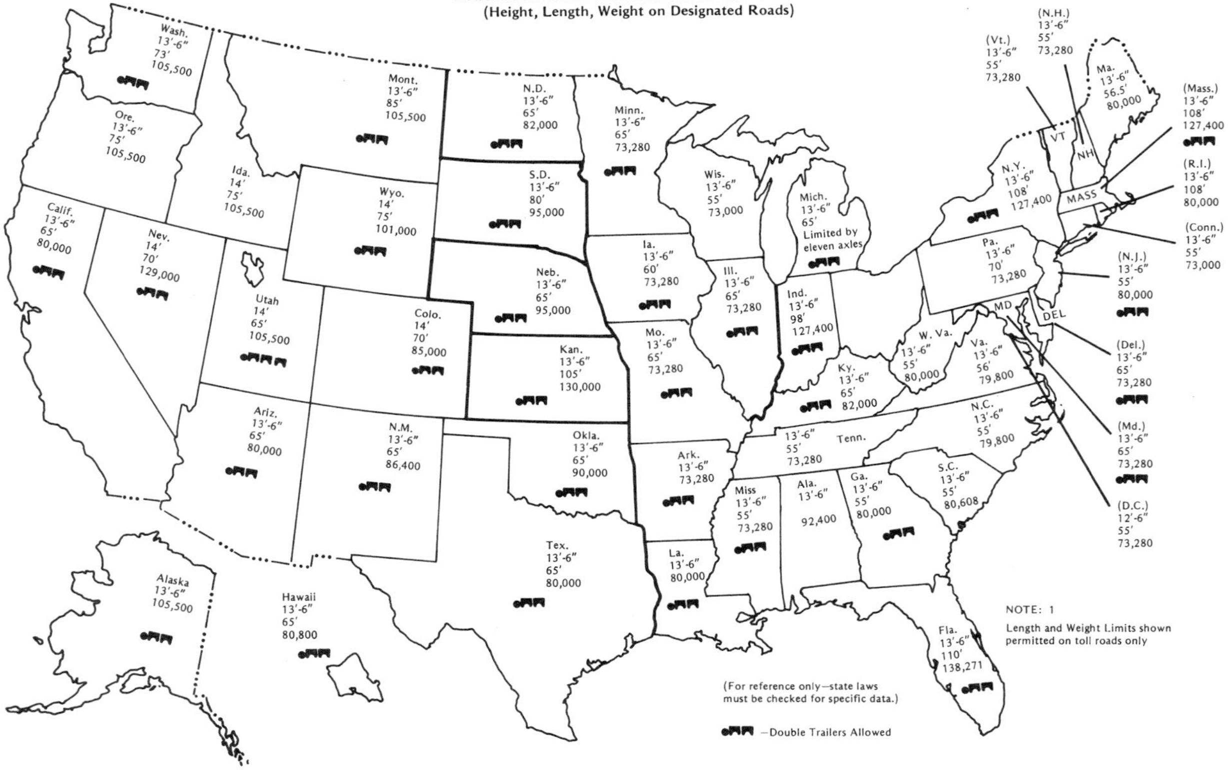

NOTE: 1
Length and Weight Limits shown permitted on toll roads only

(For reference only—state laws must be checked for specific data.)

⬛⬛ —Double Trailers Allowed

State limits (Height, Length, Weight):

- (N.H.) 13'-6", 55', 73,280
- (Vt.) 13'-6", 55', 73,280
- (Mass.) 13'-6", 108', 127,400
- (R.I.) 13'-6", 108', 80,000
- (Conn.) 13'-6", 55', 73,000
- Me. 13'-6", 80,000
- (N.J.) 13'-6", 55', 80,000
- (Del.) 13'-6", 65', 73,280
- (Md.) 13'-6", 65', 73,280
- (D.C.) 12'-6", 55', 73,280
- N.Y. 13'-6", 108', 127,400
- Pa. 13'-6", 70', 73,280
- Va. 13'-6", 55', 79,800
- N.C. 13'-6", 55', 79,800
- S.C. 13'-6", 55', 80,608
- Fla. 13'-6", 110', 138,271
- W. Va. 13'-6", 55', 80,000
- Ky. 13'-6", 65', 82,000
- Tenn. 13'-6", 55', 73,280
- Ga. 13'-6", 55', 80,000
- Ala. 13'-6", 92,400
- Miss. 13'-6", 55', 73,280
- La. 13'-6", 80,000
- Mich. 13'-6", 65', Limited by eleven axles
- Ind. 13'-6", 98', 127,400
- Ill. 13'-6", 65', 73,280
- Wis. 13'-6", 55', 73,000
- Ia. 13'-6", 60', 73,280
- Mo. 13'-6", 65', 73,280
- Ark. 13'-6", 73,280
- Minn. 13'-6", 65', 73,280
- N.D. 13'-6", 65', 82,000
- S.D. 13'-6", 80', 95,000
- Neb. 13'-6", 65', 95,000
- Kan. 13'-6", 105', 130,000
- Okla. 13'-6", 65', 90,000
- Tex. 13'-6", 65', 80,000
- Mont. 13'-6", 85', 105,500
- Wyo. 14', 75', 101,000
- Colo. 14', 70', 85,000
- N.M. 13'-6", 65', 86,400
- Wash. 13'-6", 73', 105,500
- Ore. 13'-6", 75', 105,500
- Ida. 14', 75', 105,500
- Utah 14', 65', 105,500
- Nev. 14', 70', 129,000
- Ariz. 13'-6", 65', 80,000
- Calif. 13'-6", 65', 80,000
- Hawaii 13'-6", 65', 80,800
- Alaska 13'-6", 105,500

DEPENDABILITY

Dependability was defined as the mode's ability to perform as anticipated over time. In comparison to other modes, trucks are potentially less dependable than pipelines and railroads, more dependable than air, and equally as dependable as water. Four factors reduce trucks' dependability: weather, traffic congestion, terminal handling on LTL shipments, and service to remote locations. Weather and congestion vary by seasons and by time. Congestion can sometimes be avoided, but trucks often encounter severe problems with pickups and deliveries in urban locations. Severe weather during the winter months in the northern part of the country reduces the dependability of trucks significantly. LTL shipments, small shippers, remote origin and destination points, scheduling, and terminal handling often reduce the dependability of the mode.

CAPABILITY

Capability was defined as a mode's ability to handle particular transportation requirements. Trucks are somewhat limited in capability in comparison to railroads and water. Although trucks can carry almost any type of product (liquids, gases, solids, irregular shapes, perishable and refrigerated products), load sizes are limited by law and the size of individual pieces is limited by highway configuration. Thus, trucks are not suited for handling intercity movements of coal, grains, and other bulk materials; neither are they able to handle large pieces of machinery or other bulky units.

FREQUENCY

Frequency was defined as the number of times a mode can pick up and deliver during a particular period. Because trucks are relatively fast and carry relatively small loads, their frequency is good. Daily deliveries of up to 200 miles by the same truck are not unusual. With shorter distances, many trips can be made in the same day. This latitude in frequency allows trucks to be integrated more efficiently into the overall distribution process. Trucks are able to adapt to the rest of the system rather than requiring the system to adapt to them.

COST

Cost was defined as the amount that must be paid for a movement including the freight rate, loading and unloading, the probability of damage in transit, and the cost of carrying inventory. In comparison to other modes, truck freight rates per ton-mile are more expensive than pipelines, water, and railroads, but less expensive than air. In 1977, the average revenue per ton-mile for ICC-regulated truck carriers was 12.1 cents, compared to 34.2 cents for air, and

2.29 cents for railroads.[16] The ton-mile revenue for pipelines and water is less than that of rail. Truck carriers load and unload, and the probability of damage in truck transit is comparatively low. Given the speed and frequency of trucks, inventory costs in transit are low.

Even with the apparent cost disadvantages, the demand for trucking services is high and continues to grow. Shippers are willing to pay the premium rates to gain speed and frequency, which have significant effects on overall distribution system performance. In other cases, shippers must pay the premium rates because the other modes are severely limited in their ability to ship between any two origin and destination locations.

Thus, truck transportation's major advantages are completeness and speed. The major drawback is cost. Trucks are most often used for relatively small, short-distance moves. Trucks also begin and end movements for other modes and totally dominate local pickup and delivery.

The Role of Government

As with the other modes, various levels of government play an integral role in trucking through promotion and regulation. The government's promotion of trucks is discussed in this section, and regulation will be discussed in Chapter 11. As with other modes, the introduction, ownership, and growth of truck transportation has been accomplished through private enterprise. However, as with water, the network has been provided by the government. The roads in the United States are provided, owned, and maintained primarily by state governments.

Public ownership of roads is based on English common law. With the exception of a few privately owned turnpikes during the 1800s, the government has provided roads since the country was settled. Before the twentieth century, however, the government gave little thought to road construction. With the growth in the number of automobiles, the increase and dispersion of the population, and the need for transportation to and from railroad terminals, more attention was given to planned road construction. States began to create road departments to oversee road design, construction, and maintenance. In 1916, the federal government made its first major monetary commitment by making funds available to states on a proportional basis for road construction. To be eligible for the money, the states had to create a road department, and the proposed roads had to meet minimum construction requirements.

Since that time, the federal government has become increasingly involved in road construction, but the states still play a major role in financing. The federal

[16] *Air Transport 1978* (Washington, D.C.: Air Transportation Association of America, 1978), p. 30.

government owns only roads on federal land. Even though the federal government contributes large sums of money to construction (90 per cent of the interstate system and up to 70 per cent of others), the completed roads are owned by and become the responsibility of the individual states. In addition to state-level jurisdiction, roads are often owned and maintained by county and local government units. A rural/urban breakdown of government road ownership is given by the Federal Highway Administration.

Twenty-two per cent of the (rural) mileage is under state control, 70.5 per cent is under local control (cities, towns, counties, etc.), and 7.3 per cent is under federal control (in federal parks, forests, and the like). The urban roads and streets were found to be 86.6 per cent under local control and 13.4 per cent under state control.[17]

It has been estimated that more than one half trillion dollars has been spent on highway construction by all levels of government since the turn of the century. More than half of that has been spent since 1956, with the federal government spending approximately one third and state and local governments spending the balance. For the most part, road funding has been on a pay-as-you-go basis. Various federal user taxes on fuels, registrations, vehicle sales, and parts have supported highway development. In 1956, the Federal Highway Trust Fund was created to be the source of federal funds for highway development, and slightly more than $100 billion has been placed in the fund. In 1978 the Highway Trust Fund collected almost $8 billion and had a cash balance of nearly $11 billion.

With similar types of taxes, it is estimated that state and local governments have collected more than $210 billion since 1957. In 1978, all levels of government received and disbursed $31.8 billion. Of this total, $21.1 billion came from user taxes and the balance came from property taxes, general funds, bond sales, and miscellaneous fees.[18] Disbursements included $14.1 billion for construction, $9 billion for maintenance and traffic services, and the balance for administration, research, law enforcement, debt retirement, and safety.[19]

Thus, government's promotion role in the trucking industry has been exclusively one of providing highways. The use of highways is not free to the trucking industry. However, the dollars paid in user taxes equal only about 35 per cent of total highway cost.

Future

Primarily because of continuing energy problems, the future role of trucks in the domestic freight transportation system is less clear today than it was a few

[17] *Research Review*, op. cit., p. 5.
[18] *Research Review* (Washington, D.C.: American Trucking Associations, Department of Economics, February 15, 1979, Number 207), p. 3.
[19] Ibid.

decades ago. However, other influences such as the overall demand for truck services, technology, government, competition, and ecology also must be considered. Each of these areas, also uncertain, will be reviewed to outline the possible directions the trucking industry may take and its anticipated impact on the domestic freight transportation system in the future.

As discussed in previous chapters, the demand for all transportation services is expected to increase over the next two decades. That portion of the demand that is serviced by truck—the discrete, relatively small, fast movements—will grow in proportion. And if history is any indication, the demand for truck services will grow faster than the demand for other modes. Truck services can be broadly classified as (1) intercity, when trucks are the only mode used; (2) supportive, when the trucks begin and end moves for other modes; and (3) intracity. In the last two categories, trucks are the only mode available, and the demand for intercity truck services is forecasted to increase. In summary, the demand will be present for truck services in the future, but the fact that demand will exist does not necessarily mean that trucks will continue to play the major role they have in the past.

Technological gains can affect the future of trucks, but some barriers must be considered. To satisfy the anticipated increases in demand without increasing rates, trucks must become more efficient. Many methods exist to increase efficiency. Some of those methods have been exploited successfully but, in other cases, the potential gains are being thwarted by other factors. For instance, truckload capacity could be increased. But the length, height, and gross weight of trucks are not inhibited as much by engineering as they are by government and safety regulations. The width of highway lanes, height of underpasses, weight-bearing capacity of bridges, and road configurations that limit maneuverability are serious limitations. To allow trucks to expand beyond current physical limits would require a complete redesign and reconstruction of the highway network, which is not likely to occur in the near future. Safety must also be considered because trucks must share the highways with other vehicles. The speed of trucks has also been reduced. Lowered speed limits, initially conceived to save fuel and then recognized as a significant safety factor, are not expected to increase again in the future. Thus, some technological gains that could benefit trucks are limited, at least for the immediate future, because of other considerations.

Other methods to increase efficiency are being explored, such as a communication network that would post the truck shipments available in a particular area to reduce empty backhauls. Uniform restrictions across all states as to the weight, size, and configuration of vehicles would also improve efficiency. Although these changes would help handle the anticipated increases in demand, their impact is expected to be small.

Although the government's role in the promotion of trucks is limited to the creation and maintenance of highways, government regulations have a significant impact on the industry. As discussed before, government-imposed regulations on speed limits, load capacity, truck size, and highway configuration may hinder the growth of the industry. Because drastic changes in government posture on safety and ecology are not anticipated, further gains in efficiency may be slowed.

The impact of competition appears to be less severe for the future. Just as the railroads are sandwiched between the water and truck modes, trucks are sandwiched between the air and rail modes. Although air freight has grown significantly over the last few decades, the amount of traffic carried remains less than 0.2 per cent of total ton-miles. There are no indications that air traffic will grow at a sufficient rate to cut into the demand for trucks. On the other side, primarily because of their instability, railroads currently pose a limited threat to trucks. Energy and technological gains may improve the railroads' position, but these gains will more likely reduce the rate of decline rather than increase their competitive posture. Thus, trucks are not expected to be threatened competitively by other modes in the future.

Probably the most important factor affecting the future of the truck industry will be the availability of fuel. All trucks require some form of oil-based fuel, and no technology currently exists that will significantly shift this dependence. The cost of fuel, although a serious consideration, will not have a significant impact on the rates charged for service. A more critical concern is the availability of fuel at *any* cost. Opinions as to the amount of oil available worldwide vary greatly. Nevertheless, the threat of fuel rationing continues to be a serious issue affecting the truck industry.

Ecological concerns facing the truck mode center on road construction and pollution. To date, forces promoting ecology have changed the routes of proposed roads and, in some cases, have stopped construction altogether. At the very least, the rate of road development has been slowed. Increasing attention is also focusing on the control of emission and noise pollution. Although the proposed controls are not necessarily insurmountable, technology must be developed and money must be spent to achieve compliance.

Overall, the future of trucks in the transportation system is bright. The demand will be present and the main competitive threats will be weak. However, significant increases in efficiency to satisfy growing demand are doubtful. Technological gains are approaching their limit or are being hindered by regulatory issues and physical constraints. The availability and cost of energy pose a serious threat, particularly when coupled with ecological considerations. Although the trucking industry is not expected to decline in importance, its growth will not be as easy or as spectacular as it has been over the past thirty years.

Summary

Trucks are relative latecomers to the overall transportation system. Since World War II, the number of trucks has grown sixfold, and today trucks generate the highest revenue of any transportation mode. The highway system is the largest of all modes, which allows trucks to service almost every point in the continental United States. This characteristic, coupled with its good speed, has increased the demand for truck service in spite of its comparatively high cost. Trucks complete the moves of many other modes, are the only mode for intracity movements, and play a major role in intercity movements. Because of these diverse services, trucks can move almost all goods, but find their greatest competitive advantage in higher-valued, manufactured freight.

On an industry basis, trucks are the most competitive of all modes. Ease of entry and low capital requirements have resulted in more than 15,000 regulated trucking firms and an unknown number of private and exempt shippers. A shipper has many trucking alternatives, including common, contract, and private carriage, which can be chosen and switched with relative ease. The government's assistance has been limited to supplying and maintaining the ways, which has aided the competitive position of the industry by eliminating costly investments. Although the trucking industry has grown rapidly and, for the most part, enjoys economic prosperity, the future of the mode is in question, primarily because of fuel availability. Nevertheless, trucks will continue to play an integral role in the overall transportation system even though industry gains may be slower and more difficult in the future.

Questions for Chapter 6

1. Discuss the problems that the various state restrictions on vehicle weight, length, and configuration cause the trucking industry.
2. What performance characteristic is the single greatest asset of the truck mode?
3. Compare the economic characteristics of rail and trucks. How do they differ and what effect do these differences have on their operations?
4. Describe the competitive situation within the trucking industry.
5. Define private, common, contract, and exempt truck operators.
6. Why has there been a continued move toward private truck operations?
7. Discuss the assistance that has been given to the truck industry by the federal government.
8. What factors will probably have the greatest impact on the future of the truck mode?
9. What is the greatest competitive threat to trucks in the future?
10. Discuss the type of freight that is best suited for movement by truck.

11. Discuss the possible consequences of the ICC granting private operators common or contract certificates to fill their backhauls.
12. Why are shippers willing to pay the high rates charged by truck carriers rather than to ship by rail?

7

Pipeline Transportation

ROLE OF PIPELINES
Amount Shipped and Revenue
Network
Freight Shipped

PIPELINE INDUSTRY CHARACTERISTICS
Size and Ownership
Cost Characteristics
Competition

PERFORMANCE CHARACTERISTICS
Speed
Completeness
Dependability
Capability
Frequency
Cost

THE ROLE OF GOVERNMENT

FUTURE

SUMMARY

Pipeline transportation has several unique characteristics that set it apart from all other modes. First, it is a limited product mode. At this time, the only products that can be moved through pipelines are gases, liquids, and limited slurries. Movement of natural or manufactured gas is considered energy transmission, not transportation. Slurries, which are solids such as coal, wood pulp, or sand suspended in a liquid, represent a limited amount of pipeline movement. Most pipeline movements consist of crude oil and related products.

The second unique characteristic of pipeline transportation is its low public visibility. Although almost 230,000 miles of pipeline carry about 23 per cent[1] of all ton-miles shipped in the United States, the public is generally unaware of the industry's presence. Third, the mode has the fewest number of users because of its ties to the concentrated structure of the oil industry. Fourth, the mode has no vehicles. The pipeline is the way, the pumps are the "vehicle,"

[1] *Transportation Facts and Trends*, 15th ed. (Washington, D.C.: Transportation Association of America, July 1979), pp. 8 and 31.

102

and products flow within the pipe. Therefore, maintenance and investment are reduced and no backhaul problems exist. Fifth, the industry is highly automated. Product flow can be controlled from hundreds of miles away, and computers schedule the monitor operations.

With these unique features as background, let us consider the role of the mode, the industry and its performance characteristics, the role of government, and the future of the mode.

Role of Pipelines

Pipelines continue to play an increasingly important role in the transportation system. Originally, pipelines were used to feed other modes such as rail or water. But as the industry grew and technology became more sophisticated, trunk lines were constructed and oil moved without the help of other modes. Today, the industry ships crude oil and a variety of oil products through an extensive network, often totally independent of other modes.

AMOUNT SHIPPED AND REVENUE

Pipelines account for 23.3 per cent of all ton-miles moved in the United States. Table 7–1 shows the ton-miles shipped and the percentage of total ton-miles since 1945. The growth of the industry in amount shipped and share of market has been steady. Since 1945, the amount shipped has increased 340 per cent from 129 billion ton-miles to 568 billion ton-miles, and the share of the

TABLE 7–1. Pipeline Transportation

Year	Ton-Miles Shipped (Billions)	Percentage of Total Transportation Ton-Miles
1945	129	12.4%
1950	129	12.1%
1955	203	15.9%
1960	229	17.4%
1965	306	18.7%
1970	431	22.3%
1975	507	24.5%
1977	546	23.6%
1978	568	23.3%

Source: *Transportation Facts and Trends,* 15th ed. (Washington, D.C.: Transportation Association of America, July 1979), p. 8.

103

total transportation market has increased about 90 per cent from 12.4 per cent to 23.3 per cent.

As would be expected, industry revenue has grown but still remains a small percentage of the total money spent on transportation. Table 7–2 shows the revenue and the percentage of the total freight revenue since 1960. Although revenue has grown 195 per cent since 1960, as a percentage of total transportation revenue spent, it has remained constant. The large number of ton-miles versus the small amount of revenue reflects the very low cost per ton-mile of pipelines. Like water, pipelines are capable of shipping a ton-mile for less than 1 cent.

TABLE 7–2. Pipeline Revenue

Year	Revenue (Millions of Dollars)	Percentage of Total Transportation Freight Revenue
1960	895	2.0%
1965	1,051	1.7%
1970	1,396	1.7%
1975	2,220	1.8%
1976	2,532	1.8%
1977	2,641	1.6%

Source: *Transportation Facts and Trends*, 15th ed. (Washington, D.C.: Transportation Association of America, July 1979), p. 4.

NETWORK

In 1977 the pipeline network in the continental United States was 228,243 miles. Network growth since 1945 is shown in Table 7–3. The pipeline network has two classifications: crude lines and product lines. Crude lines carry oil in its natural form from the source to the refineries, whereas product lines carry the refined oil output from refineries to the market. In 1978, approximately 125,000 miles of crude lines and 105,000 miles of product lines existed.[2] Recently, growth in the number of product lines has been greater than the growth of crude lines. In 1950 there were only 21,000 miles of product line. Originally, pipelines primarily moved crude oil because it was difficult to move products. As the problems of moving products were reduced and the ability to locate refineries at the market became more difficult, refineries located near the source of crude oil. Generally, this trend continues today.

[2] U.S. Department of Transportation. Estimates from William F. Gay, *Energy Statistics: A Supplement to the Survey of National Transportation Statistics* (1975), p. 11, Table 1–4.

TABLE 7–3. Pipeline Network

Year	Miles of Network
1945	137,545
1950	158,472
1955	188,540
1960	190,944
1965	213,764
1970	218,671
1975	224,811
1976	227,066
1977	228,243*

*Estimate.
Source: *Transportation Facts and Trends*, 15th ed. (Washington, D.C.: Transportation Association of America, July 1979), p. 31.

Crude lines can be further classified as gathering lines or trunk lines. Gathering lines collect the oil from various oil fields and bring it to a refinery or to a crude trunk line. In 1978 there were approximately 67,000 miles of gathering lines and 58,000 miles of trunk lines.[3] The diameter of pipelines varies from three inches to forty-eight inches. Crude gathering lines are usually less than six inches in diameter, crude trunk lines are usually twenty-four inches or more, and product lines vary from three to forty-eight inches.

Geographic locations of the network for crude and product lines are shown in Figure 7–1. Locations of pipelines are a function of the source of supply and the market. Before 1900, both the sources and the markets were predominantly in the eastern part of the United States. Since then, sources and markets have moved west steadily. As more oil is imported, offshore wells increase production, and Alaskan oil is shipped to the West Coast, new network patterns will emerge.

FREIGHT SHIPPED

Pipelines carry crude oil and oil products such as gasoline, kerosene, and jet fuel. Of all oil moved in the United States in 1976, crude and product pipelines moved 59.7 per cent of all ton-miles. In terms of oil moved by other modes, water transported 35 per cent, railroads moved 13.3 per cent, and motor carriers hauled 3.7 per cent.[4] Pipelines carry more than 70 per cent of all crude oil ton-miles, with most of the remainder moved by water. For instance, crude oil from the Southwest can be moved by water to refineries in the East, and Alaskan oil is being shipped by tanker to the West Coast.

[3] Ibid.
[4] *Transportation Facts and Trends*, op. cit., p. 32.

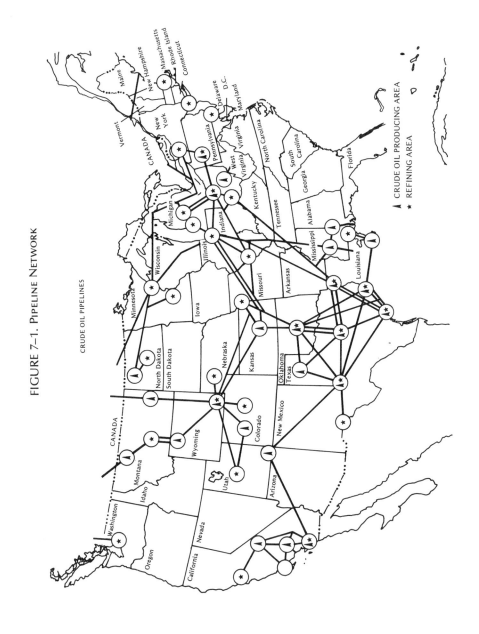

FIGURE 7-1. Pipeline Network

CRUDE OIL PIPELINES

▲ CRUDE OIL PRODUCING AREA
★ REFINING AREA

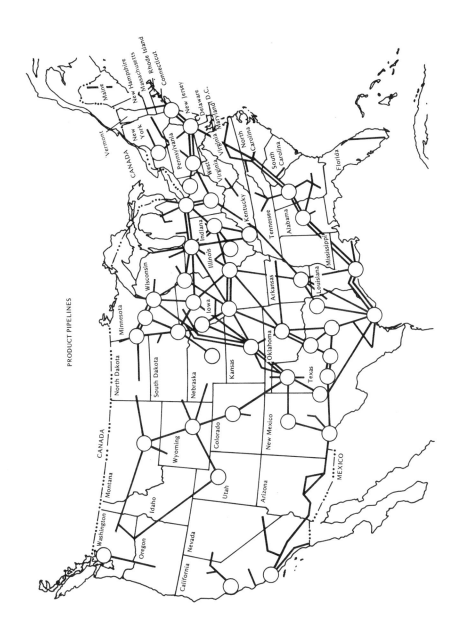

PRODUCT PIPELINES

107

Although product lines are growing faster than crude lines, they account for only about 30 per cent of all refined petroleum ton-miles. A large part of the remainder is moved by truck. Although motor carriers accounted for only 3.7 per cent of the ton-miles moved in 1976, they accounted for 28.7 per cent of all tons moved.[5] These figures support the observation that trucks are used to move refined oil products from the end of the pipeline to the point of use or resale.

Pipelines play a significant and unique role in the overall transportation system. They move almost 24 per cent of the ton-miles shipped, but collect less than 2 per cent of the revenue. They are not generally visible to the public but have a network of almost 300,000 miles. Probably the most unique feature of pipelines is their one-product orientation. The next section examines industry characteristics.

Pipeline Industry Characteristics

Industry characteristics are as unique as the mode's role in the transportation system. It is the only mode that is an integral part of a single industry. Originally, pipeline companies were independent carriers moving crude oil from fields to rail or water transportation. As the pipeline network grew, the oil companies, particularly refineries, foresaw the advantages and constructed or bought their own lines. By the turn of the century, most pipelines were owned and controlled by a few oil companies. In 1906, the Hepburn Act made most pipelines for-hire carriers. This action, however, did not change ownership patterns, and today most pipelines are owned by oil companies. Let us now examine the ownership, cost characteristics, and competition in the pipeline industry.

SIZE AND OWNERSHIP

All pipelines are owned by private enterprises. The federal government owned two lines during World War II, but these were sold to private companies at the end of the war. In 1977, 107 pipeline companies offered for-hire service and carried about 85 per cent of all ton-miles. The remaining 15 per cent were carried by approximately twelve private companies. The vast majority of the for-hire pipeline companies are owned by the oil industry. However, recently, some ownerships have shifted to nonoil industries. Several railroads, particularly in the Southwest, own pipelines. Because of the substantial investment required, the efficiencies of large-diameter pipelines, and the inefficiencies of

---

[5] Ibid.

108

parallel lines, many pipelines are owned by more than one company. A notable example is the Alaska Pipeline, which is owned and operated by the Alyeska Pipeline Service Company, a consortium of seven oil producers and pipeline companies.

COST CHARACTERISTICS

The pipeline industry is similar to the railroad industry from an economic perspective. It has high fixed costs, low capital turnover, and must provide its own network. Other characteristics, however, are quite different. Because pipeline companies must provide the network, fixed costs are high. But once the network (pipe, pumps, and storage) is completed, no vehicles are necessary. Without vehicles, operating costs are very low and consist mainly of the cost to operate pumps. Labor costs are low because pipeline operations are highly automated. Over the last twenty years, pipeline mileage has grown, but the pipeline labor force has been reduced. Maintenance costs are also low. Little maintenance is required because most pipelines are underground and there are no vehicles to service. Given these characteristics, pipelines have the highest proportion of fixed costs, more than 80 per cent of total cost.

The pipeline industry requires large capital expenditures. It must obtain the right to install pipes, and the engineering characteristics of pipe make construction expensive. A twelve-inch line may cost 50 per cent more than an eight-inch pipe to construct, but the twelve-inch line will carry more than twice the volume of an eight-inch line. Thus, it is more efficient to build larger lines. Again, the Alaska Pipeline is a good example. A forty-eight-inch pipeline 800 miles in length costs more than $9 billion. These capital requirements result in very low capital turnover (approximately once every four years) and low operating ratios (the lowest of all modes).

COMPETITION

Competition can be viewed as existing within the industry and between pipelines and other modes. Within the industry, all indicators point to an oligopoly. A small number of companies exist in the industry, and only a few companies carry more than 50 per cent of the ton-miles. Entry into the industry is very difficult, not because of regulations, but because of the high and steadily increasing capital requirements. In addition, as discussed earlier, the more efficient large-diameter pipelines are often owned by two or more oil companies, and construction of smaller parallel lines is inefficient. However, these oligopolistic tendencies have been restricted by government regulation of the for-hire pipelines. The amount of return is controlled for crude and product pipelines and, although rates are not set, they must be approved by the government.

Competition exists between pipe and other modes, particularly the water and rail modes. Over the last two decades, the trend in the shift of oil transportation between modes has been constant. Pipelines and trucks have increased the tons and ton-miles shipped, but water and rail movements have decreased. Once a pipeline is constructed between two points, it is difficult for other modes to compete for those movements. Pipeline rates are lower, particularly in comparison to railroads, dependability is higher and, in most cases, storage requirements at shipping and receiving points are much smaller. Pipelines are also attempting to become competitive for nonoil products. The most promising application is coal slurry lines to replace railroad movements. To date, these attempts have not posed a competitive threat to other modes.

All pipelines are privately owned, and about 85 per cent are for-hire. Most of the pipelines are owned by oil companies, but nonoil companies have been buying and investing in pipelines. The industry has high fixed costs and high capital requirements. Of all modes, pipelines are the most automated, and labor costs are low. Oligopoly, rather than competition or monopoly, best characterizes the industry. The next section examines the service characteristics of pipelines. Again, like the mode's role and industry characteristics, the service characteristics are unique in the transportation system.

Performance Characteristics

As discussed earlier, pipelines are not the only mode to move oil and oil products. Shippers, particularly oil product shippers, must evaluate the performance characteristics of the mode in light of other alternatives. As with the other modes, speed, completeness, dependability, capability, frequency, and cost will be examined.

SPEED

Speed was defined as the elapsed time from when freight is given to a transportation mode until the movement is completed. Oil moves through pipelines at three to four miles per hour. Although this is the slowest of all modes, it is usually not a reason for choosing an alternative mode. Speed in transportation becomes critical when demand cannot be forecast or when the value of the item in transit is absorbing high inventory costs. Neither of these conditions apply to crude oil moving from the well to the refinery. As the value of the oil product increases after refining and it moves closer to the market, the speed of the pipeline becomes more critical. However, even with product movements where inventory costs are higher, total cost versus higher speed usually favors the pipeline mode.

COMPLETENESS

Completeness was defined as the extent of the modal network and the amount of required involvement of other modes. Although the pipeline network is almost 300,000 miles, it cannot service any random pair of locations. Pipelines have no geographical flexibility. As with the water and rail modes, once the network is in place, locations cannot be shifted easily. Unlike other modes, however, the source location for pipelines is known for several years and refining locations are fixed for a long period of time. Therefore, from well to refinery, the mode is complete and other modes are not usually involved. Finished product pipelines are somewhat different. Although refining locations are fixed and intermediate distribution points are quite stable, the location of ultimate consumers will change over time. For the most part, product pipeline movements must be completed by other modes, usually trucks. Consequently, pipelines are less complete for products than they are for crude oil.

DEPENDABILITY

Dependability was defined as the mode's ability to perform as anticipated over time. Pipelines are the most dependable of all modes. They are not affected by weather because, for the most part, they are belowground. The mode's dependability is also the result, in part, of the high degree of automation and network scheduling. Shippers forecast their transportation requirements, and shipment schedules are determined with little variation. The probabilities of loss or damage in transit are very low. Pipeline construction technology has advanced to the point where failures and ruptures are rare. Consequently, the product usually will move as scheduled, and shipment will be received when promised.

CAPABILITY

Capability was defined as the mode's ability to handle particular transportation requirements. Given that pipelines can handle only liquids or gases, the mode must be considered the least capable. The technology is developing to move other products by pipeline, such as slurries and solids, but the amount of goods shipped in this form is small at the present time. Another factor affecting capability is the volume of goods shipped. Pipelines are large-volume movers. For shipments from fields to refineries and from refineries to distribution points, this is an asset. But as the product moves closer to the ultimate consumer and the amount shipped to one location decreases, this asset becomes a liability. At the present time, pipelines move only 30 per cent of product shipments. Trucks move most of the remainder and usually move products from distribution points to ultimate consumers or retail outlets.

111

FREQUENCY

Frequency was defined as the number of times a mode can pick up and deliver during a particular period. The large shipment size and slow speed of pipelines reduce frequency. However, frequency of movement is not a critical factor because of advance scheduling and the low cost of storage.

COST

Cost was defined as the amount of money a shipper or receiver must pay for movement. Cost includes the freight rate, inventory costs, and the probability of damage in transit. Of all modes, pipeline freight rates are the lowest per ton-mile. In 1976, the average revenue for pipelines was 0.41 cents, whereas water was 0.74 cents, and rail, 2.2 cents per ton-mile. Trucks and air were considerably higher.[6] Averages, however, can be deceiving. Pipeline costs decrease as the size of the pipe increases, and costs increase as the value of the product increases. Thus, crude oil moved in large-diameter pipes is least costly, and product shipped in small-diameter pipes is the most costly. Water is the closest competitor. Large tankers moving crude oil can be very cost-competitive and, depending on the pipeline diameter, the cost of water movement can be lower than pipe.

Low cost and high dependability are the major advantages of the pipeline mode. Its capability, which limits product forms and demands large volumes, is its major disadvantage. Thus, low-value, high-volume liquids become the major market for pipeline transportation. The next section examines the promotional role of government in the development of pipelines.

The Role of Government

The promotion/provision role of government is discussed here, and government regulation will be discussed in Chapter 11. Of all modes, pipelines have received the least government assistance. At the federal level, the government became involved for a short period during World War II. During that time the president of the United States could, for national defense reasons, grant rights of eminent domain for pipeline construction. During the war, the federal government constructed two pipelines from the Southwest to the East Coast to move crude oil and product to support the war effort. The "big inch" line was a twenty-four-inch crude line, and the "little big inch" was a twenty-inch prod-

[6] U.S. Department of Transportation, *National Transportation Statistics* (September 1978), p. 44.

uct line. After the war, the federal government sold these lines and has not owned pipelines since. To date, there has been no additional federal assistance. State government involvement has been limited to granting rights of eminent domain. Thus, the pipeline industry has received little or no government promotional help. There has been some discussion about granting eminent domain for coal slurry lines but, in 1978, federal legislation to grant this power to the federal government was defeated.

This lack of government support is primarily the result of the financial stability of the industry. Tied so closely to the oil industry, pipelines have always had financial support. It appears that this situation will continue and will affect the future of pipelines, which is the topic of the next section.

Future

The future of the pipeline industry, as with all other modes, depends on many factors. In discussing those factors, which include demand, technology, competition, government, energy, and ecology, let us keep in mind the dependence of pipelines on the oil industry.

The demand for pipeline transportation is tied to the demand for, the availability, and the sources of oil. The overall demand for oil is uncertain but, at the very worst, demand will remain constant. However, constant demand will depend on the availability of oil more than any other factor. Because of the economic characteristics of pipelines, movement over many years must be forecasted before an investment is feasible. Unlike other modes, pipelines are not flexible geographically or by product carried. As the sources of crude oil shift to offshore or imports, the demand for pipeline construction will increase, but total ton-miles moved in the system may not increase.

The demand for oil pipeline transportation is expected to grow. About 30 per cent of oil products are shipped by pipe, and refineries are beginning to locate near oil sources instead of near the markets. Growth in this area will come primarily at the expense of other modes. Demand for pipeline transportation of nonoil products such as coal, pulp, and other raw materials is expected to grow, but how fast this part of the pipeline industry will grow in the face of competition and ecology is unknown. Thus, even though the future supply of crude oil is uncertain, the demand for pipeline transportation looks promising.

Technological gains in the pipeline industry have been impressive over the last few decades. Large-diameter pipes have been proven to be effective, the problems of mixing two batches of liquid in transit have been overcome, pipeline construction has been shown to be possible under extreme conditions, and automated pipeline operation is increasing. The most promising area for future technological advances is in the movement of slurries and solids. If significant gains are made in these fields, the industry will be able to move new forms of product, and the future of pipelines could become promising.

It appears that pipelines will give other modes more competition than other modes will give pipelines. From a service perspective, pipelines are closest to water transportation. Both are capable of moving large quantities of products at very low cost. However, only the largest oil tankers can compete directly with large pipes. Furthermore, water routes are often longer in distance between the same two locations. In some situations, no substitution is possible between the two modes because of the lack of waterways or the inability of pipelines to cross large bodies of water. Even though it might appear to be a standoff, pipelines have the advantage. The same can be said for pipelines in comparison to railroads. Therefore, pipelines should not be threatened significantly by the water or rail modes in the near future. However, pipelines will threaten railroads and water in nonoil product areas. If this develops, water and rail modes will be the victims. Thus, pipelines will threaten competitively rather than be threatened.

As discussed, government has not played a major role in the promotion/provision of pipelines. This is not expected to change. The federal government may grant eminent domain to pipeline companies but will not pursue other forms of promotion, such as providing way, ownership, or subsidies as it has with the other modes. In some ways, this lack of government support could be seen as a competitive disadvantage.

Pipelines are efficient energy users. Among all modes, they require the least amount of energy to move products. Therefore, as energy concerns increase, pipeline movement will become more favorable. Pipelines are the least visible of all modes and have no problems with air or noise pollution. However, development will be slowed by ecological considerations. Objections focus on construction and the possibilities of ruptures. These considerations were evident during the construction of the Alaskan Pipeline and were a major factor in the delay of pipeline construction to carry Alaskan oil from the West Coast to the rest of the country.

Overall, the future of pipeline transportation is bright, even in the face of stabilizing or declining oil resources. The technology is developing to move slurries and solids, and the cost of pipeline transportation is attractive.

Summary

The pipeline industry has grown substantially in the last three decades and has doubled its market share to almost 25 per cent of total ton-miles shipped. The network has grown tenfold to more than 300,000 miles. Almost 100 per cent of the shipments by pipe consist of crude oil and oil products. The industry, which consists of approximately 85 per cent common carriers, is primarily owned by private, oil-related companies. Although a few firms control a large portion of the industry, government regulation has maintained some competition within a naturally oligopolistic industry. Because they must provide the network and no vehicles are involved in movement, pipelines have high capital requirements with associated high fixed costs. This balance of fixed-to-variable cost is the result of a high degree of automation. Of all modes, pipelines cost the least to move a ton-mile. The closest competitor is the water mode's supertankers. From a performance perspective, pipelines have low cost, speed, and capability, acceptable completeness and frequency, and high dependability. Except for a period during World War II, there has been no governmental assistance. In spite of energy and ecology problems, the pipeline industry should grow, and its future appears bright.

Questions for Chapter 7

1. Describe the economic characteristics of pipeline transportation that make it different from the modes discussed thus far.
2. How does a high degree of automation and a relatively small labor force affect the pipeline industry?
3. What is the difference between a crude line and a product line?
4. Discuss the major drawbacks of shipping petroleum and petroleum products by pipe.
5. With the exception of the Alaska Pipeline, the industry is practically invisible to the general public. What are the advantages and disadvantages of this posture?
6. Discuss the major competitive threats to the pipeline industry in the future.
7. Describe the ownership situation in the pipeline industry that makes it unique in comparison to the other modes discussed. What are the consequences of this ownership?
8. Discuss the performance characteristics of pipeline transportation.
9. Discuss how the role of government may slow the growth of pipelines in the future.
10. Discuss the nature of competition between pipelines and the other modes.
11. Define a slurry pipeline. What effect might this technology have on the transportation system?
12. Discuss the future of pipelines. What will be their role if energy problems continue?

8

Air Transportation

ROLE OF AIR
Amount Shipped and Revenue
Network
Freight Shipped

AIR INDUSTRY CHARACTERISTICS
Fleet Size and Ownership
Cost Characteristics
Competition

PERFORMANCE CHARACTERISTICS
Speed
Completeness
Dependability
Capability
Frequency
Cost

ROLE OF GOVERNMENT

FUTURE

SUMMARY

Air transportation was the most recent mode to be developed. Today it represents approximately two tenths of one per cent of total ton-miles shipped.[1] This small tonnage, however, misrepresents air freight's importance in the domestic freight transportation system. Its unique service characteristics make air transportation the only possible mode for certain types of essential movements. Unlike other modes, air transportation did not develop because of a need for its service. The airplane was the result of man's desire to conquer flight. When the Wright brothers proved heavier-than-air flight was possible, the airplane was considered a curiosity rather than an essential, useful means of transportation. The first successful use of airplanes was by the military during World War I. Once the practical application had been proved, interest in the mode increased. Airplanes slowly became an accepted means of moving people and mail. However, the movement of freight by air is a fairly recent phenomenon.

[1] *Transportation Facts and Trends*, 15th ed. (Washington, D.C.: Transportation Association of America, July 1979), p. 8.

116

Freight movements have grown at a rapid rate, but they remain only a small portion of total air transportation.

The small amount of freight shipped reflects the mode's newness and its service characteristics. From a service perspective, air transport stands almost alone. Its fast speed, high cost, and limited capabilities make it unique and suited for special types of products and circumstances.

This chapter will look at the role of air freight transportation, the industry's economic characteristics, competition, and performance characteristics. The government's role in the industry's development and the future of air transportation will be discussed.

Role of Air

Although the amount of cargo shipped is extremely small compared to other modes, in absolute terms the industry's growth has been rapid over the last thirty years. The airport network has grown, and the assortment of freight shipped has increased accordingly. Certain types of air freight transportation are indispensable. The mode adds a dimension to the overall transportation system that the total ton-miles shipped do not reflect.

AMOUNT SHIPPED AND REVENUE

In 1978 domestic air carriers shipped 5.21 billion ton-miles of cargo, which represented 0.21 per cent of the total transportation ton-miles shipped by all modes. Table 8–1 shows the ton-miles shipped and the percentage of total ton-miles since 1945. Although the amount of ton-miles is extremely small, growth within the industry has been rapid.

For statistical purposes, air cargo is divided into three categories: (1) the *United States mail*, the air cargo of the United States Postal System, (2) *freight*, commodities of all kinds, and (3) *express*, priority freight. In 1977, the United States mail represented about 19 per cent of air's total ton-miles. From 1968 to 1977, the United States mail ton-miles increased 32 per cent. During the same time, freight and express shipments increased 76 per cent.[2] The significant increase in freight and express movements indicates that the mode is becoming accepted by business firms and that air freight is viewed as an integral part of the domestic freight transportation system.

Air revenue has increased in terms of total revenue, as a percentage of total revenue spent on all freight movements, and on a ton-mile basis. Table 8–2

[2] *Air Transport 1978* (Washington, D.C.: Air Transport Association of America, 1978), computed from pages 13–15 for domestic scheduled airlines.

TABLE 8–1. Air Freight Transportation *

Year	Ton-Miles (Billions)	Percentage of Total Transportation Ton-Miles
1945	0.09	0.01%
1950	0.30	0.03%
1955	0.49	0.04%
1960	0.89	0.07%
1965	1.91	0.12%
1970	3.30	0.17%
1975	3.73	0.18%
1977	4.91	0.21%
1978	5.21	0.21%

*Includes mail and express.
Source: *Transportation Facts and Trends*, 15th ed. (Washington, D.C.: Transportation Association of America, July 1979), p. 8.

lists air freight revenues and their percentage of total revenue from 1950 to 1977. Revenue increased more than 1100 per cent since 1950, even though the amount spent on air freight was still less than 1 per cent of total revenue. Revenue per ton-mile increased from 20 cents in 1968 to a little over 34 cents in 1976.[3] Thus, in all respects, the air cargo industry has grown significantly since its inception.

TABLE 8–2. Air Freight Revenue

Year	Revenue (Millions of Dollars)	Percentage of Total Transportation Freight Revenue
1950	$ 123	N/A
1955	139	N/A
1960	220	0.4%
1965	428	0.7%
1970	720	0.9%
1975	1,073	0.9%
1976	1,247	0.9%
1977	1,484	0.9%

Source: *Transportation Facts and Trends*, 15th ed. (Washington, D.C.: Transportation Association of America, July 1979), p. 4.

[3] Ibid., p. 30.

NETWORK

The air network consists of the airways and airports. The airways are literally aerial highways. These navigational highways connect airports and are under the control of the Federal Aviation Administration (FAA). The network has grown tenfold in forty years. In 1939, there were 31,162 miles of network, and in 1976, there were 332,662 miles.[4] Although the network's growth has been largely in response to passenger traffic demands, it nevertheless facilitated an increase in air cargo.

In 1977, there were 14,117 airports. The majority of these airports were extremely small and used primarily for private flying. Of that total, 629 had scheduled airline service and 427 had FAA control towers.[5] Twenty-five hub airports handled the bulk of air freight. An estimated 70 per cent of all air freight was handled by these hub airports.

At first glance the air network appears to be quite extensive. However, the limiting factor is not the number of miles but the number of airports. Except for a few, most airports are incapable of handling the large aircraft that are the backbone of air freight operations. Smaller airports ship and receive air freight, but their operations represent only a small percentage of total ton-miles. Thus, the effective network size for freight transportation is significantly less than the total miles of airways and the number of airports implies.

FREIGHT SHIPPED

Until a few years ago, air transport was considered a mode limited to emergency service. Within the last decade, however, air transport became a legitimate alternative to other modes, particularly trucks, as an integral part of some firms' distribution systems. For the most part, air transport is suited for high-value, low-weight, low-volume products, for extremely perishable freight such as flowers and lobster, and for highly marketable products such as high fashion apparel. Air transport is also well suited for seldom needed critical parts. From a total cost perspective, it may be less expensive to move a part by air freight when it is needed than to hold it in a warehouse in anticipation of its eventual use. Thus, the type of freight moved by air can be defined by product characteristics, market conditions, or a total distribution system cost perspective. Within these boundaries, air freight transportation involves a variety of products. Manufactured products shipped by air freight include communication products and parts, apparel and related products, rubber and plastic products, instruments, photo equipment, motors and clocks, machinery and parts, and electrical products and supplies.

[4]*Transportation Facts and Trends*, op. cit., p. 31.
[5]*Transportation Facts and Trends*, p. 8, and *Air Transport*, pp. 13–15 op. cit.

Air transport is beginning to play an integral role in the overall freight transportation system. The growth of the industry in terms of ton-miles, revenue, and network has been dramatic even though shipments and revenue still account for less than 1 per cent of the total. Several factors contributing to this growth are discussed in the next section.

Air Industry Characteristics

This section examines the economic characteristics of air transportation, including the number of firms, type of ownership, competition, and cost structure. One characteristic of air transport that must be remembered is its relative proportion of freight to passengers and its simultaneous movement of people and freight. Pipelines and trucks move only freight. The water and rail modes move small numbers of people, but freight and passenger operations are separate. In air transportation, almost 90 per cent of all revenues result from passenger operations and, in some cases, freight moves on the same planes that carry passengers.

FLEET SIZE AND OWNERSHIP

The airline industry consists of three categories of carriers: scheduled, nonscheduled, and air taxi. Each category is briefly discussed.

Scheduled airlines carry 91.5 per cent of all air freight moved. Table 8–3 shows the amount of freight and the percentage carried by each airline group. Within the scheduled airlines group, there are eleven domestic trunk lines, twelve local service carriers,[6] two intra-Hawaii lines, five intra-Alaska lines, three helicopter lines, and three all-cargo lines. The size of these carriers varies widely. For instance, three carriers, United Airlines, American Airlines (both domestic trunk), and Flying Tiger (all-cargo) carry 50 per cent of all freight shipments. The fleet size of the scheduled carriers in 1977 was 2,229 aircraft,[7] of which fifty-six were all-cargo.[8]

The *nonscheduled* or supplemental airlines account for approximately 7.5 per cent of air cargo ton-miles. Within this group, seven carriers were primarily passenger charters. Collectively, they operated eighty-four aircraft, of which twenty-six were designated as all-cargo.[9]

---

[6] Includes Air Midwest and Air New England, which the Civil Aeronautics Board (CAB) classifies as regional carriers, and Aspen and Wright, which the CAB classifies as "other."

[7] *Air Transport*, op. cit., p. 26.

[8] U.S. Government Printing Office, *Civil Aeronautics Board Reports to Congress, Fiscal Year 1977 and Transitional Quarter* (1977), p. 139.

[9] Ibid., p. 139.

TABLE 8–3. Freight Carried by Scheduled Airlines * 1977

Airline Classification	Ton-Miles (Millions)	Percentage of Total
Domestic Trunk	3,219,309	83.1%
Local	117,382	3.0%
Intra-Hawaii	7,252	0.2%
Intra-Alaska	35,229	0.9%
Helicopter	3	negligible
All-Cargo	495,841	12.8%

*Includes mail and express.
Source: Air Transport, 1978 (Washington, D.C.: Air Transport Association of America, 1978), pp. 13–15.

In 1977, 3,535 air taxis were in operation. Of this group, 242 were categorized as commuter air carriers, accounting for about 1 per cent of all cargo ton-miles. Air taxi operators are restricted to aircraft of thirty seats and a payload of 7,500 pounds or less. They operate between small airports or between small and large airports as feeder lines. In 1977, the 242 commuter airlines operated at 764 airports. Their primary business is passenger carriage, but they often move freight and mail. Those air taxis not classified as commuter lines are nonscheduled charter operators carrying mostly passengers and small amounts of cargo.

Except for the military and other government operations, there is no government ownership of air carriers. By the time the air transportation industry developed, private ownership of transportation was well established. Thus, air freight is moved by privately owned, for-hire carriers. More than 90 per cent of all air cargo is moved by scheduled carriers, with the remainder shipped by supplemental and air taxi carriers.

COST CHARACTERISTICS

From a cost perspective, the airlines are higher per ton-mile than all other modes. However, as with the water and truck modes, the airlines are not responsible for provision of the network and therefore most costs are variable. Unlike trucks, however, the initial investment is significant, particularly for the vehicles.

It is difficult to be specific regarding fixed versus variable cost rates because of the time frame involved. In the short run, once a schedule has been committed, planes purchased, and crews and terminals are in place, more than 75 per cent of the costs have been fixed. Thus, the cost to carry additional cargo beyond the break-even point is low because variable costs are basically reduced to handling and billing. Once the time frame is expanded, however, the carrier has the ability to change capacity, which would be reflected in aircraft costs,

121

crews, and other operating expenses. Under these conditions, fixed costs, such as terminal facilities and overhead, become a smaller portion of the total.

The airlines are not as capital-intensive as pipelines and railroads, but are more capital-intensive than trucks. Capital turnover (annual revenues/investment) is approximately 1.2. Trucks are approximately 4; water is 1; rail, 0.7; and pipe, 0.25. The higher the capital turnover, the higher the operating ratio (operating expenses/operating revenues) can be and still allow a return. For instance, because trucks turn capital approximately four times per year, they can make acceptable returns with an operating ratio of 0.95. However, with a capital turnover of one, the operating ratio should be lower. The operating ratio for the air transportation industry has fluctuated over the last fifteen years from 0.93 in 1968 to as high as 0.99 in the early 1970s. In 1977, the operating ratio was 0.95.

COMPETITION

As with the other modes, competition must be examined both within the industry and among modes. The industry structure is oligopolistic rather than competitive. A small number of firms carry the bulk of the traffic, entry is difficult from a capital perspective, and for certain types of cargo there are few substitute carriers. In 1977, the Civil Aeronautics Board (CAB) relaxed the economic regulations imposed on the air cargo industry. According to the CAB, the move was taken to ". . . produce an industry more promptly responsive to the workings of the marketplace, less tethered by regulations, and hence more responsive to the real needs of the public."[10]

It is too soon to determine the impact deregulation will have on the air cargo industry. Several factors, however, may indicate a direction:

Before complete economic deregulation in November 1978, seventy-three carriers were certified for unrestricted all-cargo service.

Air cargo rates have increased 20 per cent in fourteen months. It is not clear, however, if this is a result of inflation or monopolistic practices.

Air cargo freight ton-miles increased 13.7 per cent in 1978 over 1977, the largest gain in freight traffic during the 1970s.

At the present time these indicators are somewhat contradictory. However, it appears that economic deregulation has spurred competition within the industry, and perhaps to that extent the marketplace will be better served.

If competition exists at all between air and other modes, it is between air and truck transportation. Although it has been forecasted for years that air would

[10] Ibid., p. 1.

become competitive with trucks on a cost per ton-mile basis, generally this has not happened. In some specific comparisons, line-haul costs of the two modes are converging, but extensive competition between the two modes is not evident. Air freight is still best suited for special product movements.

In summary, more than 90 per cent of all air freight is moved by a few scheduled, for-hire carriers. From an economic perspective, air is most like the truck mode: the way is provided, capital turnover is relatively good, variable costs are a high percentage of total costs, and competition is healthy.

Performance Characteristics

This section will examine air freight transportation in terms of performance characteristics: speed, completeness, dependability, capability, frequency, and cost to the shipper. Unique characteristics make each mode best suited for particular types of products and movements. Between certain modes, such as water and railroads, railroads and pipelines, and railroads and trucks, the performance characteristics are somewhat comparable. That is, some products that move by rail can be moved by water with few adjustments in the distribution system. This is not so with air transportation. There is no modal substitute for some products that move by air, such as highly perishable goods. In other situations, to shift traffic to other modes would require significant changes in the distribution system, such as warehouse additions. Thus, from a performance perspective, air transport stands virtually alone, as you will see in the following discussions.

SPEED

Speed was defined as the elapsed time from when freight is given to a transportation mode until the movement is completed. The line-haul speed of air transport is more than ten times that of its closest competitor. Jet-propelled aircraft, which comprise almost 100 per cent of the air fleet, travel faster than 500 miles per hour. However, the entire shipment is not made at this speed because other modes, usually trucks, must begin and end the shipment. Even though this reduces overall speed, there is no comparison between the speed of air transport and other modes. It is not unusual for cargo to leave one coast at the end of one working day and be at the other coast at the beginning of the next working day. Freight movements that would require days if moved by another mode can be completed by air within hours. Thus, speed is the strongest asset of air transportation and, if products or movements demand such speed, no substitute exists.

123

COMPLETENESS

Completeness was defined as the extent of the modal network and the amount of required involvement of other modes. In one respect, air transportation is fairly complete because products can be moved from coast to coast and border to border. However, the number of airports limits the mode and, unless shippers and receivers are located at airports, another mode must begin and end the move. The location of airports away from population centers is another limiting factor. Unlike railroads, airports are usually located on the fringe of population centers because of their recent development, their need for large tracts of land, and for environmental concerns. Although there are more than 14,000 airports in the United States, only about twenty-five originate and terminate the vast majority of air freight. Therefore, completeness is air transport's greatest drawback. The greater the involvement of other modes, the lower the completeness of the air mode.

DEPENDABILITY

Dependability was defined as the mode's ability to perform as anticipated over time. Of all modes, air is the most susceptible to adverse weather. Fog, wind, and storms can delay or stop air movements altogether. Although increasingly sophisticated navigation systems have improved air traffic performance, certain weather conditions can still stop air traffic. Another factor affecting the dependability of air is the importance of minor delays. Because speed is air transport's major asset, slight variations in anticipated performance become critical. A delay of several hours or one day, when the move was scheduled to take only an hour, can be disastrous.

CAPABILITY

Capability was defined as the mode's ability to handle particular transportation requirements. Air transport is limited by its lift capabilities and physical size. The largest plane in commercial service today is the Boeing 747 with a payload of 117 tons. This is only a fraction of the capacity of a water tow or a train, and equal to that of about three truckloads. The majority of the air fleet consists not of 747s but of smaller craft with considerably less cargo capacity. The physical dimensions of the plane also limit the type of cargo; bulky items do not fit inside. Thus, the capability of air transport is limited.

FREQUENCY

Frequency was defined as the number of times a mode can pick up and deliver during a particular period. Because of their speed, airplanes have a high frequency potential. However, waiting time to complete a cargo move can reduce the desired frequency. Measures of frequency in comparison to other modes are difficult because of the speed factor. The frequency of air transportation under most circumstances can be more than one departure and arrival per day. However, even that level of frequency may be insufficient at times. Overall, air transport is more frequent than other modes, but a one-to-one comparison of air with other modes can be deceiving.

COST

Cost was defined as the amount a shipper or receiver must pay for the movement. Air transport freight rates per ton-mile are the highest among all modes. The major costs in air transport are the rates paid to the carrier and the inventory costs in transit. For all modes, these costs are complementary but, because of the characteristics of air transport, this tradeoff becomes the most visible. In 1977, the cost to move a ton-mile by air was 34.21 cents. The cost to move a ton-mile by truck was 12.1 cents; by rail, 2.29 cents; and pipe and water were less than 1 cent. If speed is air transport's greatest asset, cost is its greatest liability. However, the actual cost for air and trucks, for instance, is closer than the ton-mile figures would indicate. Someone must pay for the freight while it is in transit. Inventory costs are incurred by either shippers or receivers. The longer the shipment is in transit, the greater the costs. Thus, inventory costs are traded off against speed. For some products, particularly those of high-value and low-weight, the reduced costs of inventory more than offset the high transportation rates. Another offsetting factor is distance. The greater the distance, the greater the comparative advantage air has over other modes.

When all service characteristics are considered and compared to other modes, air transport seems best suited for high-value, low-weight, low-volume products or perishable products that must be moved long distances. This observation is borne out by the type of air freight being shipped today and an average air freight haul of 1,075 miles in 1976.

Role of Government

Various levels of government have been involved in the development of air transportation. The regulatory role will be discussed in Chapter 11. The promotion/provision role is discussed in this section. The government has been more involved in the development of air than in any other mode for several reasons. Air was the last transportation mode to develop and by that time the government had a policy—if not stated, at least through its actions—to participate in the development of the transportation system. Also, the first practical application of airplanes was for military purposes. The government was directly involved and was able to see the potential. The first nonmilitary application was movement of the United States mail. The government moved the mail at first but later contracted with private carriers. One of the stipulations of receiving a mail contract was that facilities be available to move passengers as well. Therefore, even though the government's only direct involvement with air freight transportation from 1918 to 1925 was mail movement, it was the prime contributing factor in the development of the mode. Since then, government has continued to assist the mode by providing airways, airports, research, and subsidies. In examining these areas, it must be remembered that movement of passengers was the government's major concern. Nevertheless, the facilities and assistance given also benefited freight movement.

The federal government, through the Department of Transportation (DOT) and the Federal Aviation Administration (FAA), owns, operates, and maintains the airway system. That system, the equivalent of the highways for trucks, is designed to guide and control air traffic to, from, and between airports. The federal government initiated the system in 1926. In 1976, it monitored 332,622 miles of airways and operated control towers at 426 airports. The airway system costs $2 billion per year. About half of that money comes from user charges and the balance is accumulated mostly from general public tax revenues.

Airports, the terminals for air transportation, are provided by governments at various levels. State and local governments, with some federal assistance, provide the bulk of the money for construction, operation, and maintenance. Before 1940, all airports were provided solely by state, regional, and local governments. In 1946 the federal government initiated the Federal Aid to Airports Program. The amounts of money provided by this program were small in comparison to total expenditures, and restrictions were placed on the use of the money. At first, federal money could be used only for certain capital expenditures. Over the last three decades, however, the amount of money has been increased and restrictions on the use of funds have been relaxed. In 1976, the Congress appropriated $2.7 billion for five years for airport development and lessened restrictions even further. Funds to support this program come from the Aviation Trust Fund, which is supported by user charges.

A major aspect of government aid has been research and development. Historically, the government led the way and paid for technological advances in communication, navigation, and aircraft design. In addition, the industry has often used aircraft developed for the military but modified for commercial use. The amount of money this represents is impossible to determine, but extensive research costs have been avoided by commercial airlines, and airplane manufacturers have enjoyed economies of scale by producing for both military and commercial aviation. The commercial industry can expect less assistance of this type in the future because the operational needs of military and commercial aircraft have diverged and now have fewer similarities. The spillover will continue, however, and most technological gains will be paid for by the federal government.

Government aid has also included direct subsidies. When the federal government contracted with private carriers to move the mail, passenger service facilities were stipulated as well. Since then, the federal government's policy has been to subsidize airlines over the designated mail routes as long as they were not profitable. Over the years, certain operators became profitable and lost their subsidies. Since 1959 no domestic trunk line has received a subsidy, and the only subsidies given in 1977 were to local service carriers. Although there is no direct relationship between subsidies and air freight movement, the subsidies have helped carriers develop and remain in business, and, of course, this facilitated the growth of the air cargo industry.

Thus, the government has supported the overall air carrier industry rather than just freight transportation. That was not so for other modes. The government's role in air freight development cannot be pinpointed directly, but without its assistance, progress would have been much slower.

Future

The future of the air freight industry is extremely bright in spite of energy-related problems. Unlike other modes, air transport is still developing and has yet to reach maturity and full integration into the overall distribution system. Continued development will depend on several factors: demand, technology, competition, government, energy, and ecology.

The demand for air carrier services will continue to grow and will come from two sources. First, because the overall demand for transportation will increase, the demand for air transport will grow at least proportionately. Therefore, demand will increase even though the share of market may remain the same. Second, the share of market should increase primarily as a result of increased sophistication in distribution systems and the discovery of new applications. Although some of the increases may come at the expense of other modes, particularly trucks, most gains will come from new transportation requirements. Increased recognition of air transportation will come with more fully integrated distribution systems. The mode will become a viable alternative means of movement rather than merely a supplemental or emergency mode. Of course, the industry must be able to respond to this demand.

Significant technological gains have been made in the industry over the last thirty years. The transition from propeller-driven aircraft to jets and the increased size of airplanes have increased overall efficiency. At the present time, speed and size have reached their outside limits, and only minor improvements can be expected in the foreseeable future. Other technological gains of great impact, such as alternative and more efficient fuels, speeds in excess of Mach 1 without environmental consequences, or lighter-than-air planes capable of increased loads, are even further in the future. Therefore, although technology

127

will continue to add to efficiency for the next twenty to thirty years, revolutionary changes are not likely.

Little or no competitive threat exists between modes. Trucks are the only mode capable of competing for some traffic, such as short-haul movements. As the hauls become longer, however, truck competition drops off because of speed limitations. Truck speed is restricted by law, and the physical constraints of the way as well as urban congestion further limit the mode's speed. Within the air industry, the emphasis on competition should serve to increase the efficiency of the mode. The industry must be more responsive to market forces to fulfill the anticipated increases in demand.

The government's economic regulatory role has been sharply reduced. From a promotional perspective, however, the government's role may be inhibiting. As overall government expenditures increase, greater emphasis is placed on having all segments of society pay their own way. Debates continue as to whether air carriers should pay more of the total promotional bill. If this occurs, as it did recently in the water industry, air transportation's greatest drawback, cost, will become more disproportionate. Consequently, rates would increase and the number of potential movements would decrease.

Of all modes, air transportation requires the most horsepower to move one ton of freight. Because the only fuel used is petroleum-based, the industry will be more affected by petroleum shortages than any other mode. Some technological gains are being made in fuel efficiency, but the air carriers' total dependence on petroleum will continue for some time. That is definitely a limiting factor to the future of air freight transportation. Increased fuel prices will have a lesser effect than shortages will, but the extent of the impact is purely speculative at this time.

The impact of ecological considerations is more certain, and some results are already known. Supersonic aircraft have been limited in the United States, in part because of air quality and noise level considerations. Airport expansion has been slowed and, in some cases, stopped for ecological reasons. The air industry cannot operate invisibly, and ecological considerations will continue to slow development.

Even though energy, ecology, and government actions will slow growth, competition and demand for air freight will have a counterbalancing effect. If new technologies can help solve energy and ecology problems, the air freight industry should continue to grow rapidly.

Summary

The role of air freight in relation to other modes is small in terms of ton-miles moved and revenue. Less than two tenths of one per cent of all ton-miles are moved by air, and less than 1 per cent of all freight revenue goes to air carriers. However, the mode has grown faster than all others. Ton-miles, market share, revenue, and network size and capacity have risen dramatically over the last three decades. The industry's minor role but rapid growth are a result of the mode's recent entrance into the transportation system and its unique performance characteristics. Because of the high speed, high cost, and limited completeness and capability, air freight shipments predominantly consist of high-value, low-volume, low-weight products or perishable items. Once considered a supplemental or emergency mode, air freight is becoming an economically viable transportation alternative and an integral part of the overall distribution system.

Of almost 4,000 commercial air carriers, approximately twenty move almost 95 per cent of all freight. Nevertheless, competition has been active in the industry, particularly after the deregulation of air freight during the late 1970s. Government at all levels plays an important role in air transportation. It has aided the development of the mode through the provision of airways, airports, research, and direct subsidies. In spite of energy and ecology considerations, the future of air freight transportation is bright. It should continue to grow at a rapid rate and become more and more an integral part of the overall domestic freight transportation system.

Questions for Chapter 8

1. You are a manufacturer who must rush a shipment to an important customer. It is now 3 P.M. and the customer, who is located 200 miles away, needs the goods when business opens at 9 A.M. tomorrow. Should you ship by truck or air? Discuss.
2. Describe how the shippers' view of air transportation has changed over the last thirty years.
3. Discuss the types of freight and movement situations that are best suited for air transportation.
4. Speed is seen as air freight's greatest performance advantage. What factors must be considered to determine the true speed of air transportation?
5. Describe the competitive environment in the air freight industry before deregulation.
6. Discuss the possible effect that deregulation will have on competition within the air industry.
7. Does air transportation pose a competitive threat to any other mode?
8. Discuss the unique situation in the air industry as to fixed and variable costs.
9. Describe the assistance role that government has played in the development of air transportation.
10. Under what conditions would the air freight industry stabilize or grow rapidly in the future?
11. Discuss those performance characteristics of air transportation that are drawbacks to increased usage.
12. Discuss how the cost of holding inventory becomes involved in the decision to ship freight by air.

9

Special Transportation Arrangements

From a shipper's perspective, the transportation goal is to move freight between a given pair of locations in the most efficient manner. Each mode is ideally suited for particular types of products and movement situations. Thus, shippers attempt to match their specific transportation requirements with the service characteristics of the transportation modes. For the past fifty years, the domestic freight transportation system in the United States has been a five-mode system. Never in history have so many alternative types of transportation services been available. On the other hand, never before has our society been so complex or the demand for specific transportation services so diverse. Thus, all shipper demands cannot be met efficiently by the five major modes. Special transportation arrangements have evolved to respond to diverse requirements.

This chapter will first review the performance characteristics of the five modes and summarize the relative growth and shift in position from 1945 to 1978. Two modal limitations that such comparison reveals—unmet service demands and small shipment handling—are then discussed. Intermodalism, a service combination of two or more modes, is also described. Finally, specialists who solve the small shipment situation are discussed.

Modal Comparison

Discussions of the five basic modes in Chapters 4 through 8 have illustrated that each mode is best suited to handle specific freight. Despite the vast range of transportation supply provided by the basic modes, they do not meet all demand requirements without special arrangements.

TABLE 9–1. Performance Characteristics—Modal Comparison

Charac- teristic	Mode Water	Rail	Trucks	Pipe	Air
SPEED	Very slow	Slow	Fast	Slowest	Fastest
COMPLETENESS	Least complete	Moderately complete	Most complete	Moderately complete	Incomplete
DEPENDABILITY	Moderately dependable	Moderately dependable	Undependable	Most dependable	Least dependable
CAPABILITY	Most capable	Very capable	Moderately capable	Least capable	Incapable
FREQUENCY	Least frequent	Moderately frequent	Very frequent	Infrequent	Most frequent
COST	Very low cost	Low cost	High cost	Lowest cost	Highest cost
PRODUCT	· large volume · raw materials	· large volume · raw materials · manufactured goods	· moderate volume · manufactured goods · raw materials · begin/end other modes	· oil · oil products · limited slurry	· low volume · low weight-high value products · perishable products

Table 9–1 presents an overview of the performance characteristics of the five modes. Table 9–2 presents the modal growth comparison from 1945 until 1978. The remainder of this chapter points out modal limitations and how unfilled transportation demands are satisfied.

Modal Limitations

An examination of service characteristics and strengths of each mode reveals two major limitations. Some service demands cannot be met adequately by any of the modes. Also, no basic mode is well suited for transporting small shipments such as parcels or books.

TABLE 9–2. Modal Growth Comparison Between 1945 and 1978

	Ton-Miles (Billions)				
	Water	Rail	Truck	Pipe	Air
1945	143	691	67	127	0.09
1978	389	873	602	568	5.21
Change (Ton-Miles)	+246	+182	+535	+441	+5.12
Change (Per cent)	+172	+26.3	+799	+347	+5689

	Share of Ton-Miles (Per cent)				
	Water	Rail	Trucks	Pipe	Air
1945	13.9%	67.2%	6.5%	12.4%	0.01%
1978	15.9%	35.8%	24.7%	23.3%	0.21%
Change of Share	+2.0%	−31.4%	+18.2%	+10.9%	0.20%
Change (Per cent)	+14.4%	−46.7%	+280 %	+88.0%	+2000 %

Source: *Transportation Facts and Trends*, 15th ed. (Washington, D.C.: Transportation Association of America, July 1979), p. 8.

UNMET SERVICE DEMANDS

First, all five modes have service limitations. For instance, water and railroads are low-cost but slow and require large volumes of product. Pipelines are low-cost but are limited to liquid products. Trucks are fast and complete, but they are costly and carry relatively small loads. Air is fast but costly and incapable of handling very large loads. Although all modes have some limitations, as a system they offer a variety of services. However, given diverse shipping demands, some needs are unmet. A shipper who needs the speed of trucks and the load capacity of railroads, or the dependability of pipelines and the capability of water, cannot be satisfied efficiently.

SMALL SHIPMENTS

The second limitation revealed by a modal comparison is the inability of any mode to handle small shipments efficiently. Small shipments are loads that do not fill either the weight or cubic capacity of the vehicle. The ICC defines a small shipment as less-than-vehicle-load and less than 10,000 lbs.[1] However, the average weight of all small shipments is slightly more than 100 lbs.[2] Therefore, more realistically, small shipments can be considered to be in the less

---

[1] *Small Shipments a Matter of National Concern*, prepared for the Department of Transportation by the American University, School of Business Administration (Washington, D.C.: Transportation Research Center, 1974), p. 4.

[2] Ibid., p. 27.

than 500-lb. range. For shipments of this size, carrier operations are significantly different than for vehicle-load shipments. Vehicle-load shipments can move directly from shipper to receiver, and the vehicle is fully utilized. For small shipments, many shipments must be consolidated to gain vehicle utilization. Consolidation and the subsequent unloadings require special operations, equipment, facilities, and procedures.

Even though individual modes are not inherently designed to overcome unmet service demands and handle small shipments, the transportation system has responded to these modal limitations in an effort to increase service and lower costs. Intermodalism, a combination of two or more modes taking advantage of the best service characteristics of each mode, is one response to unmet service demands, and small shipment specialists have evolved to respond to the demand for less-than-vehicle-loads. Intermodalism will be discussed first, followed by an examination of small shipment specialists.

Intermodalism

Historically, freight shipments have always been made by a combination of modes. The first railroads were designed to assist water traffic. The first pipelines fed the railroad and water modes. Today, trucks play an important role in beginning and/or ending moves for all other modes. This use of more than one mode, however, does not constitute intermodalism. *Intermodalism* can be defined as *cooperation and coordination of two or more modes in moving a single shipment*. Such cooperation and coordination can take many forms such as through rates, single billings, or physical facilities that aid the interchange between modes. The advantages, arrangements, and future of intermodalism are examined in the following sections.

ADVANTAGES OF INTERMODALISM

The overall purpose of an intermodal arrangement is to take advantage of the best service characteristics of two or more modes. For instance, trucks are the most complete mode but are costly. Railroads are somewhat incomplete but are low-cost. The combination of these two modes is lower than the cost of an all-truck movement and overcomes the incompleteness of all-rail transportation. Thus, if two modes create facilities that accommodate rapid transfer and compatibility of equipment, decreased cost and/or increased service will result. The advantages accrue to all parties. Shippers gain from the reduced cost of paper work and negotiation, increased service such as door-to-door delivery or reduced transit time, and the availability of more service options. Carriers gain because they can perform those services for which they are best suited rather

133

than attempt to perform services for which they are not designed. Inter-modalism also benefits society as a whole by more efficient movements.

INTERMODAL ARRANGEMENTS

The most popular and visible intermodal arrangement is between trucks and railroads. Either a trailer-on-flatcar (TOFC) or a container-on-flatcar (COFC) is utilized in what is popularly called piggyback. The basic concept is simple and has been available in one form or another for many years. Trucks are used to pick up the shipment. The trailer or container is then placed on a railroad car for a portion of the line-haul move. At the destination, the trailer or container is placed on a truck for the remainder of the move. Over the last twenty years, piggyback car loadings have increased significantly and now represent the second largest car loading category, surpassed only by coal shipments. Six major piggyback plans offer combinations of equipment ownership, service, billing, and rates. Table 9–3 describes these plans.

Figure 9–1 illustrates the trends in piggyback from 1972 to 1977. The most popular arrangement by far is Plan 2½, with more than 50 per cent of the loadings. Plans 1, 3, and 4 are growing steadily, Plan 5 is stable, and Plan 2 is declining.

Other intermodal combinations exist. However, none are the size of piggyback. Trailers and containers can be moved in arrangements of truck or rail and water, railroad cars can be moved in combination with water, and special airline containers can be combined with trucks.

FUTURE

Although the concept of intermodalism is not new, its development has been most rapid over the last twenty-five to thirty years. Without constraints, inter-

---

TABLE 9–3. Piggyback Plans

Plan 1.	Motor carrier trailers, carrier pickup and delivery, motor carrier bills of lading, motor carrier rates.
Plan 2.	Railroad trailers, railroad pickup and delivery, railroad billing, rates similar to Plan 1.
Plan 2½.	Railroad trailers, shippers, freight forwarders, or motor carrier pickup and delivery.
Plan 3.	Shipper or motor carrier trailers, flat charge rate to move trailer, regardless of contents.
Plan 4.	Shipper or motor carrier trailers and railcar, flat rate to move car and contents.
Plan 5.	Joint railroad-truck rates; either mode can solicit traffic.

FIGURE 9–1. TRENDS IN PIGGYBACK PLANS (Trailers and Containers Loaded)

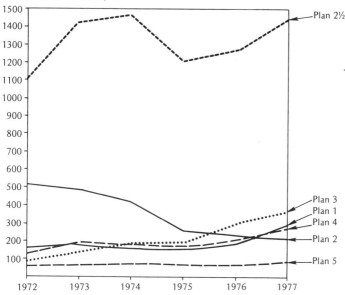

Source: Adapted from: Tom Foster, "Piggyback—Good News and Bad," *Distribution Worldwide* (April 1978), p. 48.

modalism is an important source of transportation system efficiency. Historically, the transportation modes in the United States developed autonomously and were often in conflict. At the same time, regulation and regulatory policies encouraged competition rather than cooperation. As a consequence, the growth of intermodalism has been slowed. There are some indications that transportation policy will swing in favor of intermodalism, but rapid growth is not anticipated immediately.

Intermodalism offers the best of two or more alternatives without significant sacrifices. The productivity of the transportation system can be increased to the benefit of all parties—shippers, carriers, and society. Given the present trends in policy and regulation, the future of this concept is bright.

Small Shipment Specialists

Small shipments present a special problem to all modes. Operations and facilities must change to meet these demands. As a consequence, a variety of organizations has evolved to move small shipments. This section first looks at the problems encountered and the operational changes necessary to move small shipments efficiently. Then, the organizations—small shipment consolidators and package specialists—that have evolved to move this freight will be discussed.

SMALL SHIPMENT PROBLEMS

From the carrier's perspective, the most efficient operation occurs when a vehicle is loaded to capacity and shipments move directly from shipper to receiver. When a shipment is smaller than the vehicle's capacity less-than-truckload (LTL), additional carrier operations are necessary. For a truckload (TL) movement, activities occur as illustrated on the left-hand side of Figure 9–2. The vehicle is loaded at the point of origin, moved directly to the destination, and unloaded. This type of move is very efficient. The vehicle is used to capacity, only two handlings are necessary, and only one pickup and one delivery location exist. In comparison, an LTL move requires the activities shown on the right-hand side of Figure 9–2. Small shipments are picked up at more than one location and are moved to a central location where they are consoli-

FIGURE 9–2. COMPARISON OF TRUCKLOAD AND LESS-THAN-TRUCKLOAD SHIPMENTS

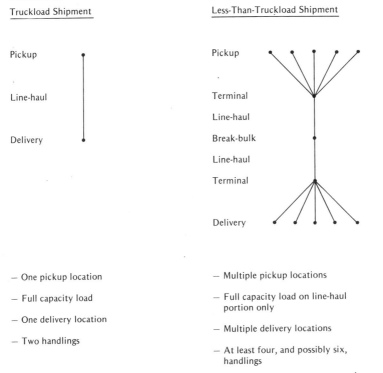

Truckload Shipment

Less-Than-Truckload Shipment

Pickup

Line-haul

Delivery

Pickup

Terminal

Line-haul

Break-bulk

Line-haul

Terminal

Delivery

— One pickup location

— Full capacity load

— One delivery location

— Two handlings

— Multiple pickup locations

— Full capacity load on line-haul portion only

— Multiple delivery locations

— At least four, and possibly six, handlings

dated into a line-haul vehicle. More than likely, a break-bulk operation occurs during the line-haul. In a break-bulk operation, the contents of several fully loaded trailers are shifted between the vehicles at a terminal to gain a greater degree of commonality in destinations. After break-bulk, the accumulation of small shipments then goes to a terminal close to the destination where the individual shipments are unloaded and delivered. In comparison to TL movements, much more effort and time are required. First, shipments must be picked up and delivered at a variety of locations. Second, shipments do not go directly to destinations but to terminals and through break-bulk operations that result in time delays and two or more handlings. Third, the only time the vehicle's full capacity is used is during the line-haul.

The railroads have consciously avoided less-than-carload (LCL) business and have moved toward larger rather than smaller loads. The trucking industry has not reacted as drastically. Motor carriers prefer a balance of approximately fifty/fifty on TL and LTL shipments. Two other types of organizations have also responded to the demand for moving small shipments: small shipment consolidators and package specialists.

SMALL SHIPMENT CONSOLIDATORS

Small shipment consolidators serve as operational intermediaries between shippers and carriers. They include surface freight forwarders, shipper associations, and air freight forwarders. These consolidators take less-than-vehicle-load traffic from shippers, consolidate the shipments into vehicle loads, and arrange for their shipment with carriers. The justifications for these consolidators are the rate structure of the modes, the decision by some carriers such as rail to solicit only volume business, and the services that carriers may not be willing or able to provide.

As discussed previously, vehicle loads require less effort than less-than-vehicle-load shipments. The rate structure of the modes has been designed to reflect these differences. Vehicle-load shipments move at lower rates per hundredweight (cwt) than do less-than-vehicle-loads. This difference was recognized by a group of shippers at the beginning of this century. Rather than tender their shipments to the railroads individually and pay high rates, the shippers consolidated their shipments into carloads that moved at substantially lower rates. This early collection behavior on the part of shippers represented the origins of freight forwarders and shipper associations.

The railroads initially objected to such practices, but shipper consolidation could not be stopped legally. Although the railroads had the opportunity to compete directly with these agencies by offering their own consolidation service, they chose instead to concentrate on volume business, and the small shipment consolidators became a permanent part of the system. As truck transportation grew, these agencies began to consolidate LTL shipments into truckloads.

The benefit to shippers of using consolidators is usually not in the rates. Consolidators charge the shipper the less-than-volume rates and move the shipments at volume rates, taking their margin from the difference. (In some situations, consolidators charge rates below the less-than-volume rate, but this is not their major differential advantage.)

The advantages to the shipper are faster transit times, which could be interpreted as lower cost, and services from the consolidators. As described earlier, the procedure to move less-than-vehicle-load shipments requires multiple pickups and deliveries, consolidation, and break-bulk, all of which result in extra handling and costs. If a mode is not organized to perform these activities, if volume is insufficient between two points, or if such traffic is considered secondary business, the small shipments take significantly more time than do vehicle loads. Consolidators do not consider small shipment traffic as secondary, have sufficient volume, and are organized to move such traffic. Consequently, transit times are shorter, and the consolidators can perform additional services, such as billing and tracing.

All small shipments do not move through consolidators. In fact, only about 5 per cent of all small shipments move this way. Unlike the railroads, the motor carrier industry competes for a large portion of this business, especially at the 1,000-lb. to 15,000-lb. weight levels.

There are three types of consolidators: freight forwarders, shipper associations, and air freight forwarders. Freight forwarders are primarily surface shippers that use trucks, railroads, and water for the line-haul movements. They are common carriers subject to economic regulation by the ICC. They are permitted to own and operate pickup and delivery vehicles but must use common carriers for line-haul movement. Approximately 150 Class A freight forwarders exist, each with more than $100,000 in annual operating revenues. The majority operate on a regional basis, and less than ten operate nationally. Three forwarders handle about 50 per cent of the traffic. Competition comes from motor carriers and small shipment specialists. Economically, freight forwarders are a high-variable-cost industry. About 75 per cent of their revenue goes toward purchasing line-haul services, and the investment in pickup and delivery vehicles and terminal facilities is modest.

Shipper associations are organizations that arrange to transport the freight of association members. A group of shippers with a common foundation, such as a specific product or type of operation, create an association to consolidate their shipments and take advantage of vehicle-load rates. These organizations are nonprofit and pay in proportion to their share of the freight moved. In addition to a greater degree of control, association members may enjoy lower rates than those of freight forwarders.

Air freight forwarders perform the same function as freight forwarders and shipper associations, except that they use air freight for the line-haul move. In 1976, 366 air freight forwarders had total revenues of approximately $1.2 billion. Approximately 37 per cent of all air freight is arranged through air freight

138

forwarders. As with the freight forwarders, the air freight forwarder industry is concentrated, with more than half of the revenue generated by three companies. Competition, however, comes from the air carriers and from small shipment specialists.

Small shipment consolidators play a vital role in the overall transportation system. They provide a service that carriers and shippers are unable or unwilling to perform. In addition to consolidators, the movement of small shipments is handled by package specialists.

PACKAGE SPECIALISTS

As previously indicated, the weight for small shipments ranges from 1 to 10,000 lbs. Within this range, there is a great demand to move packages whose weight ranges from 1 to approximately 100 lbs. For example, in 1978, more than half of all air freight shipments weighed less than 70 lbs. To meet this demand, several specialized carriers have evolved, such as the United States Postal System, United Parcel Service, bus service, and Federal Express, which is an airline specializing in package shipments. These carriers concentrate on moving packages of low weight and limited physical size. Collectively, they offer a variety of small shipment alternatives and vary in the size and weight of packages accepted, pickup and delivery services, geographic reach, speed of service, and cost.

The United States Postal Service, which, through its own earlier inefficiencies helped create all other package specialists, has displayed a renewed interest in the package business. It offers services that guarantee a delivery time or all or a portion of the cost will be refunded. Three services are offered with different speeds and costs: express, priority, and parcel post. Express mail offers the fastest service. Shipping arrangements and insurance are custom designed for each shipper, and express service guarantees that if a package is received by the post office for shipment before 5 P.M., delivery at the destination will be no later than 3 P.M. the following day. Priority mail offers two-day delivery service. Parcel post, the least expensive option, requires several days for shipment and has an erratic delivery time.

United Parcel Service (UPS) is a private organization that was formed originally to deliver small packages from stores to homes in the same geographic area. It now handles intercity movements and covers the forty-eight contiguous states. About five million parcels are handled daily through 2,000 facilities, with a fleet of about 4,000 trucks. Similar to the Postal System, UPS offers more than one service. Blue label service offers two-day delivery beyond 2,000 miles, and regular service varies according to the distances shipped.

Intercity buses are naturally suited for small shipments. Packages are stowed with passenger luggage and move on the passenger schedule from location to location throughout the United States. Packages can be transferred among most bus lines and, in many cases, bus companies cooperate with other modes, such as air, for delivery to remote locations. They offer two services based on speed of delivery.

A fourth small package specialist is air express, which concentrates on shipping small packages. An example is Federal Express, which began operations in the early 1970s. This category of specialist is expected to grow rapidly in the 1980s.

Although these four are the only types of carriers who specialize in small packages, airlines and air freight forwarders also offer small package services and compete directly with the small package specialists. Table 9–4 lists the small package shipment alternatives, limitations, services, and approximate shipping times for each carrier. Although small shipments are considered a problem by some modes, agencies and small shipment specialists see them as an opportunity. Collectively, they serve shippers' demands and fill the service void left by the five modes.

TABLE 9–4. Small Shipment Alternatives

Carrier	Maximum Weight	Maximum Size	Limits	Minimum Charge	Pickup and Delivery	Typical Transit Time		
						300 Miles	750 Miles	2000 Miles
UNITED PARCEL SERVICE Regular Service	50 lbs. per carton	108" length and girth	100 lbs. per day	None	Door-to-door	2 days	4 days	7 days
Blue Label Service	50 lbs. per carton	108" length and girth	100 lbs. per day	None	Door-to-door	---	---	3 days
U.S. POSTAL SYSTEM Parcel Post	1st carton– 40 lbs.; 2nd–70 lbs.	100" length and girth	None	None	Door-to-door	3 days	5 days	8 days
Priority Mail	70 lbs. per carton	100" length and girth	None	None	Door-to-door	2 days	2 days	2 days
Express Mail	40 lbs. per carton	100" length and girth	None	None	Door-to-door P.O.-to-P.O.	1 day	1 day	1 day
BUS* Regular	100 lbs. per carton	141" one side not to exceed 60"	5 cartons/ shipment	Yes	Terminal-to-terminal	2 days	4 days	6 days
Expedited (First Bus Out)	100 lbs. per carton	141" one side not to exceed 60"	5 cartons/ shipment	Yes	Terminal-to-terminal	1 day	2 days	3 days
AIR FREIGHT FORWARDER FORWARDERS AND AIRLINES* Regular	50 lbs. per carton	90" length and girth	None	Yes	Door-to-door	Over-night	Over-night	Over-night
Expedited	50 lbs. per carton	90" length and girth	None	Yes	Door-to-door	Same day	Same day	Same day
FEDERAL EXPRESS Priority 1	70 lbs. per carton	108" length and girth	None	None	Door-to-door	Over-night	Over-night	Over-night
Priority 2	70 lbs. per carton	108" length and girth	None	None	Door-to-door	2 days	2 days	2 days

*Restrictions, services, and times vary with individual carrier.

Summary

Although the United States has had a five-mode transportation system offering a wide range of services for more than fifty years, there are certain demands for service that cannot be performed efficiently by any of the modes. Each mode has limitations that can be overcome in part by intermodalism, which is a combination of two or more modes taking advantage of the best performance characteristics of each. Piggyback is the most popular form of intermodalism, although intermodal arrangements are also available between truck and air, truck and water, and rail and water.

Another major limitation of the transportation system is the inability to move small shipments. Small shipments are less-than-vehicle-loads, with the majority weighing less than 500 lbs. Small shipment consolidators are intermediaries who consolidate less-than-vehicle-loads for line-haul. Consolidators include freight forwarders that are common carriers primarily using surface modes, shipper associations that are typically private carriers moving the freight of association members, and air freight forwarders that are for-hire and use air freight transportation for the line-haul. Package specialists concentrate on the movement of packages weighing up to 100 lbs. These specialists include the United States Postal System, United Parcel Service, buses, and various air express carriers. Each offers a variety of services, differentiated primarily by speed. Although these carriers specialize in package shipments, airlines and freight forwarders offer services that compete for the same business.

Questions for Chapter 9

1. Why is rail considered to be somewhat in the middle on performance characteristics?
2. Looking at all modes, which represents the greatest source of competition for each of the others?
3. The modal comparison revealed two weaknesses of the transportation system. Discuss each.
4. Define intermodalism. How does it affect the efficiency of the transportation system?
5. In addition to the intermodalism combinations discussed, what other combinations might have potential?
6. Describe the various piggyback plans presently in use. Why are they all not used equally?
7. Define a small shipment.
8. Describe how trucking operations change when moving truckloads or less-than-truckload shipments.

9. What is a break-bulk operation?
10. Explain the role of small shipment consolidators. How do they make a profit?
11. Discuss the role and operations of small shipment specialists.
12. Compare the services offered between UPS Blue Label and Federal Express. Under what conditions would one be chosen over the other?

three

Transportation Environments

Transportation is accepted universally as an economic activity performed in the public interest, similar to other areas such as utilities, food processing, and drug administration. Performance of these activities invites governmental supervision to protect society's interests.

Part III reviews the governmental influences on the transportation system. National transportation policy—its evolution from non-existent guidelines, to implied and expressed policies based on legislative activities, to a congressionally authorized policy—is explored in Chapter 10. In addition, attention is given to the federal government's effort to mold the future development of transportation.

Policies can be implied from or directed by laws. Transportation laws receive in-depth coverage in Chapter 11. State and federal government involvement in transportation is better understood after a review of the legislative attention given to it.

Legislation demands a regulatory system for enforcement. The regulatory system, its institutions, and its procedures, is examined in Chapter 12. Other regulatory influences on transportation, such as the Federal Trade Commission and the court system, are introduced as well.

10

Transportation Policy

A policy of some kind is desired when any continuous activity occurs and affects, or is affected by, many different people or segments of society. Its purpose is to provide all participants in any joint behavior with a set of performance guidelines. Without a policy, actions may be haphazard, inconsistent, and biased. Policies are desirable for business firms if consistency in operations is to be achieved. However, policies are not limited to commercial activities. They appear whenever a number of people are involved in joint performance, such as in religious institutions, community programs, educational institutions, and governmental bodies. This chapter discusses the nature of policy, the need for an expressed transportation policy, and the evolution of the present national transportation policy. The chapter concludes with a set of criteria regarding development of an improved national policy.

What Is a Policy?

The word *policy* has many connotations and is seldom used in its proper context. Its meaning has been modified through simplification or through common practice. Often it is used synonymously with *rule, practice,* or *procedure.* A department store clerk may tell you, "It is our policy to make no refunds for items purchased on sale." What is meant is that the store has a *rule* to that effect. Similarly, a student who has received no response on an admission application to a university may be told that, "Our policy is to process applications on a first-come, first-served basis." What is meant is that the university's *procedure* is to handle applications that way. In another instance, a hospital intern may tell the mother of a sick child that the policy of the emergency room is to treat incoming cases on a degree-of-severity basis. Again, this refers to the emergency room's *practice,* not policy.

Technically, a policy is broad in scope and provides guidelines by which daily decisions are made. All of the aforementioned rules, practices, and procedures are derived from a high-level policy, established by the management of the institutions involved. A statement of policy expresses top management's intent to accomplish the overall objectives of a firm. It is a guide for carrying out actions or answering questions, rather than an action in itself.

In this context, a *policy* is a statement that provides guidelines and directions for carrying out activities intended to accomplish an overall objective. It would not be unusual for a firm to be following a course of action that *implies* a policy that has not been stated explicitly. Such a situation is undesirable because no assurance can be given that all the firm's components and individuals will direct themselves toward the same objective. An *expressed,* or stated, policy gives it official status.

Need for Transportation Policy

The transportation industry contains all the characteristics of an establishment that requires an expressed statement of policy. Transportation touches all segments of society. Within the industry, many firms are in competition for the same traffic volume and limited carrier services. Many decision makers are involved, both within the industry and without. Unless a policy is followed by all participants, so many decision makers could cause chaos in the industry. A look at the past provides the best support that a strong national policy is required for the transportation network to be efficient and to provide essential services to the economy.

146

PREREGULATION ERA

During the formative years of the United States, an urgent need for a transportation policy did not exist. The industry was in its infancy, and alternatives were not available. Although a policy was not expressed, federal government actions during the early 1800s reflected implied policies toward transportation. As discussed earlier, water transportation was the first mode to open the door to increased industrialization of the United States. The implied federal policy was promotional, with emphasis on expansion of transportation capacity. Land grants to expand navigable waterways and canals represented the first implied transportation policy.

Promotional activities by the federal government encouraged development of transportation facilities during the first half of the nineteenth century. At that time, the highway system consisted of little more than dirt roads. Private toll roads were built by individuals for their own business purposes, and a charge was assessed to other users. The federal government then adopted an unofficial policy of free provision of roadways, giving financial assistance to local communities for the development of public roads. Thus, the implied policy of *promotion* was modified to include *provision*. The difference between the two implied policies of promotion and provision lies mainly in the form of ownership and is important to the study of national transportation policy. In its promotional efforts, the federal government allowed and encouraged private ownership of transportation companies and facilities and offered financial assistance, such as land grants. The policies related to provisional efforts, however, made transportation service available through the facilities owned by various local, state, and federal governments, such as roadways and waterways, which also were used by the general population.

During this same era, the promotional policy continued to encourage development of the railroad industry. Initially, railroads were constructed by individuals who used short rail lines to move goods from production locations to the closest navigable water. Growing commercial activities, coupled with the federal government's desire to increase railroad development, led to more land grants for expansion. These grants began in 1850 and ended in the 1870s. Approximately 131 million acres were given in land grants to private enterprises for railroad development.

The government's implied promotion policy toward water and railroad transportation was intended and has continued to be the government's philosophy. The provision policy toward road development had a different perspective, however. Water and rail were used exclusively for commercial development. Highway improvement was different; its benefits would accrue to the general population.

Throughout the early developmental stage, it was important to the economy that transportation service expand as much as possible. New companies were formed and many small carrier firms began to grow. The government did not

147

interfere with this development. Thus, another policy was implied: *laissez-faire*, the doctrine that government should not interfere with commerce. Each carrier offered transportation services in a free enterprise environment. The preregulation era, therefore, had three separate implied government policies: promotion, provision, and laissez-faire.

ATTITUDE MODIFICATION

As discussed in Chapter 3, a new generation of freight transportation resulted from the development of the railroad industry. Small railroads began to merge, forming larger railroads that eventually covered the eastern half of the United States. By 1870, the entire nation was connected by railroads. The inherent characteristics of railroads, described in Chapters 5 and 9, permitted economical movement of large quantities of raw materials and finished goods to all developed territories. Those favorable characteristics, along with the rapidly increasing demand for transportation service, allowed the railroad industry to become powerful and influential in the economic progress of the nation. Mergers reduced competition in developed areas, and the railroad companies, through sheer size and importance, became quasimonopolies. In some instances, mergers resulted in only one carrier serving a particular community, giving it geographic monopoly status in providing transportation service.

Their dominant economic position gave the railroads the power for potential exploitation. In some situations, railroad industry actions were damaging to the competitive environment. Unfair business practices on the part of railroad management forced some businesses to close and increased costs for the consuming public. These practices, described in Chapters 11 and 12, forced a change in attitude by the federal government in the interest of public protection.

The federal government continued its implied policies of promotion and provision, but modified its laissez-faire policy. The new policy toward transportation, especially railroads, became one of monopoly control through federal legislation. The government recognized it would be difficult to protect the general public as well as private businesses if it allowed railroads a free hand to do as they pleased. After years of public complaints, the Congress passed the Act to Regulate Commerce in 1887. This act was the government's first venture into private enterprise, and it effectively ended the laissez-faire policy. The railroad industry would be controlled from that time forward. The policy of monopoly control protected not only individual businesses competing with each other, but the existence of competition as well. The first part is referred to as *protection of competitors*, and the second part is identified as *protection of competition*. It is important to remember that all federal policies for transportation up to that time were implied—that is, derived from actions, rather than expressed. No formal statement of national transportation policy had been pronounced.

POST REGULATION ERA

After the first transportation legislation was enacted in 1887, several additional laws were passed that affected railroad operations. These legislative actions served to control the railroad industry's rates, routes, equipment allocation, service, and extent of operation. At that time, the railroad industry had no competition for overland movements. This situation prevailed until World War I.

The United States Congress added pipeline transportation to the federal government's regulatory control with the Hepburn Act of 1906. However, pipelines were not viewed as competitors for the railroads because of the extremely limited number of commodities that could be shipped and the few locations served by pipelines. Thus, railroads remained the major surface carrier through the first two decades of the nineteenth century.

The importance of the railroads to the well-being of society was evidenced by the fact that the federal government assumed management of railroad operations during World War I. With the takeover, the government realized that railroad facilities were inadequate for the steadily increasing traffic volumes and would be unable to handle the required tonnages for postwar recovery. When railroad operations were returned to private industry following the war, supporting legislation was passed. The Transportation Act of 1920, designed to improve rail transport facilities, introduced the implied policy of *adequacy* to ensure a capable railroad network.

The climate for freight transportation changed considerably after the war. In the early 1920s, the federal government accelerated its provision policy, placing emphasis on highway development. The policy was implemented through federal and state legislative acts that levied taxes to finance highway improvement. (These acts are discussed in Chapter 11.) This sudden influx of funds allowed a new form of freight movement to emerge: truck transportation. Improved roadways allowed trucks to move rapidly and on schedule between communities. This form of transportation became extremely popular for shipping small quantities to destinations not served directly by railroads.

A NEW ERA-POLICY OF CHOICE

The federal government's policy regarding truck transportation was an extension of its implied railroad policy. The policy of control was implemented through the Motor Transportation Act of 1935, which became Part II of the Interstate Commerce Act (previously known as the Act to Regulate Commerce). The Motor Transportation Act was intended to protect competitors within the trucking industry. The trucking industry also had to be protected from direct price competition by the railroads. That was accomplished when the federal government set minimum freight rates that the railroads could charge, thereby effectively eliminating price as the major competitive factor between the two modes. At this point, another implied transportation policy emerged: the policy

149

of *choice*. This policy complicated the transportation network of the nation. With its initial venture into regulation of railroad operations, the government sought to protect the carriers from themselves and to assure fair business practices. Competition between carriers of the same mode, that is, one railroad competing with another railroad for the same traffic volume, is known as *intramodal competition*. The government then moved to protect competition between trucking firms.

With the policy of choice, a higher level of protection emerged. The federal government was then expected to protect competition between the railroad and trucking industries. This type of competition is known as *intermodal competition*, that between two different modes for the same traffic volumes. When railroads were the only major mode, regulation was aimed at control over monopoly power. Competition from the trucking industry ended that monopoly, and control of the trucking industry through the Motor Transportation Act became similar to railroad control. It did not consider two competing modes, loss of monopoly power, or the different characteristics of the two modes.

A national policy of choice created many difficult issues. The first related to the nature of the implied scope of federal policy. In fact, monopoly power no longer existed. However, the regulatory posture was that both modes should be controlled as if they were monopolies. Also, the task of controlling the trucking industry, with its thousands of participating carriers, was more difficult from an administrative standpoint than was the control of approximately 500 railroads. Railroad regulation was total, because all rail competitors were considered common carriers. A different situation existed within the trucking industry in that many companies were exempted from regulation, depending on their method of operation. Any attempt to provide an economical and efficient transportation system by regulating all railroads and only some trucking firms was destined to fall far short of its goal. Finally, comparison and evaluation between these two modes was difficult because of the differences in the manner by which each mode provided for its total operating expenses.

Federal aid to the railroad industry ended by 1870 with the final land grant privileges. However, the trucking industry was experiencing rapid growth. As a result, local, state, and federal programs for highway improvement were accelerating. Railroad companies were providing facilities and the maintenance of equipment and rights-of-way, paying local and state taxes on all properties owned. Efficiency measurements and comparisons of the two modes could not be accurate. These differences were not taken into consideration in the regulatory procedure.

POLICY EXTENSION

The implied transportation policies expanded further after the application of monopoly control and choice was adapted to trucking. Attention then focused on the revived water transportation system and the growing airline industry. The federal government recognized the interrelationship of water carriage and the overall transportation network and extended its authority by enacting the Merchant Marine Act of 1936. Interestingly, the framework was similar to that applied to the trucking industry, wherein the act's sphere of influence was limited because of the total coverage of the carriers affected. The total amount of water carriage placed under government jurisdiction was estimated at less than 15 per cent. In addition, the water industry received some level of local and federal subsidies with free rights-of-way and terminal facilities that could be rented, rather than owned, by water carriers. Any comparison with other modes was difficult. The implied policy of choice became expressed when water carriers were included among the other modes under the federal government's control. The Merchant Marine Act stated, "It is hereby declared to be the policy of the United States to foster the development and encourage the maintenance of such a merchant marine." The phrases *foster the development* and *encourage the maintenance* also clearly indicate a promotional policy.

Federal transportation policy reached air transportation during the 1930s with the Civil Aeronautics Act of 1938. Although safety matters were expressed in the conditions set forth, continuation of the promotion policy was evident in the act's stated objective to encourage the development of air transportation. With the inclusion of air, all transportation modes had come under the various and unrelated policies of the federal government.

The shortcoming in the initial development of federal influence was the absence of an expressed, comprehensive national transportation policy. Initially, the implied policy was promotion. Provision then followed as a separate and unrelated policy. During that time, laissez-faire also was a federal policy. The federal government then adopted an implied policy of monopoly control, dropping the previous laissez-faire. The entry of the trucking industry allowed the federal government to continue its policies of promotion, provision, and monopoly control, and to add an implied policy of choice. Those same policies continued when both water and air transportation were included. For those two modes, the federal policy of promotion was expressed clearly. With many federal policies being applied and many modes competing among and between themselves, the need for an expressed national policy that encompassed all modes became critical.

Expressed National Transportation Policy

The economic climate of the United States changed drastically during the 1930s. All forms of transportation experienced federal intervention in one way or another. The country was recovering from its worst economic decline in history, the Great Depression, and the federal government was involved in various projects intended to increase employment. Although the country was not involved in military conflict during the 1930s, industrial activity increased rapidly to help provide weapons to allied nations. The transportation system faced unprecedented demands for movement. The time was ripe for an expressed overall national policy that included all forms of transportation. The federal government began to move in that direction in 1940.

THE TRANSPORTATION ACT OF 1940

A distinction has been made between an implied and an expressed policy. An implied policy is derived from various actions. An expressed policy, on the other hand, is stated in specific terms. The transportation policies already discussed here were implied in some cases and expressed in others. Expressed policies appeared in the legislation regulating water and air transportation. Transportation policies are advocated often by United States presidents, usually in their State of the Union messages. Although these are expressed policies, they merely reflect the administration's attitudes and sometimes offer direction to congressional representatives. Because presidents cannot mandate law, their policy statements do not have the same impact as legislation enacted by Congress. Congressional legislation has greater impact because it provides the foundations for regulatory bodies to effect regulatory operations and decisions.

The first legislatively expressed national transportation policy in history was enacted in 1940. It was and remains the only formal intermodal policy enacted into law by the Congress. The preamble to the act contained a legislatively approved policy directed to the coordination of all for-hire transportation in the United States. Congress attempted to assert, in one paragraph, its intention to provide a unified transportation system with a commonly accepted objective.

Until 1940, overall transportation had been controlled by a patchwork of regulatory bodies. The Interstate Commerce Commission (ICC), created by the Act to Regulate Commerce of 1887, initially implemented policy for railroads and some water movements. Pipelines were added in 1906. The Motor Transportation Act of 1935 added truck companies to the regulatory process. The Merchant Marine Act of 1936 created the Federal Maritime Board (FMB), which acted as the regulatory body for water transportation that was not under the authority of the ICC. The Civil Aeronautics Act of 1938 created the Civil Aeronautics Authority (CAA), which regulated air transportation. Thus, three separate federal agencies were carrying out implied and expressed national transportation policies. A significant problem was the lack of coordination among these three federal agencies, as well as the enabling legislation.

The one-paragraph national transportation policy legislated into law in 1940 read as follows:

It is hereby declared to be the national transportation policy of the Congress to provide for fair and impartial regulation of all modes of transportation subject to the provisions of the Act, so administered as to recognize and preserve the inherent advantages of each; to promote safe, adequate, economical, and efficient service and foster sound economic conditions in transportation and among the several carriers; to encourage the establishment and maintenance of reasonable charges for transportation services, without unjust discriminations, undue preferences or advantages, or unfair or destructive competitive practices; to cooperate with the several States and the duly authorized officials thereof; and to encourage fair wages and equitable working conditions; and all to the end of developing, coordinating, and preserving a national transportation system by water, highway, and rail, as well as other means, adequate to meet the needs of the commerce of the United States, of the Postal Service, and of the national defense. All of the provisions of this Act shall be administered and enforced with a view to carrying out the above declaration of policy.[1]

On the surface, this appeared to be exactly what was needed to foster coordinated action between transportation carriers and regulatory bodies. However, as future events would prove, the initial expressed policy was little more than a broad statement of intent. The intention was to provide a comprehensive policy to guide the future development of a total transportation system in the United States. The limitations contained in the expressed policy and the use of ambiguous terms prevented this intention from resulting. Subsequent interpretations of those words have become major obstacles to implementation. Some of the most serious flaws are the following:

1. *Scope:* The intent was to establish national transportation policy. Yet, by including only water, rail, and highway, the act made the ICC solely responsible for implementation. The act gave the commission some additional authority over water movements, but the CAA and the FMB retained influence over their respective modes. As such, the act might more appropriately have been labeled "the Interstate Commerce Commission Policy Act of 1940."
2. *Interpretation:* Too many ambiguous terms were used. There is still no commonly accepted interpretation of such words as *fair, impartial, adequate,* and *reasonable.*
3. *Definition:* Closely related to interpretation is the problem of definition. It is not possible to ". . . recognize and preserve the inherent advantages . . ." if the method of determining those advantages is lacking because of the inequities in aid among modes.
4. *Application:* Because of the problems listed, the policy has limited, if any, application. There is little in the expressed statement that provides guidelines for future regulatory decisions or total network development.

Although the expressed policy was of little, if any, practical value in implementation, it reflected the critical need to bring order to a chaotic situation. Congress acted to show its interest in the development of a unified and efficient transportation system for the country.

---

[1] Transportation Act of 1940, 54 Stat. 899.

POST EXPRESSED POLICY ERA

Many significant policy-related events occurred during the 1940s and 1950s. The nation experienced a second world war, with its associated demands upon the transportation system. The trucking industry grew rapidly and became the primary carrier of many shipments that previously moved by rail. Railroad market share declined, and financial difficulties became commonplace among rail carriers. The Korean conflict of the early 1950s placed additional strains on the transportation network. During that period, railroad problems became more severe. Noticeably absent until 1958 was any formal attempt to develop and implement an expressed national transportation policy or to develop one that offered more specific goals.

TRANSPORTATION ACT OF 1958

The worsening railroad situation during the 1950s led to the implementation of a part of the expressed National Transportation Policy contained in the Transportation Act of 1940. Earlier decades had witnessed policies of promotion, provision, laissez-faire, monopoly control, adequacy, and choice. The expressed National Transportation Policy contained in the Transportation Act of 1940 did little to formalize these policies. Many railroad companies were on the verge of bankruptcy. Declining railroad traffic volumes and profits were inadequate to attract investors, and railroad equipment and tracks could not be repaired or replaced because of insufficient capital. Thus, the next course of action was to resort to the expressed National Transportation Policy, which states, in part, ". . . to recognize and preserve the inherent advantages of each; . . .". This expressed policy was implemented to preserve the railroads, as well as to continue the implied choice policy. The importance of railroad transportation to the general economy of the United States demanded further federal action to ensure continued railroad operations by any available means. The Transportation Act of 1958 was an example of the federal government's concern for the viability of railroad transportation.

With the Transportation Act of 1958, the government guaranteed repayment of loans made to the railroads. The objective was to attract funds to renovate equipment and facilities. This act is interpreted as having originated in the Transportation Act of 1940, which stated that its policy was to preserve the system. A financial commitment was made to stabilize railroads as an integral part of the transportation network. The act also committed the government to continued support of private enterprise in the railroad industry.

ADMINISTRATION POLICIES

As mentioned earlier, transportation problems have captured the attention of United States presidents. At various times, statements have originated from the president's office, or from those representing the administration, expressing concern about the direction of the transportation system. Although these statements do not have the impact of an expressed legislated policy originating in the Congress, they do have considerable influence upon transportation development. One of the most famous transportation statements was made in 1962 by President John F. Kennedy. The president said:

An efficient and dynamic transportation system is vital to our domestic economic growth, productivity, and progress. Affecting the cost of every commodity we consume or export, it is equally vital to our ability to compete abroad. It influences both the cost and the flexibility of our defense preparedness, and both the business and recreational opportunities of our citizens. This Nation has long enjoyed one of the most highly developed and diversified transportation systems in the world, and this system has helped us to achieve a highly efficient utilization of our manpower and resources.

Transportation is thus an industry which serves, and is affected with, the national interest. Federal laws and policies have expressed the national interest in transportation particularly in the last 80 years: through the promotion and development of transportation facilities, such as highways, airways, and waterways; through the regulation of rates and services; and through general governmental policies relating to taxation, procurement, labor, and competition. A comprehensive program for transportation must consider all of these elements of public policy.[2]

The basic objective of our Nation's transportation system must be to assure the availability of the fast, safe, and economical transportation services needed in a growing and changing economy to move people and goods, without waste or discrimination, in response to private and public demands at the lowest cost consistent with health, convenience, national security, and other broad public objectives. Investment or capacity should be neither substantially above nor substantially below these requirements—for chronic excess capacity involves misuse of resources, and lack of adequate capacity jeopardizes progress. The resources devoted to provision of transportation service should be used in the most effective and efficient manner possible; and this, in turn, means that users of transport facilities should be provided with incentives to use whatever form of transportation which provides them with the service they desire at the lowest total cost, both public and private.[3]

The thrust of this proposal was directed to competition in the marketplace rather than to federal intervention. However, the request for policy actions to implement this perspective received no serious congressional support.

The situation changed dramatically in 1980. In his State-of-the-Union message in January, 1980, President Jimmy Carter asserted that legislation to reregulate the carriers must be enacted by mid-year or he threatened to release the ICC to apply more liberal attitudes to foster greater competition and loosen the rigidities of transportation regulation. In subsequent actions during that year, the trend in tight governmental control was reversed, indicating a swing back toward laissez-faire. Further discussion is deferred to Chapter 11 on Transportation Law.

However, the approach toward coordinated transportation thus far has been fragmented, and attempts at a comprehensive policy have been largely unsuccessful. After years of contemplation and discussion, another governmental

[2] 108 Cong. Rec. 5985.
[3] Ibid.

body was created as an attempt to provide a centralized authority on transportation matters.

DEPARTMENT OF TRANSPORTATION

The federal government's interest in improving the country's transportation network resulted in the creation of the Department of Transportation (DOT) in 1966. Congress instructed the DOT at its inauguration ". . . to develop and recommend to the President and to the Congress for approval national transportation policies and programs to accomplish these objectives." Living up to the charges, policy recommendations have been made by many of the secretaries of the DOT. The statements have been made to the Congresses so that legislation can be enacted to improve the system consistent with the late President Kennedy's 1962 statement. Secretaries Volpe, Brinegar, and Coleman made policy statements during the 1970s that mirrored the Kennedy views, encouraging user fees, reduced subsidies, and less federal intervention in transportation. These policy statements have not been acted on by the Congress.

The most recent DOT policy statement was issued by former Secretary Brock Adams in 1978.

> Our energies must focus on the improvement and integration of the services of the various transportation modes, on increasing operational efficiency and on eliminating wasteful redundancy in existing facilities. Federal transportation policies and programs will have to reflect an approach that treats all elements of the national transportation system as a whole and thus transcends the parochial interests of any single mode of transport.[4]

His message focused on the need to improve the current network, and gave further expansion a low priority. Clearly, the statement had guidelines that could be implemented. The degree to which former Secretary Adams' direction will ultimately become a national transportation policy rests with the Congress.

With the creation of DOT, selected authority that had been scattered in major and minor agencies within the federal bureaucracy was centralized in one organization. However, no new powers were allowed the DOT, and it was not given authority over regulatory matters. This action was based on the doctrine of separation of powers. Because the secretary is a presidential appointee, the entire industry could conceivably be subject to the personal preferences of the president through his secretary.

The DOT was given authority over transportation safety matters and was free to conduct various studies related to allotment of a coordinated transportation system. The DOT, as presently constituted, functions in an advisory capacity to the president. Proclamations that originate with the president are influenced by

---

[4] "Transportation Policy for the Future Revealed by DOT Secretary Adams," *Traffic World*, Vol. 173, No. 7 (Feb. 13, 1978), p. 23.

DOT recommendations. However, such statements do not carry the impact of congressional policy.

A *New National Transportation Policy*

A number of implied transportation policies and the only expressed legislated intermodal policy statement in the history of freight transportation have been reviewed. An urgent need still exists for a national transportation policy. Before any new policy is legislated, however, a great deal of forethought is necessary. Consideration must be given to priorities, ownership types, degree of subsidies, and implementation.

PRIORITIES

It must be determined which matters should receive priority in the formation of a new policy. For example, if low costs are the prime consideration, then attention can be focused on the modes that enjoy lower variable costs, such as railroads and pipelines. If transit speed is the prime concern, then efforts should concentrate on the highway and airline systems. If, on the other hand, energy conservation is critical, then highway and airline traffic will have to play a minor role in the system. Without a determination of priorities, any policy to coordinate a satisfactory network will fail.

OWNERSHIP

The new policy must provide direction for the ownership arrangements desired. Historically, private ownership has dominated transportation. If this ownership philosophy is continued, then competition will have to be encouraged and control over the modes will have to be loosened. Otherwise, the federal government will continue to be a silent partner for those carriers suffering financial difficulties.

DEGREE OF SUBSIDIES

Recognized inequities exist in the subsidies currently given to the different modes. These must be resolved. In the last decade, criticisms of the transportation industry have focused on the subsidy program. Substantial support exists for more equitable user charges or greater charges to be assessed to those modes that can take advantage of governmental budget allocations for maintenance of highways, waterways, and airways. If all modes share equally in the total cost of operations, then each will face a competitive environment from the same start-

157

ing point. If subsidies are made more equitable, then policy can be developed fairly.

IMPLEMENTATION

Finally, the administrative format for efficient implementation of a new national transportation policy must be determined. A coordinated effort is required. If it is to put the policy into practice, the federal government must face two major issues, and the answer to the second issue is dependent on the first. First, it must be decided what degree of regulatory control will be exercised by the government over each mode. If the reins are to be tight, and the trend seems to be reversing, then the second issue concerns the method of control. The separate control authority that exists today must be revised so that a single agency oversees the entire network. Lacking this single agency, coordination will continue to rest with individual agency decision makers.

IDEAL POLICY REQUIREMENTS

A new national transportation policy must avoid the pitfalls of the past. When such a policy is drafted, the responsible parties must keep in mind that it must be designed to provide defined guidelines that can be implemented in future efforts to attain desired objectives. Without implementation possibilities, policies have little usefulness.

The new policy must originate from the designated authority—the Congress of the United States. The policy must have the force of law and the Congress must consider implementation. Finally, the policy must have support. Those who affect, or are affected by, the policy should understand the necessity for such a statement. Without support, implementation will be difficult, if not impossible. The administrative unit with the responsibility to enforce the law will have to make decisions unfavorable to some transportation participants. All laws are susceptible to violations. The history of transportation has demonstrated the need for enforcement. Chapter 11 examines transportation laws that have been passed and their enforcement problems.

Summary

A policy of some kind is desirable when any continuous activity occurs and affects, or is affected by, many different people or segments of society. No legislated, expressed statement of national transportation policy existed until 1940. Implied federal transportation policies of promotion, provision, and laissez-faire had prevailed before then. After federal intervention, implied and quasiexpressed policies of monopoly control, adequacy, and choice were followed. The legislated, formal national transportation policy was ineffective in scope, interpretation, definition, and application. Application of the expressed policy of preservation developed after 1958.

The need for a new national transportation policy continues. Before a new policy is stated or legislated, however, consideration must be given to priorities, ownership types, degree of subsidies, and implementation.

Questions for Chapter 10

1. What is the purpose of a policy?
2. Describe the difference between the federal government's implied promotion and provision transportation policies of the 1800s.
3. By what action did the federal government end its laissez-faire policy?
4. What were the issues that were created from the federal government's transportation policy of choice?
5. By what means did the federal government express its promotion policy toward water transportation?
6. In what manner did the federal government adopt an official national transportation policy?
7. What flaws can be cited in the legislatively enacted national transportation policy?
8. What was the intent of the Transportation Act of 1958?
9. What changing transportation policy attitudes emerged since the creation of the Department of Transportation?
10. What considerations should be given to future attempts to adopt a revised national transportation policy?
11. Railroad monopoly power existed through the first half of the twentieth century. Do you agree? Why, or why not?
12. How does the scope of government jurisdiction over the railroad, truck, and water transportation modes differ?

11

Transportation Law

160

Chapter 10 explored national transportation policy. It was emphasized that only one legislatively expressed intermodal policy has existed since the commercial beginnings of transportation. That policy was stated as the preamble to the Transportation Act of 1940. Usually, it could be expected that laws would follow from such a policy. A policy's objective is to provide guidelines for overall direction. However, many laws passed after 1940 did not follow the stated national transportation policy. For reasons discussed earlier, the legislated policy did not favor enactment of specific laws because of its lack of application.

This chapter examines transportation law. Because hundreds of transportation laws have been enacted, it is beyond the scope of any introductory text to review all of those laws.[1] However, we will review the major laws and some of their results.

Role of Transportation Law

Usually, the term *law* connotes an elaborate procedure whereby a government body proposes a bill, it is discussed and argued, and, finally, a vote is taken to determine whether the bill will become law. Actually, beyond common law, which is commonly accepted societal behavior, three categories of laws exist: administrative, judicial, and legislative. Administrative laws result from mandates issued by administrators of various government agencies and departments. For example, when the Food and Drug Administration questioned the safety of saccharin, it issued a "law", that saccharin and all products containing it as an ingredient be properly labeled warning the public of possible health hazards. Judicial law results from court decisions wherein judges hear all sides of a case and then issue a decree, which has the impact of law in governing future actions. Legislative law results from bills that are submitted to and voted on by a body of elected representatives. Presidential approval of successful bills makes them binding laws.

Transportation law encompasses all three categories. The regulatory bodies, as described in Chapter 12, are given congressional authority to pass administrative laws. Their orders are binding on the carriers under their jurisdiction. Under certain circumstances, the regulatory bodies' decisions may be appealed to the court system and, in other cases, transportation issues may go directly to the courts, bypassing the regulatory bodies. The courts' decisions have the force of judicial law and are binding on all future actions. Transportation legislative laws are discussed in this chapter. The development of administrative and

---

[1] For a more thorough discussion of transportation law, see John Guandolo, *Transportation Law*, 2nd ed. (Dubuque, Iowa: William C. Brown Company, Publishers, 1965).

judicial laws will be examined in the discussion of regulatory institutions in Chapter 12.

The nature of the transportation industry makes it subject to more specific laws than perhaps any other industry in the economy.[2] First, it is the most visible of all industries in that most commercial activities could not exist without transportation. Second, the industry is made up of many carriers within each mode, each competing with the other. Third, the different modes within the transportation industry are affected by the actions of the others. Finally, the transportation industry contributes substantially to this nation's standard of living. Society depends on the industry to provide those products so necessary to existence. This all-encompassing nature of the transportation industry makes it vulnerable to many conflicts. With so many different interests represented, it is not surprising to find many laws regulating its activities.

Before Transportation Law Era

During the early years of transportation development in the United States, no governing laws existed. Transportation was conducted primarily by individual businesses to move products owned by those businesses. Water vessels were owned by individuals and mine operators, and the earliest roads were built by individuals and private businesses to transport their products between communities or to seaports. The earliest railroads were constructed by private businesses for the same purpose.

If others wished to use the private roads, a fee had to be paid to the owner. The payment usually was not high because the owner was satisfied to cover the expenses involved in building and maintaining the roadway. During this early period, common law generally prevailed, with the user expecting to pay a nominal fee to the owner and the owner expecting to receive some payment for the use of personal property.

The growth of the United States economy was the result, in large part, of the transportation system that developed. Communities began to link together, then regions, then states and, finally, the entire country. This development occurred because the growth of various modes made it easier to transport products. With larger volumes of products moving between communities, transportation became a major business activity in its own right, and companies were formed for the sole purpose of providing transportation service. Conflicts arose because the providers of transportation wanted to make as much profit as possi-

---

[2] The body of business law can be found in Len Young Smith and G. Gale Roberson, *Business Law: Uniform Commercial Code*, 4th ed. (St. Paul, Minn.: West Publishing Company, 1977).

ble and the users wanted to pay low fees to increase their own profitability. These early conflicts planted the seeds for transportation law.

The conflicts expanded with industry growth. The obvious profitability in providing transportation services for a rapidly growing economy encouraged others to enter the transportation industry. With more than one organization providing identical services to the same group of users, additional conflicts developed. Conflicts occurring among companies providing transportation service and the difficulties users faced in choosing among several transportation firms contributed further to the need for transportation law.

STATE CONTROLS

The earliest transportation controls involved rail carriers. Individual railroads were required to obtain state charters that permitted them to conduct business within the state. This type of activity is known as *intrastate transportation*. Although common law generally governed railroad operations, individual states were obligated to intercede when the public interest was involved. Formal regulation started in 1839 when Rhode Island became the first state to establish a commission to improve its railroad system.[3] Not long after, New Hampshire, Connecticut, Vermont, Maine, and Massachusetts established similar commissions. Neither state charters nor the railroad commissions had direct power over the fees railroads charged to shippers. However, other activities attracted attention. For example, the first commission was established because a railroad favored a steamboat carrier with which it was affiliated over other competing water carriers. Other commissions were established to allow and encourage rail carriers to connect with other rail lines to provide a better transportation system within the state and to formulate safety regulations. Still other commissions were formed to establish procedures by which rail carriers could purchase property when the original owners refused to sell.

The continued growth of the industry led to pressure on the railroad commissions to recommend rate control laws. One major problem was that the competing railroads would not cooperate with each other to set joint rates for the benefit of the users. Users were required to pay charges to each rail carrier participating in the service. These charges often were unreasonably high and a financial burden to the users.

It is impossible to generalize on the state laws passed because of the variety of legislation. Each state dealt with problems of greatest local importance. For example, the Virginia Law of 1837 was the first general law enacted in the South. It made it mandatory that a charter be obtained to operate a railroad in that state. In New York, the General Railroad Act passed in 1850 covered similar

---

[3] The subject of state railroad commissions is covered in depth in Edward Chase Kirkland, *Men, Cities, and Transportation: A Study in New England History, 1820–1900* (Cambridge, Mass.: Harvard University Press, 1948), Ch. 22.

charter requirements and also limited the profit that could be earned by the railroads. New York also passed the Free Railway Law that same year to protect the public from any abuses resulting from the railroad monopoly.

One of the earliest state laws dealing with discrimination was passed by the state of Illinois in 1861, and several other states followed as the issue became more serious.[4] Discrimination resulted when railroads could charge any rate they wished. In many cases, some shippers were charged higher rates for short-haul movements than preferred users were charged for longer hauls. Also, rates charged for identical movements were higher for some users than for others. These situations led to a variety of state laws intended to protect shippers, but these laws were limited to railroad operations within the state boundaries.

ADDITIONAL RAILROAD PROBLEMS

During the 1870s, a new concern developed. The rates charged by rail carriers for interstate movements came under violent attack. The major thrust of this attack came from the Grange, an organization of farmers in the midwestern states. The movement adopted the name of the organization and became the Granger Movement. Farmers, the primary victims of the rail carriers, needed the carrying capacity of railroads to transport their product to market or processing areas. The cost of transportation directly influenced the profitability of farm operations. In the opinion of the farmers, rail carriers were reaping unreasonably high profits. This exploitation was particularly severe when only one rail carrier served a geographic area.

The objective of the Granger Movement was to reduce high rates. The benefits to be derived were obviously in the public interest for both the farming community and the final consumers. State commissions began pressing for laws that would regulate the level of rates on a "just and reasonable" basis. State laws complied with these requests, in spite of the rail carriers' protests that rate regulation deprived individual businesses of the rights inherent in possession of private property. The landmark Supreme Court decision validating state regulation of private property in the public interest was *Munn* v. *Illinois.*[5] Ironically, the decision did not involve the railroad industry. The issue resolved by the Court's decision concerned the high rates charged to the farmers for grain storage by warehouse operators. The Supreme Court ruled that grain storage was in the public interest and, therefore, was subject to governmental regulation. This decision led to enforcement of the state laws regarding railroad rates because that activity also involved the public interest. The regulation

---

[4] State laws pertaining to railroad transportation are discussed in Lee Benson, *Merchants, Farmers, and Railroads: Railroad Regulation and New York Politics, 1850–1887* (Cambridge, Mass.: Harvard University Press, 1955); Solon Justus Buck, *The Granger Movement* (Lincoln, Neb.: University of Nebraska Press, copyright by Harvard University Press, 1913); and Maxwell Ferguson, *State Regulation of Railroads in the South* (New York: AMS Press, 1968).

[5] 94 U.S. 113.

again was restricted to intrastate activity and had no impact on interstate business transactions.

In addition to the freight charge discriminations practiced by the railroads, several other activities occurred during the 1870s and 1880s. A major problem arose from the apparently unethical practices used to attract rail shipments away from competitors. Some railroads charged the established fee common to all carriers for a shipment between two identical locations. However, after collecting the total charges, a portion of the payment was returned to the shipper. This was known as a *rebate*. In effect, the user was favored and was inclined to use that same rail carrier again rather than its competitors.

Another practice common during that time was the preference shown to major users by supplying railcars, particularly during periods when cars were in short supply. In effect, a competitive advantage was given to the preferred shippers. Other users suffered because of the lack of railroad cars.

In other instances, railroads did not assess extra charges to shippers equally. For example, a charge was imposed, and still is, for detention of railcars. Each user is given a specified time period to load or unload a car. Once this time period is exceeded, an extra daily charge, known as *demurrage*, is attached to the shipment. Several railroads overlooked the charge to earn the loyalty of shippers.

INTRASTATE-INTERSTATE CONFLICT

The growing economic interaction between states would have a significant impact on the formulation of laws to protect users on shipments that originated in one state and were delivered in another. This type of movement is known as *interstate commerce*. By the 1880s, state regulation of the railroads was common, but railroad transportation problems did not subside. Another major issue arose regarding rate levels.

The Wabash, St. Louis & Pacific Railway discriminated against a shipper who had tendered a shipment in Illinois destined for New York State. The shipper was assessed a higher fee than that charged for a similar commodity from a more distant point in Illinois to the same point in New York. Although the state's court ruled this practice was in violation of its regulatory law, the Supreme Court of the United States overturned the decision in 1886.[6] Regulation of interstate commerce was given to the federal government through the United States Constitution. Therefore, the state of Illinois had no authority to regulate the issue and the decision was nullified. The Wabash Case was the final straw. Federal intervention to regulate interstate railroad transportation became necessary to protect the public interest.

---

[6] 118 U.S. 557.

Federal Intervention

The problem of railroad regulation changed from intrastate in the mid-1800s to interstate by the 1870s. In 1874, the Congress established the Windom Committee to investigate the railroad industry, including the feasibility of government ownership.[7] No legislative action resulted from this investigation. The continuing problems, however, forced yet another investigation by Congress. This special group, the Cullom Committee, reported in 1886 that its investigation favored regulation of the railroads for interstate commerce.[8] This report, coupled with the Supreme Court decision discussed earlier, initiated legislative action. The federal government was on the verge of passing the first piece of national regulatory legislation.

Act to Regulate Commerce of 1887

The call for federal regulation was widespread. Several state commissions had appealed for federal intervention to help solve the regulatory problems they faced. The Supreme Court had made decisions that called for federal legislation to resolve discriminatory practices. Two major committee reports had called for federal action. In addition, some of the railroads had appealed directly to the Congress for regulation of the unfair discriminations practiced by other railroads. With the pressures coming from all sides, the federal government saw fit to enact a law regulating the railroad industry. The Act to Regulate Commerce, later to be known as the Interstate Commerce Act, was approved on February 4, 1887.[9] This act was intended to limit the abuses resulting from the railroads' monopoly control.

SCOPE OF THE ACT

In drawing up the legislation, Congress attempted to address two problem areas: freight charges and equity.

FREIGHT CHARGES

The first section of the law dealt with freight charge problems. The law stated that all charges to the users must be "just and reasonable." This state-

[7] Hugh S. Norton, *National Transportation Policy: Formation and Implementation* (Berkeley, Calif.: McCutchan Publishing Corp., 1966), chap. 2.

[8] Ibid.

[9] Act to Regulate Commerce, 24 Stat. 379.

ment eventually caused many problems because the definition of "just and reasonable" is open to many interpretations. Nevertheless, the act's first section made every unjust and unreasonable charge unlawful. The sixth section required that all railroad freight charges be commonly known. Exact charges had to be published so that all parties were aware of the fees and could be sure that all others were paying the same amount.

EQUITY

Four sections of the act dealt with the issue of equitable treatment. The second section disallowed any monetary discrimination toward any individual or any business firm. The third section addressed other types of discrimination. The railroads were not allowed to favor one shipper over any other. However, the preference had to be significant to be illegal. As discussed earlier, railroads charged a preferred shipper a lower fee for a long-haul shipment than they charged another user for a shorter movement over the same route. The fourth section of the act made this practice illegal. Equal treatment was thus assured. The fifth section required that all railroads be forced to compete on an equal basis. This section disallowed pooling agreements, arrangements made between two or more railroads to use joint facilities for transportation or division of revenues. This practice would have given some railroads a competitive advantage over those who were not part of the agreement.

INTERSTATE COMMERCE COMMISSION (ICC)

To enforce the provisions in the act, Congress established the Interstate Commerce Commission. Although the subject of regulation will be covered in Chapter 12, it is important to understand that the ICC was established to hear complaints of violations and to correct illegal activities.

Bear in mind that the provisions of the Act to Regulate Commerce and the actions of the ICC were restricted to shipments *between* states. The individual states reserved the right to enact laws to govern railroad operations within their geographic boundaries.

Corrective Laws

Any first attempt is likely to be far from perfect. The federal government's first venture into transportation regulation was no exception. The Act to Regulate Commerce was not clear enough to end the problems that had led to its enactment. Attempts to apply the provisions of the law to the railroads' daily operations uncovered several problems that could not be resolved by the courts. Several corrective laws emerged that attempted to remove the confusion, broaden coverage, and re-emphasize the intent of the Congress in passing the original regulatory law.

ELKINS ACT OF 1903

Although the practice of rebates was no longer permitted under Section 2 of the regulatory act, it was not stated specifically. The practice continued in secret. Thus, those railroads trying to follow the intention of the original act were losing business to carriers who continued the illegal practice. The offended railroads appealed to Congress to pass a law that spelled out the illegality of such actions. The Elkins Act of 1903[10] appeared as the first corrective act. It not only held the railroads responsible for any rebates given to any user, but it also made anyone who asked for or received a rebate equally in violation of the law.

Both parties to the rebate, railroad and recipient, would be guilty of a misdemeanor and subject to a fine. All users were to be assessed the identical charge for similar shipments, and no deviations were allowed. Thus, the intent of the initial law was stated in more specific terms.

HEPBURN ACT OF 1906

The original act called for "just and reasonable" freight charges. However, these words were not easy to define and became a matter of personal judgment. Problems surfaced after the ICC tried to exercise its control over the level of rates, a matter not stated specifically in the regulatory act. The Hepburn Act,[11] passed in 1906 to clarify the freight charge issue, explicitly gave authority to the ICC to set the maximum amount that could be charged for a particular movement. If a difference of opinion between the ICC and the railroad occurred, the decision of the commission prevailed, subject to court review.

Some of the railroads were not pleased with the requirement to compete fairly. After passage of the initial regulatory act, some carriers published new charges to take effect immediately. Competing railroads did not have adequate time to reduce their charges and lost business. The Hepburn Act required railroads to give a thirty-day notice of any change in freight charges so that all railroads would have an opportunity to adjust to the new charges if they wished.

Occasionally, the railroads would not cooperate with each other to provide through routes and a single freight charge for a shipment that involved two or more railroads. The ICC was given authority to establish a through route and a single freight charge if the carriers would not cooperate. This act also contained a *Commodities Clause* that prohibited railroads from transporting commodities

[10] P.L. 57–103.
[11] P.L. 59–337.

they produced or in which they had a financial interest. Many railroads owned manufacturing firms. If they were allowed to haul their own products, the railroads could favor themselves in service or freight charge levels. The Commodities Clause eliminated this competitive advantage.

The authority of the ICC was extended to other agencies by this act. Until that time, only operating railroad companies were under control of the commission. Express, storage, and sleeping car companies, as well as the pipeline industry, were brought under the umbrella of federal regulation. This began the extension of regulation beyond railroads. Although some major issues had been clarified, problems continued.

MANN-ELKINS ACT OF 1910

The last major law before World War I that attempted to clarify railroad regulation was passed in 1910. Two prominent issues were resolved by the Mann-Elkins Act.[12] The issue of higher freight charges for shorter distances had been addressed in the fourth section of the Act to Regulate Commerce. That section came to be known as the *Long- and Short-Haul Clause.* According to that section, the practice was made illegal ". . . under substantially similar circumstances and conditions." Interpretation of that phrase had caused many problems. The Mann-Elkins Act removed the phrase altogether, eliminating any conditions under which a higher charge could be assessed for a shorter haul than for a longer freight haul over the same route.

The other major problem concerned reduction of freight charges. Whenever a freight charge violation was reported to the ICC, an investigation had to be made. However, the accused railroad could continue with the alleged violation until the investigation was completed. If the issue remained unresolved, the railroad could take the matter to the courts and gain more time and business until the legal process was completed. Although the Expediting Act of 1903[13] gave ICC cases a high priority in the court system, time lags still occurred. The Mann-Elkins Act gave the ICC the authority to suspend the questionable charge, and the railroad had to continue to assess the previous charge until the matter was resolved. Thus, other railroads would not lose additional business during the legal process.

POST-WORLD WAR I ERA

Although minor acts were passed after the Mann-Elkins Act, relative calm prevailed in the industry during World War I. During the war, the federal government assumed management control of the railroads, and efforts were directed mainly to transporting the materials necessary to support the national

---

[12] P.L. 61–218.
[13] P.L. 57–82.

effort. As soon as the war ended, transportation problems again emerged and captured the attention of Congress.

TRANSPORTATION ACT OF 1920

A major issue was confronted at the end of World War I. Because the federal government had managed the railroads during the war, several members of the Congress believed the railroads should not be returned to private owners. Nevertheless, private ownership prevailed and the old system was revived. Congress passed the Transportation Act of 1920[14] that changed the federal attitude toward the railroads. First, more profitable railroad operations were desired. The ICC was asked to prepare a plan to consolidate the many railroads into major systems to reduce the overall cost of railroad transportation. The previous ban on pooling arrangements were altered to allow those arrangements if they led to better service. This action also was directed to reducing overall railroad transportation cost.

The second area of change related to freight charges. As noted earlier, the ICC was permitted to set maximum freight charges through the Hepburn Act of 1906. The Transportation Act of 1920 gave the ICC authority to set *minimum* freight charges. The intent was to maintain financial stability within the industry. Some argued that this action also allowed the ICC to protect the competition created by the motor transportation system, a topic to be discussed later. In any event, this new clause, called the *Rule of Rate Making*, stated that the ICC should set minimum charges to allow a reasonable profit return on the railroads' investments. An interesting aspect of the Transportation Act of 1920 was contained in the *Recapture Clause*. This clause allowed the ICC to collect one half of all railroad profits that exceeded 6 per cent of the return on the railroads' investment. These profits were used to set up a fund to help financially troubled railroads.

EMERGENCY TRANSPORTATION ACT OF 1933

The next significant railroad law was passed during the Great Depression. The Emergency Transportation Act of 1933[15] aided the railroads' poor financial condition resulting from the depression. Its aim was to avoid duplication of facilities by encouraging railroad consolidations. The ICC was given the responsibility to approve all railroad consolidations and to ensure that these combinations followed the general pattern of the commission's railroad plan. The Emergency Transportation Act of 1933 also repealed the Recapture Clause of the Transportation Act of 1920.

The acts mentioned in this section were directed toward preserving the railroad network. Railroad monopoly and profitability were issues no longer. The impact of the Great Depression and the entrance of motor freight transpor-

---

[14] P.L. 66–152.
[15] P.L. 68–72.

tation in the 1930s made preservation of the railroad industry a continuing prime concern.

POST-WORLD WAR II ERA

The nation's economy recovered from the Great Depression as the country supplied the allies in World War II, and railroads profited from the increased traffic volumes. After the United States entered the war, traffic volumes increased even more. During the war years, material shortages prevented the railroads from adding new equipment, and the demand for the use of railroad cars prevented adequate repair of the existing fleet. After the war, the railroads' financial condition did not permit significant investments in transportation equipment. Profitability declined further as the trucking industry made great inroads into the freight hauling business. Once again, the railroad industry required federal assistance.

REED-BULWINKLE ACT OF 1948

In order to avoid railroads competing with each other by reducing freight charges on shipments that could be hauled by more than one railroad, agreements were made that each railroad would charge the same fee for movements of identical commodities between the same two points. Also, each railroad was allowed to express opinions on any rate reductions for points served by only one carrier. The major features of these agreements were as follows:

1. Competition on the basis of freight charges would be avoided. If, for example, a profitable railroad wanted to attract more freight shipments between two points, it might set its freight charge lower than that of its competition. The competitor would then be forced to reduce rates or lose business. If the competitor was having financial problems, the reduced revenue would cause further losses. If the charge was not reduced, shipments would be lost and total revenue would be lower. Also, if both reduced their charges similarly, less revenue would be received than would be possible if both remained at the higher level. By assessing identical charges, the railroads could compete on the basis of service and could realize the maximum revenue from users.

2. If a railroad reduced its charges on shipments where no competition existed, there would be no price competition with other railroads. However, the structure of freight charges on similar commodities for approximately the same distance might be affected. For example, the distance between Detroit, Michigan, and Cleveland, Ohio, is approximately the same as the distance between Cleveland and Pittsburgh, Pennsylvania. If railroad X reduced its freight charge from Detroit to Cleveland and railroad Y hauled the same commodity from Cleveland to Pittsburgh for another shipper, the second user might pressure railroad Y for a reduction in

charges. The logic was that charges should be approximately the same for similar distances and commodities.

3. Another reason for these agreements is illustrated by the example of two railroads serving the same destination point with similar shipments starting at different points of origin but of approximately the same distance. If railroad X reduced its rate from an origin point, the shipper would have a competitive advantage over shippers at other origin points. The shipper served by railroad X would be able to sell the commodities at a lower price because the transportation charge would be lower.

To remove these inequities, railroads were permitted to establish rate bureaus in which each railroad serving a particular region was represented. Planned rate changes could be discussed to determine their overall impact. The majority opinion of the committee prevailed on all proposed changes.

The bureau system kept all carriers in agreement with all freight charges. However, these agreements violated the Sherman Antitrust Act of 1890, which prohibited any agreements between companies that would tend to lessen competition. Additional legislation was required to allow the bureaus to operate in order to protect the railroads' financial condition. Congress passed the Reed-Bulwinkle Act of 1948,[16] the major railroad legislation of the 1940s, which exempted railroad rate bureaus from the Sherman Antitrust Act of 1890. This act permitted railroads to avoid price competition and maintain financial stability. As will be explained in Chapter 13, although this act allowed rate bureaus, it also allowed individual carriers to propose independent action.

Critics of the bureau system have existed as long as the system itself. Supporters of unrestrained competition believed the system kept freight charges higher than they would have been if each carrier had set its own charges. This same argument was used to oppose the Reed-Bulwinkle Act. Because the bureau system attracted so many criticisms as being anticompetitive, the reregulation legislation enacted in 1980 did, in fact, modify the antitrust immunity aspects of that procedure.

PRESERVATION PERIOD

The railroad industry continued to suffer financial instability. The trucking industry was making greater dents in the volume previously handled by the railroads. Declining profits prevented rail carriers from modernizing plants and equipment, service was below par, and investors were not attracted to the railroad industry. The federal government had to intercede to keep the railroads from disappearing. The preservation period reached its high point during the 1970s, but was evident as early as the 1950s.

Many laws had been passed by various United States Congresses to ensure

[16] P.L. 80–662.

172

that trains will continue to run. During the 1970s, it seemed that more and more laws were proposed to save the industry from total collpase. With so many laws proposed and/or enacted, it is not possible to discuss each one, but we will examine three major laws that demonstrated the federal attitude of preservation.

TRANSPORTATION ACT OF 1958

During the business recession of the mid-1950s, the only way to ensure that railroads could obtain loans to update their equipment was to have the federal government guarantee repayment. With the Transportation Act of 1958,[17] the federal government agreed to guarantee up to a total of $500 million outstanding at any one time. The loans could not be for periods of more than fifteen years.

In addition, the act modified the regulation of railroad freight charges. There had been many complaints that the minimum charges set by the ICC were unusually high in order to protect the trucking industry's high rates. If the gap between the railroads' charges and the trucking companies' rates was too wide, shippers would not be attracted to truck transportation. Whether or not the argument was valid, the Rule of Rate Making was amended by the Transportation Act to ensure that the ICC did not consider other modes' rates when prescribing minimum charges for the railroad industry.

REGIONAL RAIL REORGANIZATION ACT OF 1973

One of the major railroad laws of the past decade was the Regional Rail Reorganization Act of 1973.[18] The financial condition of many railroads serving the northeastern and midwestern sections of the country was so poor that several carriers were in the midst of bankruptcy proceedings. To allow them to discontinue operations would have left many communities without rail service. Also, only two major railroads would remain to provide freight transportation in those regions, which would strengthen their monopoly power. The Regional Rail Reorganization Act of 1973 allowed the insolvent railroads to merge into the Consolidated Rail Corporation (Conrail). Financial assistance was provided for the new system. Many claim that Conrail is a form of a national railway system because of the continued federal funds to keep the carrier solvent.

RAILROAD REVITALIZATION AND REGULATORY REFORM ACT OF 1976

Another major act was passed by the Congress in 1976. The financial problems of many railroads prevented significant expenditures to improve their physical facilities. Also, there was a growing belief that the regulation procedures were bogging down the railroads. Again, the federal government was

---

[17] P.L. 85–625.
[18] P.L. 93–236.

called upon for major legislation to assist the industry. With the Railroad Revitalization and Regulatory Reform Act,[19] several actions occurred. First, the federal government guaranteed loans made to the railroads to improve their physical facilities. Second, the railroads were given more freedom in adjusting freight charges. Third, new procedures were established that would allow mergers between carriers. These actions were taken in the hope of revitalizing the railroad industry, but not enough time has passed to evaluate the success of the act.

Further regulatory reform activity occurred during 1980. The federal government's attitude during the 1970s had been shifting toward more regulatory freedom. The 96th Congress prepared legislation (H.R. 7235, S. 1946) to allow railroads to compete more freely, both intramodally and intermodally. This proposed legislation allowed the carriers to set rates, modified the antitrust immunity of the bureau system, permitted railroads to operate both as common and contract carriers, and modified various ICC procedures.

In summary, the railroad industry has received more federal attention and assistance than any other industry in the economy. Judging by recent actions, it can be assumed that the attention has not ended. Unless circumstances change drastically and the volume of traffic handled by the railroads increases significantly, more federal assistance will be necessary to keep the industry operating.

Other Transportation Laws

Fortunately, the other transportation modes have not had as many problems as the railroad industry. In most cases, laws pertaining to regulation of the other modes were designed along the same patterns as those for the railroads. The other modes do not require as much federal attention because most of them do not possess the same degree of monopoly potential as the railroads. That is, many communities are served by only one railroad because of the huge investment required to set up operations and maintain the rights-of-way and equipment. Because many communities do not have sufficient traffic volume to justify more than one railroad, users are subject to that railroad's monopoly power.

PIPELINE TRANSPORTATION LAWS

The pipeline industry perhaps has been least affected by federal laws. Pipelines were brought under the regulatory power of the ICC by the Hepburn Act of 1906. The only problems posed by the pipeline industry relate to obtaining

---

[19] P.L. 94–210.

land on which to install new lines. If land must be purchased and the property owner does not wish to sell, the right of eminent domain has to be exercised. Eminent domain is the right of the government to force the sale of property when the land can be used for the greater benefit of society. The Cole Act of 1941[20] gave this power to the president. It also authorized the federal government to construct interstate pipelines when necessary for national defense.

Additional legislation was enacted in 1977 that affected the regulatory status of pipeline transportation. The Department of Energy Act of 1977[21] transferred economic regulatory responsibility to the Department of Energy from the ICC. The Federal Energy Regulatory Commission was established to handle the regulatory activities.

Pipeline regulation is justified by the mode's monopoly power. The degree of power is not as great as that of the railroads because of the limited number of products transported and the relatively few possible users. Nevertheless, the power exists and is permitted because of the large investment necessary to build lines and because only one facility is necessary to handle the traffic flow. To allow competing lines to exist would duplicate facilities and add to the cost of pipeline transportation.

HIGHWAY TRANSPORTATION LAWS

Throughout the first two decades of the twentieth century, only the railroads and pipelines were federally regulated. The trucking companies did not yet carry a large percentage of traffic volume, and interstate motor transportation was uncommon before the 1930s, so there was no demand to regulate the industry at that time. This is not to say, however, that no laws pertained to motor transportation. The federal government's promotion policy was evident in the Federal Aid Road Act of 1916[22] and the Federal Highway Act of 1921.[23] The first act allowed the federal government to pay for one half of the cost of road improvements, with the other half funded by the individual states. The second act supplemented the 1916 law and allowed the federal government to select a system of highways to connect the various states. Both of these laws contributed to the growth of trucking companies as a major mode of freight transportation.

As the trucking industry grew, problems occurred similar to those of the railroads. The state regulatory commissions had no power to control operations when the truck shipments involved interstate commerce. Also, more and more trucking companies were being formed and price-cutting became a problem. In addition, the federal government believed that the excessive duplication of fa-

---

[20] P.L. 77–197.
[21] P.L. 91–95.
[22] P.L. 64–156.
[23] P.L. 67–87.

cilities wasted resources. A law to control interstate motor operations became necessary. In 1935, the Congress passed the Motor Carrier Act,[24] which became Part II of the Interstate Commerce Act. Interstate bus shipments were included in the act.

The Motor Carrier Act was modeled after the Interstate Commerce Act. For example, motor carriers were required to charge "just and reasonable" rates. Charges had to be published and could not be changed without thirty days' notice. Mergers between carriers required ICC approval and had to be in the public interest. The carriers had to publish minimum rates, and the ICC was given the power to set rate levels. However, some notable differences existed between railroad and truck regulations.

The first difference was the handling of interstate matters. An issue that involved less than four states could be settled in a meeting of representatives of those areas. If the matter involved four or more states, the ICC would decide how the issue was to be resolved. In railroad regulation, all matters that involved interstate transportation were handled by the ICC. Another difference involved control of the number of trucking companies allowed to operate. Because of the small capital requirements, thousands of motor carriers were being formed. To control the number of firms, the law required that each new company must obtain a *Certificate of Public Convenience and Necessity* (CPCN). To obtain a certificate, the company had to show that it was able to perform the transportation service and that the service was necessary. The certificate spelled out the areas to be served, the commodities to be hauled, and the routes to be used. The ICC could turn down an application if it believed that adequate competition existed in a given area. Considerable modifications in entry approval were part of the 1980 re-regulation enactments.

Another notable difference between railroad and motor carrier regulations was the extent of regulation. Although all railroad carriers were regulated until the late 1970s, the motor carriers enjoyed exemption from regulations under certain circumstances. For example, motor carriers hauling unprocessed agricultural products were exempted from economic regulations, as were motor carriers providing local transportation services. The local service had to both originate and terminate within the same geographic area, known as a *commercial zone*. Commercial zones are defined by the regulatory bodies and are not generally the same as political boundaries. Usually the commercial zone extends beyond the city's boundaries to include those outlying areas that participate in commercial activities with the city. This type of exemption considerably reduces the burden of regulation, considering the number of truck movements usually occurring within any city among vendors, buyers, and stocking locations. Other economic exemptions have been granted for specific types of products hauled, in addition to the general agricultural exemption. For example,

[24] P.L. 74–255.

vehicles used to transport newspapers, livestock, and fish are free from economic regulations.

In railroad transportation, all carriers were considered common carriers. The trucking industry was unique in that different types of companies existed, as described in Chapter 6. The Motor Carrier Act defined and classified the trucking companies in five major groups: (1) common, (2) contract, (3) private, (4) brokers, and (5) exempt. Carriers were not allowed to operate in two of these forms in any area, with exceptions allowed only by the ICC. Some major activity occurred in this regard in the late 1970s that was to be reflected in the 1980 re-regulation legislation. An ICC decision in 1978, which became known as the *Toto decision*, allowed a private carrier to transport commodities for another company. The decision was highly contested and proceeded through the court system well into 1980. The 1980 trucking enactment changed the regulatory posture to allow a private carrier to haul for other companies in the same corporate family if the parent firm maintained a 100-percent ownership in the companies for which the transportation service was being provided.

On July 1, 1980, President Jimmy Carter signed into law the Motor Carrier Act of 1980[25] which was the most sweeping trucking regulation activity since the Motor Carrier Act of 1935. Some of the provisions have been cited above. The more lenient attitudes toward economic regulation demonstrated by the ICC during the late 1970s were manifested in this legislation. Under provisions of this new legislation, carriers no longer have to prove a *necessity* for providing transportation service from a competitive standpoint, but only that they are "fit, willing, and able" to do so. Prior to this act, requests for certification to provide transportation service between two points could be refused on the basis of the number of carriers authorized to operate in that realm. Previous entry controls provided a method to limit competition in an effort to make the service profitable for the trucking companies which had certification. Certification no longer is restricted to specific commodities and is granted on broad product groupings or classifications. Common carriers are allowed to transport between two points, as opposed to shipping from one location to another. In other words, any back hauls to the origin point are permitted from the initial destination. Any locations between the two points can be served by that carrier. Individual certification for specific types of shipment gave way to consolidated authority into just one of a few certificates. Contracts between carriers and users no longer have to state the exact locations to be served and can provide transportation service from and to any point for the user stated in the contract. In some cases, only counties, as opposed to specific cities, can be named in the certification, allowing more points to be served. Also, the procedures allowing for mergers between trucking companies were expedited and more lenient rules are applied. In addition, pooling agreements between carriers explicitly were legalized, subject to the approval of the ICC because of the potential anticompetitiveness of these arrangements.

Interestingly, the trucking re-regulation thrust is carried down to the intrastate level. On the same day as the re-regulation legislation was signed into law by the President, the state of Florida deregulated economic controls over that industry. All trucking companies operating in intrastate activity were completely freed from rate, route, commodity, and entry controls, establishing a totally free competitive system. The ICC commissioned a special study of the future results of this action, and if the reports are favorable, future re-regulation or deregulation thrusts may be in the offing.

A new federal attitude is demonstrated by the legislation of 1980. Although an intermodal national transportation policy has not resulted, a policy with regard to the trucking industry surfaced. The federal government has demonstrated its desire to conserve the use of scarce resources. It also has shown a desire to free the industry from tight economic regulation and increase competition. The future results of this sweeping legislation will be the subject of many future studies. Any statement regarding the ultimate impact is only a matter of conjecture at this time.

AIR TRANSPORTATION LAWS

With the Motor Transportation Act of 1935, all land carriers were brought under some form of regulation. As discussed earlier, the federal government's implicit policy toward the airlines was promotion. Up to the present time, air freight transportation had not been prominent and therefore had not required tight control of its operations. The major concerns in air carrier regulation have been promotion, safety, and maintenance of the airways.

The many airlines in existence after World War I were hurt financially by the Great Depression. Many faced bankruptcy and the federal government had to act. In the Civil Aeronautics Act of 1938,[26] the federal government took over the regulation of interstate commerce by airlines. Many of the regulation matters included in earlier laws were adopted in this act. For instance, the airlines were not allowed to discriminate between users. Rates had to be published and could not be changed without a thirty-day notice. The airlines also had to obtain a CPCN before participating in interstate commerce, and mergers had to be approved.

The major difference in this newest form of transportation regulation was establishment of a separate regulatory body. Other transportation modes were regulated by the ICC. The Civil Aeronautics Act set up the Civil Aeronautics Authority (later changed to the Civil Aeronautics Board) to regulate activities.

---

[26] P.L. 75–706.

Although air freight was the last of the major modes to be regulated from an economic standpoint, it was the first to feel the impact of the re-regulation thrust of the late 1970s. The first law was passed in 1977[27] and a second followed in 1978.[28] In combination, these laws set the stage for economic deregulation of both passenger and freight transportation service.

WATER TRANSPORTATION LAWS

Water transportation was the first form of freight transportation in the United States, so it is not surprising to find federal laws dealing with this mode. However, the early laws were not legislated to *control* the activities of the mode. Laws that dealt with regulation of the other modes often included some aspect of water transportation, which resulted in a patchwork of legislation. Total definition of water transportation regulation was the last to be of concern to the federal government and did not occur until all other modes had been affected by national regulatory laws.

As stated, a patchwork of legislation covered water transportation. For example, with the Act to Regulate Commerce in 1887, water carriers were placed under control of the ICC when a shipment was a water-rail combination. The Hepburn Act of 1906 gave the ICC power to establish joint water-rail routes and rates and to set the maximum level of charges for those carriers that came under ICC jurisdiction. The Panama Canal Act of 1912[29] made it illegal for any railroad to have any interest in water carriers operating through the Panama Canal. It was believed that those railroads with controlling interests in water carriers would enjoy lower costs and would lower their rates on some movements, placing other railroads at a competitive disadvantage.

The most extensive water transportation law passed in the early 1900s was the Shipping Act of 1916,[30] which was concerned primarily with international water movements. It increased the number of water carriers subject to federal regulation, allowed some activities, and disallowed others. The act did the following:

1. Created the United States Shipping Board and gave it regulatory power over water common carriers in interstate and foreign commerce and on the Great Lakes. This power did not extend to water carriers under ICC control.
2. Legalized agreements between water carriers, called *conference agreements*, which fixed a set rate to be charged to users. These agreements did not violate the Sherman Antitrust Act if they were filed with the Shipping Board.

[27] P.L. 95–163.
[28] P.L. 95–504.
[29] P.L. 62–337.
[30] P.L. 64–260.

3. Declared to be illegal:
   a. Certain practices that might tend to destroy competition and lead to monopoly power.
   b. Granting special rates or privileges to selected users.
   c. Offering rebates to selected users.
   d. Any other acts of preference or discrimination to particular users.
4. Required that affected carriers publish their maximum rates.
5. Required that all rates be "just and reasonable."

The major objectives of this act were to protect the water carriers from unfair competition and to protect the users from discrimination. However, only a limited number of water carriers were affected by this act and most water transporters remained out of the reach of federal control.

The railroads were not willing to cooperate with water carriers because they saw them as major competitors for certain traffic movements. The Denison Act of 1928[31] allowed the ICC to force the railroads to establish joint water-rail routes and rates for shipments on the Mississippi River. It also required water carriers on the Mississippi River to obtain a CPCN. This act brought more carriers under federal regulation and served to limit the number of competitors for freight volume on the Mississippi River.

The Intercoastal Shipping Act of 1933[32] was intended to offer stronger controls over competition for water freight transportation on intercoastal shipments moving through the Panama Canal. It was amended later to include water shipments moving along the coasts of the United States and on the Great Lakes. This applied to both common and contract carriers. The law required that both common and contract carriers file the *actual* rates they would charge rather than the maximum rates, and that a thirty-day notice be given on any rate changes. Again, this requirement was added to stabilize the pricing competition common in water transportation.

The structure of regulatory control over water freight transportation was changed significantly in the Water Carrier Act of 1940,[33] which became Part III of the Interstate Commerce Act. That act brought all water freight transportation within the continental United States under the jurisdiction of the ICC. Regulatory control of transoceanic shipping remained with the Maritime Commission, which succeeded the Shipping Board. The act allowed the ICC to control all minimum, maximum, and actual rates charged by water carriers, although no control was allowed over the operations of contract carriers. In that regard, the act prohibited a water carrier from operating as both a contract and a common carrier. The act also made consolidations or mergers subject to ICC approval to prevent any attempts to gain monopoly control. However, no con-

---

[31] P.L. 70–601.
[32] P.L. 72–415.
[33] P.L. 76–785.

trol was exercised over abandonment of operations, which made it easier for water carriers to leave the industry. To conform with the regulatory procedures applied to other modes, the act required all regulated carriers to publish all rates and to give a thirty-day notice of any intended rate changes.

One provision of the act that made the legislation virtually ineffective was a list of exemptions. Exempted from the act were the following:

1. Any shipments of commodities in bulk containing less than four commodities on one vessel.
2. All shipments of liquid cargoes in bulk.
3. All shipments by contract carriers.
4. All shipments by private carriers.
5. All shipments by small craft, with definition of the type of vessels stated in the act.

Thus, despite all the legislation, less than 15 per cent of all water freight shipments are under regulatory control. Consequently, the entire regulatory system of water freight transportation remains a hodgepodge of laws that do not regulate effectively.

Exemptions

The description of transportation laws has included various types of services or products that have been exempted from economic regulation. The general posture has been to exempt carriers when regulation would serve no useful purpose or would be an undue burden on performance of the transportation service.

Although each mode has some degree of exemption because private transportation is exempt in every mode, the extent of economic regulation exemption varies by mode.

The water industry enjoys the greatest degree of freedom, with less than 15 per cent of its volume subject to regulation by either the ICC or FMC. The railroad industry did not enjoy regulatory freedom until the 4–R Act of 1976. In that act, the deregulation attitude appeared in what was commonly referred to as the "Yoyo Clause," which allowed railroads to raise or lower their rates to a maximum of 7 per cent without the ICC's approval. In 1978, through a provision allowed in the 4–R Act, the ICC began to free rail carriers from regulations in specific instances when it believed that regulation would serve no useful purpose, represent an undue burden, and have no material effect on competition. The new attitude undoubtedly will affect the extent of economic regulation of rail carriers during the 1980s, a subject to be explored further in Chapter 18.

Motor carriers have been subject to the revised regulatory attitude. Exemptions from restrictions on private carrier backhauls started to appear in the late 1970s. Also, as a result of an ICC task force study, the commission proposed a new concept in 1979 known as *master certification,* wherein motor carriers would have been granted regulatory exemptions on commodities shipped in twelve different producing industry segments. The proposal specifically was outlawed in the trucking re-regulation enactment of July 1, 1980. However, the concept of master certification illustrates the ICC's attitude toward freeing the industry from tight control.

Air freight transportation has also enjoyed certain exemptions from economic regulation. As will be discussed in Chapter 12, air freight transportation was freed from most economic regulation in 1978. Before that, however, the CAB had been allowed to exempt air carriers when it was believed that regulation would represent an undue burden and serve no useful purpose.

The various laws discussed here have described the economic regulations imposed on each major transportation mode. In several instances, however, exemptions have reduced the burden on regulatory institutions and allowed some operating freedom for the carriers.

Department of Transportation Act

The final national law to be discussed was an attempt to coordinate all regulatory aspects of freight transportation. The many laws dealing with freight transportation resulted in three major regulatory bodies. The Interstate Commerce Commission was established to control the activities of the railroads, motor carriers, pipelines, and some domestic water carriers. The Civil Aeronautics Board controls the airline industry. The Federal Maritime Commission, formerly known as the United States Maritime Commission and the United States Shipping Board, controls other aspects of water transportation.

Many criticisms had been leveled against having three separate major agencies involved in regulating freight transportation. With such a fragmented approach, it was unlikely that a consistent policy toward transportation could be achieved. The idea of a single regulatory authority gained support. A single agency could coordinate all transportation activities and try to achieve the general objectives of the national transportation policy stated in the Transportation Act of 1940. After much discussion and debate, the Department of Transportation Act was passed by Congress in 1966.[34]

[34] P.L. 89–670.

The initial intention of the movement toward this act was not realized once it reached its final form. The creation of the Department of Transportation (DOT) placed that office in the cabinet of the president of the United States. Critics feared that too much power would be exercised by the president because the department secretary is a presidential appointee, and the political implications would be detrimental to the well-being of this important economic activity. Thus, the DOT materialized as much less than its original intended purpose. The department's role became administration of government policy toward the transportation industry. It was given no regulatory powers, except for safety matters pertaining to all modes.

In passing the act, many separate government agencies were combined, and various state commissions were to be coordinated by the DOT. The establishment of DOT grouped together the United States Coast Guard (USCG), the Federal Aviation Administration (FAA), the Federal Highway Administration (FHWA), the Federal Railroad Administration (FRA), the Urban Mass Transportation Administration (UMTA), the National Highway Traffic Safety Administration (NHTSA), and the St. Lawrence Seaway Development Corporation (SLSDC). In addition to operating administration for those agencies, DOT provided coordination for the Materials Transportation Bureau (MTB), which is responsible for hazardous materials and pipeline safety activities. The DOT was ordered to develop national policies and to make recommendations to the Congress that would result in a coordinated effort toward a balanced transportation system.

The separation of regulation and administration has often caused conflicts between the DOT and several regulatory agencies. Also, most of the recommendations forwarded to Congress generally have not resulted in legislation. However, the DOT has not been a complete failure. At the very least, the many agencies that once operated on their own are now under a single controlling unit.

Summary

The transportation conditions that existed in the last half of the nineteenth century led to the need for railroad transportation regulatory laws. State regulatory laws were established first, but these laws did not apply to shipments between states. Thus, a federal law was enacted to regulate interstate commerce. After passage of the Act to Regulate Commerce, several problems continued that required additional legislation to clarify the intent of the original act and to expand regulatory authority.

Regulatory authority eventually extended to pipelines, truck companies, water carriers, and airlines, with separate acts bringing these modes under control. The various laws resulted in three major regulatory bodies. The Department of Transportation, established in 1966 with the Department of Transportation Act, became the single controlling unit for many agencies that once operated on their own.

A new re-regulation effort emerged in the late 1970s and resulted in some sweeping legislation and proposals in the late 1970s and in 1980 relating to airline, motor, and rail transportation service.

To be effective, a policy requires law to ensure that objectives can be achieved. Then, some administrative procedure must be established to enforce those laws. In the history of transportation, various policies have been followed and many laws passed. Chapter 12 examines the regulatory system, the procedure for enforcing the laws that have been passed.

Questions for Chapter 11

1. For what transportation reasons were state regulatory commissions established?
2. What was the main impact of the *Munn* v. *Illinois* Supreme Court decision?
3. What major transportation regulation issue was presented in the Supreme Court's Wabash Case decision?
4. What kinds of pressures led to enactment of the Act to Regulate Commerce of 1887?
5. Detail the scope of the Act to Regulate Commerce of 1887.
6. What were the provisions of the Elkins Act of 1903?
7. By what manner did the Rule of Rate Making and the Recapture Clause of the Transportation Act of 1920 intend to preserve the financial stability of the railroad industry?
8. In what way were railroad rate bureaus exempted from antitrust violations?
9. Name the major legislative acts of the 1970s dealing with the railroads' financial condition and describe their provisions.
10. Discuss the notable differences between the regulatory aspects of the Act to Regulate Commerce of 1887 and the Motor Carrier Act of 1935.
11. Name the governmental bodies legislatively established to regulate the major transportation modes.
12. List the types of water transportation shipments that were exempt from regulation.

12

Regulatory Institutions

Chapter 11 reviewed some of the major legislative laws affecting transportation. Those laws would be ineffective unless some method existed to ensure compliance and to protect the rights of all involved parties. This chapter examines the major federal institutions involved in the transportation regulatory process.

It should be noted at the outset that during the late 1970s the status of the regulatory bodies and transportation regulation began to undergo drastic revisions. This text describes the regulatory climate as it existed in the middle of 1980 and incorporates changes that had occurred up to that time. Undoubtedly, revisions in regulation will occur more rapidly than ever before as the 1980s unfold.

Necessity of Regulatory Institutions

With each of the major laws through which the federal government intervened in transportation activities, a regulatory body was assigned or created to oversee the modes and to ensure compliance with the legislation. In addition to the major regulatory agencies, other governmental units, such as the Federal Trade Commission and the Department of Justice, affected transportation regulation. Often, various court decisions outside the regulatory stream have had an impact on carrier operations as well.

The regulators of the transportation network of the United States have been given the authority and responsibility to ensure that industry participants comply with the variety of regulations in existence. Enforcement is intended not only to protect the rights of the participants, but also to ensure the well-being of society through an efficient transportation network.

In performing their functions, regulatory institutions exercise a great deal of control. The regulatory functions can be classified as entry, rate, structural, financial, operating, and enforcement controls.

ENTRY CONTROL

If too many competitors exist within a single mode, competition suffers because each carrier's market share may be too small to justify providing the service. Each carrier invests large amounts of money to maintain facilities and vehicles. If the assets are underutilized, freight charges must be higher to cover total costs. Carriers maintain similar types of assets in order to service users. For simplicity, assume that the cost of facilities maintained between two cities is $1,000 per year for each carrier. Also, assume that there is a total of 1,000 tons to be transported each year between the two cities. Table 12–1 shows the minimum charge that must be assessed to cover facility costs.

186

TABLE 12–1. Freight Charge Comparison Based on Number of Carriers

Number of Carriers	Tons Per Carrier	Minimum Freight Charge
1	1,000	$1.00
2	500	2.00
4	250	4.00

In an attempt to keep too many carriers from competing for the same volume of traffic and increasing transportation costs, *entry control* is exercised by the regulators. This control keeps out of the competitive arena more carriers than are economically necessary to perform the desired level of transportation service.

Before a carrier is allowed to perform a transportation service between two locations, a Certificate of Public Convenience and Necessity (CPCN) must be obtained from the appropriate regulatory body. Application for a CPCN must be supported by proof that the carrier is "fit, willing, and able" to perform the service. Before the late 1970's deregulation thrust and the 1980 legislation, applications for CPCN's also had to prove that a need for the service existed. If carriers were currently providing adequate service to the users, there was no public need for another competitor. By exercising entry control, the regulating body protects both the public and the competition from high transportation costs. However, the 1980 legislation described in the previous chapter relaxed these entry controls considerably.

RATE CONTROL

A large part of the need for regulatory control over transportation carriers arose from rate issues. In some cases, rates charged to users were unreasonably high, which exploited freight shippers and discouraged product movements. In other cases, different rates were charged for identical shipments. In still other cases, shippers were charged higher rates for shorter hauls than other users were assessed for longer movements over essentially the same routes. For these reasons, the regulatory institutions were given authority over *rate control*.

In some cases, this control involves the power to set maximum rates. By exercising this power, the regulators can prevent undue exploitation of users who need the service and have no alternative method of shipment. The regulatory bodies were also given authority to set minimum rates. Doing so prevents carriers from undercharging on some shipments to gain a competitive advantage. In some cases, regulators have the authority to set actual rates. This aspect of rate control concerns the *level of rates*, control of which has been attacked vigorously by deregulation proponents.

Various transportation laws gave regulators the power to require that rates be published thirty days in advance. This gives other carriers and shippers the opportunity to protest the action if they so wish. This aspect of rate control concerns the *public knowledge of rates.*

In the past, carriers had favored some shippers over others by charging lower rates. This extended to favoring some industries over others, especially if the carriers were selective about the types of commodities they wished to haul. To avoid such favoritism, regulators were given authority to ensure that no discrimination was practiced that favored specific shippers. In particular, all users were to be charged the same rates for identical shipments, and no deviations were permitted. This aspect of rate control concerns the *consistency of rates.* In other industries, the Federal Trade Commission (FTC) is responsible for protection from discrimination. Transportation deregulation proponents believe that the FTC can continue to do this, which would shift the responsibility from one regulator to another.

STRUCTURAL CONTROL

The structure of transportation carriers within a mode, that is, the physical characteristics of the carriers, has been controlled by the regulatory bodies. For example, if a rail carrier wanted to extend service into another city by adding new tracks, permission was necessary. Usually, this involved a CPCN. Although this form of authority could be considered entry control, it also affects the physical characteristics of participating carriers.

The past two decades have seen a rash of various types of carrier mergers and consolidations within a single transportation mode. Whenever two or more carriers combine their operations and form a single company, the structure of both the competition and the carriers is changed. There is less competition within a community if carriers combine, and the potential for monopoly power increases. Another type of structural change involves physical facility arrangement. Duplicate tracks and other facilities can be combined into one operation. Therefore, any consolidation or merger had to be approved by the regulatory body to ensure that the public interest was protected.

Another type of combination is known as a *pooling agreement.* These agreements are in violation of the Interstate Commerce Act. The act makes illegal any contract, agreement, or combination of carriers for the purpose of pooling, or combining, arrangements to offer transportation service. Efforts of the carriers to divide potential volume among themselves so that each services particular customers in a given territory was also illegal. Similarly, any division among the carriers of revenues or profits based on such action is illegal. The trucking re-regulation of 1980 legalized pooling agreements between and among carriers if they would be in the interest of better public service or of economy of operation.

FINANCIAL CONTROL

Financial matters are a major concern in transportation, particularly because the financial condition of the carriers has been taken into consideration in rate increase requests, as mandated in the Transportation Act of 1920. Accounting practices differ from company to company in the same industry, as well as among industries. Also, the methods of handling various costs have a great deal of flexibility in application. If the carriers used this information in attempting to obtain increased rates, then the method by which the data were recorded must have some degree of consistency. Then, each factor in accounting reports could be compared between companies and would have the same meaning for all involved parties. The regulatory bodies, therefore, were given control to guide the financial reporting systems of all carriers within their jurisdiction. They were allowed to dictate the accounting methods and standards to be used by all carriers in preparing financial reports. Items such as depreciation receive a great deal of attention, because the methods used to account for them could have a significant impact on the alleged financial condition of any company.

The regulators could also require any types of financial reports from any carriers within their jursidiction, particularly to determine the financial condition of the company and its stability within the industry. In addition, any carriers' actions relating to securities were to be approved. If a carrier were to issue additional stock on the open market or to purchase back large blocks of securities from the open market, the action would have to be approved by the appropriate regulatory agency as well as meet the requirements of the Securities and Exchange Commission (SEC). Because financial controls exist for any corporation listed in the United States stock exchanges, proponents of deregulation suggest that transportation financial controls be handled by the SEC. This is another instance of transferring the responsibility from one regulator to another.

OPERATING CONTROL

Each regulatory institution was made responsible for the ability of the modes under its jurisdiction to perform the transportation service demanded by the public and the various governments. The safety and adequacy of that service was to be ensured. To carry out these responsibilities, the regulators were given control over the operations of the carriers. For highway shipments, the regulatory body could dictate which routes could be driven by trucks serving two points. It also could dictate the maximum number of hours a day a driver could drive so as to protect the safety of other highway users. The trucking re-regulation legislation removed the ICC's authority to restrict the routes to be followed by motor carriers, allowing them to apply the most direct method to provide the required transportation service.

Operating controls extended to the other transportation modes, particularly railroad transportation. The regulators could dictate exactly which routes to follow for any shipment. Those routes could be changed on short notice if a need arose. Short-notice route changes could be ordered to avoid an unsafe bridge or to return empty rail cars rapidly.

Other operating controls extended into such areas as equipment standards, insurance, and transportation of hazardous materials. Unsafe tracks can cause a catastrophe in any community if a derailment occurs. Thus, the regulators could dictate minimum equipment standards to protect the public. Transportation users are entitled to some assurance that the commodities turned over to the carriers are reasonably protected. Therefore, the regulators could dictate the required level of insurance coverage. Transportation of hazardous materials is potentially the most dangerous type of shipment. Therefore, strict standards have been enforced by the regulators with regard to vehicle types and condition, containers used, bracing required, and any other necessary safeguards. Under the deregulation thrust, operating control responsibility is transferred to the Department of Transportation and implemented after the president declares a state of emergency. Thus, the carriers would be much freer to conduct daily operations. Whether operating effectiveness would be improved is a question still not answered.

ENFORCEMENT CONTROL

Both the laws passed by Congress and the orders, rules, and regulations issued by the regulatory bodies had to be enforced if they were to have any effect. Thus, the regulators were given broad *enforcement control*. In exercising this control, regulatory institution representatives can make routine checks on any carriers within their jurisdiction. These policing powers allow a regulator representative to visit any carrier location to check the records being maintained on all shipments, accounting practices, condition of facilities and equipment, and all other aspects of transportation service. If performance does not conform, the investigator can issue orders for compliance. The order might range from a simple request for adjustments to prosecution of the violating carrier.

Enforcement control includes investigations resulting from complaints forwarded to the regulatory institution by shippers or other carriers. In the investigation, the regulator seeks out relevant facts and attempts to resolve the issue. The regulator attempts to resolve disputes between carriers or issues between carriers and shippers in a manner satisfactory to all involved parties. However, if this is not possible, a formal procedure can be used, which will be discussed later in the chapter.

This section has described the conditions that partially justify the existence of regulatory institutions and has detailed the types of control that have been exercised by those agencies. Not all modes have been regulated in the same manner or to the same extent. The degree of control over each mode will be discussed later in this chapter in a review of specific agencies. Let us first examine the status of regulatory institutions.

Status of Regulatory Institutions

Transportation regulatory institutions have had a tremendous amount of responsibility in contributing to the well-being of the economy, society, and living standards in addition to ensuring an adequate transportation system. They have had to ensure that all communities who needed and wanted freight transportation would have adequate service. They have had to ensure that carriers maintain both a required level of service and the equipment and facilities to provide that service on a regular basis. Through regulatory actions, they have been responsible for an efficient transportation system with the lowest possible cost and the best use of available resources. They have had to be sure that society was not in danger from the transportation equipment used or the service level offered. In their long-range planning efforts, the regulatory bodies have been responsible for the continuing progress of the carriers so that the total transportation system remains the best and most advanced in the world.

Within the industry, regulating institutions have to ensure that fair and reasonable carrier charges are assessed. They also ensure that the competitive environment is free from unfair business practices so that carriers can compete equally, and that industries are treated with fairness so that no one is placed at a competitive disadvantage. The regulators are responsible for the financial stability of the industry and the financial soundness of the carriers. Finally, the regulatory institutions are responsible for resolving transportation disputes and seeing that all violations have been corrected.

Because of the magnitude of these responsibilities, the American public attaches considerable status to the regulatory institutions and to the members who make up the executive and administrative staffs. Those staffs are expected to be well qualified to carry out stated responsibilities. The commissioners, the highest ranking officials in regulatory institutions, are expected to be experts in their respective fields because their actions and decisions have such far-reaching effects.

In carrying out their responsibilities, it is important that the commissioners and their staffs be totally free from prejudices or favoritism. They cannot be biased for or against any particular carrier within a mode. Nor can preferences be allowed in the treatment of one mode or another, or any shipper or industry over another. In addition, the regulatory institutions are required to be free of outside influences, including that of the federal government. Political control cannot be exercised over regulatory bodies. Commissioners are appointed for long terms by the president, with Senate approval. They cannot be relieved of their duties without proper cause, which is defined as malfeasance, or mispractice of their office. Thus, even the president cannot exercise influence over the regulatory institutions.

Regulators act mainly as fact finders. They conduct investigations and hearings to determine facts, and all decisions, rules, and orders are based on that factual evidence. All such decisions are considered binding. Congresses have given the regulatory bodies the authority to make rules and issue decisions, and the courts will not intercede. However, any rules or decisions based on *interpretation* of laws, rather than *administration* of laws, are subject to further court actions. Only the courts are allowed to interpret the laws passed by the United States Congress. Although the regulatory institutions have been given the authority to rule on interpretation of evidence without the appeal to the courts by the offended party, it is recognized that any issue's technicalities make almost all cases subject to appeal. Legal maneuvering can, in fact, press most matters as interpretation of laws.

The regulatory institutions have no power or authority to legislate, that is, to make laws. However, they regularly recommend legislation needed to achieve the major objectives of regulation. For example, the Elkins, Hepburn, and Mann-Elkins Acts, described in Chapter 11, were remedial laws suggested to correct misinterpretations or to relieve problems created by the original Act to Regulate Commerce. These laws were processed by Congress, the only body with the power to legislate. In all cases, laws recommended by the transportation regulatory institutions have been directed to achieving a unified, smoothly operating network.

Until now, regulatory institutions have been discussed in general terms, dealing with those topics that apply to all transportation regulation and are common to all of the regulatory bodies. Let us now examine the individual regulatory institutions.

Major Transportation Regulatory Institutions

As it became necessary for the federal government to intercede in transportation activities, enforcement procedures were developed. As previously stated, an enforcement procedure is required to guarantee that the laws are not ignored or violated. Thus, as each transportation mode came under federal control, the authority and power of enforcement had to be assigned to a responsible agency. As government organizations exist today, three major agencies, the Interstate Commerce Commission (ICC), Federal Maritime Commission (FMC), and

Civil Aeronautics Board (CAB) are primarily responsible for regulating transportation. Although these three agencies have many similarities, they differ in several important respects.

In addition to these three major regulating agencies, several other governmental units have been involved in one way or another in transportation regulation. For example, the Federal Trade Commission (FTC) has made decisions that affect the structure and operations of the transportation network, as has the court system. These matters will be discussed later in the chapter.

The Interstate Commerce Commission (ICC) is the oldest, largest, and, perhaps, most important transportation regulation institution. The major transportation modes under the jurisdiction of the ICC are the railroads, motor carriers, inland and Great Lakes water carriers, and freight forwarders. The ICC is the only regulatory institution that has maintained its original name throughout its history.

The Federal Maritime Commission (FMC) oversees common carriage by water carriers in domestic offshore and overseas transportation and water terminal operations. It has limited control over the entire water transportation network, as discussed in Chapter 11. The FMC, the latest of several regulating institutions involved with water transportation, has undergone a series of name changes.

Air transportation regulation was affected dramatically by some major laws of the 1970s. In 1977, Congress modified the Federal Aviation Act of 1958 with a new law[1] that reduced the regulation of air freight. This was followed by the Air Deregulation Act of 1978,[2] which had a greater impact on deregulating air freight transportation. The Civil Aeronautics Board (CAB) regulates air freight transportation. As with the FMC, the CAB has had a series of name changes throughout the history of air freight regulation.

Interstate Commerce Commission

As the federal government takes on new functions, it needs some way to administer the additional authority and duties. After years of investigations, discussions, and debates, the federal government moved into the area of transportation regulation. The ICC, established to fulfill the responsibilities assumed through the Act to Regulate Commerce of 1887, has become the largest transportation regulating agency in the United States. This section will review the origin, composition, authority, organization, operating procedures, and budget of the ICC.

[1] P.L. 95–163.
[2] P.L. 95–504.

ORIGIN

The Act to Regulate Commerce stated ". . . that a Commission is hereby created and established to be known as the Inter-State Commerce Commission, which shall be composed of five Commissioners, who shall be appointed by the President, by and with the advice and consent of the Senate."[3] With this act, the Forty-ninth Congress established the first transportation regulatory commission in the United States. Totally free enterprise in interstate transportation had come to an end. As discussed in Chapter 11, the act resulted from pressure exercised by state commissions, the Granger Movement, several railroad companies, and many shippers.

COMPOSITION

Initially, the ICC was composed of five commissioners. As regulatory problems increased, the number of commissioners was increased to seven, and today there are eleven seats on the ICC. The commissioners serve a term of seven years. The act also stated that "any commissioner may be removed by the President for inefficiency, neglect of duty, or malfeasance in office."[4] Before 1970, the chairman's position rotated among the commissioners. Since then, the chairman of the ICC has been appointed by the president. However, the influence of the executive branch ends at that point. The agency is independent of reporting authority to any federal office or department and is answerable only to the Congress.

AUTHORITY

At first, the ICC's authority was loosely defined. The act stated:

that the Commission hereby created shall have authority to inquire into the management of the business of all common carriers subject to the provisions of this act, and shall keep itself informed as to the manner and method in which the same is conducted, and shall have the right to obtain from such common carriers full and complete information necessary to enable the Commission to perform the duties and carry out the objects for which it was created.[5]

Different parts of the original act listed some of the specific areas that were to be influenced by the ICC, and the remedial acts described in Chapter 11 defined additional areas of authority more explicitly. Generally, the ICC's power has been exercised in all of the entry, rate, structural, financial, operating, and enforcement controls described earlier in this chapter. As described by the ICC, the agency's functions and responsibilities include the following:

---

[3] Act to Regulate Commerce, 24 Stat. 383.
[4] Ibid.
[5] Ibid.

1. Issue rules for the protection of consumers who move household goods.
2. Aid the consumer whose only other recourse in a transportation dispute would be to go to court.
3. Offer rail and bus passengers an alternative channel for complaints other than the carriers themselves.
4. Assure stability of service so that shippers and the general public can have a dependable transport system at reasonable prices.
5. Protect the public against unlawful carrier practices.
6. Certify that carriers have the necessary fitness to serve the public.
7. Provide assurance that carriers must be properly responsible in case of loss or damage.
8. Require common carriers to serve everyone who wishes to purchase transportation.
9. Settle disputes between shippers and carriers and among carriers.
10. Ensure that small towns and communities receive service.
11. Prevent shippers from wringing unlawful concessions out of carriers.
12. Protect the public against monopoly pricing and destructive competition.
13. Ensure through rate regulation that new products can be developed and marketed.[6]

At the time of the original act, not many modes were competing for freight traffic. Therefore, the act applied to all railroad companies performing in interstate commerce. Water common carriers also came under the ICC's jurisdiction when shipments were rail-water combinations. As time passed, pipelines, motor carriers, and inland water common carriers were added, along with freight forwarders, which were included officially in 1950.

In regulating the activities of the common carriers under its authority, the ICC has several duties. These duties are defined by Professor Charles A. Taff as follows:

1. Duty to grant carriers operating authority, which includes, for railroads, authority to construct or abandon lines.
2. Duty to prescribe rules governing the publication of rates, fares, and charges, together with power to conduct investigations and hold hearings to determine the justness and reasonableness of new or changed rates.
3. Duty to authorize consolidations and mergers, the issuance of securities, and—in the case of railroads—approval of reorganizations in bankruptcy.
4. Duty to provide uniform systems of accounts and to ensure compliance therewith, set up depreciation rates to determine the costs of rail transportation, and maintain inventories of original costs and land values of railroads and pipelines.
5. Duty to prescribe regulations governing the publication and filing of rates and charges, and ensure compliance therewith; and adjudicate complaint proceedings involving tariff interpretation, justness and reasonableness, and discrimination.

[6] U.S. Interstate Commerce Commission, *Interstate Commerce Commission 1977 Annual Report*, p. 4.

6. Duty to prescribe and administer regulations governing the filing of liability insurance by motor carriers and freight forwarders.
7. Duty to prescribe regulations governing the use, control, distribution, and interchange of locomotives and cars, and ensure compliance therewith.
8. Duty to investigate violations by carriers of the Interstate Commerce Act and related acts, and assist the Department of Justice in the prosecution thereof.
9. Duty to provide statistical information and analyses of carrier finances, physical characteristics, operations, and traffic to afford guidance in regulatory problems.
10. Long-range planning and public counsel service through Rail Service Planning Office.[7]

The duties of the ICC did not change substantially over the initial years of its operation. However, during the 1970s the interpretation and performance of ICC duties became more relaxed. For example, all railroad transportation freight movements had been under strict regulation. During the late 1970s, however, the ICC authorized the exemption of certain movements if it could be determined that regulation served no useful purpose. Also, merger attempts were viewed more favorably by the ICC in an effort to improve the financial stability of the railroad industry. During the late 1970s, the ICC began to allow private motor carriers to contract for backhauls that otherwise would have been empty mileage. In addition, the ICC began to apply more liberal decisions regarding transportation issues in keeping with the formal announcement by President Carter that he intended to push for drastic re-regulation of motor freight transportation.[8]

ORGANIZATION

It should be obvious that the ICC's scope of authority and duties require a substantial organizational structure. Human resources must be made available to accomplish whatever tasks are required to carry out responsibilities. If the responsibilities are extensive, then many people are needed. As the number of people is increased, the duties are separated into categories and an organizational structure is developed. As the number of regulated freight carriers increased and traffic volume grew, the ICC regulatory system expanded to accommodate the growth. The result was a sophisticated organization with divided responsibilities, all integrated to carry out the ICC's full authority. The organizational arrangement shown in Figure 12–1 can be divided into two areas: administrative and operational.

ADMINISTRATIVE

The ICC's administrative arm consists of eleven commissioners appointed by the president. One of these commissioners is appointed as chairman, also by

[7] Charles A. Taff, *Management of Physical Distribution and Transportation*, 6th ed. (Homewood, Ill.: Richard D. Irwin, Inc., 1978), p. 560.
[8] "Key Senator Says Trucking Deregulation Faces 'Problems' as Carter Launches Bill," *Wall Street Journal* (June 22, 1979), p. 5.

FIGURE 12–1. INTERSTATE COMMERCE COMMISSION ORGANIZATION[1]

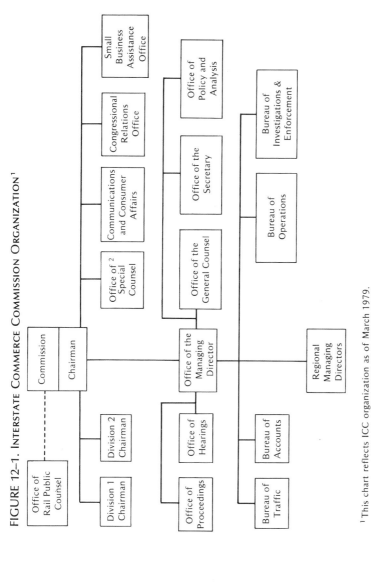

[1] This chart reflects ICC organization as of March 1979.
The text of the Annual Report reflects organization prior to October 1, 1978.

[2] Subject to administrative supervision of the chairman but in all other respects shall be accountable to the Commission.

– – – – – – Independent Office

197

the president, and serves as the executive head of the ICC. He has general responsibility for the following:

1. Overall management and functioning of the Commission.
2. Formulation of plans and policies designed to assure the effectiveness of the Commission and the administration of the Act.
3. Identification and early resolution of major regulatory problems.
4. Development and utilization of effective staff support to carry out the duties and functions of the Commission.[9]

A vice chairman, elected annually by the commissioners, fills in for the chairman when necessary. The other nine commissioners take part in formal proceedings, which will be described later in this chapter. In addition, each commissioner serves on one of the two administrative divisions shown in Figure 12–1. Prior to 1977, the ICC maintained three divisional sections, each with specific interests regarding the nature of issues in which it became involved. Division I handled operating rights matters; Division II was concerned with rates and practices issues; and Division III concerned itself with financial and service problems. Under that arrangement, three commissioners served on each division. In late 1977, the number of commission appointments was reduced by administration decision. At the end of 1979, only seven commissioners served on the ICC, although eleven still are permitted by law, and the divisional structure was revised. Two divisions emerged, with assignment to each made on a rotating basis. Cases are assigned to either division alternately, with neither division specializing in a particular area of concern. The nature of the matters handled by these divisions is described later in this chapter.

OPERATIONAL

The administrative arm of ICC needs a great deal of support service to aid in its operations. These services are provided by eleven offices and five bureaus.

OFFICE OF THE MANAGING DIRECTOR. The managing director is a permanent employee of the ICC. This office, perhaps the most important in the ICC, coordinates the activities of all components of the commission. It directs the activities with regard to personnel, money, materials, and methods.

OFFICE OF THE SECRETARY. All ICC orders and decisions are issued through this office, which is the custodian of the seal and all records. This office is the issuances and documentations center of the ICC.

OFFICE OF THE GENERAL COUNSEL. Legal advice is provided to the ICC by this office. The advice relates to various laws that affect, or are affected by, the ICC's orders and decisions. It also defends ICC actions in court, if necessary.

OFFICE OF HEARINGS. Any hearings required to discuss both sides of an issue confronting the ICC are conducted by this office. The issues may involve any of the ICC's areas of responsibility and authority. This office is staffed by administrative law judges.

[9]*Interstate Commerce Commission 1977 Annual Report,* p. 5.

OFFICE OF PROCEEDINGS. All formal and informal proceedings are processed through this office. All applications are examined and documentation validated here. It prepares official notification of ICC activities as required by law.

OFFICE OF COMMUNICATIONS AND CONSUMER AFFAIRS. Any public or consumer requests for information or aid are handled through this office. A newsroom is maintained for press assistance.

SMALL BUSINESS ASSISTANCE OFFICE. Small businesses are assisted in finding required transportation services through this office. It also assists companies wishing to participate in providing transportation service.

OFFICE OF RAIL PUBLIC COUNSEL. This office was created in 1976 to ensure that the public interest would be protected during and after the restructuring and combination of bankrupt railroads in the northeast quadrant of the United States. Its function continues by assisting the ICC in determining the nature of the public interest.

OFFICE OF CONGRESSIONAL RELATIONS. This office is responsible for maintaining relations with all members of Congress, apprising them of ICC activities and direction. It also reviews suggestions and recommendations from Congressional representatives.

OFFICE OF SPECIAL COUNSEL. The ICC is aided in determining the public interest through this office. The ICC's responsiveness to public need is increased through this office's efforts.

OFFICE OF POLICY AND ANALYSIS. Future surface transportation needs are studied in this office. It also coordinates the ICC's policy and planning function for long-range plans. It currently assists the ICC in analyzing major railroad networks and the impact of potential mergers as they fit into a major railroad network.

BUREAU OF ACCOUNTS. Carrier accounting procedures and practices are this bureau's major concern. Uniform accounting rules have been prescribed so that all carriers can be evaluated on the same basis. This bureau also reviews carriers' financial reports and audits their books.

BUREAU OF ECONOMICS. Transportation research, economic, and statistical studies are performed by this bureau. The ICC must be aware of the economic climate of the country or an industry if it is to perform its function properly. (Not illustrated in Figure 12–1.)

BUREAU OF INVESTIGATIONS AND ENFORCEMENT. This bureau is the ICC's prosecutor. It is responsible for investigating any violations of transportation statutes and assisting in the prosecution of violators after developing facts and issues.

BUREAU OF OPERATIONS. This bureau monitors the operations of regulated carriers. It ensures that operations are in compliance with ICC rules and regulations and develops suggestions on needed ICC orders to maintain adequate service.

BUREAU OF TRAFFIC. This bureau's area of responsibility concerns the freight rates charged by carriers. It maintains carriers' tariffs, suspends proposed rate

199

changes if an investigation is necessary, and offers advice concerning tariff and rate applications.

It is evident that regulation of any industry is a complex task, involving many people and large sums of money. However, if it is determined that an industry must be regulated, the proper vehicle must be provided to perform the required regulatory activities. All of the ICC offices and bureaus are involved in a regular routine of activities to ensure compliance with the desired level of regulation. The following section describes some of the procedures employed to decide the issues brought before the ICC.

PROCEDURES

The large number of regulated carriers has assured a steady stream of issues brought before the ICC. Fortunately, the full eleven-member commission has not been required to resolve each matter. In fact, only matters of general transportation importance have ever reached the full commission. More than twenty three-member boards, composed of high-ranking individuals with transportation expertise, have been created to resolve most of the issues brought before the ICC. After investigating the matter, these boards render a decision, which stands as if decided by the full commission. The decision may be appealed to one of the two administrative divisions mentioned earlier. If the division agrees to review the decision, the matter is investigated and a decision is then rendered by the division. The same opportunity exists to appeal this second decision. If the issue is of general transportation importance, the full commission may agree to review the issue. If the full commission agrees, all evidence is presented, and the commission renders a final decision after a hearing. The matter may be appealed to the courts only if it is a question of *interpretation of the law*. An appeal cannot be made to the court system if the issue is *interpretation of the evidence*. The courts have ruled that the Congress has given the ICC full authority to interpret evidence related to transportation matters, and it respects the ICC's level of expertise in this regard.

Two procedures have been used to resolve issues forwarded to the ICC: the *informal* and the *formal* procedure. In addition, the formal procedure may be handled by a *modified* (or *shortened*) procedure, at the discretion of the ICC. The specific details of each procedure are described in the *General Rules of Practice Before the Interstate Commerce Commission*.[10] These rules are in compliance with the Administrative Procedures Act of 1946.[11]

INFORMAL

Many times, a complaint received by the ICC against a carrier has not been serious, or was not a matter that required a hearing. For example, a shipper

[10] U.S. Interstate Commerce Commission, *Interstate Commerce Commission General Rules of Practice*, 1977.
[11] P.L. 79–404.

200

may complain that an empty railcar for loading was not provided within a reasonable time period. Such isolated situations are not matters that require hearings between the carrier, shipper, and ICC personnel. Under the informal procedure, the carrier is notified of the complaint by mail. The carrier responds to the ICC by mail, and the complainant is notified. Several letters may be exchanged before the matter is finally resolved. If an issue exists and the ICC makes a decision, the shipper or carrier may appeal the decision by requesting a formal procedure. The appeal must be made within six months of the initial decision.

The informal procedure has many advantages. First, it is handled entirely by letter, and all evidence is stated in writing by the involved parties. Second, the matter generally will be resolved in a short time. Third, a greater number of issues can be resolved, which reduces the backlog of open cases. Finally, savings in time, effort, and money are substantial for all parties involved, including the ICC. In contrast, the formal procedure is much more time-consuming and expensive for all parties.

FORMAL

Matters of greater significance than those handled by the informal procedure are processed formally. A complaint must be forwarded on an ICC form established specifically for that purpose. The carrier's response is sought and both sides of the issue are reviewed. A decision is then made as to whether a modified procedure should be used. Generally, the involved parties are asked to approve the use of the modified procedure, but the ICC can insist that it be used, and the other parties must abide by that decision. Under the modified procedure, all facts and relevant information are requested to be sent by mail. A hearing may be held for a specific item in the complaint but not on the entire matter. After a review of all evidence, a decision is rendered and is final, unless appealed to one of the ICC's divisions.

The formal complaint procedure is much more complicated than the informal. The issue is given a docket number, a chronological numbering system used to identify complaints or issues. The carrier is notified of the issue and is given a stipulated period of time in which to respond. A hearing date is set and then conducted before an administrative law judge. At the hearing, the opposing views are presented and all relevant information, data, and evidence are offered. At these hearings, other parties not named in the complaint may testify before the law judge. For example, if a carrier wants to reduce rates between two points and a complaint has been made by other carriers, a shipper may testify that the reduced rate is necessary. At the end of the hearing, the law judge sets a date by which each party must submit a brief, a summary of position and evidence. After deliberating the briefs and hearing transcripts, the administrative law judge renders a tentative decision. This decision is final, unless changed by the commission or appealed by either party. If the appeal is granted, an ICC division may hold a hearing, requiring all parties to gather once more. The division's decision may be appealed to the full commission. If the issue is of general transportation importance, the full commission will hold a hearing. Its decision may then be appealed to the courts if a matter of law interpretation is involved.

The formal procedure is more complicated than the modified or informal procedures. Several months may pass before a formal hearing is scheduled, and some issues have taken years to be resolved. The procedures described here, as well as the vast array of offices and bureaus required to perform the ICC's activities, require substantial budgets and personnel.

BUDGET

The ICC represents the largest expenditure for transportation regulatory institutions. Table 12–2 lists the budget for the ICC's activities since 1950. Also shown is the average number of employees for those years. The budget has increased more than 500 per cent, although the number of employees has not changed drastically. It should be noted that because the budget alloca-

TABLE 12–2. Interstate Commerce Commission Statement of Budget and Average Employment, 1950–1978

Year	Appropriation	Average Employment	Year	Appropriation	Average Employment
1951	$11,408,200	2,072.3	1966	$27,540,000	2,375.8
1952	11,264,035	1,889.5	1967	*27,169,000	†1,928.9
1953	11,003,500	1,849.4	1968	23,846,000	1,899.0
1954	11,284,000	1,837.9	1969	24,664,000	1,808.1
1955	11,679,655	1,859.1	1970	27,742,660	1,801.9
1956	12,896,000	1,902.2	1971	28,442,000	1,730.7
1957	14,879,696	2,090.1	1972	30,640,000	1,676.2
1958	17,412,375	2,237.8	1973	33,720,000	1,765.4
1959	18,747,800	2,268.1	1974	40,681,000	1,873.7
1960	19,650,000	2,343.6	1975	44,970,000	1,985.6
1961	21,451,500	2,386.1	1976	52,455,000	2,049.0
1962	22,075,000	2,399.7	TQ	12,290,000	2,135.7
1963	23,502,800	2,412.8	1977	60,786,000	2,116.6
1964	24,670,000	2,407.8	1978	65,575,000	2,110.0
1965	26,715,000	2,339.1	1979	70,400,000	2,103.0

*Excludes $1,310,000 transferred to the Department of Transportation (Public Law 89–670) approved Oct. 15, 1966, and determination order of the Director of the Office of Management and Budget which authorized transfer of funds as of Apr. 1, 1967.

†Excludes average employment for those functions transferred to the Department of Transportation effective April 1, 1967.

Source: Interstate Commerce Commission 1978 Annual Report (Washington, D.C.: U.S. Government Printing Office, 1978), p. 130.

N.B. TQ on the above table indicates the transitional quarter when some of the ICC activities were transferred to the DOT.

TABLE 12–3. Interstate Commerce Commission Activities: 1978–1980

	1978 (Actual)	1979 (Estimate)	1980 (Estimate)
1. Formal Proceedings			
A. Formal Cases	11,000	11,500	13,000
B. Informal Cases	21,640	23,850	23,850
2. Compliance and Enforcement			
A. Enforcement Actions	602	691	740
B. Insurance Reviews	5,560	5,650	5,890
C. Consumer Complaints Handled	90,720	94,320	98,630
D. Investigations and Compliance Surveys	9,894	10,229	10,320
3. Financial Oversight; Audits and Analyses	2,266	2,317	2,337
4. Tariff Examination			
A. Tariffs Filed	389,642	370,000	370,000
B. Consumer Examinations	246,346	250,000	250,000
C. Rule Relief Applications Processed	5,199	5,298	5,300
D. Interpretations and Complaints Handled	5,096	4,909	4,966

Source: Appendix to the Budget of the United States Government for Fiscal Year 1980, p. 928.

tions do not measure constant dollars, the inflationary rise of the dollar is not considered.

To give you a better understanding of the number of issues handled by the ICC that justify the budget and personnel, Table 12–3 summarizes the activities involved in one year's operation and the estimates for 1979 and 1980.

Federal Maritime Commission

Water transportation has never been under the exclusive jurisdiction of one regulatory body. You will recall that the ICC was given regulatory authority over water transportation in the Act to Regulate Commerce of 1887, if the shipment was in conjunction with a railroad haul. Since that time, the ICC has retained regulatory authority over some types of water transportation, particularly domestic interstate shipments over the Great Lakes and other inland waterways. But a separate regulatory agency with jurisdiction over other types of water transportation has existed since 1916. The United States Shipping Act created the United States Shipping Board. The Board's jurisdiction covered

American flag vessels involved in foreign commerce. Its economic regulatory powers were minimal, concerned mostly with establishing maximum rates. Its major activities focused on the operation of vessels and the protection of water carriers from unfair or discriminatory practices. A greater degree of economic regulation came about with the creation of the United States Maritime Commission, now known as the Federal Maritime Commission (FMC). This section will review the origin, composition, authority, organization, operating procedures, and budget of the FMC.

ORIGIN

The Merchant Marine Act of 1936 created the United States Maritime Commission to enforce the water transportation regulatory powers contained in the act. Both the name of the commission and its scope of authority have changed many times since then. The United States Maritime Commission replaced the United States Shipping Board, which had been in existence since 1916. The Maritime Commission remained in existence until it was abolished in a federal reorganization plan in 1950. The Federal Maritime Board (FMB) was created in its place and was placed in the Department of Commerce for administrative purposes. Another federal reorganization plan, this time in 1961, abolished the FMB and replaced it with the Federal Maritime Commission (FMC). At that time, the FMC became an independent regulatory agency not placed within any other federal department. Thus, no political influence can be exercised over its regulatory practices or decisions.

COMPOSITION

The number of members of the water transportation regulating agency has changed more often than the institution's name or scope of authority. For instance, the United States Shipping Board, which was created in 1916, had five members. The membership was increased to seven by the Transportation Act of 1920, but then was decreased to three by the Intercoastal Shipping Act of 1933. When the United States Maritime Commission was created by the Merchant Marine Act of 1936, it specified five members. This was reduced to three when the FMB was created in 1950. Then, the 1961 reorganization that created the FMC provided for a membership of five.

Currently, the FMC has five commissioners. They are appointed by the president for a five-year term, and the appointments must be approved by the United States Senate. No more than three commissioners may be from the same political party, in order to provide some balance in its regulatory direction. As with other regulatory agencies, the president appoints the chairman.

AUTHORITY

Not all water transportation carriers are under the jurisdiction of the FMC. As stated earlier, the ICC exercises regulatory responsibility over interstate freight water transportation within the United States. The FMC's authority extends to water carriers engaged in trade with foreign countries. It also has regulatory responsibility for domestic offshore trade, which involves water transportation between the continental United States, Alaska, Hawaii, and all United States possessions. The FMC's functions and scope of authority are in the following principal areas:

1. Regulation of services, rates, practices, and agreements of common carriers by water and certain other persons engaged in the foreign commerce of the United States.
2. Acceptance, rejection, or disapproval of tariff filings of common carriers engaged in the foreign commerce of the United States.
3. Regulation of rates, fares, charges, classifications, tariffs, regulations, and practices of common carriers by water in the domestic offshore trades of the United States.
4. Licensing independent ocean freight forwarders.
5. Investigation of discriminatory rates, charges, classifications, and practices of common carriers in the waterborne foreign and domestic offshore commerce, terminal operators, and freight forwarders.
6. Issuance of certificates evidencing financial responsibility of vessel owners or charterers of American or foreign vessels, having accommodations for fifty or more passengers and embarking passengers at United States ports, to pay judgments for personal injury or death, or to indemnify passengers holding tickets in the event of nonperformance of voyages or cruises.
7. Issuance of certificates evidencing financial responsibility of vessel owners, charterers and operators of every vessel over three hundred gross tons, using any port or place in the United States to meet the liability to the United States for the discharge of oil and hazardous substances.
8. Rendering decisions, issuing orders, making rules and regulations governing and affecting common carriers by water, terminal operators, freight forwarders, and other persons subject to the Commission's jurisdiction.[12]

ORGANIZATION

As in the ICC, many offices and bureaus exist to carry out the functions of the FMC. As shown in Figure 12–2, four major offices report directly to the FMC chairman. These are the offices of the secretary, general counsel, administrative law judges (hearing examiners), and managing director. The duties of each closely resemble their counterparts in the ICC.

The FMC's managing director has direct authority over its five bureaus and three less prominent offices, as Figure 12–2 indicates. Again, each has its counterpart in the ICC, and the duties are virtually the same.

---

[12] U.S. Federal Maritime Commission, *Federal Maritime Commission Fifteenth Annual Report*, p. 1.

FIGURE 12–2. FEDERAL MARITIME COMMISSION ORGANIZATION

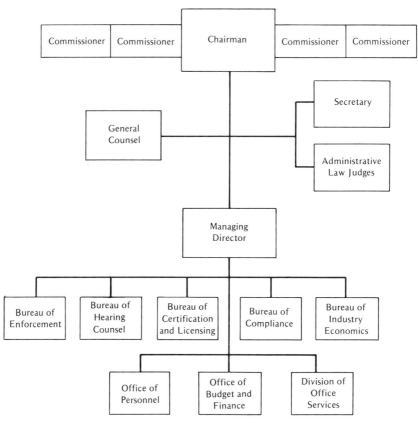

PROCEDURES

Regulation of water transportation requires a procedure to process complaints lodged by users of the carriers' service. As with the ICC, the FMC has two types of procedures by which complaints are processed: *informal* and *formal*. The specific procedures are outlined in the Administrative Procedures Act of 1946 and are summarized briefly here.

INFORMAL

You have already seen the many benefits possible from handling complaints on an informal basis. Most complaints received by the FMC are handled informally. As an example, the FMC received 267 informal complaints in fiscal year 1977, and 236 were carried over from the 1976 fiscal year. At the end of the 1977 fiscal year, only 154 informal complaints remained open.[13] All others

[13] U.S. Federal Maritime Commission, *Federal Maritime Commission Sixteenth Annual Report*, p. 62.

had been resolved through the informal procedure. In comparison, the FMC was able to conduct formal hearings on five complaints and closed out thirty-four other complaints in the same time period.[14]

The informal complaint procedure is almost identical to that used by the ICC. The complaint is handled by the Office of Informal Complaints in the Bureau of Enforcement. The carrier is informed by mail of a complaint received against it and replies to the FMC. If the complaint borders on violation of any of the water transportation statutes, an investigation may be instigated by the FMC. However, if no illegal matter is involved, the issue is resolved entirely through correspondence. As already stated, the majority of complaints is handled through the informal procedure.

FORMAL

Matters that cannot be handled by correspondence or issues that are of general water transportation significance are processed formally. The procedure closely follows the guidelines of the Administrative Procedure Act. Generally, a pre-hearing conference is held at which the case is organized and the issues are defined. Dates are set for each party to submit relevant information and exhibits, and a hearing date is set. The hearing is conducted by an administrative law judge and testimony is taken from all parties. At the conclusion of the hearing, the judge sets a date by which all briefs are to be received. After reviewing the briefs and the hearing record, the judge renders a decision. The full FMC may review this decision if requested by either party. If granted, the FMC then reviews all pertinent information and issues its decision. Either party in the action may request a reconsideration, at which time the FMC will request answers from the other involved party. After another review, a final decision is issued. Again, if a matter of law interpretation is involved, the decision may be appealed to the courts.

This procedure is time-consuming and expensive. Expenses are incurred by the involved parties for travel and legal representation. The FMC's expenses are not directly measurable because of the large number of people involved in the preparation, processing, and closing of any formal proceeding. Not surprisingly, the FMC requires a large staff and budget, although the limited number of regulated carriers and movements does not warrant as large a staff and budget as that of the ICC.

BUDGET

The FMC is given a yearly budget by the Congress. The budget includes funds for conducting research, investigations, and proceedings, and the required personnel to support these activities. FMC budget and personnel data from select years since 1962 are presented in Table 12-4. If the appropriations

---

[14] Ibid., p. 30.

appear large, it might help to review some of the activities in which the FMC becomes involved. Table 12–5 is a summary of the Bureau of Enforcement activities in fiscal year 1977. Judging from the number of investigations and closed cases, it appears that the regulatory process is required and that the United States will continue to support the activities of the agency.

Civil Aeronautics Board

Air freight transportation is a twentieth century phenomenon. Air transportation's early development centered on passenger travel. As the industry grew, freight was transported on a space-available basis. Before 1938, the only regulations imposed on air carriers concerned safety matters. Safety inspections were conducted by the Department of Commerce by authority established in the Air Commerce Act of 1926. Not long after, the need arose to impose economic regulations of air transportation for both freight and passenger travel, and a new regulatory institution was born. This section will review the origin, composition, authority, organization, operating procedures, and budget of the Civil Aeronautics Board (CAB).

TABLE 12–4. Federal Maritime Commission Statement of Budget and Personnel, Select Years

Year	Budget (In Thousands)	Personnel
1962	$ 1,306	188
1964	2,575	249
1966	3,173	261
1968	3,600	271
1970	4,008	252
1971	4,658	290
1972	5,267	287
1973	5,679	294
1974	6,385	311
1975	7,400	321
1976	8,040	321
1977	8,640	321
1978	9,724	351
1979*	10,880	360
1980*	11,217	365

*Estimates.
Sources: Budget of the Federal Government and Appendix to the Budget of the United States Government, various issues.

TABLE 12–5. Bureau of Enforcement Field Investigations, Fiscal Year 1977

Investigations	Total	Malpractices	Tariff Violations	Forwarders and Other Matters
Pending 9/30/76	662	234	240	188
Opened FY 1977	608	208	83	317
Completed FY 1977	470	59	146	265
Pending 9/30/77	800	383	177	240

Source: *Federal Maritime Commission Sixteenth Annual Report, 1977* (Washington, D.C.: U.S. Government Printing Office, 1977).

ORIGIN

There is a history of changes with regard to the labels attached to air transportation's regulatory agencies. The Civil Aeronautics Act of 1938 created a Civil Aeronautics Authority (CAA). This agency had several components. First, a three-member Air Safety Board was established to investigate accidents and to make improvement recommendations to the CAA. The CAA was created as a five-member board with jurisdiction over both economic and safety matters. Within the CAA, an administrator was appointed solely for the purpose of promoting air transportation. The CAA was placed under the Department of Commerce, although its economic regulatory activities were conducted independently.

The CAA was changed to the Civil Aeronautics Board (CAB) in the Transportation Act of 1940. It remained independent, although it was still under the Department of Commerce for administrative purposes. The act abolished the Air Safety Board and established an administrator of the Civil Aeronautics Administration. The administrator's major responsibilities were establishment and promotion of safety rules as well as overall air transportation. The CAB was concerned with economic regulations and continued its air accident investigations.

A later law changed the regulatory agency's name but not its functions. The Federal Aviation Act of 1958 abolished the Civil Aeronautics Administration and replaced it with the Federal Aviation Agency (FAA). This act also replaced the Civil Aeronautics Act of 1938, although regulatory functions remained virtually the same. The CAB's role in economic and safety matters was unchanged.

The Department of Transportation Act of 1966 changed the labels and functions once again. This act abolished the FAA and replaced it with the Federal Aviation Administration (another FAA). The FAA was placed under the DOT and was headed by an administrator. All of the Federal Aviation Agency's functions were transferred to the DOT. In addition, the CAB's accident and safety responsibility and authority were transferred to the DOT. A National Transportation Safety Board (NTSB) was created and given responsibility and authority over safety matters. The CAB retains its control over economic regulations. At this writing, another change appears imminent.

The CAB may face discontinuation. During the latter half of the 1970s, the Carter administration attempted to live up to its promise to trim the federal bureaucracy. Statutes were enacted in 1977[15] and 1978[16] that aimed to phase out economic regulations over a period of time. Depending on the success of these attempts, the CAB is slated to be abolished by the year 1985, ending economic regulations for either passenger or freight transportation. Achieving this objective depends on the attempts to phase out regulation and the ensuing problems. If it appears that the industry is not capable of managing totally free competition in air transportation, the regulations will be continued, and any further deregulation attempts will be stopped.

COMPOSITION

Since passage of the Civil Aeronautics Act of 1938, the CAB's composition has remained stable. Like the FMC, the CAB has five commissioners and is supported by a number of bureaus and offices. Commissioners are appointed for six-year terms. All appointments are made by the president and must be approved by the Senate. Like the other regulatory agencies, a political balance is desired. No more than three commissioners can be from the same political party.

AUTHORITY

The CAB's regulatory authority extends to interstate and foreign air transportation. Its primary responsibilities and duties closely resemble those described for the other regulatory agencies. Generally, the CAB's scope of authority surrounds the same entry, rate, structural, financial, operations, and enforcement authority granted to the other regulatory bodies over their respective modes. The extent of regulatory responsibility is similar.

ORGANIZATION

The CAB has had ten offices and five bureaus. But changes are occurring regularly as the effort to phase out takes place. The major organizational difference in the CAB is the managing director's status. The director reports to the commissioners, just as in the other agencies. However, unlike the other agencies, all offices and bureaus report to the managing director.

The CAB's offices and bureaus are shown in Figure 12–3. As mentioned, the CAB's plans to phase out regulation will undoubtedly continue to change

[15] P.L. 95–163.
[16] P.L. 95–504.

FIGURE 12–3. CIVIL AERONAUTICS BOARD ORGANIZATION

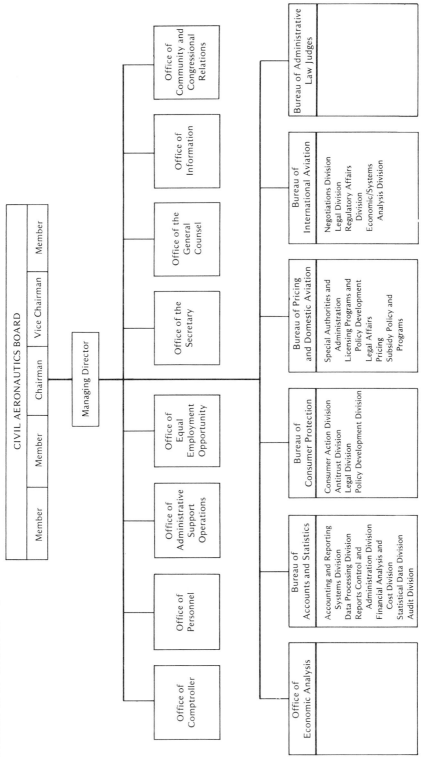

the organization. The bureaus and offices are either self-explanatory or resemble their counterparts in the ICC or FMC.

PROCEDURES

Guidelines contained in the Administrative Procedures Act are used in the CAB's complaint procedure. Complaints are handled informally through correspondence or follow the formal hearing procedure. Matters of general air transportation importance are handled formally. The involved parties have the same opportunity to appeal administrative law judges' opinions to the full commission, and the commission's rulings may be appealed to the courts if a legal interpretation is involved.

BUDGET

The CAB's budget and personnel for selected years are shown in Table 12–6. Note that federal appropriations more than doubled during the 1970s, just as with the ICC and FMC. Table 12–7 is a summary of some of the CAB's activities between 1978 and 1980. It is not surprising that a large budget and staff are required.

TABLE 12–6. Civil Aeronautics Board Statement of Budget and Personnel, Select Years

Year	Budget (In Thousands)	Personnel
1962	$ 8,887	875
1964	10,240	889
1966	11,163	628
1968	9,082	678
1970	11,395	692
1971	12,204	690
1972	13,543	707
1973	14,302	709
1974	15,607	730
1975	17,610	735
1976	19,855	770
1977	22,646	810
1978	25,267	820
1979*	28,094	847
1980*	30,700	837

* Estimates.
Sources: Budget of the Federal Government and Appendix to the Budget of the United States Government, various issues.

TABLE 12–7. Civil Aeronautics Board Selected Work Load Data: 1978–1980

	1978 (Actual)	1979 (Estimate)	1980 (Estimate)
1. Domestic Competition			
A. Operating Authority Decisions Reached	179	175	179
B. Agreements and Mergers Processed	1,860	2,674	2,483
C. Pricing Activities	2,010	1,569	1,286
2. Research and Information			
A. Information Systems Activities Completed	1,077	1,131	959
B. Policy Studies Completed	15	12	14
3. International Authority			
A. International Negotiations Conducted	63	80	81
B. Operating Authority Decisions Reached	97	109	112
4. Consumer Protection			
A. Consumer Complaints Processed	23,213	25,000	52,000
B. Investigations Completed	438	450	450
5. Community Assistance and Subsidy			
A. Essential Air Service Determinations	—	200	300
B. Section 406 Subsidy Decisions Reached	128	190	164

Source: Appendix to the Budget of the United States Government for Fiscal Year 1980, p. 872.

Other Regulation Influences

In addition to the major regulatory agencies described, transportation is influenced by decisions of other governmental units. The DOT and its jurisdiction over safety regulation matters have been discussed. Further economic regulation of a sort is imposed by the FTC, as well as by the court system. For example, the Department of Justice, in a matter investigated by the FTC, ruled that an apparel association could not assign specific carriers to serve the organization's members and the carriers could not supply the association with the names of members served.[17] In another case, the courts ruled against two unincorporated steel hauler associations that had agreed to withhold service and equipment from several steel firms.[18]

In a more recent action, the FTC imposed its position on a legislative proposal intended to conserve fuel that extended the agency's transportation regulatory arm and caused a setback in attempts to increase fuel utilization. In its statement, the FTC claimed that allowing buyers to pick up commodities

[17] "U.S. v. Greater New York Tailors' Expressmen Association, Inc.," *Trade Cases: 1961* (New York: Commerce Clearing House, Inc., 1962), pp. 78, 595–597.
[18] "U.S. Steel Corp. v. Fraternal Association of Steel Haulers," *Trade Cases: 1970* (New York: Commerce Clearing House, Inc., 1971), pp. 88, 681–694.

purchased on a delivered basis and then to deduct actual freight charges would result in price discrimination.[19] Nevertheless, the 1980 trucking re-regulation legislation allowed sellers to deduct their actual transportation charges to the buyers' locations from the selling price when buyers provided their own transportation. It was stipulated therein that any resultant charges are to be passed on to the ultimate consumer.

Several other instances can be cited to illustrate how more governmental units are involved, in one way or another, with regulatory transportation activities. Transportation regulation has been fragmented into three major agencies. However, decisions made by other governmental bodies also impinge on transportation regulation and have added confusion and inconsistency to the overall program.

The foregoing review of the regulatory agencies describe their organization and operations, budget and personnel requirements, and selected work load data. Let us now briefly explore the future of transportation regulatory institutions.

The Future of Transportation Regulatory Institutions

The regulatory bodies' future will follow the future of transportation regulation. As stated, the CAB is scheduled to be phased out as air transportation regulation is removed. Wisely, the Congress set that date for 1985. This will allow close scrutiny as to how deregulation affects the structure and operations of the air industry. If more problems are confronted during this changeover in industry activities, the CAB will still be in force and its regulatory authority and responsibility can be activated. Increasing complaints of anticompetitive practices will again bring cries for more regulation. Basically, it will be up to the industry to show it is capable of providing the desired service at just and reasonable rates.

The fate of the ICC and its regulated carriers is unknown. However, because the involved industries are different in so many respects, deregulation attempts will not be as easy. For instance, the rail and trucking industries have a much greater number of participants who would be affected by any deregulation attempts. If larger companies survive and smaller ones do not, as has been the trend in the late 1970s, then the industry's structure and service levels will be affected.

The federal government's desire to reduce transportation regulation, how-

[19] John A. Byrne, "FTC Maintains Backhaul Violates Robinson-Patman," *Supermarket News* (September 18, 1978), pp. 1, 12.

214

ever, intensified in 1979. This drive led to studies conducted by the Commerce Committees of both the House and Senate and ultimately resulted in re-regulation legislation and proposals in 1980. These results also took into consideration the formal re-regulation position which emerged from an extensive interagency task force study that offered several deregulation options. The task force was comprised of representatives of the Departments of Agriculture, Commerce, Defense, Energy, Justice, Labor, and the Treasury, in addition to the Council of Economic Advisors, Council on Wage and Price Stability, Federal Trade Commission, Interstate Commerce Commission, Office of Consumer Affairs, and the Office of Management and Budget.

Industry associations also advanced position statements, which, in some cases, were in opposition to deregulation. Reports from the American Trucking Associations, Association of American Railroads, and the National Industrial Traffic League, for example, were considered in an in-depth analysis of how far deregulation should go. The results of these studies, proposals, and legislation will have some future impact on the status and extent of the ICC.

Although it is an extreme simplification of the problem, the basic questions yet to be answered are the federal government's priorities and society's desires. If a major priority and desire is that all communities that want freight transportation service should have it, then some form of regulation may be necessary. Otherwise, no carrier could be forced to serve a particular community. In extreme cases, an entire locality could be without service. If one accepts freight transportation's role in the economy (see Chapter 2), then entire communities could suffer greatly. Major carriers might compete for the same large revenue shipments and refuse operations to outlying areas as less lucrative. Smaller carriers might—or might not—emerge to serve smaller communities, perhaps as feeder lines to the major carriers. These priorities and desires then will offer guidelines as to the extent of further re-regulation effort, and may lead to total deregulation or a reversal to stricter controls.

These are the kinds of dilemmas that the deregulation issue confronts. It is not a simple problem with a simple solution.

Summary

Various congressional laws affecting transportation established regulatory institutions to implement and enforce those laws. Regulating institutions are necessary to enforce transportation laws not only to protect the rights of the industry participants, but also to ensure the well-being of society through an efficient transportation network. Regulatory functions center on entry, rate, structural, financial, operating, and enforcement controls. Three major transportation regulatory agencies exist at the present time. The Interstate Commerce Commission is the oldest, largest, and most important transportation regulation institution. The Federal Maritime Commission and the Civil Aeronautics Board closely resemble the ICC in structure and operation.

Other governmental units such as the Federal Trade Commission and the judicial system are often responsible for decisions that affect transportation regulation. The potential to phase out the CAB and the increased support for deregulation throughout the 1970s are expected to alter the future of the major regulatory bodies.

This chapter concludes the discussion of the transportation environment as it relates to transportation policy, laws, and regulating institutions. Transportation administration and management will be examined in Part IV.

Questions for Chapter 12

1. Give a brief description of the entry, rate, structural, financial, operating, and enforcement controls exercised by transportation regulatory bodies.
2. Show, with an example, how too many carriers can cause higher freight rates than would exist with fewer participants.
3. List at least five freight regulatory functions of the ICC.
4. Discuss some of the ICC's most recent actions that indicate a relaxation of the rigid regulations of the transportation modes.
5. Describe fully the administrative arm of the ICC.
6. List the differences between the ICC's formal and informal procedures to resolve transportation issues.
7. List some advantages of using the informal procedure to resolve transportation issues.
8. What is the difference between the regulatory scope of the ICC and the FMC on water freight shipments?
9. Describe the status of the CAB with regard to future air freight regulation.
10. By what method are transportation regulation commissioners selected?
11. For what reasons can the regulatory bodies' decisions be appealed to the court system?
12. In addition to the three major transportation regulatory bodies, what other governmental units influence regulation of the carriers?

four

Management and
Administration

Transportation activities occur daily. Operations are multifaceted, performed by many carriers and modes and managed by both carriers and industrial traffic personnel. Transportation operations are examined in this part.

Freight rates and documentation are integral to transportation management. Chapter 13 discusses the complexities of transportation pricing, and Chapter 14 reviews the various types of transportation documents. Familiarity with pricing and documentation leads to management and administration of transportation activities.

Chapter 15 discusses industrial traffic management, its activities and organization. Industrial traffic management interacts with transportation carrier management, which is examined in Chapter 16.

13

Freight Rates

The provision of transportation service requires many costs that must be recovered so that carriers can not only continue to operate but also make a reasonable profit. The profit level should be high enough to encourage further provision of services and to attract potential investors. Without incoming investment funds, carriers would be unable to update facilities, purchase new equipment, and incorporate new technologies that would improve service and keep costs low. Profit is only part of the revenue received by carriers; the rest of their income covers costs. Income is the charge to users for providing transportation service. The charge is based on the freight rate.

The subject of freight rates is the most complicated area of transportation. Its complexity can be appreciated if you consider the wide variety of commodities moved by all transportation modes between all cities in the United States. But the subject of freight rates is not difficult to understand if it is examined systematically. This chapter will first present an overview of the economic role of freight rates and will then proceed to the method by which rates are quoted, classified, and published. Various rate types will be described along with the factors that affect the rate level. Rate-making procedures will be explored, and the chapter will conclude with some of the persistent issues surrounding transportation freight rates.

Economic Impact of Freight Rates

Freight rates have a far greater impact on the economy than merely providing revenue for transportation carriers. They affect a wide range of economic issues. Freight rates are determining factors in location decisions, competitive conditions, and geographic development decisions.

LOCATION DECISIONS

It is difficult to imagine any commercial location decision being made without considering transportation costs, as represented by freight rates. In fact, any location decision, whether personal or commercial, must consider transportation. For example, in personal location decisions, individuals or families cannot decide on a home without investigating available transportation to schools, shopping, and employment. If transportation to and from these points is costly or difficult, the location becomes less desirable.

TABLE 13–1. Location Decision Based on Transportation Costs

	Location A (per unit)	Location B (per unit)
Inbound Materials	$ 5	$ 5
Inbound Transportation	3	2
Manufacturing	7	7
Marketing	2	2
Administration	5	5
Outbound Transportation	3	2
Total Costs	$25	$23
Selling Price	$25	$25
Total Costs	25	23
Profit	0	$ 2

220

The same principle applies to commercial location decisions. A manufacturer must consider the inbound transportation costs of the raw materials and parts used in the production process. Of equal importance is the freight rate to buyers' locations. These inbound and outbound transportation costs will determine if the manufacturer will be able to supply the market with products and still realize a profit. For example, Table 13–1 illustrates two different locations that a firm is considering for a manufacturing facility. Transportation costs are different because the sites are in different cities. All other costs are identical. If the firm chose location A, no profit would be possible. Location B is preferable because the firm would be able to earn a $2 profit per unit.

Transportation costs also affect the number of locations a company will use for its manufacturing operations. Sometimes a firm has to decide whether to establish more than one manufacturing facility to serve a particular market. Perhaps the firm wants to divide manufacturing between two different cities. By doing so, the firm would not be affected as badly if, for example, a flood should hit one of the cities. For illustration, assume that all costs except transportation are identical at the sites being considered, and the firm is weighing the advisability of two locations instead of one as insurance against a catastrophe. Referring to Figure 13–1, it is evident that one location is preferred (P_2), based solely

FIGURE 13–1. MULTIPLE LOCATION DECISION BASED ON TRANSPORTATION COSTS

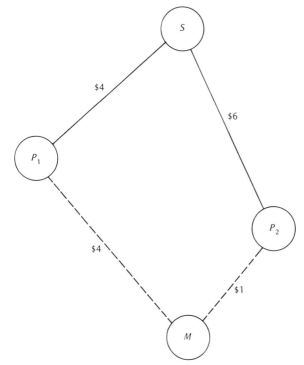

on transportation costs. This assumes one source (S) for all materials and parts used in production. If two manufacturing facilities were used, they would be located at P_1 and P_2. If one manufacturing location were used, it would be located at P_2. The market location is designated as M. Inbound transportation costs to the manufacturing operations are indicated by solid lines, and outbound transportation costs to the marketplace are shown with dashed lines. Using two facilities, P_1 and P_2, the firm would incur total transportation costs of $8 per unit for P_1 and $7 per unit for P_2. Therefore, based solely on transportation costs, only one facility should be used.

The desire for an additional facility, however, may carry a higher transportation charge as an opportunity cost. The existing freight rates will help determine the production levels that should be maintained at each facility, with larger operations at P_2 in the example used. Also, firms can use existing freight rates in negotiations for possible reductions so that equal production can be maintained at both locations and total transportation costs can be reduced.

Although the example is simplified, the concept is valid. Of course, many sources and many marketplaces involve larger calculations, but the impact of freight rates is evident. Location decisions cannot be made without carefully considering carriers' freight rates.

COMPETITION

When you think of commercial competition, you probably think of two or more firms trying to gain an advantage. When the firms are engaged in transactions requiring transportation of raw materials, parts, and finished products, the freight rate level will affect the degree of competition. Also, carriers compete to provide transportation service. And because the transportation service is to and from different geographic points, communities also compete for favorable freight rates to keep their areas active economically. Therefore, freight rates involve industrial competition, transportation carrier competition, and geographic competition.

INDUSTRIAL COMPETITION

There are two aspects to industrial competition. First, two or more firms make the same type of product with the same materials and attempt to sell to the same types of buyers. For example, American Motors Corporation, Chrysler Corporation, Ford Motor Company, and General Motors Corporation make automobiles and attempt to sell to the same car buyers. This is known as *intraindustry competition*. The freight rate levels on both inbound shipments of parts and materials and outbound shipments of finished automobiles will affect the success of these competitors. The second type of competition occurs among industries who make similar but substitutable products, using different materials. For example, furniture can be upholstered with fabric, leather, or vinyl, and these industries compete with each other to supply furniture manufacturers. This is known as *interindustry competition*. The level of freight rates will affect the degree of competition among those industries.

INTRAINDUSTRY COMPETITION. Within an industry, the firm that offers a product of comparable quality at a lower selling price most likely will be more successful in the same market than its competitors. To illustrate, assume that both Ford Motor Company and Chrysler Corporation are assembling automobiles in Detroit, Michigan. Assume that Chrysler buys its tires from a manufacturer in Akron, Ohio, and Ford buys its tires from a firm in Mansfield, Ohio, a location closer to Detroit. Assume further that the freight rate is $5 per tire from Mansfield and $10 per tire from Akron. If the buyer is indifferent to the type of car owned, then Ford has a price advantage of $25 per car because of the freight rate difference on five tires (including the spare) per car. As long as the manufacturing price at each tire factory is the same, Ford definitely has the competitive advantage. Thus, the level of competition within an industry is affected by the freight rate.

INTERINDUSTRY COMPETITION. Television cabinets can be made of either wood or hardened plastic. Assume, for the moment, that both of those raw materials are available at the same origin point for the same price. If the freight rate to the manufacturing point is lower for wood than for hardened plastic, then the manufacturer most likely would use wood, giving a boost to that industry. This assumes, of course, that buyers are indifferent to the kind of finish used in television sets.

Now, assume that the price of wood is higher than that of hardened plastic. For both the wood and plastic industries to compete as suppliers of raw materials to make television cabinets, the freight rate must be higher for hardened plastic between the same origin and destination points. If the freight rate is the same for both, or if the rate on hardened plastic is lower, then the manufacturer would tend to prefer it over wood. Table 13–2 illustrates this. In situation A, the freight rate for plastic is higher than for wood, making both raw materials competitive because of the identical delivered cost. In situation B, the freight rates are identical, giving plastic a comparative advantage over wood. This example illustrates the effect of freight rates on interindustry competition.

TABLE 13–2. Effect of Freight Rate on Demand

| | Situation A | | Situation B | |
	Wood	Plastic	Wood	Plastic
Selling Price	$10	$ 6	$10	$ 6
Freight Rate	2	6	2	2
Delivered Price	$12	$12	$12	$ 8

CARRIER COMPETITION

Freight rate setting is not done in a vacuum. In most situations, transportation users have carrier alternatives. An area may be served by two or more trucking companies able to provide service between that area and several other points. Thus, each carrier must consider the freight rates charged by other carriers when setting its rate. Otherwise, too high a rate will drive the business to the other carrier. The community may be served by railroads as well. The trucking companies must then be concerned with the rates charged by the railroads. If the area is served by water, then both the trucking companies and the railroads must be concerned with the water carriers' rate levels. Thus, two types of carrier competition exist: *intramodal competition* and *intermodal competition*.

INTRAMODAL COMPETITION. If a city is served by only one carrier, it is captive to the rates charged by that carrier. Users must pay the freight rates demanded by that carrier or go without the service. Assume that the carrier is a trucking company and the transportation needed is from El Paso, Texas, to Albuquerque, New Mexico. Because it is the only trucking company going to Albuquerque from El Paso, the carrier has great pricing freedom. However, if two trucking companies serve both points, then each carrier is able to handle the shipment and must be concerned with the rate charged by the other if it wants the business. The problem is magnified if one of the carriers is handling a shipment from Phoenix, Arizona, to Dallas, Texas, and is going through Albuquerque on its way back to home base. In that case, the carrier could reasonably charge a lower rate because it is already going in that direction and any revenue is better than returning empty. This complicates the rate setting by the other carrier, unless it is also on a return trip. Obviously, rate setting is not an easy task in intramodal competition.

INTERMODAL COMPETITION. Major cities located near navigable waterways enjoy transportation services from several modes. These modes serve many of the same destinations to which freight is moved from those cities. Thus, each carrier must be concerned with the rates set by other carriers in that same mode, as well as the rates charged by the other modes. For example, when a shipment of ore arrives in Chicago, Illinois, from Duluth, Minnesota, on a seagoing vessel, several options are available to move that ore to St. Louis, Missouri. The ore can be transferred from the vessel to barges in Chicago and towed to St. Louis. Or it can be loaded into railcars and attached to a train destined for St. Louis. Railroads cannot ignore the barge option when setting the ore rate from Chicago to St. Louis, because the user will favor the carrier that keeps its costs low. Thus, railroads must consider water rates when setting the level of charges for the shipments.

In this case, as in most others, the charge does not have to be identical, as long as total transportation costs are reasonably close. Water shipments incur additional transfer and transport costs that are not necessary for rail transportation. Handling costs are incurred in Chicago as well as in St. Louis, and these costs will affect the freight rate level. In addition, the water carrier will have to pay user fees on the Mississippi River, but no such charge will be involved in rail transportation. Table 13–3 shows how the various charges are applied to arrive at a freight rate. (The amounts shown are used only for illustrative purposes and are not the actual charges.) Notice that the freight rate for a rail shipment is higher than for a barge shipment, but the total transportation cost is the same. If, however, the rail rate were $8 instead of $7, the user would prefer the water shipment for which total transportation costs are less. As the charges change for the other components, such as transfer costs, then the freight rate can be adjusted to reflect those changes. However, total transportation costs must be reasonably close for these carriers to compete on the basis of freight rates in intermodal competition.

GEOGRAPHIC COMPETITION

By now, you should be convinced of transportation's important role in a community's economic survival. For the economy to thrive, freight rates on materials for production, parts for assembly, or personal items for society must be low enough to be affordable by those who need the products. High freight rates will discourage traffic movement and will damage the economy and well-being of an entire area. All finished products are drawn to communities by the demand. Demand, in turn, is influenced by price. Because freight rates are an important element of the delivered cost, high freight rates will reduce demand. Sellers will ship their goods to other areas where the freight rates—and, therefore, the delivered cost—are lower.

Similarly, the production within an area is somewhat dependent on the demand in other areas for its continued operation. Using the automobile tire example cited earlier, the city of Akron, Ohio, would be interested in a lower freight rate to Detroit, Michigan, so that its tire production would continue, keeping employment high and the economy thriving. Lower freight rates from Mansfield, Ohio, to Detroit would lead automobile manufacturers to purchase tires produced in Mansfield. Thus, there is geographic competition: each area competes with others for continued prosperity, which is affected by the freight rates on commodities, both inbound and outbound.

TABLE 13–3. Barge and Rail Freight Rate Comparison: Chicago to St. Louis

	Barge	Rail
Transfer in Chicago	$ 2	$ 3
Freight Rate	4	7
User Fee	3	—
Transfer in St. Louis	2	1
Total Transportation Cost	$11	$11

To further illustrate the importance of freight rates on economic development, consider two economically depressed areas, one in West Virginia and the other in Pennsylvania. Both have coal fields and are dependent on mining. Assume there is a demand in Atlanta, Georgia, the total of which is lower than the combined output of the two depressed regions. If the freight rate to Atlanta is higher for Pennsylvania than it is for West Virginia, then Pennsylvania's coal will not be purchased by the Atlanta buyers. The miners in West Virginia will be employed and will have the money to purchase additional products to raise their standard of living. A greater quantity of goods will move into West Virginia, thereby allowing the carriers to maintain low freight rates. The Pennsylvania mines, however, will remain at the subsistence level. Fewer commodities will move into Pennsylvania, and freight rates will remain high.

This discussion of the economic role of freight rates should help you appreciate the difficulties involved in establishing freight rates. It is more than a matter of determining costs and adding a certain amount for profits. Many interests, carriers, and communities are involved, and the state of the economy is at stake. Let us now consider freight rate structures and the procedures used by the carriers.

Freight Rate Categories

Most communities are involved in some type of commercial activity. Products that result from this activity must be transported to other areas. Coal mined in West Virginia, except for supplies used locally, must be transported to other demand areas. Therefore, freight rates must be established to move the coal from producing regions to industrial and residential areas. If, for example, coal produced in Beckley, West Virginia, is to be transported to 20,000 consuming points, there are potentially 20,000 coal freight rates from Beckley alone. Similarly, Hershey's chocolates, manufactured in Hershey, Pennsylvania, must be transported to all sales locations. Therefore, there are many truck and rail rates on chocolates from Hershey.

To combat the growing complexity of transportation movement, a rate classification system was developed. Even with such a system, trillions of freight rates still exist. The system was initiated by railroads, and trucking companies soon after developed their own system. Water carriers use the railroad system. The airlines and pipelines have no similar classification systems, primarily because of the limited number of freight commodities carried.

This discussion focuses on the railroad and truck classification systems. The basic plans group commodities with similar transportation characteristics into categories called classes. The use of a classification system resulted in a generalized system of rates that covers all commodities to and from all locations. To

226

provide more specific rates on large quantities and special movements, commodity and exception rates have been established. Thus, there are three major freight rate categories: *class*, *commodity*, and *exception*. A fourth category, *contract rates*, will also be discussed because of its growing importance to transportation management.

CLASS RATES

The classification system was initiated by the railroads to simplify rate publication and quotation. In 1887, railroads serving the northeastern section of the United States initiated the system. Commodities were grouped into classes based on similarities in shape, size, damage potential, value, density, and general handling characteristics. For example, gravel, stone, and crushed coal may be placed in the same class. Or large household appliances, such as refrigerators, washers, dryers, and freezers, may be placed in the same class.

The classification that a specific commodity falls within provides that commodity's *rating*. Be careful not to confuse the terms *rate* and *rating*. The rating is a commodity's classification among all other types of freight. And, as you will see later in the chapter, the rate is the charge per unit of transportation the shipper must pay.

The ratings of all commodities are related on a ratio basis to an index of 100. Each category of commodities is referred to as a specific class. Although the application is not always accurate, the historical intent was that the actual rate charged for the transportation movement would be a ratio of the 100 class rate. For example, if a commodity was placed in class 13, the rate would be 13 per cent of the rate that applied to class 100. If the class 100 rate was $10 per hundredweight, the class 13 rate would be $1.30. If the commodity fell into class 400, the rate would be $40 per hundredweight.

The rail carriers serving the southern United States collectively devised a classification system in 1891, as did the western United States carriers. Not all classifications were identical. An attempt to make classifications uniform across the country resulted in the development of the Consolidated Freight Classification (CFC) in 1919. Unfortunately, not all carriers followed the CFC, and the confusion continued. The problems this created caused the ICC to order the railroads to devise a standard classification system that would apply to all regions of the United States. This was accomplished with publication of the *Uniform Freight Classification* (UFC) in 1952. By 1956, all railroads began using the UFC. The CFC was cancelled officially in the early 1970s.

The UFC is an alphabetical listing of all commodities that could possibly be shipped by rail. These commodities are separated into thirty-one classifications, ranging from class 13 to class 400. All commodities fall into one of these thirty-one classifications.

A similar classification system developed in the motor freight industry. In 1935, when truck freight transportation became regulated, the trucking compa-

227

nies developed the *National Motor Freight Classification* (NMFC). The system closely resembled the railroads' CFC. When the railroads developed the UFC in 1952, the trucking companies instituted a revised NMFC to resemble the UFC. The 1952 NMFC is currently in use in all areas except the New England states, which have their own *Coordinated Motor Freight Classification* (CMFC). Although the truck classification system closely resembles the UFC, some differences are apparent. For example, the NMFC has only twenty-three classes. This is possible because trucks ship a smaller variety of commodities than rail. Also, the NMFC classes for heavy and bulky commodities are higher than for rail, mainly because of the unattractiveness of those commodities for truck shipments. The CMFC system used in the New England states has only five classes, based on different weights per cubic foot of the various commodities.

Rates based on the classification system are known as *class rates*. A wide variety of different class rates exists across railroad and truck tariffs. However, the determination of the applicable rate usually requires three steps. The product to be shipped must be identified in terms of its appropriate item number. The item number is used to find the appropriate classification. The classification rating is used to find the actual freight rate from the applicable tariff. Tariffs exist in many forms. They are merely price listings for transportation services. Tariffs publish charges for providing different kinds of services, such as special services, demurrage, or rates. Of immediate interest is the rate tariff. Further discussion of tariffs is contained in Chapter 14 on transportation documents.

To illustrate the determination of a class rate, an example of moving acetic acid from Kings Mill, Texas, to Celriver, South Carolina, is presented. The illustration was selected because of the complex nature of this specific rail movement, which involves several special situations. Most class rate determinations are not as complicated as the acetic acid example. All, however, require completion of the three steps outlined.

To find the class rate on acetic acid, it is necessary first to determine the rating. Figure 13–2 is taken from the *Uniform Freight Classification 13*. The *item number* for acetic acid is 2100. This item number is used to determine the commodity's rating. The item number refers to another part of the classification that describes the commodities and gives the rating. Figure 13–3 indicates that acetic acid takes a 70 rating on an LCL shipment and a 30 rating on a 30,000-lb. carload shipment. It shows that the full carload freight rate will be 30 per cent of a *rate base*. Thus, the rate can be at two different levels, depending on the size of the acetic acid shipment.

To find the rate, it is necessary to refer to the *class tariff*. In this case, freight rates between the two cities are not published. Therefore, the *National Rate Basis Tariff 1–D* lists other cities located close to the involved points to be used to determine the base. This tariff, shown in Figure 13–4, indicates that shipments to Celriver take the same rates as shipments to Rock Hill, South Caro-

FIGURE 13–2. UNIFORM FREIGHT CLASSIFICATION ITEM NUMBER FOR ACETIC ACID

STCC No.	Article	Item
08 422 13	Accroides gum	47910
35 856 20	Accumulators, ice-making or refrigerating, gas or liquid	62560,162720
35 329 10	Accumulators, mining, ore milling or smelting, hydraulic	63480,163710
35 481 10	Accumulators, rolling mill	63320
28 181 03	Acetaldehyde	21990,33800
28 181 11	Acetaldol (aldol)	21990,33800
28 151 10	Acetanilid	22000,33800
28 431 25	Acetates, fatty amine	72385
28 431 25	Acetates, fatty diamine	72385
28 186 10	Acetic acid, glacial or liquid	2100,33800
28 186 44	Acetic anhydride	22010,33800
28 189 15	Acetone cyanohydrin	22020,33800
28 181 05	Acetone, noibn	22030,33800
28 181 73	Acetonitrile (methyl cyanide)	⅋
28 132 10	Acetylene gas	45380
35 691 21	Acetylene gas generating apparatus	61810
28 181 87	Acetylene tetrachloride (tetrachloroethane)	26290,33800
28 311 10	Acetylsalicylic acid	2110,33800
32 551 65	Acid bath tanks brick	88720
33 322 10	Acid chamber residuum lead, dry	56150
33 322 15	Acid chamber residuum lead, liquid or paste	56160
35 999 24	Acid condensing sections, cast iron	63800
20 942 32	Acid fish scrap	38640
28 712 51	Acid phosphate (superphosphate) ammoniated	88450
28 712 50	Acid phosphate (superphosphate), ot ammoniated	88460
28 141 64	Acid salt, tar, crude	⅋
40 251 17	Acid sludge (an unrefined waste obtained in the refining of petroleum)	86840
40 291 70	Acid sludge containing not less than 75% water (an unrefined waste obtained in the metal finishing industry)	86845
32 551 65	Acid storage tanks, brick	88720
32 412 20	Acid-proof cement	21670
	Acids	
28 186 10	Acetic, glacial or liquid	2100,33800
28 311 10	Acetylsalicylic	2110,33800
28 186 62	Adipic	2135,33800
28 194 10	Arsenic, fused	2140,33800
28 194 14	Arsenic, ot fused	2150,33800
28 994 10	Azelaic, from animal or vegetable fats	2160,33800
28 151 60	Benzoic	2120,33800
28 194 18	Boric (boracic)	2170,33800
28 186 72	*Butyric	2130,33800
28 151 11	Carbolic (phenol)	2180,33800
28 194 22	Chlorosulfonic	2190,33800
28 194 26	Chromic	2200,33800
28 186 12	Citric, dry	2205,33800
28 151 21	Cresol (cresylic), crude	2210,33800
28 151 21	Cresylic (cresol)	2210,33800
28 186 14	Decanedioic	2215,33800

Source: *Uniform Freight Classification 13* (Chicago: Uniform Classification Committee, Agent, 1978), p. 15.

FIGURE 13–3. Uniform Freight Classification Rating for Acetic Acid

ITEM	ARTICLES	Less Carload Ratings	Carload Minimum (Pounds)	Carload Ratings
2000	ABRASIVES:			
2010	Abrasive cloth or paper, including emery or sand paper, in packages	55	36,000	37½
2020	Corundum, emery, or other natural or synthetic abrasive material consisting chiefly of aluminum oxide or silicon carbide:			
2030	Crude or lump, LCL, in bags, barrels or boxes; CL, in bulk or in packages	55	50,000	27½
2040	Flour or grain in packages	55	36,000	35
2050	Refuse, including broken wheels, wheel stubs or wheel grindings, loose, see Note, Item 2051, or in packages	55	50,000	20
2051	NOTE. –LCL shipments may be loose only in lots of 10,000 lbs. subject to minimum charge as for 10,000 lbs.; shipments to be loaded by shipper and unloaded by consignee; shipper to furnish and install all dunnage and packing material; freight charges to be assessed on basis of gross weight of article and all dunnage or packing material.			
2060	Wheels, other than pulp grinding, in barrels, boxes or crates, or on skids if weighing each 300 lbs. or over; also CL, loose packed in packing material	55	30,000	40
2070	Wheels, pulp grinding, in boxes or crates, or on skids	55	30,000	40
2085	ACIDS (see also Item 33800):			
2100	Acetic, glacial or liquid:			
	In carboys, other than Package 800	100	30,000	45
	In glass containers in boxes or in Packages 514 or 800	77½	30,000	40
	In bulk in barrels; also CL, in tank cars, Rule 35	70	30,000	30
2110	Acetylsalicylic, in barrels, boxes or Package 1157	85	30,000	45
2120	Acids, no ibn, dry:			
	In glass containers or in cans or cartons in boxes	92½	30,000	55
	In bulk in barrels, boxes, steel pails or 5-ply paper bags, or in plastic bags, see Rule 40, Section 101; or Benzoic acid in Packages 29 or 1380 or Fumaric acid or Malic acid in Package 1380, or Sulfamic acid in Package 1348	85	30,000	50

Source: *Uniform Freight Classification 13* (Chicago: Uniform Classification Committee, Agent, 1978), p. 512.

lina. As shown in Figure 13–5 the tariff indicates that shipments from Kings Mill, Texas, use the same rates as those originating in Pampa, Texas. Now it is possible to obtain a rate base. Referring to a class rate tariff, it is found that shipments between Rock Hill and Pampa have a rate base of 1374, as shown in Figure 13–6. It is then necessary to refer to the rate basis of 1374 to find the carload rate. The class tariff, as in Figure 13–7, shows that a 30 rating on rate basis under 1375 carries a freight rate of 406 cents per hundredweight ($4.06/cwt). This example shows the details involved in determining a railroad class rate. Although the procedure seems complex, it is simpler than trying to keep class tariffs between all conceivable points of origin and destination. As noted earlier, most class rate determinations are not usually as difficult to determine as the acetic acid example.

FIGURE 13–4. RATE BASIS FOR CELRIVER

Alphabetical Index of Stations by State Showing Railroad Location, Standard Point Location Code and Rate Basis Applicable					Alphabetical Index of Stations by State Showing Railroad Location, Standard Point Location Code and Rate Basis Applicable				
STATION	RR	NO	SPLC	RATE BASIS	STATION	RR	NO	SPLC	RATE BASIS
ITEM 6460000					ITEM 6460000				
			SOUTH CAROLINA					SOUTH CAROLINA	
Cartersville	SCL 2130	444656	Florence	SC	Dixiana	SCL 2985	445662	Columbia	SC
Cash	SCL 2580	441374	Cheraw	SC	Dixon	SCL 2260	444128	Dillon	SC
Cassatt	SCL 2515	441954	Camden	SC	Dobson	SCL 3915	442357	Greenville	SC
Catawba	SCL 3480	442178	Catawba	SC	Docheno	SOU 4030	443664	Belton	SC
Catawba	SOU 4485	442178	Catawba	SC	Doddville	SOU 3611	442332	Spartanburg	SC
Cave	SOU 4955	448922	Allendale	SC	Donalds	SCL 4000	446415	Belton	SC
Cayce	SCL 2975	445635	Columbia	SC	Donalds	SOU 4020	446415	Belton	SC
Cayce	SOU 4840	445635	No Rate Basis		Dorange	SOU 5210	447537	Pregnall	SC
Celriver	SOU 3801	442137	Rock Hill	SC	Dorchester	SOU 5175	447554	Pregnall	SC
Cementon	SCL 2905	445955	Giant	SC	Dover	CNL 110	442957	Clinton	SC
Centenary	SCL 2365	444467	Mullins	SC	Downs	SCL 4020	442898	Greenwood	SC
Central	SOU 4380	443484	Seneca	SC	Downs	SOU 3997	442898	Greenwood	SC

Source: *National Rate Basis Tariff 1-D* (Chicago: Western Trunk Line Committee, Agent, 1978), p. 244.

FIGURE 13–5. RATE BASIS FOR KINGS MILL

Alphabetical Index of Stations by State Showing Railroad Location, Standard Point Location Code and Rate Basis Applicable					Alphabetical Index of Stations by State Showing Railroad Location, Standard Point Location Code and Rate Basis Applicable				
STATION	RR	NO	SPLC	RATE BASIS	STATION	RR	NO	SPLC	RATE BASIS
ITEM 6490000					ITEM 6490000				
			TEXAS					TEXAS	
Kenefick	MP	14080	684540 Sandune	TX	Lawn	ATSF	10190	678870 Tuscola	TX
Kent	MP	20645	696162 Van Horn	TX	Lazare	QAP	15	673711 Quanah	TX
Kerens	SSW	2810	667624 Corsicana	TX	Le Verte	ATSF	10675	681672 Bessmay	TX
Kermit	TNM	15	694450 Monahans	TX	League City	GHH	45	686134 Houston	TX
Kerr	GRR	15	683564 Georgetown	TX	League City	MKT	4780	686134 Houston	TX
Kerr	MP	16517	683564 Georgetown	TX	League City	MP	16120	686134 Houston	TX
Kerrick	ATSF	12100	672210 Stratford	TX	Leander	SP	23985	683570 Leander	TX
Kevin	SP	22635	682963 Cleveland	TX	Lee	ATSF	12400	671995 Amarillo	TX
Kildare	MP	20060	661462 Atlanta	TX	Leesburg	LA	1225	661860 Mt. Pleasant	TX
Kilgore	MP	15625	665490 Kilgore	TX	Leevan	MKT	4577	685238 No Rate Basis	
Killeen	ATSF	10280	683267 Temple	TX	Leggett	SP	22710	681852 Moscow	TX
Kilowatt	MP	14205	684148 Orange	TX	Lehman	ATSF	13470	677550 Seagraves	TX
Kings Mill	ATSF	12380	671867 Pampa	TX	Lehr	MP	17612	687481 Pleasanton	TX
Kingsland	SP	24035	690774 Llano	TX	Lelavale	ATSF	10120	684248 Kountze	TX
Kingsville	MP	14850	689430 Bishop	TX	Lelia Lake	FWD	455	673280 Memphis	TX
Kinsloe	MP	15617	665461 Kilgore	TX	Leming	MP	17635	687917 Pleasanton	TX
Kipfer	MP	14949	689845 Harlingen	TX	Lemonville	KCS	1410	684122 No Rate Basis	TX
Kirbyville	ATSF	10665	681663 Kirbyville	TX	Lemonville	SRN	15	684122 Orange	TX

Source: *National Rate Basis Tariff 1-D* (Chicago: Western Trunk Line Committee, Agent, 1978), p. 262.

COMMODITY RATES

Certain shippers offer carriers regular large shipments of identical commodities. To attract and continue to serve these shippers, the carriers publish rates for specific commodities. These are known as *commodity rates*. For example,

FIGURE 13–6. RATE BASE BETWEEN ROCK HILL AND PAMPA

Section 1

APPLICATION OF RATE BASES

Item	BETWEEN ► (See Item 340) AND (See Item 340) ▲	Moscow	Mt. Pleasant	Nacogdoches	Navasota	Odessa	Orange	Paducah	Palacios	Palestine	Pampa	Panhandle	Paris	Pecos	Perryton	Pineland
	SOUTH CAROLINA															
29701	Graniteville	943	907	892	1054	1350	903	1252	1303	945	1316	1340	956	1424	1330	908
29702	Great Falls	1026	990	975	1137	1433	1004	1335	1204	1028	1384	1408	1038	1507	1398	991
29703	Greenville	925	889	874	1036	1332	902	1234	1102	927	1283	1307	937	1406	1297	890
29704	Greenwood	922	886	871	1033	1329	900	1231	1100	924	1280	1304	934	1403	1294	887
29705	H. & B. Jct	1019	983	968	1130	1426	979	1328	1179	1021	1392	1416	1032	1500	1406	984
29706	Hardeeville	977	941	926	1088	1384	937	1286	1137	979	1378	1433	990	1458	1423	942
29707	Hartsville	1079	1043	1028	1190	1486	1048	1388	1248	1081	1437	1461	1091	1560	1451	1044
29708	Jackson	931	895	880	1042	1338	891	1240	1091	933	1304	1328	944	1412	1318	896
29709	Kingville	1027	991	976	1138	1434	992	1336	1192	1029	1385	1409	1039	1508	1399	992
29710	Lake City	1108	1072	1057	1219	1515	1072	1417	1272	1110	1466	1490	1120	1589	1480	1073
29711	Lancaster	1025	989	974	1136	1432	1003	1334	1203	1027	1383	1407	1037	1506	1397	990
29712	Lando	1013	977	962	1124	1420	991	1322	1191	1015	1371	1395	1025	1494	1385	978
29713	Lane	1086	1050	1035	1197	1493	1050	1395	1250	1088	1444	1468	1098	1567	1458	1051
29714	Laurens	949	913	898	1060	1356	927	1258	1127	951	1307	1331	961	1430	1321	914
29715	McBee	1063	1027	1012	1174	1470	1034	1372	1234	1065	1421	1445	1075	1544	1435	1028
29716	McColl	1112	1076	1061	1223	1519	1088	1421	1288	1114	1470	1494	1124	1593	1484	1077
29717	McCormick	918	882	867	1029	1325	886	1227	1096	920	1276	1300	930	1399	1200	883
29718	Marion	1106	1070	1055	1217	1513	1070	1415	1270	1108	1464	1488	1118	1587	1478	1071
29719	Meggetts	1025	989	974	1136	1432	985	1334	1185	1027	1426	1450	1038	1506	1449	990
29720	Mullins	1114	1078	1063	1225	1521	1079	1423	1279	1116	1472	1496	1126	1595	1486	1079
29721	Newberry	960	924	909	1071	1367	938	1269	1138	962	1318	1342	972	1441	1332	925
29722	North Augusta	931	895	880	1042	1338	891	1240	1091	933	1304	1328	944	1412	1318	896
29723	Orangeburg	1006	970	955	1117	1413	966	1315	1166	1008	1379	1403	1019	1487	1393	971
29724	Pageland	1125	1089	1074	1236	1532	1096	1434	1296	1127	1484	1507	1137	1606	1497	1090
29725	Perry	998	962	947	1109	1405	958	1307	1158	1000	1371	1395	1011	1479	1385	963
29726	Poston	1116	1080	1065	1227	1523	1080	1425	1280	1118	1474	1498	1128	1597	1488	1081
29727	Pregnall	1027	991	976	1138	1434	987	1336	1187	1029	1400	1424	1040	1508	1414	992
29728	Ridgeville	1008	972	957	1119	1415	986	1317	1186	1010	1366	1390	1020	1489	1380	973
29729	Rock Hill	1016	980	965	1127	1423	994	1325	1194	1018	1374	1398	1028	1497	1388	981
29730	Russellville	1094g	1058g	1043g	1205g	1501g	1045g	1403g	1254g	1096g	1456g	1480g	1107g	1575g	1470g	1059g

RATE BASES APPLICABLE (For rates, see Section 2)

Source: *Supplement 200 to Southwestern Lines Freight Tariff SW/S-1007-A* (St. Louis: Southwestern Freight Bureau, Agent), p. 494.

coal moves in volume regularly from mining areas to industrial cities. In most cases, commodity rates are published on coal shipments. Lumber also moves in volume from the Pacific Northwest eastward for further manufacturing or construction. Thus, lumber commodity rates are usually published.

To illustrate the application of commodity rates, we will again use the example of acetic acid moving from Kings Mill, Texas, to Celriver, South Carolina. Because these shipments are regular movements, it should be determined if a commodity rate can be used rather than a class rate. The commodity tariff index in Figure 13–8 shows several commodity rates for acetic acid. Item 4025–A is an acetic acid commodity rate from Kings Mill to Celriver, as shown in Figure 13–9. The carload rate is 165 cents per hundredweight ($1.65/cwt.). As you can see, commodity rates represent a great savings over class rates for regular shipments.

FIGURE 13–7. FREIGHT RATE FROM CELRIVER TO KINGS MILL

⑩ SECTION 2–CLASS RATES IN CENTS PER 100 LBS
Part A (See Item 55000 per Application)

RATE BASIS NUMBER NOT OVER	CLASSES															
	39	38	37½	37	36	35	34	33	32½	32	31	30	29	28	27½	27
900	410	400	395	389	379	368	358	347	342	337	326	316	305	295	289	284
925	415	404	399	394	383	372	362	351	346	340	330	319	309	298	293	287
950	422	411	406	400	390	379	368	357	352	346	335	325	314	303	298	292
975	427	416	410	405	394	383	372	361	356	350	339	328	317	306	301	295
1000	435	424	418	413	401	390	379	368	362	357	346	335	323	312	307	301
1025	441	430	425	419	408	396	385	374	368	362	351	340	328	317	311	306
1050	448	436	431	425	413	402	390	379	373	367	356	344	333	321	316	310
1075	453	442	436	430	418	407	395	383	378	372	360	349	337	325	320	314
1100	459	448	442	436	424	412	401	389	383	377	365	353	342	330	324	318
1125	567	455	449	443	431	419	407	395	389	383	371	359	347	335	329	323
1150	473	461	455	449	437	425	412	400	394	388	376	364	352	340	334	328
1175	478	466	459	453	441	429	417	404	398	392	380	368	355	343	337	331
1200	486	474	468	461	449	436	424	412	405	399	387	374	362	349	343	337
1225	491	479	473	466	454	441	428	416	410	403	391	378	365	353	347	340
1250	496	484	477	471	458	446	433	420	414	407	395	382	369	356	350	344
1275	505	492	486	479	466	453	440	427	421	414	401	389	376	363	356	350
1300	510	497	491	484	471	458	445	432	425	419	405	392	379	366	360	353
1325	517	504	497	491	477	464	451	438	431	424	411	398	385	371	365	358
1350	523	510	503	496	483	469	456	443	436	429	416	402	389	375	369	362
1375	528	515	508	501	487	474	460	447	440	433	420	406	393	379	372	366
1400	535	521	515	508	494	480	466	453	446	439	425	412	398	384	377	370
1425	543	529	522	515	501	487	473	459	452	445	432	418	404	390	383	376
1450	548	534	527	520	506	492	478	464	457	450	436	422	407	393	386	379
1475	554	540	533	525	511	497	483	469	462	454	440	426	412	398	391	383
1500	560	546	539	532	517	503	489	474	467	460	445	431	417	402	395	388
1525	567	553	545	538	523	509	494	480	473	465	451	436	422	407	400	393
1550	571	557	549	542	527	513	498	483	476	469	454	440	425	410	403	396
1575	578	564	556	549	534	519	504	489	482	475	460	445	430	415	408	400
1600	585	570	562	555	540	525	510	495	487	480	465	450	435	420	412	405
1625	592	577	569	562	546	531	516	501	493	486	471	455	440	425	417	410
1650	597	581	574	566	551	536	520	505	497	490	474	459	444	428	421	413
1675	604	588	581	573	557	542	526	511	503	495	480	464	449	433	426	418
1700	611	595	587	579	564	548	532	517	509	501	485	470	454	438	431	423
1725	618	602	594	586	570	554	539	523	515	507	491	475	459	444	436	428
1750	622	606	599	591	575	559	543	527	519	511	495	479	463	447	439	431

Source: *Supplement 200 to Southwestern Lines Freight Tariff SW/S-1007-A* (St. Louis: Southwestern Freight Bureau, Agent), p. 14.

EXCEPTION RATES

The classification system gives rate quotations on any commodity that can be shipped. Commodity rates often exist for regular shipments that move in volume over a period of time. As with most rules, however, an exception often exists. The same theory applies to freight rates. The class rate may be too high to allow the freight to move between two locations. Many reasons may account for this. For example, a truck class rate between two points may be considerably lower than the rail class rate. If the railroads wish to remain competitive for this traffic, a rate adjustment has to be made. If the railroads establish a commodity rate for the shipment, it will be lower than the rail class rate. But the railroads then may have to establish commodity rates from and to all points where this commodity will be shipped. Or the rates on similar or possible substitute products may have to be reduced to keep the levels the same.

FIGURE 13–8. COMMODITY RATES FOR ACETIC ACID

INDEX OF COMMODITIES

Commodity	Item	Commodity	Item	Commodity	Item
Accelerators, rubber, other than petroleum, noibn	See Item 1250	Acetone, cyanhydrin	See Item 1250; also Items 1850, 1875, 12950	Acid—Continued	
Acetaldehyde	See Item 1250; also Item 4000			Aliphatic dicarboxylic	16350
		Acetylene tetrachloride (tetrachloroethane)	See Item 1250	Arsenic, fused	See Item 1250
Acetaldol (aldol)	See Item 1250	Acid:		Arsenic, other than	See Item 1250
Acetanilid	See Item 1250	Abietic	See Item 1250	Azelaic, from animal or vegetable fats	See Item 1250;
Acetate:		Acetic	1900, 1925,	Boric (boracic)	See Item 1250;
Butyl	4000		1940, 1950,	Butyric	also items
Ethyl	4000		2000, 2025		3700, 3705,
Isobutyl	4000		2050, 2075,		3975, 4025
Propyl	4000		2100, 2125,	Carbolic	See Item 1250
Vinyl	4000, 22700,		3725, 3825,	Carbolic (phenol)	See Item 1250;
	22725, 22750,		4000, 4025		also Item
	22775, 22800,	Acetic, glacial or	See Item 1250;		2275
	22825, 22850,	liquid	also Items	Chorosulfonic	See Item 1250
	22875, 22900,		1950, 2050,	Chromic	See Item 1250
	22925, 22950,		2100, 2125,	Citric dry	See Item 1250
	23000, 23025		3725, 3825,	Cresol (cresylic)	See Item 1250
Acetic anhydride	See Item 1250;		4000, 4025	Cresylic	2475, 2500, 2550
	also Items	Acetylsalicylic	See Item 1250	Cresylic (cresol)	See Item 1250
	1925, 1940,	Acrylic	2175, 2180	Decanedioic	See Item 1250
	1950, 2000,	Adipic	See Item 1250;	Diamine-tetraacetic	9050
	2025, 2050,		also Items	Electrolyte	See Item 1250
	2075, 2100,		2200, 2225, 2250	Fluophosphoric	See Item 1250
	2125, 2150,				
	3725, 3825,				
	4000, 4025				
Acetone	4000				

Source: *Supplement 99 to Southwestern Lines Freight Tariff 357-C* (St. Louis: Southwestern Freight Bureau, Agent, 1977), p. 14.

234

FIGURE 13–9. Commodity Rate for Acetic Acid Between Kings Mills and Cel-
RIVER

SUPPLEMENT 99 TO TARIFF 357-C

SECTION 1

Item	Commodities	From	To	Rates in Cents per 100 LBS		
	COLUMN 1– Acid, acetic, glacial or liquid or acetic anhydride, in tank cars, CL, (R35). (F46) (Notes 1 and 4) COLUMN 2– Acid, acetic, glacial or liquid or acetic anhydride, in	Kings Mill . . . . TX	Celriver . . . . . . SC	⊖COLUMN		
				1	2	3
						(101)
				327	165	318
						(102)
						332
4025-A	tank cars, CL, (R35) and min wt provided therein for cars of not less than 20,000 gallon capacity, but in no case less than 170,000 lbs per car. (Notes 2 and 3) COLUMN 3– (F46) Acid, butyric or acid, isobutyric, in drums or barrels, CL, min wt 30,000 lbs; in tank cars, CL, (R35) . (Note 1) Acid, propionic, in tank cars, CL, (R35) . (Note 1) NOTE 1–Applies via Routes 112000, 112600, 112645, 112775, 112840, 113680, 113705, 113775, 113815 to Memphis, TN Gateway, thence via Routes 34265, 38510, 43165, 44090, 48595, 72340, 120190, 136305, 175579; also via Route 113690 to the New Orleans, LA Gateway, thence via Route 136000. NOTE 2–Applies via Routes 112000, 112600, 112645, 112775, 112830, 113680, 113705, 113775, 113815 to the Memphis, TN Gateway, thence via Route 136399; also via Route 113690 to the New Orleans, LA Gateway, thence via Route 136000. NOTE 3–Subject to Items 80 and 85 only via Route 112000 to Memphis, TN Gateway, thence via Route 136399. NOTE 4–Not applicable when rate in Column 2 applies. (101) Does not apply on acid, propionic. (102) Applies only on acid, propionic.					

Source: *Supplement 99 to Southwestern Lines Freight Tariff 357-C* (St. Louis: Southwestern Freight Bureau, Agent, 1977), p. 23.

Whenever such a circumstance occurs for a particular movement or shipment, the carriers may publish an *exception rate*, which is excepted (removed)
from the regular classification system. Exception rates may apply to one commodity or to several commodities. Or they may apply to only one carrier or to
all carriers. Generally, the exception rate will be lower than the class rate but
higher than the commodity rate. Because the exception rate is a substitute for
the prevailing class rate, it takes precedence.

Still another category of rates exists that does not fall into the described systems. In specific situations, contract rates can play an important role in product
distribution.

CONTRACT RATES

When permitted by law, a carrier may negotiate a rate for a specific shipper.
Approval by one of the regulatory bodies is needed. The negotiations include
the commodity to be shipped and the specific points between which the shipments will occur. In most cases, common carriers would have the legal author-

ity to perform the movement under class rates. However, circumstances may require a separate negotiation between the shipper and carrier. For example, specialized transportation equipment or individualized hours or times of delivery may be necessary. Whatever the reason, the carrier and shipper negotiate and prepare a contract for the intended service. The result is known as a *contract rate*. As long as it covers operating costs, the rate is not subject to the regulatory body's approval and does not have to be published as do the other rate categories.

Contract rates are common in the motor carrier and water transportation industries, but not in the other transportation modes. However, with the lessening of government regulations, the future may bring a greater number of contract arrangements. In the past, the availability of common carriers to perform transportation services has made separate contracts difficult to negotiate. The future, however, may see completely different schemes for freight rate development and publication.

FREIGHT RATE LEVEL FACTORS

Freight rates are established to produce revenue for the carriers. The rates should be set at a level that attracts shippers and allows traffic to move between the desired points. However, the rate to be charged is not left to the carrier management's judgment. All costs relevant to performing the transportation service must be covered or the carrier cannot expect to remain in business. The rate also must include part of the cost of the carrier's offices and management that are not directly associated with commodity movement. Profit must be included in the rate to allow carriers to update equipment, install new technology, and attract investment funds. Many factors are involved in setting the rate *levels*, including costs, operating and product characteristics, and demand.

Costs

Whatever the commercial activity, costs are incurred and must be covered by the revenue generated from that activity. Usually, many elements are involved in determining total costs. If you go to an optician to have a pair of glasses fitted, the price you pay for those glasses includes all costs of providing the service. For example, there are material costs for the frames and lenses, costs for maintaining the optician's office and laboratory, inventory costs for all materials stored for future business, and sample products such as frames.

The cost categories are *fixed* and *variable*; the terms *direct* and *common* are also used to describe the same costs.

FIXED COSTS. Some costs occur once an investment or commitment has been made and do not change with different levels of activity. These costs are known as fixed costs because they are fixed at the amount of the commitment for a certain length of time. For instance, if a railroad buys a new locomotive for

$600,000, that cost is constant. Whether it sits in a terminal or pulls loaded freight cars, the locomotive's cost remains at $600,000. If a water carrier buys a container for $15,000, the dollar cost is fixed and does not change if the container is used or sits idle in a water terminal. Many administrative costs are fixed. Managers, telephone operators, filing clerks, and other administrative employees are paid a regular salary. These salaries do not change according to the traffic volume handled by the carrier. Rent on the office space is also fixed. Transportation *fixed costs*, then, are defined as those expenditures that remain unchanged regardless of traffic volume.

VARIABLE COSTS. Some costs will vary with the amount, value, or volume of traffic handled. For example, seaway tolls or highway turnpike tolls vary, depending on the number of vehicles using the seaway or turnpike. In some instances, the commodity's value may affect the toll's level. In any event, the tolls may be considered a variable cost because their total is affected by the number of shipments involved. If a trucking company sends five trucks containing the same commodity across a turnpike that has a $2 toll, a total toll cost of $10 has been incurred. These costs vary with the volume handled. Fuel is another example of varying costs. The further the vehicle travels, the more fuel is used. The more fuel that is used, the higher is the fuel cost. Therefore, fuel costs vary with distances traveled. *Variable costs*, then, are defined as those costs that change with different volumes of tonnage or changes in distance.

The combination of fixed and variable costs makes up the total cost of providing transportation services. Freight rate setting would be fairly simple if only variable costs were involved. Fixed costs complicate rate setting because of the difficulty in allocating a portion of those costs to each shipment.

OPERATING CHARACTERISTICS

Carriers experience different operating costs on different commodities. The differences are reflected in different rate levels for shipments moved between the same two locations. If it costs more to transport one commodity than another between the same origin and destination, it is reasonable that the rates should differ. For example, the carrier's liability is higher on some commodities. Assume that the same freight train carries a carload of refrigerators and a carload of sand. If a derailment occurs, the carrier's insurance must reimburse the owner of the refrigerators a much higher amount than the owner of the sand. Thus, the freight rate for refrigerators should be higher to cover the increased liability.

Distance traveled is another operating factor that affects the actual freight rate. The rate difference here is not solely attributed to additional fuel consumed or wages. Some portion of the freight rate must cover fixed costs. Variable costs will increase with distance, but the increase is not in direct relationship to distance. Assume that the freight rate on a rail carload of wood chips is $4 per ton for a shipment of 600 miles. If distance costs were directly

237

TABLE 13-4. Freight Rate Comparison for
Two Different Distances

	600 Miles	1,200 Miles
Freight Rates	$4 per ton	$6 per ton
Weight	50 tons	50 tons
Total Revenue	$200	$300
Fixed Cost	$100	$100
Variable Cost	$100	$200

proportional, the rate would be $8 per ton for a distance of 1,200 miles. Each carload is assigned a certain amount for fixed costs, with the balance covering variable costs. Therefore, the rate for a 1,200-mile shipment may be only $6 per ton. The carrier may wish to assign a flat cost of $100 to each carload to cover fixed costs. The variable cost is smaller than the fixed cost, so the rate is not necessarily twice as high for double the distance. This example is illustrated in Table 13–4. A flat charge of $100 per carload is assessed for fixed costs. The freight rates are $4 per ton for a 600-mile shipment and $6 per ton for a 1,200-mile shipment. The variable cost is twice as much for the longer movement, but the freight rate is not, and all costs are covered. This aspect of freight rate level is referred to as the *tapering principle.*

Directly related to the distance factor is the facility utilization factor. A motor carrier may complete a shipment using only one terminal at the origin point and another at the destination. Another shipment may have to interchange through three or more terminals and may even be of shorter mileage. Because a portion of the freight rate is assigned to cover the fixed costs (terminal use), then the freight rate for a shorter distance could conceivably be higher than the rate for a longer haul.

Another operating characteristic that affects the freight rate level is volume. Commodities that move in greater volume will enjoy lower freight rates than the less frequently handled products. This is possible because greater equipment utilization will reduce the costs assigned to each shipment. For example, assume that the XYZ Trucking Company maintains a terminal in Oakland, California, and another in San Francisco. The monthly cost is $10,000 for the Oakland terminal and $15,000 for the San Francisco terminal. Because a portion of each rate covers these common costs, the freight rate level will depend on the volume handled at each terminal. Table 13–5 illustrates this. The Oakland terminal processes 1,000 trucks per month. The San Francisco terminal is much busier; it processes 2,000 trucks each month. Because of the greater utilization of the San Francisco terminal, a shipment originating or terminating at that facility could reasonably have a lower freight rate than one using the Oakland terminal because of the fixed cost allocation.

Thus, operating characteristics have a considerable impact on freight rate

TABLE 13–5. Utilization Effect on Freight Rate Levels

	Oakland	San Francisco
Monthly Terminal Cost	$10,000	$15,000
Shipments Processed	1,000	2,000
Fixed Cost Per Shipment	$10	$7.50

levels. These characteristics can include carrier liability, distance traveled, facility utilization, and volume. In addition to operating characteristics, certain product features affect the freight rate level.

PRODUCT CHARACTERISTICS

All products have different characteristics, such as size, shape, density, and value. These characteristics have a bearing on the freight rate that will be charged for transportation. More small products can be placed in a truck trailer than large products. Oddly shaped products take up more space than those that are more compact. For example, a great deal of dead space exists in a truckload shipment of motorcycles because of the way the cycles are constructed. However, the same truck can haul more stereo speakers because of the compactness of the product. Another closely related feature is the density of the products. A dense product may carry a lower freight rate than lighter products because greater revenues can be achieved by hauling heavier loads. The carriers' charges are based on a unit freight rate times the weight of the shipment. It is to the carriers' advantage to load as much as is physically possible in the transportation vehicle.

For instance, assume the same truck could be used to carry either stereo speakers or stereo tuners. Both commodities are compact and the trailer's full cubic capacity would be used with either product. But the tuners are much heavier, and more weight can be loaded in the trailer if the carrier hauls the tuners. Table 13–6 shows the same number of units to be transported. With an identical freight rate, the carrier is much better off hauling tuners. The freight rate on the speakers would have to be twice as much to give the carrier an identical amount of revenue.

Another product characteristic that affects freight rate levels is the value. As mentioned earlier, the carrier's liability affects the rate level. A higher-valued product may also need special handling such as theft protection or additional bracing (dunnage). The greater the possibility of damage, the more expensive the effort to deliver the commodities in good condition.

Products with special features that require care during transit also affect the rate level. A shipment containing perishable food may require refrigeration or icing to keep it fresh. This process requires labor and materials and, if an additional charge is not assessed, the cost must be built into the rate. The same

TABLE 13–6. Density Effect on Freight Rate Levels

	Stereo Tuners	Stereo Speakers
Number of Items	1,500	1,500
Weight Per Item	40 lbs.	20 lbs.
Total Weight	60,000 lbs.	30,000 lbs.
Freight Rate Per Cwt	$3	$3
Total Freight Revenue	$1,800	$900

concept applies to cattle that must be fed on long-distance shipments. Commodities such as dairy products might have to be shipped in more expensive refrigerated equipment, and the cost must be included in the freight rate. You may be able to think of other products with special features that must be considered when determining proper rate levels.

DEMAND CHARACTERISTICS

Thus far, the discussion has centered on the costs of providing transportation service. Another factor that affects freight rate levels is demand. Chapter 2 explained that communities prefer low freight rates so that they can purchase products from other areas and ship their manufactured items to regions where they are in demand. Given identical products, most people will buy the one with the lower price tag. Transportation costs represent a portion of the final price paid for any product. If the transportation cost from all producing points is high, total demand may decline. Demand also affects freight rate setting.

Those factors that enter into each freight rate-setting decision are costs (both fixed and variable), operating characteristics (carrier liability, distance traveled, facility utilization, volume handled), product characteristics (size, shape, density, value, special handling requirements), and demand characteristics (the quantity demanded at any particular location). You can see that the decision is not easy. Many variables affect the rate charged by carriers. Let us now discuss the various types of freight rates that exist among transportation modes.

Freight Rate Types

Freight rates are based on some unit of measure, which is most often weight, but not always. For example, it is possible to rent an entire train for a year. Some rates, such as contract rates, may be based on mileage. Rates are also charged on a mileage basis to move privately owned freight cars back to the owners after unloading. The main basis for rates is a cents-per-weight formula, such as 86 cents per hundredweight. In addition, most rates are quoted with a minimum weight per shipment, which ensures a certain minimum total revenue for the carrier on each shipment. One exception to the weight basis is the pipeline rate, which is assessed on a per-barrel basis. Most pipeline rates carry a minimum quantity, with 500 barrels the most popular minimum. In all cases, if the minimum is not achieved for the shipment, the shipper must pay the stated minimum.

To illustrate, assume a rate is quoted on sawdust. The rate may be 20 cents per hundredweight with a minimum weight of 40,000 pounds. If the total shipment weighs only 36,000 pounds, the shipper would have to pay the full $80, because that is the minimum weight acceptable to the carrier. For pipelines, the shipper would have to pay the full 500-barrel minimum, even if only 100 barrels were shipped.

A variety of rate types exists. Because of the many conditions involved in freight transportation and the many products transported, carriers attempt to publish rates to accommodate many users. This section will discuss two types of rates: line-haul rates and accessory rates.

A *line-haul rate* is a charge for providing freight transportation service between a point of origin and a point of destination. It takes its name from the fact that it is a charge for a haul along the line of the carrier. The class, commodity, and exception rates discussed earlier are all line-haul rates. Line-haul rates are either carrier line-haul rates or product line-haul rates. An *accessorial rate* is a charge for services provided by carriers other than for line-haul.

CARRIER LINE-HAUL RATES

Carrier line-haul rates are not separate rates but describe the procedure involved in arriving at the freight rate for a particular shipment. These particular rates are described as carrier line-haul rates because they reflect the way the product is handled in actual movement, independent of the product being hauled. The carrier classification of line-haul rates is based on operational features.

LOCAL RATE

Many shipments are transported by a carrier that also serves the point to which the shipment is destined. For example, if a carload of brick is loaded in Pueblo, Colorado, by a shipper served by the Missouri-Pacific Railroad, and it is shipped to a buyer in Kansas City, Missouri, who is also served by the Missouri-Pacific Railroad, the shipment probably will remain on that one railroad until it is delivered. The rate charged is a single carrier rate and is known as a *local rate*, a transportation charge for a shipment along the line of a single carrier.

JOINT RATE

Not all freight shipments originate and terminate with the same carrier, so the shipment must be interchanged along the way. For example, a carload of lumber originating in Seattle, Washington, with a shipper served by the Burlington-Northern Railroad, is destined to a buyer in Los Angeles, California, who is served by the Southern Pacific Railroad. Because Burlington-Northern does not serve Los Angeles, the shipment must be interchanged along the way. The rate charged for this shipment is known as a joint rate, because it has been set by the two involved carriers. A *joint rate* can be defined as a transportation charge for a shipment along the lines of two or more carriers.

COMBINATION RATE

In the preceding example, assume the shipment will move from Seattle to Sacramento, California, where it will be interchanged to the Southern Pacific to complete its journey to Los Angeles. If there is no joint rate from Seattle to Los Angeles, the separate rates for this shipment must be combined. That is, the rate from Seattle to Sacramento must be added to the rate from Sacramento to Los Angeles. This type of rate is known as a *combination rate*, a total freight rate that is the result of combining two or more separate rates.

THROUGH RATE

The existence of a through rate eliminates the need for a combination rate. In the preceding example, if a rate exists from Seattle to Los Angeles and is published in that format, it is known as a through rate, which would be the same as a joint rate. A *through rate* is defined as a single rate published for a shipment transported from point of origin to point of destination. It may be known as a local rate or a joint rate, as well.

PROPORTIONAL RATE

Combination rates are reached by adding the freight charges from origin to midpoint, and from midpoint to destination. In some cases, no published rate may exist from origin to destination or from origin to a midpoint, but a rate may exist from midpoint to ultimate consignee. Thus, there must be some way to determine the rate from origin to actual destination. The proportional rate method of determining the freight charges can resolve this problem and is best described by referring to Figure 13–10. In this illustration, a shipment is originating at point B and is destined for point D. However, no rate is published from B to D or from B to C, the midpoint, which prevents application of a combination rate. Yet, a rate does exist from point A to point C. In this hypothetical example, the rate from A to C is $3 per unit. From point C to point D, the final destination, the rate is $4 per unit. Through pricing analysis, it is known that the $3 rate from point A to point C is comprised of two portions. From A to B, the rate proportion is $1.50 per unit, and from B to C the proportion is $1.50 per unit. The freight rate on the shipment from B to D is determined by combining the proportion of $1.50 from B to C with the $4 rate from C to D to arrive at a $5.50 per unit rate from B to D. This is known as a *proportional rate*, a transportation charge obtained by adding a part of the

FIGURE 13–10. Proportional Rate Illustration

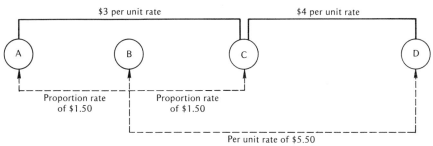

freight rate between two points to a total freight rate between two other points to obtain its total.

Arbitrary Rate

There are instances wherein proportional rates need not be computed to arrive at the total freight charges between two points where published rates do not exist. In these cases, the carrier will add a fixed amount to the rate published to or from the closest point involved in the shipment. Suppose, for example, a shipment is being made from New Orleans to Weatherford, Texas. Rates are published from New Orleans to Fort Worth, Texas, but none to Weatherford, which is a short distance west of Fort Worth. The carrier might assign an additional amount, such as 20¢/cwt for the additional mileage to be serviced. Rates of this type are known as *arbitrary rates*.

Differential Rate

Many times, a shipper may desire the slowest possible route from origin to destination. Several reasons may account for this, such as additional seasoning enroute or to relieve congestion at either the origin or destination points. In these cases, where the applicable tariffs allow, the carrier will assign a fixed amount to the rate that applies by a more direct route. For example, the freight rate on fresh apples from Tacoma, Washington, to St. Louis, Missouri, may be $6/cwt. However, the apples are harvested green and will ripen enroute. The shipper may desire a more roundabout route to ensure ripening and will specify routing instructions through Albuquerque, New Mexico; Dallas, Texas; and on to St. Louis, Missouri. The carrier may charge an additional amount, say 30¢/cwt, for the privilege of using the longer route. This additional amount is known as a differential, and the resulting charge is a *differential rate*.

PRODUCT LINE-HAUL RATES

Many rates are tailored to a specific commodity or industry. However, the following discussion focuses on the product freight rates commonly used and applicable across a wide range of products and industries.

VEHICLE-LOAD RATE

Earlier, the carrier's desire to use the transportation vehicle's full capacity was discussed. To encourage this, the carriers publish vehicle-load rates that give the users exclusive use of the vehicles. A high minimum is attached to the published rate, which encourages shippers to load as much as possible in the vehicle. For example, a full truckload of Tupperware kitchen aids most likely would not meet the weight capacity of a truck. In an effort to encourage the heaviest possible load and also to meet the minimum revenue desires of the trucking company, a rate may be published on a 32,000-lb. minimum weight. Any weight less than 32,000 lbs. would be billed to the user, and the difference in charges between the actual weight and the minimum rate assessed by the carrier is known as *dead freight*.

LESS-THAN-VEHICLE-LOAD RATE

Many times, shippers are unable to meet the minimum set by the carriers, but the commodities must be shipped. In such cases, the shippers will share the vehicle space with other users shipping in the same direction. A higher rate per hundredweight than vehicle-load is quoted, and the carrier collects commodities from several users to consolidate a large load. The carriers will charge a higher unit rate to cover the additional time and effort. These rates are known as *less-than-carload* (LCL) for rail and *less-than-truckload* (LTL) for highway shipments.

INCENTIVE RATE

Some rates are in between the vehicle-load and less-than-vehicle-load rates. Rates may be published that set a rate and weight minimum. However, once the minimum is reached, the unit rate is lower for any weight that exceeds the minimum. For example, the quoted rate may be $5 per unit on 32,000 lbs. and $3 per unit for any weight beyond 32,000 lbs. This is known as an incentive rate, because the shipper is given an incentive to load a heavier shipment. Otherwise, the overflow held for another shipment would cost the user $5 per unit. Incentive rates may be published in one of two ways. In the preceding example, the shipper is responsible for a $5 rate on the first 32,000 lbs. contained in the vehicle. The $3 rate applies on all weight in excess of 32,000 lbs. In the first type of incentive rate, a shipper may load 50,000 lbs. in one shipment. The freight charges on the shipment would total $2,140, as shown in Table 13–7. This is classified as a *one-break incentive rate*.

A *two-break incentive rate* presents some interesting possibilities. Assume for purposes of illustration that a rail carrier publishes a two-break incentive rate on a particular commodity between two points. Assume rates of $9 per cwt. on a 44,800-lb. minimum and $6.50 on an 80,000-lb. minimum. The lower rate on the higher minimum is intended to encourage heavier loading of the rail-car, resulting in better equipment utilization. In actuality, the shipper need not load 80,000 lbs. in the railcar to enjoy the lower unit rate. In the two-break

TABLE 13–7. One-Break Incentive Rate 50,000 lb. Shipment

Freight Rate	Minimum Weight	Freight Charge
$5	32,000 lbs.	$1,600
$3	18,000 lbs.	$ 540
Total Freight Charge		$2,140

rate structure, the user is responsible for the rate that would result in the lower total freight charges. Thus, in the example, if the railcar is loaded to 80,000 lbs., total freight charges would amount to $5,200, as shown under (A) in Table 13–8. A saving could be realized after a certain weight, between 44,800 lbs. and 80,000 lbs., is achieved. In this example, an 80,000-lb. shipment would result in railroad revenue of $5,200, as shown in (A) of Table 13–8. Suppose a railcar is loaded to 57,780 lbs. As (B) in Table 13–8 shows, either rate assessed would result in almost identical revenue for the rail carrier. If the railcar is loaded beyond 57,780 lbs., the user would realize a freight saving by paying the lower rate on an 80,000-lb. shipment, absorbing dead freight for the weight difference between the dead freight over 57,780 lbs. and the 80,000-lb. minimum weight needed to guarantee use of the lower freight rate. With shipments meeting the lower of the two-break weights, it unquestionably would be advantageous to pay the higher freight rate. But, in all instances of two-break freight rates, there is a weight breakpoint at which the lower rate on the higher weight is cost-beneficial and should be applied. This is illustrated in (B) of Table 13–8. In this example, all shipments weighing more than 57,780 lbs. should be paid at the 80,000-lb. rate.

VOLUME RATE

During the past two decades, the carriers have used another method to attract business to their modes. Lower rates are published if the shipper uses

TABLE 13–8. Two-Break Incentive Rate

(A)		
Freight Rate	Minimum Weight	Revenue
$9.00	44,800 lbs.	$4,032
$6.50	80,000 lbs.	$5,200

(B)			
Freight Rate	Shipment Weight	Dead Freight	Cost
1) $9.00	57,780 lbs.	0	$5,200.00
2) $6.50	57,780 lbs.	22,220	$5,200.00

more than one vehicle at a time. The practice is common among the railroads and is occasionally used in modified form by trucking companies. In the rail industry, a shipper may hire a full train for a one-time shipment or on a yearly basis. Generally, there is a flat charge plus a rate per mile that is accepted by the user only when it is economically feasible. Shippers do not have to rent an entire train to take advantage of volume rates. Many rates are lower per unit if five, ten, or twenty carloads are tendered at one time, in one day, at the same origin, and going to the same destination. Volume rates are justified because of the lower operating costs in handling several carloads at one time.

FREIGHT-ALL-KINDS RATE

It is common practice to publish rates on a single commodity moving between two points. Occasionally, a shipper is unable to ship a full vehicle load of one commodity from one origin to one destination at one time but does not wish to share the vehicle space with other shippers. The carriers publish rates that allow shippers to load several different commodities in one vehicle. These are known as freight-all-kinds rates (FAK) or all-commodity rates (ACR). They are usually higher than rates published for a full load of one commodity but lower than the less-than-vehicle-load rates that otherwise would apply.

CONTAINER RATE

Rates are published for containers loaded with merchandise. The shipper loads a large container with all the commodities to be transported. The large container then requires only a single handling by the carrier to put it in the transportation vehicle. The one rate quoted is known as a container rate. This practice is extremely popular in water transportation. Very large containers are also used for railroad transportation. The box is put on a flat railcar and transported to its destination. These rates are known as container-on-flatcar (COFC) rates.

TRAILER-ON-FLATCAR RATE

Intermodal shipments have become increasingly popular during the last two decades. Truck trailers are loaded and driven to railroad terminals. The tractors remain in the city of origin and the entire trailer is placed on a flat railroad car. At its destination, the trailer is hooked to another tractor and driven to its final point. To encourage acceptance of this practice, the railroad established trailer-on-flatcar (TOFC) rates and has several variations of this method. The available arrangements were discussed in Chapter 9.

GROUP RATE

To eliminate problems with competitors seeking favored rates over other competitors, carriers have established group rates, or rates to and from entire regions. The same rate applies from any origin point within the grouping of cities or states or to any destination point within a grouping of cities or states. The entire country could be divided into six or eight groups. For instance, the rate might remain the same on lumber from any of the producing states in the Pacific Northwest to Memphis, Tennessee. Then, all producers at the place of origin would be in the same competitive posture to sell lumber in Memphis.

Import-Export Rate

It is common to find lower rates on commodities moving to or from cities enroute to seaports if those products are exported or have been imported. For example, the corn rate from Omaha, Nebraska, to Chicago, Illinois, may be lower if the corn is to be loaded on a seagoing vessel and exported to Great Britain than it would be if the corn is to be processed in Chicago for domestic consumption. Lower freight rates on exported commodities encourage foreign trade and assist in a favorable balance of trade.

Transit Privilege Rate

It is not always necessary to fill a transportation vehicle at one origin point or unload the total contents at one destination point. Carriers will allow a vehicle to be partially loaded at one location and to stop off at another city to add more products before completing its journey. The rate charged will be from origin point for the total contents delivered at the final destination. The total charges are less than they would be if a less-than-vehicle-load rate were charged for each portion of the total load. Similarly, a fully loaded vehicle can stop at one point, partially unload, and continue to another destination for final unloading. Then, the rate charged is for the entire shipment to the farthest point. These rates are known as *stop-off rates*, a form of transit privilege rates. An accessorial charge, discussed later, will also be assessed.

Another transit privilege allows for changes in the form of the commodity. Raw wheat may be shipped from a gathering area to a milling location, processed into flour, and then shipped to a consuming or manufacturing location. Lumber and several other commodities also use this method. In these cases, the through rate from the origin point to the final destination point applies. The rate level is for the higher-rated commodity. If wheat carries a higher rate than flour, the wheat rate from origin to the delivery point of the flour is assessed. This service, known as *milling-in-transit*, carries an accessorial charge as well. The higher through rate can be justified because it eliminates paying fixed costs twice, which would occur for two separate rates.

Section 22 Rate

The final product line-haul rate is a special rate that applies to any commodity shipped by the United States government. These commodities are shipped at lower rates than those charged to any other user between the same two points for the same quantity. The rates are known as *Section 22 rates* because they are sanctioned by Section 22 of the Interstate Commerce Act. The lower rates are justified because of the government's substantial investment in transportation facilities, from the original land grants to the subsidies that continue today. In addition to line-haul rates, the carriers have special rates for other services not directly involved in line-haul movement. The charges are assessed to those who require something extra when shipping commodities.

ACCESSORIAL RATES

In daily operations, carriers are often called upon to provide services beyond moving commodities between two points. Because these services are accessory to the primary movement function, accessorial rates are assessed. The carriers usually provide any additional or accessorial service that will secure a shipper's business. Some of the more common services for which accessorial rates are charged are diversion, reconsignment, demurrage and detention, reweighing, transit privileges, car ferry, feeding, and icing.

DIVERSION

Business conditions and demand situations change frequently. Sometimes, emergencies may require that destinations be changed for shipments that have already left their origin point. A destination change on a shipment while it is enroute is known as a *diversion*. If the new destination is out of line from the original destination, the shipper may have to pay a combination rate. Otherwise, a through rate to the new destination will be charged. In either event, the carrier will assess an accessorial charge for changing the shipment.

As an example, assume that a full carload shipment of jams, jellies, and preserves is enroute from its production location in Orrville, Ohio, to a supermarket chain's distribution center in Pittsburgh, Pennsylvania. As a practice, the distribution center carries a minimum two weeks' supply to ensure that its retail outlets are never out of stock. It is learned that a flood has destroyed the complete inventory of another major buyer in Buffalo, New York, and a request is made to the seller for a rush shipment to the Buffalo location, where it will be stored in a public warehouse that was not damaged. To supply immediate customer service, the shipper can contact the rail carrier and request a diversion of the full carload shipment to the Buffalo buyer. The rail carrier will locate the shipment along its line and redirect it to Buffalo, and the shipper loads another full railcar for the original buyer. As long as the initial shipment is not out of the route usually followed on shipments from Orrville to Buffalo, the through rate will apply. If the shipment is out of the legal route, the shipper has the option of paying a combination rate for the diversion. In either case, the carrier will assess an accessorial charge in addition to the freight charges for making the desired change.

RECONSIGNMENT

Closely related to diversion is changing the receiver of a shipment in the destination city. Suppose a shipment is made from Atlanta, Georgia, to company

A in Jacksonville, Florida. For some reason, the shipper may decide the shipment should go instead to company B in Jacksonville. Before the shipment is delivered, the shipper may request the change. This is known as a *reconsignment*, and an accessorial charge is assessed.

The practice of reconsigning rail shipments is popular in speculative industries. For example, assume there is a steady, heavy demand for Idaho potatoes in the Chicago metropolitan area. The many buyers may be food processing companies or large retailers with many outlets. An agricultural products broker may make a long-term purchase of a large quantity of Idaho potatoes from a large grower and will request that shipments be made on a regular basis to Chicago. Because selling prices on potatoes can change daily, the broker may want to delay final delivery instructions so as to realize the highest price at the time of delivery. In such a situation, the broker will issue initial shipping instructions showing the consignee to be the broker in Chicago. The broker knows the time it takes to ship a full carload from the Idaho producer to Chicago. Shortly before the shipment's arrival, the broker will contact the rail carrier and issue delivery instructions that the railcar be delivered to the firm with whom the broker negotiated a sale while the potatoes were enroute. The broker follows this same procedure for every shipment. In each case, the rail carrier will issue a reconsignment charge to the broker in addition to the regular freight charges.

DEMURRAGE AND DETENTION

The primary function of a truck, railcar, barge, or vessel is to move commodities between two points. When an empty vehicle is placed at a shipper's location for loading, or a loaded vehicle is placed at a receiver's location for unloading, the carrier expects the loading or unloading to be accomplished within a reasonable time. Time limits are placed on the shipper and receiver for loading and unloading, and there is no additional charge if the activity is completed within that time limit. If the allowed time limit is exceeded, an accessorial charge known as *demurrage* for rail or water vehicles and *detention* for trucks is assessed. The extra charge is based on daily rates for railcars and hourly rates for water vessels and trucks.

Many times, demurrage or detention are unavoidable. For example, a consignee may not have sufficient storage space in which to place the contents of a railcar and must wait until some stored items are shipped out. In such a case, it would be less costly to delay unloading and pay the demurrage charge. Otherwise, the shipment would have to be moved to a public warehouse, where further handling would be necessary to unload and then reload the shipment later. It is usually cheaper to pay the daily demurrage charge, provided the delay is not excessive.

In other instances, demurrage is avoidable, but the receiver wishes to leave the shipment intact. Several reasons can justify this practice, even though the railcar, in effect, becomes a storage container rather than a transportation vehicle. For example, some steel-making facilities use large quantities of coal in their operations. Incoming coal shipments may be in a few railcars or as many as a trainload. If the coal is unloaded to a stockpile, additional handling will be required later to reload the coal into railcars to move it to furnaces. The steel company may prefer to hold the loaded incoming cars and schedule them directly to the furnaces when required, thereby avoiding the expense of unloading, stockpiling, and reloading. As long as the demurrage charges are lower than the additional operating expenses, the steel company enjoys lower costs by paying demurrage.

REWEIGHING

Freight rates are based on a monetary amount and the total weight of the commodities. The weight of the empty vehicle is known. To determine the weight of the vehicle contents, the vehicle is weighed after it is loaded. The weight of the empty vehicle is known as the *tare weight*; loaded vehicle, *gross weight*; and contents weight, *net weight*. If the shipper or receiver wants to verify the weighing report, a reweighing can be requested. If the difference between the two weighings exceeds the established tolerance (an insignificant difference), no charge will be made for reweighing. If the reweighing is within the tolerance, an accessory charge will be made.

TRANSIT PRIVILEGES

A previous section described the transit privileges of stop-off and milling-in-transit. In either case, the user is better off with the special line-haul rates. Carriers will assess an additional accessorial charge for performance of these services.

CAR FERRY

The shortest distance between two points is a straight line, and it would be beneficial to transport commodities that way. Unfortunately, a river or lake may lie between those two points. When the service is available, a shipper may request that a railcar be transported across water by car ferry to save time in transit. An accessorial charge may be assessed by the carrier for this service.

FEEDING AND ICING

Earlier, it was illustrated that product chracteristics influence rate levels. Some commodities, such as frozen food or cattle, need additional services. When these services are not incorporated in a higher-rate level, the carrier will assess the user an accessorial charge to compensate for the extra expense.

Let us now examine the rate-making process, the basic method by which freight rates are established, put into effect, and changed.

Rate-Making procedures

You have seen how freight rate levels can affect the economy of an entire community. Rates affect the products brought into an area as well as the commodities produced in a community and shipped elsewhere. Freight rate levels can also affect an individual company within an industry. If a firm must pay higher freight rates for inbound and outbound shipments than other companies in the same industry but located in different areas, the firm may not be able to remain competitive. Similarly, when two industries produce possible substitute products such as aluminum and steel, the industry with lower freight rates has an advantage. Consequently, many separate entities are interested in establishing reasonable freight rates or lowering unreasonable rates. Carriers are interested in higher freight rates to increase their revenue, but they sometimes want to reduce published rates to develop new movements.

Because of these many aspects of rate making, a regular procedure is necessary to handle freight rate matters. This section describes the most common procedures employed to set up or change freight rates.

RATE BUREAUS

Chapter 11 explained that carriers recognize the destructiveness of competing on the basis of freight rates. If one carrier reduced its rate, the others would have to follow or lose business. If all carriers reduced their rates in a competitive contest, then all would lose revenue. The carriers therefore decided to act collectively on rate matters. Groups of carriers engaging in transportation services in each region of the country were formed to act on all rate matters. Membership is not mandatory. At least one representative from each member carrier has a vote in these groups, known as rate bureaus. The country is sectioned so that rate matters are handled in the region involved, rather than on a national basis. One central organization would be hard-pressed to handle the volume of rate matters from all parts of the country. The rate bureaus serve as clearing houses. They receive rate-setting and rate-changing requests and inform all members of each matter. Members express opinions and vote on the matter. Any member may request that the rate be investigated further or that it be discussed at a meeting of the group.

In addition to acting as clearing houses, the bureaus act as publishing agents for the rate tariffs. This frees carriers from publishing their own tariffs on all rates. The rates common to all carriers who may participate in the haul are known as *agency publications*. The bureaus also publish tariffs that apply only to one carrier; these are known as *local tariffs*. Rates that apply to two carriers are known as *joint tariffs*. All such tariffs are published by the rate bureaus. The territorial divisions of railroad rate bureaus are shown in Figure 13–11.

251

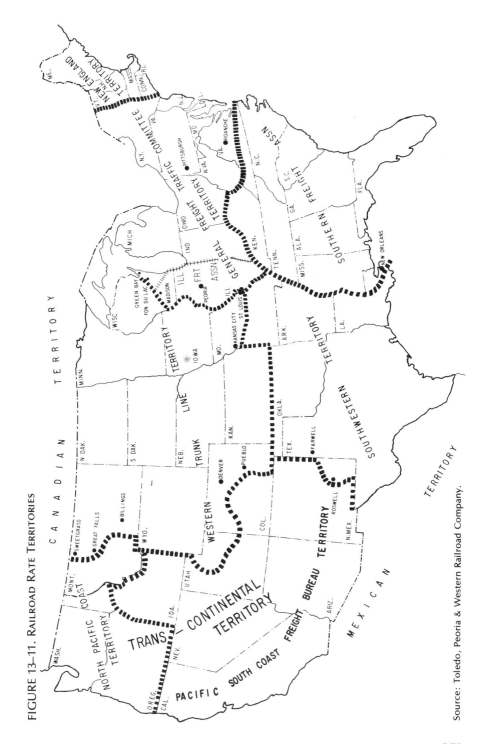

FIGURE 13–11. Railroad Rate Territories

Source: Toledo, Peoria & Western Railroad Company.

252

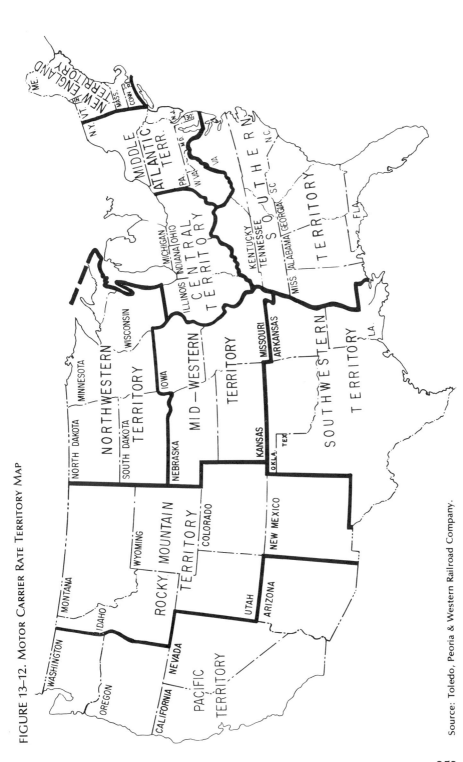

FIGURE 13–12. MOTOR CARRIER RATE TERRITORY MAP

Source: Toledo, Peoria & Western Railroad Company.

253

The motor freight bureau regions are shown in Figure 13–12. The respective bureaus review rate matters pertaining to activities performed within their geographic regions.

RATE REQUEST FLOWS

Although many people, communities, business firms, and carriers are directly affected by freight rate levels, requests to set new rates or change old ones usually originate from two sources: shippers or carriers. Carrier requests usually stem from shipper needs, so all requests are user-based in effect. A breakdown of the procedure will illustrate the different reasons for requests and the slight modifications in the procedures.

SHIPPER REQUESTS

Shippers have a variety of reasons for requesting that carriers establish a new rate or lower an existing one. A shipper may have had to pay a class rate because adequate volume has not existed for any other arrangement. But a change may occur and large volumes of a commodity may enter the traffic flow. A lower rate would help the additional shipments, and the shipper may request that a commodity rate be established. This type of request usually goes directly to the rate bureau. The bureau proceeds with its usual information dissemination procedure and may consult the classification committee. The committee would definitely be involved if the request concerned reclassification of a commodity.

A shipper may feel at a competitive disadvantage because of proportionately higher rates from sources to markets than other firms pay. This type of issue usually involves specific points, and the shipper may approach one or more carriers with a rate reduction request. If the carriers agree to the request, the proposal is forwarded to the bureau so that all member carriers can be informed of the intended change. The voting procedure is followed or the matter may be reviewed at a general meeting.

In some cases, an entire industry may request rate changes. This is handled by an industry association, an organization whose members participate in a particular activity. The association forwards the request to the involved bureau and the rest of the procedure is the same as with a shipper request. Generally, industry requests are of greater importance and are reviewed at a regular bureau meeting.

CARRIER REQUESTS

The more common rate requests originate with one or more carriers. Several reasons exist for carrier-sponsored rate requests. Most individual shipper requests are discussed informally with carrier rate representatives to gain support for the change within the transportation mode. If the carrier believes that the request has merit, a formal rate change request proposal is prepared and forwarded to the appropriate bureau.

A carrier may sponsor a rate change request because of a competitive disadvantage with another transportation mode. If, for example, water carriers are shipping large traffic volumes of a particular commodity, a rail carrier may initiate a rate-reduction request so that the railroad can compete for the business.

When individual railroads publish rates between two points in local tariffs, one carrier's rate may be lower than the other carrier's rate in the same mode. The carrier with the higher rate might request a rate reduction in order to be competitive.

Although many other reasons exist for carrier-sponsored rate requests, the foregoing are the general types of requests. In most cases, the request is forwarded to the involved bureaus. All changes are sent to member carriers, who are allowed to express their opinions. If the proposed change involves other bureaus' territories, the information is sent to those bureaus and their members are notified. Each bureau is allowed to act on the proposed change.

RATE REQUEST ACTION

Rate changes affect shippers and carriers alike. Therefore, any affected party can have a voice in the outcome. The bureaus notify respective members, and users are notified by various transportation magazines that publish proposed changes on a regular basis. Responses to the proposed change are subject to a time limit. If no negative responses are received, the bureau will publish the rate change in a new tariff with an effective date of at least thirty days after the publication date. In rare cases, a change may be expedited with a shortened procedure and can take effect as quickly as within one day. All rate changes are forwarded to the appropriate government regulatory body. The regulator checks the changes to be certain they are in compliance with the laws and that they are properly worded. Barring any problems, the new rate can take effect.

Proposed changes may run into snags. A complaint may be received by the bureau from a shipper or another carrier. If the change is opposed, it will be sent to one of the bureau's committees for further investigation and may also be put on the agenda for discussion at the next general meeting. The bureau's subsequent decision on the change is binding at this stage of the process. The change may be approved, disapproved, or modified. Anyone dissatisfied on either side of the issue can appeal directly to the regulatory agency. If that happens, the formal complaint procedure is followed. For example, a shipper may request a rate reduction that will increase its firm's business volume. In the shipper's opinion, the rate reduction request is justified economically, but the bureau rejects the request. Because the regulatory bodies are endowed with the authority to determine a rate's reasonableness, a formal complaint may be filed. According to the procedure described in Chapter 12, the bureau may be requested to justify its rejection in a hearing before a three-person board, and then an official decision is rendered. Or, a single carrier may take independent action and announce that a reduced rate will be published. A competing carrier may believe that the proposed rate is lower than the variable costs involved with the particular movement and will so protest to the regulatory body. The investigation and suspension procedure allows the regulatory body to suspend the proposed rate pending further investigation. After the investigation, the three-person board renders a decision as to the proposed rate's reasonableness. As explained in Chapter 12, this decision may be appealed to a higher level in the regulatory body for further consideration and an ultimate final decision.

The change may be approved by all parties, but the regulatory agency may block the change. The regulator may believe the change needs to be explored further to be certain that the proposed lower rate covers the carrier's operating cost. Or it may stop the change's effective date to investigate whether the long- and short-haul clause of the Interstate Commerce Act is being violated. In any event, the change can be suspended pending an investigation. This procedure is known as an *Investigation and Suspension Ruling* (I&S). The regulatory body may request a formal hearing if there are sufficient reasons. After investigation, the change may be approved, disapproved, or modified by the regulatory body. Its decision is then binding, subject to possible judicial review. An individual carrier may not want to participate in any shipments in which a reduced rate is involved. It will then make its position known to the tariff bureau, and the published rate will indicate that the rate does not apply to that carrier. This is known as flagging-out on the rate.

A carrier's proposed change may be disapproved by the bureau to the detriment of that carrier. It is permissible, although infrequent, for the carrier to bolt from the bureau's decision and order the bureau to publish the rate, as sanctioned by law. This is known as independent action and can take effect unless disapproved by the regulatory agency. The regulators will prevent the action if the rate is found to be unreasonable or discriminatory. Naturally, the carrier's standing with other bureau member carriers is damaged and the carriers' cohesiveness in the industry is weakened. The fact that such a rigorous rate-changing system exists is subject to much criticism.

Rate Issues

The complexity of freight rate setting raises some major issues. To the unfamiliar, it might appear unreasonable that transportation pricing should be so complicated. The answers, unfortunately, are not as easy as the criticisms. Let us explore the major issues of bureau, differential, competitive, and contribution pricing.

BUREAU PRICING

After reviewing the rate-making procedures, you may question the necessity for collective action on transportation pricing. In the free enterprise system, each firm attaches a price to its services, independent of outside influences, as long as the action is within legal guidelines. The regulatory system prevents the carriers from overcharging for their services, a practice that was common before transportation regulation. Undercharging is also prevented by the regulatory system. But should the carriers be allowed to act collectively in setting charges? The action was made legal by the Reed-Bulwinkle Act of 1948, which exempted the bureaus from antitrust violations. It is true that free competition would allow each carrier to set rates, as long as costs were covered. But that point in itself is controversial because of the many methods used to compute costs. From the earlier discussion you can see how fixed and variable costs add to the computation difficulty. Therefore, carriers might go according to the desirability of the traffic volume and favor the more lucrative movements in their pricing methods. This leads to another aspect of the pricing problem. Price wars would have a detrimental effect on the financial stability of the industry. Maintaining an adequate and updated transportation system becomes less likely without a healthy industry. The existence of bureaus tends to reduce the temptation to enter price wars. Also, consistency in transportation pricing is achieved because the carriers must justify prices to their competitors. Comparison pricing becomes easier.

Pressures were put on the bureau system during the late 1970s. Proponents of transportation deregulation attacked its collusive pricing practices, and efforts to repeal the Reed-Bulwinkle Act gained momentum. What the end result of these efforts will be remains unknown at this time.

DIFFERENTIAL PRICING

Freight rates on commodities moving between identical points by the same transportation mode sometimes differ greatly. This is called differential pricing. One side of the issue is the argument that the cost of providing line-haul service is the same for all commodities. Except for the product characteristic differences described earlier in this chapter, the argument has some validity. On the other side of the argument, freight charges can be no higher than those that allow the traffic to move. Exceedingly high rates will prevent some commodities from being transported. For example, a $20 freight charge attached to moving a refrigerator 500 miles will not prevent the movement because the rate may be only 5 per cent of the value of the $400 refrigerator. However, a $20 freight rate on a ton of coal may be too high if the coal is valued at $80 per ton. In that case, the rate is 25 per cent of the commodity's value. Thus, some products are able to absorb a freight charge that would be prohibitive for another product. The *value of service* is higher for the refrigerator, thus the higher rate. This disregards the *cost of service*, which is roughly the same. Which is the correct approach?

COMPETITIVE PRICING

Carriers take into consideration intraindustry and interindustry competition when setting freight rate levels. The arguments on both sides of the issue resemble those for differential pricing. Should the carriers be concerned with external factors or should all rates be based on cost of service? Resource locations are not dispersed evenly across the country, and yet demand for these resources may be distributed evenly. Therefore, freight charges must reflect the differences in demand variations and the ability to absorb freight charges. Competitors within an industry are dispersed and still require the same resources to continue operations. If rates were charged strictly on the basis of providing service, some competitors could not afford the higher costs and would go out of business. If the traffic does not move, fixed costs still have to be absorbed. Ultimately, the remaining competitors would incur higher freight rates because of the lower volumes moving in the transportation stream.

The same concept applies to interindustry competition. Not only is employment created by the many industries that make products for which substitutes exist, but a greater variety of products is available for the consuming public. If freight charges were identical, one of the industries might not be able to afford the proportionately higher freight charges. Lower rates are available to one industry because the other pays higher charges. That is possible because of differences in other costs incurred by both industries. In the final analysis, freight rates move commodities. Can this be fulfilled by ignoring industry characteristics?

CONTRIBUTION PRICING

Both differential and competitive pricing occur because of *contribution theory*. This theory allows rates to be set at a level to cover at least variable costs. If variable costs are not covered, the firm cannot afford to stay in business. In contribution theory, total charges are based on variable costs plus some contribution to fixed costs. The issue involved is whether each shipment should contribute the same amount to fixed costs. Differential pricing is possible because some commodities pay a larger proportion of fixed costs than others. With fully distributed costs, each shipment pays an equal share of fixed costs and all variable costs. However, with different operating procedures and accounting systems, there is no perfect method to determine equality in fixed costs. Even if it were possible to determine the proportion to be shared equally, the question of whether all shipments will continue to move emerges again.

258

The issues raised here are by no means the only ones faced in rate setting. However, they pose theoretical questions that must be addressed each time rate issues are discussed. At the beginning of this chapter, it was stated that the freight rate subject is the most complicated in the transportation industry. This examination of some of the issues confirms that many problems exist. As with almost any topic, the questions are easy. The answers are much more difficult.

Summary

The subject of transportation freight rates is complex. Freight rates play an economic role in location decisions and in the competitive arena, where they affect industrial, carrier, and geographic competition. Freight rates are divided into class, commodity, exception, and contract rates. The major factors that influence freight rate levels are fixed and variable costs, and operating, product, and demand characteristics. Specific freight rate types are line-haul rates (both carrier and product), and accessorial rates.

A regular procedure for setting or changing freight rates exists that involves rate bureaus, carriers, and shippers, all of whom have an opportunity to respond to the proposed rate. Major issues that affect freight rate setting, center on bureau, differential, competitive, and contribution pricing.

Transportation management requires an understanding of not only freight rate structures and procedures, but also various types of transportation documentation, which is the subject of Chapter 14.

Questions for Chapter 13

1. Explain how freight rates affect both intramodal and intermodal competition.
2. Distinguish between a freight commodity's rating and its rate.
3. Briefly describe the differences among class, commodity, exception, and contract freight rates.
4. Use an example to distinguish clearly between transportation fixed and variable costs.
5. Describe operating characteristics that affect freight rate levels.
6. In what way does the extent of facility utilization affect freight rate levels?
7. What reasons can you give for a product's characteristics to affect its freight rate level?
8. Define line-haul rates.
9. Explain the conceptual difference between combination rates and proportional rates.
10. Give a one-sentence definition of the following freight rate types:
    a. Vehicle-load
    b. Incentive

    c. Volume
    d. Freight-all-kinds
    e. Group
    f. Transit privilege
11. What is the difference between reconsignment and diversion?
12. Distinguish clearly among local, joint, and agency tariffs.

14

Transportation Documents

Your day-to-day life routinely involves a lot of paper work. Writing a check and maintaining a checkbook requires paper work. When you buy a new appliance or automobile, you receive a warranty, a contract with the seller or manufacturer, that involves paper work. As a student, you take lecture notes, write exams, outline text chapters, and fill out various forms. A list of the various kinds of paper work in which all are involved and documents that all maintain on a regular basis is endless.

It is not surprising, then, that business firms are even more involved than individuals in paper work. Every business function requires documents and records. The method of issuing documents and keeping records may vary from industry to industry and even from firm to firm, but it is done by all. The transportation industry is not exempt from the paper work requirement. Because of the industry's complexity, however, the paper work and documentation is often assumed to be much more elaborate than it is. This is not to say that transportation documentation is not a burden. But considering that at least three separate entities—shippers, carriers, and receivers—are involved in every transaction, the paper work is not overwhelming.

This chapter will describe the most common forms of documentation and paper work directly used in daily transportation operations, and some management documents relating to transportation service that are used by both carriers and shippers. All of the documents that involve both carriers and shippers may be separated into three categories: shipment documents, supporting documents, and management documents.

Shipment Documents

The transportation industry is unique in comparison to almost all other types of commercial activity. In all common or contract carriage, the owner of property turns it over to someone else who performs a service by delivering that property to another party. The owner may or may not retain title to the property, but the carrier takes physical possession until transportation is completed. Thus, some kind of documentation is necessary to verify legal rights to the property. The carriers perform a service based on the expectations of both the shipper and the receiver, and some form of documentation is required to state those expectations. The carriers have responsibilities and limitations that must be stated explicitly to avoid disagreements after the fact. Again, documentation is required.

In performing the transportation service, carriers move commodities between two locations and must keep records regarding the movement. The carriers expect to receive revenues for performing this service, so documentation is required to prepare an invoice. The common documents used to record these functions are known as bills of lading, waybills, and freight bills.

BILLS OF LADING

Whenever two separate parties with self-interests negotiate to trade something of value for something else of value, it is wise to have a contract. A contract is a legal document that details what is to be exchanged and what is to be per-

262

formed. Exchanges occur in transportation. Commodities are physically exchanged from the shipper to the carrier. Often carriers need to exchange commodities among themselves in the process of providing the transportation service. To complete the transportation move, the delivery carrier must exchange commodities with the receiver. Also, either the shipper or the receiver will eventually exchange something of value, money, with the carrier for something of value, transportation service. Because of these exchange and ownership situations, a contract is mandatory. The transportation contract is known as a *bill of lading*.

PURPOSES OF BILLS OF LADING

A bill of lading is the most common, widely used, and important document in freight transportation. Before industry regulation, each carrier had its own form of documentation. Different documents were used by different carriers to perform the same service. As the railroad industry stabilized, documentation became more standardized. Rail carriers issued documents to protect both the users and themselves. Bills of lading have three major purposes: receipt for goods, contract of carriage, and evidence of title.

RECEIPT FOR GOODS
The bill of lading, properly completed and endorsed, becomes a receipt for goods. Although the commodities are in the carrier's physical possession, legal title remains with the holder of the receipt, the bill of lading. The shipper can use the bill of lading as proof that the commodities were turned over to the carrier. This receipt also shows that the commodities were received in good condition, which may be important if any damage occurs during movement.

CONTRACT OF CARRIAGE
The bill of lading serves as a contract of carriage between the shipper and carrier, documenting that the carrier has contracted to deliver the commodities as directed by the shipper. The bill of lading also provides standard terms and conditions that clarify the carrier's obligations. Limitations of such obligations are included in the contract as well. For example, the carrier is expected to deliver the shipment in a reasonable amount of time, but acts of God such as floods or earthquakes cannot be used to blame the carrier for nonperformance. As a contract of carriage, the bill of lading identifies the parties involved in the transaction (shipper, carrier, and receiver) and the terms and conditions under which the carrier is obligated.

EVIDENCE OF TITLE
Title to any item depends on the terms of the transaction. If, for example, you buy a television set from a discount store, you take title to the set at the store, cart it away, and set it up yourself. If, however, you buy a console model

at a department store, you may or may not take title immediately, but you will not take immediate possession if the terms of sale include delivery and proper tuning of the set. In this instance, you pay a certain sum of money for installation. If the purchase price includes installation, both title and possession remain with the seller until the set is in good working condition in your home. Actual title to the property is merely paper work and may not be visible. Physical possession, on the other hand, is quite visible.

If the seller's terms with the buyer are based on free on board (f.o.b.) origin, the title reverts to the buyer as soon as the goods are turned over to a carrier. If the terms are "f.o.b. delivered buyer's location," then title remains with the shipper until the carrier has satisfactorily delivered the merchandise to the buyer. In either event, title stays with either the shipper or the receiver, but possession goes to the carrier. The bill of lading serves as evidence regarding who retains title. The holder of the bill of lading, in most cases, can use that document to substantiate a valid claim to ownership of the merchandise.

The bill of lading's importance is evident. It is the basic transportation document by which the involved parties agree to conduct operations. It serves as a receipt for goods, contract of carriage, and evidence of title. A separate bill of lading is prepared for each shipment made by common carriers.

TYPES OF BILLS OF LADING

Many kinds of bills of lading exist. All contain the same basic information, such as origin, destination, receiver, commodity, and dates. But the bills of lading for different modes vary in format. Bills of lading for water or air transportation are not the same as those used in rail transportation. Because water carriers do not have a standard bill of lading form, the format may differ among carriers within that mode. The railroad industry uses standard bill of lading forms, regardless of which railroad provides the service.

Standardization in the railroad bill of lading forms did not happen by accident. During the early railroad era, each carrier used its own form. In 1922, the ICC prescribed a standard format for bills of lading as part of its regulatory function. The ICC has not prescribed standard formats for the other transportation modes. Therefore, the bills of lading referred to in this discussion relate mainly to the railroad industry. Some bills of lading used by other modes will be reviewed, but the main thrust will be on the five major kinds of railroad bills of lading: uniform straight bills of lading, uniform order bills of lading, uniform livestock bills of lading, through export bills of lading, and government bills of lading.

Uniform Straight Bill of Lading

Regular rail freight shipments usually require the standardized bill of lading, which is the most commonly used. The form, as prescribed by the ICC, contains all relevant information necessary to complete the transportation service.

FIGURE 14–1. Uniform Straight Bill of Lading

UNIFORM STRAIGHT BILL OF LADING

Original—Not Negotiable

(To be Printed on "White" Paper)

Shipper's No..........

Agent's No............

Company

RECEIVED, subject to the classifications and tariffs in effect on the date of the issue of this Bill of Lading,

at..., 19...

from..

the property described below, in apparent good order, except as noted (contents and condition of contents of packages unknown), marked, consigned, and destined as indicated below, which said company (the word company being understood throughout this contract as meaning any person or corporation in possession of the property under the contract) agrees to carry to its usual place of delivery at said destination, if on its own road or its own water line, otherwise to deliver to another carrier on the route to said destination. It is mutually agreed, as to each carrier of all or any of said property over all or any portion of said route to destination, and as to each party at any time interested in all or any of said property, that every service to be performed hereunder shall be subject to all the conditions not prohibited by law, whether printed or written, herein contained, including the conditions on back hereof, which are hereby agreed to by the shipper and accepted for himself and his assigns.

(Mail or street address of consignee—For purposes of notification only.)

Consigned to...

Destination...State of.........................County of.........................

Route...

Delivering Carrier...Car Initial.......................Car No.................

No. Pack- ages	Description of Articles, Special Marks, and Exceptions	*Weight (Subject to Correction)	Class or Rate	Check Column	Subject to Section 7 of conditions, if this ship-

Subject to Section 7 of conditions, if this shipment is to be delivered to the consignee without recourse on the consign- or, the consignor shall sign the following state- ment:

The carrier shall not make delivery of this shipment without pay- ment of freight and all other lawful charges.

(Signature of consignor.)

If charges are to be pre- paid, write or stamp here, "To be Prepaid."

....

Received $..............
to apply in prepayment of the charges on the property described hereon.

....
Agent or Cashier.

Per.........................
(The signature here acknowl- edges only the amount prepaid.)

*If the shipment moves between two ports by a carrier by water, the law requires that the bill of lading shall state whether it is "carrier's or shipper's weight."

Note.—Where the rate is dependent on value, shippers are required to state specifically in writing the agreed or declared value of the property.

The agreed or declared value of the property is hereby specifically stated by the shipper to be not exceeding

Charges advanced:

$..................

....per..

....Shipper.   ....Agent.

Per..   Per...

Permanent postoffice address of shipper...

A copy of the form, known as a *uniform straight bill of lading*, or just straight bill of lading, is shown in Figure 14–1. Although the railroads are legally responsible for preparing the bill of lading, shippers actually fill out the forms and present them to a railroad representative for inspection and validation. The railroad's representative is required to sign the document, which is tantamount to preparing it, and the signature makes it legal. As you can see in Figure 14–1, all information regarding the commodity and the desired transportation service is contained in the straight bill of lading.

The shipper may insert an identification number in the upper right-hand corner. The most important sections to be completed are the origin point and date, which are inserted on the first full line, followed by the shipper's name. The name of the receiver, also known as the consignee, and the exact location should be filled in completely to avoid any misunderstandings. The shipper may include the exact routing for the shipment to follow. However, if the exact routing is specified, the freight rate applicable to that route will be applied, even if it is higher than the rate for an alternate route. If the route is not speci-fied by the shipper, the carrier is responsible for choosing a route with the lowest freight rate between the two involved points. In the body of the bill of lading, the preparer should include the number of packages, the contents' ac-cepted description, the weight (if known), and the classification or rate. The bottom of the bill of lading contains space for the shipper's name and its repre-sentative's signature, as well as the carrier's certification.

The right-hand column refers to freight charges. An often-neglected part of the bill of lading on the right-hand side relates to section 7 of the terms and conditions. This section is sometimes referred to as the "without recourse clause." Generally, if a shipment is "collect," freight charges are billed to the receiver (consignee) for payment. If the consignee does not pay freight charges to the carrier, the original shipper is responsible for payment. However, if the shipper (consignor) signs the section 7 clause, the carrier cannot bill the con-signor if the consignee does not pay the freight bill. In other words, delivery is made "without recourse." The additional sections in the right-hand column also relate to payment of freight charges.

One distinguishing characteristic of the uniform straight bill of lading is that it spells out the responsibilities and liabilities of the contracting parties. The back of the form contains a description of all terms and conditions. However, it is not mandatory that all bills of lading contain these terms and conditions, as the following section explains.

SHORTENED FORM. A modified form of the uniform straight bill of lading is permissible. The abbreviated form is known as a short, or shortened, bill of lad-ing. The legal ramifications of the uniform straight bill of lading and the short form are identical. The short form does not list the terms and conditions, but it does contain a statement to the effect that normal terms and conditions apply to the shipment and the existence and content of those stipulations is acknowl-edged. Regular shippers are aware of the terms and conditions that need not be

266

FIGURE 14-2. STRAIGHT BILL OF LADING—SHORT FORM

STRAIGHT BILL OF LADING—SHORT FORM

ORIGINAL — NOT NEGOTIABLE
(To be printed on white paper)

Shipper's No..........

Carrier's No..........

_____
(Name of Carrier)

RECEIVED, subject to the classifications and tariffs in effect on the date of the issue of this Bill of Lading,

At..., 19....

From...

the property described below, in apparent good order, except as noted (contents and condition of contents of packages unknown), marked, consigned, and destined as indicated below, which said carrier (the word carrier being understood throughout this contract as meaning any person or corporation in possession of the property under the contract) agrees to carry to its usual place of delivery at said destination, if on its route, otherwise to deliver to another carrier on the route to said destination. It is mutually agreed, as to each carrier of all or any of said property over all or any portion of said route to destination, and as to each party at any time interested in all or any of said property, that every service to be performed hereunder shall be subject to all the terms and conditions of the Uniform Domestic Straight Bill of Lading set forth (1) in Uniform Freight Classification in effect on the date hereof, if this is a rail or a rail-water shipment, or (2) in the applicable motor carrier classification or tariff if this is a motor carrier shipment.

Shipper hereby certifies that he is familiar with all the terms and conditions of the said bill of lading, including those on the back thereof, set forth in the classification or tariff which governs the transportation of this shipment, and the said terms and conditions are hereby agreed to by the shipper and accepted for himself and his assigns.

Consigned to...
(Mail or street address of consignee—For purposes of notification only.)

Destination.............................State...........County..........Delivery Address ★......................
(★To be filled in only when shipper desires and governing tariffs provide for delivery thereat.)

Route..

Delivering Carrier ....Car or Vehicle Initials..........No..........

No. Packages	Kind of Package, Description of Articles, Special Marks, and Exceptions	*Weight (Subject to Correction)	Class or Rate	Check Column	Subject to Section 7 of Conditions of applicable bill of lading, if this shipment is to be delivered to the consignee without recourse on the consignor, the consignor shall sign the following statement:
....	....	....	....	....	The carrier shall not make delivery of this shipment without payment of freight and all other lawful charges.
....	....	....	....	....	
....	....	....	....	....	(Signature of consignor.)
....	....	....	....	....	If charges are to be prepaid, write or stamp here, "To be Prepaid."
....	....	....	....	....	
....	....	....	....	....	....
....	....	....	....	....	Received $.............. to apply in prepayment of the charges on the property described hereon.
....	....	....	....	....	
....	....	....	....	....	.... Agent or Cashier.

*If the shipment moves between two ports by a carrier by water, the law requires that the bill of lading shall state whether it is carrier's or shipper's weight.

Note.—Where the rate is dependent on value, shippers are required to state specifically in writing the agreed or declared value of the property.

The agreed or declared value of the property is hereby specifically stated by the shipper to be not exceed-

ing...per............................

Per.....................
(The signature here acknowledges only the amount prepaid.)

Charges advanced:

$.....................

....:Shipper.   ....Agent.

Per.....................................   Per..

Permanent postoffice address of shipper...

repeated on every bill of lading. As long as the document's intent and legal responsibility are clear, printing costs can be saved by using shortened bill of lading forms. A copy of the shortened form of a uniform bill of lading is shown in Figure 14–2.

SHIPPER BILL OF LADING. Carriers are responsible for proper completion of a bill of lading. They are also responsible for providing blank bills of lading. However, shippers often find it economical to print their own bills of lading to avoid duplicate clerical efforts.

Costs can be saved if the shipper's name, address, location, and commodity do not have to be inserted on each bill of lading. If several commodities may be shipped, a listing of the options can be included on the preprinted form and used in an abbreviated format. An example of a shipper preprinted short bill of lading is shown in Figure 14–3. Note that the name, location, and mailing address of the shipper are preprinted. Also, a list of commodities usually shipped is printed. In the contents description section, the shipper can use a code number that identifies the legal commodity classification. Much time and effort can be saved with this form. Note also that the carrier and route section contains a fine-print statement acknowledging the terms and conditions of the uniform straight bill of lading. Usually, all preprinted shipper bills of lading use the shortened form.

Both the uniform straight bill of lading and the short form are nonnegotiable. That is, they cannot be sold to a party not named in the document to claim the shipment. The only parties who can legally claim the contents of a shipment are the original consignor and the consignee. Consequently, the consignee does not have to surrender the bill of lading to other carriers before delivery is completed. If the business transaction involved with a shipment requires that a bill of lading be produced before delivery is made, another bill of lading form can be used.

UNIFORM ORDER BILL OF LADING

Business conditions may require a negotiable instrument for the contents of a freight shipment. A few examples illustrate how a negotiable bill of lading can facilitate business operations and provide efficient and timely transportation.

Suppose that a regular supply of lumber is available in the Pacific Northwest. Also assume that a constant demand for lumber exists in the northeastern and southeastern quadrants of the United States. To reduce storage costs and speed up cash flow, owners in the Pacific Northwest may want to begin shipments to the eastern markets, even though sales to specific buyers have not been negotiated. Several days can be saved if the shipment is enroute while business negotiations are completed. To illustrate, assume the shipper filled out a bill of lading that indicated a lumber broker in Chicago as the receiver. Before the carload of lumber arrives in Chicago, the shipper arranges to sell to a different Chicago business firm. The shipper could reconsign the shipment but could

FIGURE 14–3. SHIPPER PREPRINTED SHORT BILL OF LADING

Shipper's No. __31628__

RECEIVED, subject to the classifications and tariffs in effect on the date of the issue of this Bill of Lading.

The property described below, in apparent good order, except as noted (contents and condition of contents of packages unknown), marked consigned, and destined as indicated below, which said carrier (the word carrier being understood throughout this contract as meaning any person or corporation in possession of the property under the contract) agrees to carry to its usual place of delivery at said destination, if on its route, otherwise to deliver to another carrier on the route to said destination. It is mutually agreed, as to each carrier of all or any of said property over all or any portion of said route to destination, and as to each party at any time interested in all or any of said property, that every service to be performed hereunder shall be subject to all the terms and conditions of the Uniform Domestic Straight Bill of Lading set forth (1) in Official, Southern, Western and Illinois Freight Classifications in effect on the date hereof, if this is a rail or a rail-water shipment, or (2) in the applicable motor carrier classification or tariff if this is a motor carrier shipment.

Shipper hereby certifies that he is familiar with all the terms and conditions of the said bill of lading, including those on the back hereof, set forth in the classification or tariff which governs the transportation of this shipment, and the said terms and conditions are hereby agreed to by the shipper and accepted for himself and his assigns.

(Name of Carrier)

Subject to Section 7 of conditions of applicable bill of lading, if this shipment is to be delivered to the consignee without recourse on the consignor, the consignor shall sign the following statement:

The carrier shall not make delivery of this shipment without payment of freight and all other lawful charges.

From **CONTAINER CORPORATION OF AMERICA** _____ **CONTAINER** _____ DIVISION

at _____ **FORT WORTH, TEXAS** _____ 19 ____

(Signature of consignor.)

If charges are to be prepaid, write or stamp here, "To be Prepaid."

CONSIGNED TO _____ (Mail or street address of consignee—For purposes of notification only.)

Rec'd $ _____ to apply in prepayment of the charges on the property described hereon.

DESTINATION _____ STATE _____ COUNTY

Agent or Cashier.

ROUTE

Per _____ (The signature here acknowledges only the amount prepaid.

DELIVERING CARRIER _____ CAR OR VEHICLE INITIALS _____ NO.

Charges advanced:

$

No. Pkgs.	Kind of Package, Description of Articles, Special Marks, and Exceptions	* Weight (Sub. to Cor.)	Class or Rate	No. Pkgs.	Kind of Package, Description of Articles, Special Marks, and Exceptions	* Weight (Sub. to Cor.)	Class or Rate
Bdls. Units Pallets	Fibreboard Boxes, Corrugated, K. D. F.			Bdls. Cases Pallets	Fibreboard Boxes, Other Than Corrugated, K. D. F.		
Pkgs.	Fillers, Partitions or Platforms, for Packing, N.O.I. Fibreboard, Not Corrugated, K. D. Flat			Loose	Wooden Skids		
Pkgs.	Dunnage, Freight Loading Rubber Pneumatic, Deflated			Bales	Scrap Paper		
Pkgs.	Store Display Racks or Stands density less than 4 pounds per cubic foot density 4 pounds or greater per cubic foot KDF			Bdls. Rolls Skids	Pulpboard, N.O.I.B.N. Fibre Contents Consisting of Not Less Than 80% Wood Pulp, Waste Paper, or Straw Pulp. (Not Corrugated)		
Size Car Ordered	Dunnage				The description and weight indicated on this Bill of Lading are correct, subject to verification by the Governing Weighing and Inspection Bureau according to agreement:		
Size Car Furnished	Total Wgt.						

CONTAINER CORPORATION OF AMERICA, Shipper

Per _____ _____ Agent

Permanent postoffice address of shipper   P.O. Box 1441, Fort Worth, Texas 76101   Per _____

*If the shipment moves between two ports by a carrier by water, the law requires that the bill of lading shall state whether it is carrier's or shipper's weight.
NOTE—Where the rate is dependent on value, shippers are required to state specifically in writing the agreed or declared value of the property. The agreed or declared value of the property is hereby specifically stated by the shipper to be not exceeding

per

not arrange for title transfer under the terms and conditions of a straight bill of lading.

In another example, suppose that a transaction is made between a shipper of a carload of tomatoes and a food processor who makes catsup. The shipper has not dealt with the buyer before and is uncertain about the buyer's credit standing. The shipper would like some assurance of payment for the carload. A straight bill of lading cannot ensure that payment will be made.

In the two examples given, a negotiable bill of lading can be used to facilitate the business transaction. The document is known as a *uniform order bill of lading*, sometimes referred to as an order/notify bill of lading. Shippers can prepare a uniform order bill of lading that commits the receiver to payment before the shipment is released by the carrier. The order bill of lading assures payment to the shipper for the shipment's value before the carrier releases the merchandise.

As stated, the order bill of lading is a negotiable instrument. Therefore, the shipper can consign a shipment to the order of another party, and the merchandise can be obtained by paying the shipment's value. Returning to the earlier examples, the shippers can prepare an order bill of lading for a specific shipment. The order bill of lading can be processed through the shipper's bank to a bank at the destination city. A broker or buyer in the destination city can obtain possession of the shipment by paying for the shipment's contents to the destination city's bank. That bank will then transfer the funds to the shipper's bank. The shipper is thus assured of payment, and the business transaction is completed.

The major difference between the straight bill of lading and the order bill of lading is negotiability. The form differs in that the order bill of lading carries a notice of its negotiability and a separate space for the name of the party to be notified before delivery. In many cases, that designee differs from the party that actually receives the shipment. As Figure 14–4 illustrates, the basic format for an order bill of lading is similar to a straight bill of lading, except that space is allotted for a possible third party. Whether or not a third party is involved is unimportant. The major purpose of an order bill of lading is payment of the shipment's value before the commodities are released for further use. Order bills of lading are used primarily in railroad transportation.

UNIFORM LIVESTOCK BILL OF LADING
Carriers are not always held completely responsible for the full value or well-being of all commodities transported. In some cases, the carriers' responsibility is limited. For the shipment of livestock, such as cattle, carriers are responsible for exercising reasonable care during transportation. Feeding and watering may be included in the usual freight rate or arranged for a fee. However, carriers are not held responsible for the health of the cargo, which may be affected by kicking, overcrowding, or fright. A separate shipping document, known as a *uniform livestock bill of lading*, is used for such shipments. The major difference between a straight bill of lading and a livestock bill of lading is the limitation of carrier responsibility, which is detailed in the bill's terms and conditions. Order bills of lading are not used for livestock shipments. A copy of a uniform livestock bill of lading is shown in Figure 14–5.

270

FIGURE 14–4. Uniform Order Bill of Lading

UNIFORM ORDER BILL OF LADING
ORIGINAL
(To Be Printed on "Yellow" Paper)

Company

Shipper's No..........

Agent's No............

RECEIVED, subject to the classifications and tariffs in effect on the date of the issue of this Bill of Lading, at..., 19...
from..

the property described below, in apparent good order, except as noted (contents and condition of contents of packages unknown), marked, consigned, and destined as indicated below, which said company (the word company being understood throughout this contract as meaning any person or corporation in possession of the property under the contract) agrees to carry to its usual place of delivery at said destination, if on its own road or its own water line, otherwise to deliver to another carrier on the route to said destination. It is mutually agreed, as to each carrier of all or any of said property over all or any portion of said route to destination, and as to each party at any time interested in all or any of said property, that every service to be performed hereunder shall be subject to all the conditions not prohibited by law, whether printed or written, herein contained, including the conditions on back hereof, which are hereby agreed to by the shipper and accepted for himself and his assigns.

The surrender of this Original ORDER Bill of Lading properly indorsed shall be required before the delivery of the property. Inspection of property covered by this bill of lading will not be permitted unless provided by law or unless permission is indorsed on this original bill of lading or given in writing by the shipper.

Consigned to ORDER of..
Destination..State of.........................County of.......................
Notify..
At..State of.........................County of.......................
Route..
Delivering Carrier..Car Initial.........................Car No.................

No. Pack- ages	Description of Articles, Special Marks, and Exceptions	*Weight (Subject to Correction)	Class or Rate	Check Column	Subject to Section 7 of conditions, if this shipment is to be delivered to the consignee without recourse on the consignor, the consignor shall sign the following statement:
					The carrier shall not make delivery of this shipment without payment of freight and all other lawful charges.
					(Signature of consignor.)
					If charges are to be pre-paid, write or stamp here, "To be Prepaid."
					....
					Received $............. to apply in prepayment of the charges on the property described hereon.
					Agent or Cashier.
					Per.....................

*If the shipment moves between two ports by a carrier by water, the law requires that the bill of lading shall state whether it is "carrier's or shipper's weight."

(The signature here acknowledges only the amount prepaid.)

Note.—Where the rate is dependent on value, shippers are required to state specifically in writing the agreed or declared value of the property.

The agreed or declared value of the property is hereby specifically stated by the shipper to be not exceeding

....per...........................

Charges advanced:

$....................

....Shipper.   ....Agent.
Per..   Per..
Permanent postoffice address of shipper...

271

FIGURE 14–5. Uniform Livestock Bill of Lading

UNIFORM LIVE STOCK CONTRACT

This form of contract to be used for shipments of Live Stock and Wild Animals instead of Uniform Bill of Lading

DUPLICATE ORIGINAL.—NOT NEGOTIABLE

Company

......................................Station, ..., 19...

THIS AGREEMENT, made this ....day of......................, 19..., by and between the

....COMPANY,

party of the first part, hereinafter called the carrier, *and...

....(Shipper's name)

part.... of the second part, hereinafter called the shipper;

WHEREAS, The classifications and tariffs under which this agreement is made require that, for the purpose of applying the lawful rate of freight, the shipper must declare the shipment to be "Ordinary Live Stock," specifying the kind or kinds of animals, or if not "Ordinary Live Stock" he must declare the kind and value of each animal, space for such declaration being provided below:

NOW, THEREFORE, THIS AGREEMENT WITNESSETH, That the carrier has received from the shipper, subject to the classifications and tariffs in effect on the date of issue of this agreement, the live stock described below, in apparent good order, except as noted, consigned and destined as indicated below, which the carrier agrees to carry to its usual place of delivery at said destination, if on its road or on its own water line, otherwise to deliver to another carrier on the route to said destination. It is mutually agreed, as to each carrier* of all or any of said live stock over all or any portion of said route to destination, and as to each party at any time interested in all or any of said live stock, that every service to be performed and every liability incurred in connection with said shipment shall be subject to all the conditions, whether printed or written, herein contained, including the conditions on back hereof, and which are agreed to by the shipper and accepted for himself and his assigns.

Consigned to...

Destination........................., State of......................, County of.........................

Route..

Car Initials and Numbers,...

ORDINARY LIVE STOCK	OTHER THAN ORDINARY LIVE STOCK
Ordinary live stock means all cattle, swine, sheep, goats, horses, and mules, except such as are chiefly valuable for breeding, racing, show purposes, or other special uses. On shipments of ordinary live stock no declaration of value shall be made by the shipper, nor shall any values be entered on this bill of lading. I (We) declare the shipment covered by this bill of lading to be ordinary live stock.	On shipments of live stock chiefly valuable for breeding, racing, show purposes, or other special uses, different rates of freight are in effect dependent on the valuation placed thereon by the shipper; which valuation may be the basic value as stated in the classification, at which the lowest freight rate applies, or it may be any higher valuation up to actual value, in which event the freight rate will be higher by the amount prescribed in the tariffs or classifications. Such declared or agreed values shall be entered in the column provided therefor in this bill of lading, and in no event shall the carrier be liable for any amount in excess of such valuation. I (We) declare the shipment covered by this bill of lading to be other than ordinary live stock, and of the value herein declared, or agreed upon, and entered.
.......................Shipper.	.......................Shipper.

Note.—The shipper shall execute one of the above declarations. Upon refusal of a shipper of other than ordinary live stock to declare the values of said stock for entry in this bill of lading the shipment will not be accepted for transportation under this contract. In the event the shipment consists of both ordinary live stock and other than ordinary live stock, both of such declarations shall be executed, but values shall be declared and entered on only the other than ordinary live stock.

Number and Description of Animals	Shipper's Declared Value (If on live stock chiefly valuable for breeding, racing, show purposes, or other special uses)	Weight (Subject to correction)	Rate of Freight	
			Per 100 Lbs.	Per Car

Subject to Section 3 of conditions, if this shipment is to be delivered to the consignee without recourse on the consignor, the consignor shall sign the following statement:

The carrier shall not make delivery of this shipment without payment of freight and all other lawful charges.

....
(Signature of consignor.)

If charges are to be prepaid, write or stamp here, "To be prepaid."	**Acknowledgment to be used if freight is prepaid.**
....	Received $......................., to apply in prepayment of the charges on the live stock described hereon. ....Agent or Cashier. Per....................... (The signature here acknowledges only the amount prepaid.) Charges advanced, $.......................

Witness my hand......................, Shipper.

By......................, Shipper's Agent.

The......................Company.

....

By......................Agent.

......................, Witness.

*The word "carrier" is to be understood throughout this contract as including any person or corporation in possession of the live stock under the contract.

GOVERNMENT BILL OF LADING

Chapter 13 stated that freight rates on government shipments differ from rates on all other shipments handled by the carriers. Documents for government shipments also differ. A special form, known as a *government bill of lading*, is used. Its format differs from a straight bill of lading in that it is designed to process information needed for government record keeping. Government bills of lading are preprinted by the federal government and serve as drafts on the United States Treasury to pay for freight charges. In all other commercial shipments, carriers prepare special invoices for freight payments. No additional documents are necessary on government shipments.

UNIFORM THROUGH EXPORT BILL OF LADING

Many shipments handled by the carriers originate in the United States and are destined for a consignee in a foreign country. Such shipments would require the shipper to prepare three separate bills of lading: one for the domestic carrier, one for the ocean carrier, and one for the foreign land carrier. That would create an added burden for the shipper, because many other forms must be completed on all foreign shipments. Therefore, a special form known as a *uniform through export bill of lading* has been devised. It may be either a straight or an order type.

The shipper can include special instructions to any or all of the carriers involved in the service. However, carriers have limited liability on these shipments. Each carrier is expected to exercise reasonable care for the shipment but cannot be held responsible for negligence by any of the other carriers. The same conditions would apply if the shipper prepared three separate bills of lading. Therefore, it is in the shipper's best interest to use a uniform through export bill of lading to reduce clerical costs. A copy of a uniform through export bill of lading is illustrated in Figure 14–6.

OTHER BILLS OF LADING

Rail freight carriers are the only ones that use a standard, prescribed bill of lading, regardless of the particular railroad originating the shipment. In all other cases, carriers issue bills of lading on their own forms. The basic information contained in a railroad bill of lading also appears in forms used by other carriers, but the amount of detail included may differ among carriers in the same transportation mode.

Motor freight carriers have no prescribed format, but most use bills of lading similar to those used by the railroads, and others use a format recommended in the National Motor Freight Classification. Figure 14–7 is an example of a motor carrier bill of lading. By comparing this to the railroad bill of lading shown in Figure 14–1, you can see that only minor variations exist. Note that the bill of lading shown in Figure 14–7 is a short form containing a statement in fine print that normal contractual terms and conditions apply.

No bills of lading are used by pipeline carriers. Instead, a separate contract is

FIGURE 14–6. Uniform Through Export Bill of Lading

Bill of Lading Signature Certificate No................

    Through Bill of Lading issued in conformity with understanding [1] with the Liverpool Cotton Bills of Lading Conference (1907) Committee and the American Bankers Association.

    The word "agreement" may be substituted for the word "understanding."

UNIFORM THROUGH EXPORT BILL OF LADING
(Prescribed in Interstate Commerce Commission Orders of October 21, 1921, January 30, 1922, March 7, 1922, July 3, 1922, June 6, 1923, and June 21, 1929, as modified by decision of November 7, 1939, in Docket No. 4844.)

STRAIGHT BILL OF LADING—ORIGINAL—NOT NEGOTIABLE

The............................(Issuing)............................**Company**

IN CONNECTION WITH OTHER CARRIERS ON THE ROUTE

Export Bill of Lading No...................Lot No...................Contract Numbers............................

Dated at.....................this..........day of.., 19...

Received, subject to the classifications and tariffs in effect on the date of the receipt of the property described in this bill of

lading, at..

From..

the following property, in apparent good order (contents and condition of contents of packages unknown), marked, numbered, consigned, and destined as indicated below.

Consignee..

Destination..

Route..

Party to whom arrival notice is to be addressed..

MARKS AND NUMBERS	ARTICLES	*Weight (Subject to Correction)	Measurement (Subject to Correction)
CAR NUMBERS			

Received $.........to apply in prepayment of the charges on the property described herein.

....
By............................ Agent.
(The signature here only acknowledges the amount prepaid.)

*U. S. Law requires Agent issuing Bill of Lading to write either "Shipper's" or "Carrier's" before "Weight."

To be carried to the port (A) of...and thence by.................................

to the port (B)......................................(or so near thereto as vessel may safely get) always subject to the liberties, exceptions, terms and conditions hereinafter specified or provided for, and to be there delivered in like good order and condition as above consigned, or to consignee's assigns, or to another carrier on the route to destination if consigned beyond said port (B), upon payment immediately on discharge of the property of the freight due thereon, at the rate

(INLAND AND/OR COASTWISE) from..to...................of....................cents

per one hundred pounds gross weight, port charges, if any..................cents, and (OCEAN AND ON-CARRYING) from............................

to................of............................cents per.................................., and advanced charges ....($ ....), with

all other charges and average, without any allowance of credt or discount,........................., settlement to be made on the basis of lawful money of the United States of America, amount to be paid by receivers at current rate of New York exchange as quoted on the day the vessel is entered at the Custom House at her port of discharge.

    In consideration of the rate of freight herein named it is hereby stipulated that the service to be performed hereunder shall be subject to the contract terms and conditions, whether printed or written, herein contained, and said terms and conditions are hereby agreed to by the shipper and by him accepted for himself and his assigns.

CONTRACT TERMS AND CONDITIONS

    Any alteration, addition, or erasure in this bill of lading which shall be made without the special notation hereon of the agent of the carrier issuing this bill of lading shall be without effect and this bill of lading shall be enforceable according to its original tenor. If shipment consists of cotton or cotton linters it is mutually understood and agreed that the description of the condition does not relate to insufficiency of or the torn condition of the covering, or to any damage resulting therefrom, and that no carrier shall be responsible for any damage of such kind. The vessel shall be at liberty to call at any port or ports in or out of the customary route, to tow and be towed, to transfer, trans-ship, or lighter, to load and discharge goods at any time, to assist vessels in distress, to deviate for the purpose of saving life or property, and for docking and repairs.

    This bill of lading is not to be used on traffic from a point in the United States destined to an adjacent foreign country.

    PART I.—With respect to the service until delivery at the port (A) first above mentioned it is agreed that—

    1. (a) The carrier or party in possession of any of the property herein described shall be liable as at common law for any loss thereof or damage thereto except as hereinafter provided.

    (b) No carrier or party in possession of all or any of the property herein described shall be liable for any loss thereof or damage thereto or delay caused by the act of God, the public enemy, the authority of law, or the act or default of the shipper or owner, or for natural shrinkage. The carrier's liability shall be that of warehouseman, only, for loss, damage, or delay caused by fire occuring after the expiration of the free time allowed by tariffs lawfully on file (such free time to be computed as therein provided) after notice of the arrival of the property at destination or at the port of export (if intended for export) has been duly sent or given, and after placement of the property for delivery at the port of export, or tender of delivery of the property to the party entitled to receive it, has been made. Except in case of negligence of the carrier or party in possession (and the burden to prove freedom from such negligence shall be on the carrier or party in possession), the carrier or party in possession shall not be liable for loss, damage, or delay occurring while the property is stopped and held in transit upon the request of the shipper, owner, or party entitled to make such request, or resulting from a defect or vice in the property, or for country damage to cotton, or from riots or strikes.

274

FIGURE 14–7. MOTOR CARRIER BILL OF LADING

STRAIGHT BILL OF LADING	**JOHNSON MOTOR LINES, INC.**	SHIPPER NO.
ORIGINAL — NOT NEGOTIABLE	**(JMLS)**	CARRIER NO.
		DATE

CONSIGNEE (TO)		SHIPPER (FROM)	
NAME		NAME	
STREET		STREET	
CITY, STATE	ZIP	CITY, STATE	ZIP

ROUTE	VEHICLE NO.

NUMBER SHIPPING UNITS	Kind of Packaging, Description of Articles, Special Marks and Exceptions	Weight (Subject to Correction)	Rate	CHARGES (For Carrier use only)

REMIT C.O.D. TO:		**COD** Amt: $	C.O.D. FEE
ADDRESS			PREPAID ☐ COLLECT ☐ $

Note — Where the rate is dependent on value shippers are required to state specifically in writing the agreed or declared value of the property. The agreed or declared value of the property is hereby specifically stated by the shipper to be not exceeding

$ _____ per _____

Subject to section 7 of the conditions, if this shipment is to be delivered to the consignee without recourse on the consignor, the consignor shall sign the following statement. The carrier shall not make delivery of this shipment without payment of freight and all other lawful charges.

_____ (Signature of Consignor)

TOTAL CHARGES:	$

FREIGHT CHARGES:
FREIGHT PREPAID ☐   Check box
except when box at right if charges are
is checked ☐ collect   to be collect

RECEIVED, subject to the classifications and tariffs in effect on the date of the issue of this Bill of Lading, the property described above in apparent good order, except as noted (contents and conditions of contents of packages unknown), marked, consigned and destined as indicated above which said carrier (the word carrier being understood throughout this contract as meaning any person or corporation in possession of the property under the contract) agrees to carry to its usual place of delivery at said destination if on its route, otherwise to deliver to another carrier on the route to said destination. It is mutually agreed as to each carrier of all or any of said property over all or any portion of said route to destination and as to each party at any time interested in all or any said property, that every service to be performed hereunder shall be subject to all the bill of lading terms and conditions in the governing classification on the date of shipment. Shipper hereby certifies that he is familiar with all the bill of lading terms and conditions in the governing classification and the said terms and conditions are hereby agreed to by the shipper and accepted for himself and his assigns.
This is to certify that the above-named articles are properly classified, described, packaged, marked, and labeled, and are in proper condition of transportation, according to the applicable regulations of the Department of Transportation.

SHIPPER	CARRIER
NAME	NAME
	JOHNSON MOTOR LINES, INC.
AUTHORIZED SIGNATURE	AUTHORIZED SIGNATURE DATE

Permanent address of Shipper Street _____ City _____ State _____ Zip _____

issued for the volume to be shipped. This contract is known as a *tender of shipment* and usually covers at least the minimum quantity listed in the pipeline tariff. Each portion is known as a *run,* and all runs are recorded on the tender until the total shipment is completed. Pipeline tenders of shipment are non-negotiable.

Air freight bills of lading are known as *air bills* and are not standardized within the industry. The airlines transfer air bills to other airlines participating in a through shipment, and each airline respects the formats of all others, even though they differ. Most of the air bills are similar, so the arrangement is workable. Air bills are nonnegotiable. A copy of a uniform air bill is illustrated in Figure 14–8.

Domestic water bills of lading are not standardized, although most are similar and follow the basic format of a railroad bill of lading. Water bills of lading can be either the straight or order type. The major difference between water bills of lading and those of the railroads is the limitation of liability for water freight carriers. Railroads are held responsible for all commodities turned over to them for transportation service. Water carriers, on the other hand, are expected to exercise reasonable care but are held accountable only for negligence. Because of the extraordinary hazards of the sea, water carriers are not responsible for damages occurring through no fault of the carriers. These stipulations are contained in the bill of lading's terms and conditions.

Bills of lading are not required for private or contract carriage. In private carriage, commodities are in complete control of the owner at all times, and a bill of lading is not necessary. In contract carriage, occurring mostly with motor or water carriers, preparation of bills of lading is left to the discretion of the contracting parties. If either party wants separate bills of lading on each shipment, that stipulation should be included in the contract arrangements. Whether or not bills of lading are required usually depends on the relationship between the contracting parties. There is no regulatory or mandatory requirement for bills of lading on contract carriage.

The bill of lading represents a contract between a shipper and a carrier and is a document in which both involved parties have a role. It is used as a basis for both data gathering and for other documents used in transportation. These other uses will be described later in this chapter. Let us now examine another shipment document based on the bill of lading that is used by carriers.

CARRIER WAYBILLS

A bill of lading is prepared for a freight shipment readied for tendering to a carrier and contains all of the information necessary to complete the shipment. However, it does not contain information about the actual movement of the shipment until it is delivered. Of course, movement information cannot be recorded on a bill of lading because the document is either kept by the shipper or forwarded to the receiver, and the shipment route may be unknown at the time the bill of lading is prepared. Yet, the carrier usually wants a record of the shipment's movement between origin and destination. For very short shipments, such as air freight or motor freight carriage, movement information is not as important. In other cases, however, such as rail carloads passing through several terminals and being interchanged among carriers, a running record of

FIGURE 14–8. Uniform Air Bill

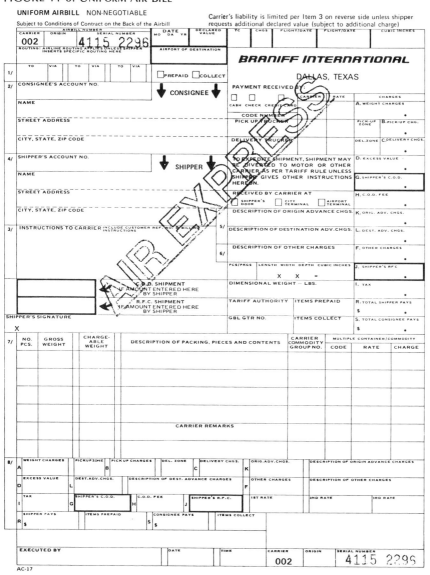

2 - ORIGIN STATION COPY

the total shipment is valuable. The rail carriers use a document known as a waybill for this purpose. A sample of a railroad waybill is shown in Figure 14–9.

Whereas the bill of lading shows the date the shipment was ready for trans-

FIGURE 14–9. RAILROAD WAYBILL

PLACE SPECIAL SERVICE
PASTERS HERE

FORM 33258 REV. 9/76

494 - MISSOURI PACIFIC RAILROAD CO.- 494
ORIGINAL FREIGHT WAYBILL
To be used for single consignments, carload and less carload, and T. O. F. C.

TRANSFERRED TO CAR		KIND	WEIGHT IN TONS			LENGTH OF CAR		MARKED CAPACITY OF CAR	
			GROSS	TARE	NET	Ordered	Furnished	Ordered	Furnished
CAR INITIALS AND NUMBER		KIND							

DATE OF SHIPMENT | WAYBILL NUMBER

T. TRAILER INITIAL AND NUMBER — LENGTH — PLAN NUMBER

O.

F. TRAILER INITIAL AND NUMBER — LENGTH — PLAN NUMBER

C. CONSIGNEE AND ADDRESS AT STOP

STOP AT _____

THIS AT _____

CAR AT _____

| TO NO. | STATION | STATE OR PROV. | FROM NO. | STATION | STATE OR PROV |

ROUTE (Show each Junction and Carrier in Route order to destination of waybill) | Route Code No.

FULL NAME OF SHIPPER, AND, FOR C. O. D. SHIPMENTS, STREET, POST OFFICE ADDRESS, AND INVOICE NUMBER | Code No

Show "A" if Agent's Routing or "S" if Shipper's Routing

| RECONSIGNED TO | STATION | STATE OR PROV. |

ORIGIN AND DATE, ORIGINAL CAR, TRANSFER FREIGHT BILL AND PREVIOUS WAYBILL REFERENCE AND ROUTING WHEN REBILLED.

AUTHORITY

| CONSIGNEE AND ADDRESS | Code No. |

C. $ .... FEE   AT _____

O. $ ....   GROSS _____

D. $ .... TOTAL

AMOUNT | WEIGHED

TARE _____

FINAL DESTINATION AND ADDITIONAL ROUTING | PICKUP SERVICE

ALLOWANCE _____

YES   NO

ON C. L. TRAFFIC—INSTRUCTIONS (Regarding Icing, Ventilation, Milling, Weighing. Etc. If Iced, Specify to Whom Icing Should be Charged.)

DELIVERY SERVICE REQUESTED

NET _____

IF CHARGES ARE TO BE PRE-PAID, WRITE OR STAMP HERE **"TO BE PREPAID"**

YES   NO

WHEN SHIPPER IN THE UNITED STATES EXECUTES THE NO-RECOURSE CLAUSE OF SECTION 7 OF THE BILL OF LADING, INSERT "YES"

Indicate by symbol in Column provided ★ how weights were obtained for L. C. L. Shipments only. R—Railroad Scale. S—Shipper's Tested Weights. E—Estimated—Weigh and Correct. T—Tariff Classification or Minimum.

No. Pkgs	Description of Articles, Special Marks and Exceptions	Commodity Code No.	★	WEIGHT	RATE	FREIGHT	ADVANCES	PREPAID

DESTINATION AGENT'S FREIGHT BILL NO.

Outbound Junction Agent Will Show Junction Stamps in Space and Order Provided. Additional Junction Stamps and all Yard Stamps to be Placed on Back Hereof.

Destination Agent Will Stamp Herein Station Name and Date Reported

FIRST JUNCTION	SECOND JUNCTION	THIRD JUNCTION	FOURTH JUNCTION

494– MISSOURI PACIFIC RAILROAD CO.—494

278

port, the waybill shows the actual date the freight car started its journey. The information on a bill of lading is also included in the waybill, but additional internal carrier information is also included. The waybill contains operational information, such as railroad junction points, intermediate stops, transfers of lading, special instructions, and transportation vehicle data. In addition, rail carriers assign a "pro number" (also the waybill number), an abbreviation for progressive numbers, to each shipment. All further references to the shipment use the pro number. When the transportation service is completed, the delivery date and the number assigned to the freight bill are noted to complete the waybill activity record. The waybill makes it relatively easy to trace a shipment's history. Rail carriers with computerized information systems use the waybills as inputs for data processing.

The waybill has many uses. If a shipper or receiver needs to determine the exact location of a shipment at any time, the waybill has that information. It is also useful to carriers who want to evaluate the service being provided shippers. Also, if a claim is filed for damage or delay, the waybill is the starting point for analysis and evaluation. The waybill can be considered a flow chart of a shipment.

Because of the characteristics of rail freight shipments, rail carriers are the primary users of waybills. Such extensive documentation is not as necessary for most other transportation modes. However, all carriers record movement information and, in many cases, a copy of the bill of lading is used for the same internal record keeping. When a shipment is completed, the waybill information becomes a matter of record. The information contained on it is used to complete record keeping and, in many cases, it is used to bill freight charges for the transportation services.

FREIGHT BILLS

In transportation service, the user may pay before or after completion of the service. In both situations, the invoice is identical and is known as a *freight bill*. If the freight charges are to be paid by the shipper, the freight bill is prepared by the carrier at origin and is submitted directly to the shipper. This is known as a *prepaid freight bill*. The shipper pays the carrier at origin before the transportation service is completed. On the bill of lading shown in Figure 14–1, the right-hand column contains a section where the shippers can indicate that they intend to pay freight charges.

Any charges paid by the shipper to the carrier at point of origin are inserted in the space provided on the right-hand side of the bill of lading, illustrated in Figure 14–1. For shipments of this nature, the buyer receives an invoice from the shipper that includes freight costs. The terms of sale in this type of transaction are known as *f.o.b. delivered*.

Many times, the carrier is not paid until the transportation service is completed. Once the shipment is delivered, the carrier submits a freight bill to the

FIGURE 14–10. Railroad Freight Bill

494 - Missouri Pacific Railroad Co. - 494

ORIGINAL FREIGHT BILL

TRANSFERRED TO CAR	KIND	WEIGHT IN TONS				
		GROSS	TARE	NET	**FREIGHT BILL NO.**	
CAR INITIALS AND NUMBER	KIND					

DATE OF SHIPMENT — WAYBILL NUMBER

| T. O. | TRAILER INITIAL AND NUMBER | LENGTH | PLAN NUMBER |
| F. C. | TRAILER INITIAL AND NUMBER | LENGTH | PLAN NUMBER |

CONSIGNEE AND ADDRESS AT STOP

STOP AT _____
THIS AT _____
CAR AT _____

TO NO.	STATION	STATE OR PROV.	FROM NO.	STATION	STATE OR PROV.

ROUTE — Route Code No. — SHIPPER — Code No.

For Charges on articles to be transported

CONSIGNEE AND ADDRESS	Code No.		WEIGHED

C. O. D.

AMOUNT $ .... AT _____
FEE $ .... GROSS _____
TOTAL $ .... TARE _____
$ .... ALLOWANCE _____

PICKUP SERVICE — YES NO

ON C. L. TRAFFIC—INSTRUCTIONS (Regarding Icing, Ventilation, Milling, Weighing Etc. If Iced, Specify to Whom Icing Should be Charged.)

DELIVERY SERVICE REQUESTED — YES NO

NET

IF CHARGES ARE TO BE PRE-PAID, WRITE OR STAMP HERE **"TO BE PREPAID"**

WHEN SHIPPER IN THE UNITED STATES EXECUTES THE NO-RECOURSE CLAUSE OF SECTION 7 OF THE BILL OF LADING INSERT YES

Indicate by symbol in Column provided ★ how weights were obtained for L. C. L. Shipments only R—Railroad Scale S—Shipper's Tested Weights E—Estimated—Weigh and Correct T—Tariff Classification or Minimum

No. Pkgs.	Description of Articles, Special Marks and Exceptions	Commodity Code No.	★	WEIGHT	RATE	FREIGHT	ADVANCES	PREPAID

DESTINATION AGENT'S FREIGHT BILL NO.

TOTAL

494– Missouri Pacific Railroad Co.– 494

buyer for the charges. This is known as a *collect freight bill*. If the prepaid section of the bill of lading is not filled in, the carrier automatically will submit a collect freight bill to the buyer. When more than one carrier is involved in providing the transportation service, the revenue is divided by the carriers among themselves, and the buyer is not involved.

A sample of a railroad freight bill is shown in Figure 14–10. Note that this freight bill is identical to the waybill shown in Figure 14–9 except for the statement in the center regarding freight charges. This standardization simplifies form preparation because the freight bill and waybill can be prepared at the same time with multipart forms. Some carriers use three-part forms and prepare the bill of lading, waybill, and freight bill at one time and in one operation, which saves a great deal of time and clerical expenses.

Many times, the freight bill is a completely different document. Figure 14–11 shows a motor carrier freight bill that is completely different from the bill of lading shown in Figure 14–7. Although the bill of lading contains freight charge information, with the exception of the government form, payment is not made until a freight bill is received. Copies of the bill of lading are used by the carrier to prepare a freight bill.

Payment for the accessorial services described in Chapter 13 may be made by either the shipper or the receiver. There is little standardization in the way these charges are submitted for payment. Some carriers include accessorial charges, such as demurrage or detention, directly on the original freight bill. Other carriers have separate forms and will prepare different documents for each service.

Another nonstandardized practice is issuance of a prepaid freight bill by a delivering carrier to the consignee. This procedure notifies the receiver that freight charges have been prepaid. All of the freight bill information is included, with a notation that freight charges have been prepaid. Although this

FIGURE 14–11. MOTOR CARRIER FREIGHT BILL

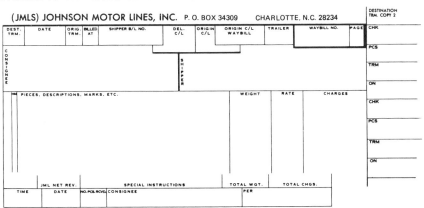

practice is intended to provide additional information to the receiver, it often leads to confusion when the consignee mistakenly remits a freight payment, even though the document shows that payment was made by the shipper. Adding to the confusion, the same freight bill form is usually used to provide this information. Once the duplicate payment is discovered, the receiver must file a freight overcharge claim to recover the payment. The claim form will be discussed later in this chapter.

This section has examined the basic documentation involved in providing transportation service between origin and destination points. Yet, still other documents are used that support the required service but are not used for all shipments by all carriers.

Supporting Documents

The documents described in the previous section are the most commonly used, although all of them are not required on all shipments. Additional documents may be required for special conditions or specific requirements. Also, problems occur that force the use of other documentation. These additional forms are called supporting documents because they supplement the basic documents used in transportation service. The more frequently used supporting documents are arrival notices, delivery receipts, inspection reports, and various types of claim forms.

ARRIVAL NOTICES

Not all shipments are completed exactly as intended by the shipper, carrier, and receiver. The shipper may originate the shipment as expected and the carrier may ship on time, but the receiver, or consignee, may not be able to accept the shipment immediately. As discussed previously, demurrage or detention charges can be assessed if unloading is delayed beyond an allotted time.

When a shipment is ready for delivery, the carrier notifies the receiver with a form known as an arrival notice. The receiver then schedules the carrier to either make delivery or hold the shipment until further notice. The arrival notice is used most often by the railroads because rail shipments are more likely to be held for longer periods of time than shipments handled by other modes.

A sample of an arrival notice is shown in Figure 14–12. As you can see, the consignee is given adequate data to identify the shipment. A statement is also included that demurrage rules will apply. In most cases, railroads cannot assess demurrage charges unless the receiver is notified in writing of the shipment's availability. The arrival notice form serves this purpose, and the date and time listed are used to determine the demurrage assessment. Usually, the receiver is

FIGURE 14–12. ARRIVAL NOTICE

FORM 35018-REV.

_____
(RAILROAD)

STATION_____

DATE_____

COPY _____

ARRIVAL NOTICE

You are hereby notified that the following cars consigned to you have been received and are ready for delivery. These cars are subject to the demurrage rules published in the tariffs lawfully on file and charges will be made as provided therein.

INITIAL	NUMBER	COMMODITY	WEIGHT	ORIGIN	SHIPPER	REMARKS

_____ Agent

Per _____

When original copy of Arrival Notice delivered and receipt refused -

Delivered to MR. _____

At _____ M, _____ 19____

By _____
Signature of Delivering Party

When original copy of Arrival Notice is served by U.S. Mail

Deposited in U.S. Mail at _____ M.

Date _____ 19____

By _____
Signature of Mailing Party

notified by telephone of the shipment's arrival and may request immediate delivery. In such cases, the arrival notice is not necessary. If, however, the receiver requests that delivery be postponed, the carrier will prepare the arrival notice.

DELIVERY RECEIPTS

The bill of lading instructs carriers to deliver to a particular consignee. Because carriers are entrusted with someone else's possessions, they often may be required to substantiate that delivery was completed. There are many reasons for this precaution. It may be difficult to process a collect freight bill if, because of a clerical error, the consignee's records do not show receipt of the merchandise. Or, the shipper's invoice for the contents may be declined for the same reasons. Therefore, the carrier may be required to substantiate delivery. These incidents are most common with motor carrier shipments where the merchandise is delivered, but the vehicle is not detained for a long period of time by the consignee. If a motor carrier submits a detention bill, the time of delivery has to be proved to substantiate the charges. For these reasons and several others, a document known as a *delivery receipt* is maintained by the carrier.

There is no commonly accepted form for a delivery receipt. Motor carriers, the most consistent users of delivery receipts, may use a copy of one of their other documents as a receipt. Bills of lading, waybills, and freight bills are prepared with many carbon copies and any of them can be used as a delivery receipt. The receiver's representative signs the document and indicates the time of receipt. This document can then be used to substantiate delivery. Under recent rule changes, an employee of the consignee is required to sign the delivery receipt. An example of a delivery receipt prepared explicitly for this purpose is shown in Figure 14–13.

INSPECTION REPORTS

Merchandise is sometimes damaged while enroute from origin to destination. Unless the bill of lading's terms and conditions indicate otherwise, the carrier is responsible for the condition of the commodities upon delivery. If the receiver claims receipt of damaged merchandise, an inspection is required before a claim can be made against the carrier. The consignee must notify the carrier of the damage, and the carrier has an opportunity to inspect the merchandise. An *inspection report* is then made out by the carrier representative. Damaged freight occurs most often in railroad and motor carriage, and each mode has its own form for inspection reports. The consignee is given a copy of the inspection report, which is then used as the basis for a claim against the carrier for the amount lost.

CLAIM FORMS

As indicated earlier, freight charges may be mistakenly paid by both the shipper and the receiver. It was also stated that merchandise may be damaged while enroute from origin to destination. In both cases, a formal claim must be filed

FIGURE 14–13. DELIVERY RECEIPT

Mclean TRUCKING COMPANY

OFFERED TO_____
           CUSTOMER NAME   ADDRESS   CITY   STATE

SHIPPER'S NO. (LOADING)_____PRO NO. (UNLOADING)_____WEIGHT_____

WAS A PREARRANGED SCHEDULED TIME SET? ☐ NO ☐ YES IF YES, TIME_____DATE_____

EXPLAIN ALTERNATIVE ARRANGEMENTS MADE WHEN PREARRANGED SCHEDULE NOT MET. _____

HELPER SERVICE REQUESTED AND USED? ☐ YES ☐ NO   TRAILER NO._____

EMPLOYEE REMAINED WITH VEHICLE TIME / DATE	**VEHICLE SPOTTED** TIME / DATE
Vehicle Released _____ _____	Vehicle Released _____ _____
☐ Loading ☐ Unloading	Vehicle Arrived _____ _____
Completed _____	Total Time Elapsed in Hours _____ _____
Began _____	
Vehicle Arrived _____ _____	
Total Time in Minutes _____	THE INFORMATION ABOVE IS HEREBY ACKNOWLEDGED AS A RECORD TO BE USED WHEN APPLICABLE IN ASSESSING CHARGES FOR DETENTION AND/OR HELPER SERVICE.
Lunch Ended _____	
Lunch Began _____	
Break Ended _____	SIGNATURE OF CUSTOMER'S AGENT_____
Break Began _____	
Net Time (Less Lunch, etc.)In Minutes _____	SIGNATURE OF DRIVER_____

INVOICE NO._____

LOADING/UNLOADING INFORMATION — DETENTION AND/OR HELPER SERVICE

Form No. 319 Rev. 9/77

against the carrier. The two major types of claims filed against carriers are for freight overcharges and for loss and damage.

FREIGHT OVERCHARGE CLAIMS

The freight charges appearing on a freight bill may not be accurate for a variety of reasons. The carrier may have used an incorrect freight rate for the commodity. Or the rate may be based on incorrect origin and destination points. Sometimes an estimated weight is used on the bill of lading, and the receiver may be able to substantiate the lower actual weight at destination. When the freight charges are based on the estimated weights and a given unit rate, an overcharge occurs. In other cases, freight charges are paid twice. The consignee may misinterpret a prepaid freight bill or a carrier may mistakenly issue a collect freight bill on a prepaid shipment. A claim may be filed if the carrier used an incorrect route for the shipment that resulted in a higher rate than that which would have applied by the correct route. Although the rate shown on the freight bill must be paid, the shipper is not ultimately responsible for the incorrect rate. In all of these situations, a freight overcharge claim is filed because excessive payments have been made.

The claim must state the reasons a refund is being sought, and all shipment details must be shown on the claim form. An overcharge claim form is shown in Figure 14–14. A claim for freight overcharges must be accompanied by the bill of lading and the original paid freight bill. There may be times when the

FIGURE 14–14. Overcharge Claim Form

SOUTHERN PACIFIC COMPANY   S-6401

FORM FOR PRESENTATION OF OVERCHARGE AND LOSS AND DAMAGE CLAIMS

To_____

| Name | Title | Date | Claimant's Number |

SOUTHERN PACIFIC COMPANY

Carrier's Number

_____
Address

This claim for $_____is made against the Southern Pacific Company for_____
in connection with the following described shipments.   overcharge—or loss or damage

DATE of W.B.	W.B. No.	CAR OR BOAT	B/L Issued By	LAST WAYBILLING POINT	DESTINATION	F. B. No. AND ROUTE

If concealed loss or damage also fill in "Prior transportation record," below.

DATE of W.B.	W.B. No.	CAR OR BOAT	B/L Issued By	*Place Where Articles Were Packed	DESTINATION	F. B. No. AND ROUTE
				*		

Shipper_____Consignee_____Commodity_____Amount Claimed_____

*If for overcharge show "as collected" charges in first 5 lines and "as should be charges" in lines 6 to 10. If Loss and Damage disregard double space ruling. Show number and description of articles, nature and extent of loss or damage, invoice price of articles, etc.

1	
2	
3	
4	
5	
6	
7	
8	
9	
10	
Total Amount Claimed	

The following documents are submitted in support of claim: ( ) 2 Original invoice or certified copy, showing
( ) 1 Original Bill of Lading   all trade and other discounts or deductions
( ) 3 Original paid freight bill   by shipper.
( ) 5 Copy F/B-B/L covering prior transpor-   ( ) 4 Inspection Report & Salvage Receipt.
tation record to waybilling point   ( ) 6 _____
Authority for rate claimed

Information Required from Shipper in Support of Claim for Concealed Loss or Concealed Damage:

Were the goods packed at last Waybilling Point?_____ (a) In event packages were opened, examined and re-

packed at last Waybilling Point, were contents found to be in good condition at that time?_____. (b) State

date such unpacking was performed_____. (c) In event not opened for examination at last
Waybilling Point, fill in "Prior transportation record," above. A copy of Freight Bill and Bill of Lading covering such prior
movement is required.

The foregoing statement of facts is hereby certified to as correct_____
                                                          Signature of claimant
IF CLAIM IS SUPPORTED WITH COPY OF INVOICE IT
SHOULD BE CERTIFIED AS TO CORRECTNESS BY AN
OFFICER OF THE COMPANY, SHOWING TITLE.   Claimant's address: (Street and number)   (City or town)

If claim filed by Traffic Bureau_____
                    Name and address of Traffic Bureau

claim's preparer does not have or cannot locate the bill of lading and/or the original paid freight bill. In these circumstances, another document must be completed to guarantee the carrier that any refunds issued in error will be returned if it is discovered that the refunds should not have been made. This document is known as a *bond of indemnity*, which protects the carrier in the event the refund should have been made to another party. This would occur if the party possessing the bill of lading and/or the original freight bill is the party that should have been paid. Examples of bonds of indemnity are shown in Figures 14–15 and 14–16.

It should be noted that not all errors on freight bills are overcharges paid to the carrier. Some of the same reasons that exist for freight overcharges pertain to freight undercharges. For example, the billed weight may be less than the actual weight. Or the rate charged on the original freight bill was not as high as it should have been because of misinterpretations of classification, origin and destination points, or routing. In cases of freight undercharges, the carrier submits a claim against the party responsible for payment of the charges. The claim form is similar to the original freight bill and is called a *balance due bill*.

LOSS AND DAMAGE CLAIMS

Often, claims must be filed against carriers because of the condition of the contents of a shipment. Damage may occur from carrier negligence in handling, or merchandise may have been stolen while the shipment was in the carrier's possession. Entire packages or parts of packages may be missing when a shipment reaches its destination. Fire or improper temperatures may completely ruin commodities. In addition, an unusually long period of time may

FIGURE 14–15. BOND OF INDEMNITY

C. 6. 5874

OVERNIGHT PRINTING CO. — HOUSTON

Claim No._____

GUARANTEE AGAINST CLAIMS ARISING FROM NON-DELIVERY of ORIGINAL FREIGHT BILL or BILL of LADING

In consideration of the_____, paying to the undersigned

$_____(more or less), in settlement of claim for Loss or Damage or Overcharge on the shipment referred to below,

without surrendering the original Freight Bill and/or Bill of Lading,_____agree to bind_____and guarantee

to reimburse the said_____whatever amount it may be required
to or may pay on other claims for overcharge or for loss or damage on same shipment, or for damages, costs or expenses, incident to or growing out of such payments, or out of refusal to pay such claims made by any parties in case of presentation of claim at any time hereafter, accompanied by the missing document referred to.

The missing Freight Bill and/or Bill of Lading cannot be submitted in support of this claim account_____

Description of Shipment_____

Dated at_____State of_____Day of_____19____

Witness:_____

NOTE: This guarantee cannot be accepted in place of original paid freight receipt, and, or, original bill of lading unless the document has been actually lost or has been presented to another railroad in support of claim on the same shipment. If document has been lost or attached to another claim, the reason must be definitely stated. The person who signs the firm or corporate name for the giver of this guarantee, must be one of authority to bind the maker, and should sign his own name in full, and state his official relation to principal.

FIGURE 14–16. Railroad Bond of Indemnity

Form 1249

ST. LOUIS SOUTHWESTERN RAILWAY COMPANY

Auditor Freight Accounts

RELEASE OF ORIGINAL BILL OF LADING OR FREIGHT BILL

....19........

....hereby guarantee to protect St. Louis
Southwestern Railway Co., or any connecting carrier or carriers, as their respective interests may appear,
against any and all loss, damage, cost, expenses and attorney's fees which may result from the payment
of our claim number...

Amounting to $...........................Auditor Freight Accounts' Number...................., for{ Loss of or Damage / or Overcharge }

To Shipment of..., Shipped by...

From...................................To...................................Covered by W. B. No............................

From...To...

Dated............................19........, the original { Freight Bill / Bill of Lading } having been requested

and...being unable to furnish same

Account..
        (Lost or Destroyed)

Signed...

Witness:...

pass from origin date to delivery date, causing the merchandise's value to be
lower than it would have been if the shipment had arrived when expected or
promised. In these cases, a claim can be filed by either the shipper or the
receiver. Loss and damage claims must be accompanied by the original bill of
lading, the freight bill, weight certificates at both origin and destination if a loss
of freight is involved, an invoice showing the merchandise's value, and an
inspection report if damage is involved. If the required documentation is not

available, bonds of indemnity must accompany the claim. The loss and damage claim form is shown in Figure 14–17. The form contains space for details that specifically identify the shipment involved. Loss and damage claims, as you might expect, usually take longer to process and settle than do freight overcharge claims. Overcharge claims are usually a matter of fact; loss and damage claims involve much more investigation and negotiation.

This section has introduced the common types of supporting documents

FIGURE 14–17. LOSS AND DAMAGE CLAIM FORM

1-66 30M

C. S. 5820

ST. LOUIS SOUTHWESTERN RAILWAY COMPANY

CLAIM PRESENTATION FORM

O S & D
No. if any______

Mail to______

______ Address | ______ Station | ______ 19__ Claimant's Number and Date of Filing

This claim for $______ is made against the ______
in connection with the following described shipments.

DATE OF W. B.	W. B. No.	Received at Destination in Car	B/L ISSUED BY	F. C. U. No.	F. B. No.	Station Claim No.
						ROUTE
				LAST WAYBILLING POINT	DESTINATION	Date Shipment Delivered
	CHECK	CL ___ LCL	TFC			

Shipper______ Consignee______ Commodity______

ARTICLES BILLED:
WEIGHT:______ NO. OF PKGS.______
ARTICLES SHORT OR DAMAGED: Visible ☐ Concealed ☐

1. Was salvage dumped?______
Attach copy of salvage W/B.
W/B No. and Date______ BRO #______

2. Was damaged article packed, repacked or inspected at waybilling point?
______ If not and damage exceeds $10.00, attach chain of billing from point where packed—if known.

3. If claim for loss, was package corded or otherwise protected against pilferage?______

4. Describe condition of container______

5. Nature, Extent and Cause of Damage: If furniture, show package nos. (1-2, etc.)

Date and by whom inspection made and loss or damage verified.

Signed______ (Inspector's Name) 19__ Date

BASIS OF CLAIM This need not be filled out if separate claim statement is submitted.

Net Amount of Claim $

GUARANTY AND CERTIFICATION

The undersigned binds and guarantees, to reimburse the St. Louis Southwestern Railway Company whatever amount it may be required to or may pay on other claims of overcharge or for loss or damage on same shipment, or for damages, cost or expenses, incident to or growing out of such payments, or out of refusal to pay such claims made by any parties in case of presentation of claim at any time hereafter, accompanied by the missing original Freight Bill and/or Bill of Lading.

The undersigned hereby certifies that this claim, if for loss or damage, does not exceed the destination value of the property, in the quantity shipped at time of delivery, or invoice prices, less discounts or allowances, if any, and that the actual allowance, if any, represents the actual value realized from sale or use of damaged property; and that missing articles have not been received from any other source.

The foregoing statement of facts is hereby certified to be correct and reasonable:

Signed______ Title______

Claimant______

Address______

Draft No.______ mailed to claimant______ 196__

AGENT'S CLAIM FOR MISCELLANEOUS CREDIT (Submit One Copy)

Station Claim No.______

Auditor of Freight Accounts:

Herewith claim papers for which credit is claimed on Form 3313, off-setting debits and credits, supporting the above payment. This will certify that claim does not exceed carrier's record of loss or damage, inspection report, Form 3005, and that the shortage, if any, has not been received by consignee from any other source. Invoice Verified, Prices, Calculations correct and reasonable.

Signed______ Agent______

used in freight transportation. Of course, most shipments do not require any of these supporting documents. But a knowledge of these documents is valuable in the event that transportation service does not occur as planned. Another group of documents not used on a regular basis relates to providing total transportation service. These documents are used in transportation management.

Management Documents

The shipment documents and supporting documents described in previous sections relate to individual shipments moving from origin to destination. Other documents exist that assist in transportation service but are not involved directly with movement. Because they involve administration of activities, they are more appropriate categorized as management documents. The major types of management documents are contracts, tariffs, average weight agreements, average demurrage agreements, and insurance policies.

CONTRACTS

As indicated previously, a separate bill of lading is required for each shipment when a common carrier is involved. When a contract is arranged between a shipper and a contract carrier, proper preparation of the contract document is important. The two negotiating parties should state all details pertaining to the arrangement in specific terms. Usually, contracts will define the length of time the contract is to be in effect, the commodities to be hauled, the origin and destination points to be served, and the rates for the service. Some contracts will include the exact time of day that pickups and deliveries are to be made. To avoid problems, the user should state any further services desired in the contract. The contract may request weight certificates substantiating the exact weight of each shipment, separate bills of lading for each movement, and delivery receipts. It should not be assumed that the contract carrier will provide all desired documentation for the shipper unless the requirements are stipulated in the negotiated contract.

When the contract does not spell out all the requirements of the shipper, conflicts may arise between the shipper and the contract carrier. Because document preparation involves additional clerical expenses and independent weighings may involve additional fees, these costs are built into the negotiated charges for performing transportation services. If the services are not stipulated in the contract and are requested after the service has begun, the transportation charges will have to be renegotiated. Or the contract carrier may not want to perform the service if too many details are involved. Thus, time should be taken to negotiate and prepare the contract document to avoid future problems.

Because of the many variables in contract carriage, no standard contract document is used. Usually, both parties will employ legal representatives to assist in completing the contract.

TARIFFS

Transportation management requires maintenance of many documents relating to transportation costs. As explained in Chapter 13, many publications list the legal charges for transporting commodities between two points, as well as for accessorial services. Thousands of tariffs exist to cover these costs. Tariff documents are maintained by all carriers for the services they provide and the commodities and points they serve. Users involved in many shipments maintain many tariffs in their files so that cost information is readily available.

Many kinds of tariffs exist, such as local, joint, agency, commodity, and class. Carriers usually maintain all tariffs relevant to their regular shipments. Shippers also maintain tariffs for their commodities and shipment locations. These tariffs provide immediate information and serve as double checks on carriers to ensure that correct freight rates are being assessed. Shippers can subscribe to agency services that supply tariffs to shippers on a regular basis. Subscribes also receive changes, known as *tariff supplements*, as they occur.

AVERAGE AND ACTUAL WEIGHT AGREEMENTS

Shippers are responsible for a freight rate between two points, based on the specific weight of the freight. Determining the exact shipment weight can be time-consuming and costly, especially with railcars that must be switched to a scale and then switched again so that the car can be attached to a train. To eliminate weighing and to expedite transportation, a document known as an *average weight agreement* can be negotiated.

An average weight agreement allows the shipper to estimate the shipment's total weight. It is commonly used when standard weights exist for the commodities being shipped. For example, if a user is shipping 50 motorcycles and each bike weighs 400 pounds, then the shipment should weigh 20,000 pounds. If the shipper has an average weight agreement with the carrier, the shipment will proceed from origin to destination without a separate weighing of the railcar or motor truck. The freight bill is prepared for a 20,000-pound shipment, and the user is responsible for those charges unless an actual weighing is made and a difference is uncovered.

Large industrial shippers may have scales capable of weighing transportation vehicles, such as trucks or railcars, at their manufacturing locations. These scales are maintained because of the large variety of inbound and outbound materials and vehicles. The carriers can accept the weight of the shipper's or receiver's scales if an *actual weight agreement* is in effect. In such situations, many carriers might question the accuracy of the scales and the weighing procedure. Therefore, independent agencies regularly inspect the weighing procedures and scales used. The Eastern Weighing and Inspection Bureau is one agency that performs this service, and similar agencies operate in all parts of the country. Inspections are performed regularly, and approval allows the carriers to accept users' weights without weighing the shipment for liability and freight billing purposes. The average weight agreement or the actual weight agreement can lower transportation time and cost.

AVERAGE DEMURRAGE AGREEMENTS

As stated previously, shippers are allowed a limited time to load or unload a shipment. If the time limit is exceeded, the shipper or the receiver is responsible for a special demurrage or detention charge. Demurrage charges for rail shipments are assessed daily in three progressive stages. For example, the railroad may charge $20 per day for each day beyond the free-time limitation. However, if the car remains more than four days beyond the free time, the rate progresses to the second stage of $30 per day for two days, then to the third stage when the user is charged $60 per day for each day.

Many reasons may force the user to require more than the allowed free time to load or unload. Production may be halted for a plant vacation or for physical inventory. Or a specific shipment may arrive earlier than anticipated. A shipper may have ordered more empty cars than it was capable of loading in the given free time. In all of these cases, the user is responsible for the demurrage rate. On the other hand, the user may load or unload cars in less than the allowed free time in any given month, making the transportation vehicles available to the railroad sooner. In such situations, the user may negotiate with the carrier and complete a document known as an *average demurrage agreement*. An example of the agreement is shown in Figure 14–18.

An average demurrage agreement allows the user to offset demurrage charges with those time periods that were less than the allowed free time. For example, a receiver may hold a car for four days before unloading. However, two other cars were received and unloaded in one day. Assuming that the free-time allowance is two days per car, the user has built up two credits, meaning that two days' less time was taken to unload the railcars. The two credits can then be used to offset the two additional days needed to unload the third car. Thus, no demurrage charge is assessed.

Usually, credits apply only to the first stage of demurrage assessment and cannot be used to offset demurrage in the later two stages. The demurrage rules existing at the time apply and may change during different periods of activity. In the past, the rules have varied, sometimes requiring two credits to offset a demurrage, or debit, day. In all situations, however, a user can use credits to offset debits only if the average demurrage document has been completed and is in force.

The charge for excessive delays in loading or unloading truck shipments, as

FIGURE 14–18. Average Demurrage Agreement

AVERAGE AGREEMENT

ST. LOUIS SOUTHWESTERN RAILWAY COMPANY

Being fully acquainted with the terms, conditions and effect of the average basis for settling for detention of cars, as set forth in..being the car demurrage rules governing at all stations and sidings on the lines of said railroad, except as shown in said tariff, and being desirous of availing (myself or ourselves) of this alternate method of settlement (I or we) do expressly agree to and with St. Louis Southwestern Railway Company that, with respect to all cars which may, during the continuance of this agreement, be handled for (my or our) account at.. (Station) (I or we) will fully observe and comply with all the terms and conditions of said rules as they are now published, or may hereafter be lawfully modified by duly published tariffs, and will make prompt payment of all demurrage charges accruing thereunder in accordance with the average basis, as therein established, or as hereafter lawfully modified by duly published tariffs.

This agreement to be effective on and after the_____day of_____, 19___ and to continue until termination by written notice from either party to the other, which notice shall become effective on the first day of the month succeeding that in which it is given, except that for any failure or refusal to pay charges lawfully accruing under this agreement, it may be terminated as of the date of written notice of termination.

                                                _____ (FIRM NAME)

                                                _____ (BY)

                                                _____ (TITLE)

Approved and accepted.............. ...., 19......., by and on behalf of St. Louis Southwestern Railway Company

                      St. Louis Southwestern Railway Company

                      By ....- -   Title

already mentioned, is known as detention. The common time limit on loading or unloading is four hours, but may vary to a maximum of twenty-four hours, depending on the nature of the shipment. Truck companies do not have average agreements allowing credits and debits as in rail transportation. Detention charges are made on an hourly basis and start once the free time has expired.

INSURANCE POLICIES

Although a contract of carriage holds carriers responsible for commodities in their possession, the extent of liability varies. Limited liability applies most often to water freight transportation. However, under certain conditions, other modes may want to limit their financial responsibility. Products of extremely high value may be accepted for shipment only if the shipper absolves the carrier from responsibility beyond a stated limit. In these instances, special freight rates, known as *released-value rates*, are charged. When the carrier's liability is limited to an amount less than the commodity value, the user would be wise to obtain additional insurance protection. Thus, if loss or damage beyond the carrier's responsibility occurs, the user is not harmed financially. These additional policies are negotiated with insurance firms not involved in transportation service. However, these firms are aware of the potential hazards of transportation, and base their rates accordingly.

Summary

Any business activity requires paper work. Documents are necessary to control the flow of activities and to maintain current and permanent records. Transportation is no exception to the paper work requirement. This chapter discussed transportation documents in three categories.

In the first group, bills of lading, waybills, and freight bills were described. Several kinds of bills of lading, for different purposes, were discussed. Waybills, the activity records, were examined. The documents in this group are used regularly and relate directly to transportation service.

The second category includes documents also directly involved with transportation service but not required on all shipments. This group includes arrival notices, delivery receipts, inspection reports, and two types of claim forms.

The third group of transportation documents, categorized as management documents, includes contracts, tariffs, average and actual weight agreements, average demurrage agreements, and insurance policies. These documents are issued infrequently and are concerned more with transportation administration than with transportation movement. This third group of management documents leads naturally to Chapters 15 and 16, which discuss carrier management and industrial traffic management.

Questions for Chapter 14

1. What are the purposes of a bill of lading?
2. Describe the difference between a uniform straight bill of lading and a uniform order bill of lading.
3. What documents take the place of a bill of lading in pipeline and airline freight transportation?
4. What is the purpose of a carrier waybill?
5. Describe the difference between a prepaid and a collect freight bill.
6. For what purpose is an arrival notice used?
7. What functions are accomplished with the use of a delivery receipt?
8. Under what circumstances would an inspection report be required?
9. Differentiate between the two major kinds of claim forms.
10. How does an average weight agreement reduce overall transportation operating costs?
11. Why is it advantageous for a firm to arrange an average demurrage agreement?
12. Why would a firm wish to arrange an insurance policy on commodities shipped?

15

Industrial Traffic Management

295

Objectives represent a goal to be achieved. But objectives cannot be realized with uncoordinated and haphazard approaches. A planned system of effort—management—is necessary to coordinate and direct many activities toward specific objectives.

A professional baseball team can illustrate the need for management to achieve objectives. If you are a baseball fan, you go to the stadium, cheer for the team during the game, and then leave. You may not appreciate all the efforts that went into the game you saw. The team's administration, composed of the owners and board members, is dedicated to providing sports entertainment to the community. Therefore, the administration's objective is to assemble a team good enough to attract and excite the fans. A business objective also exists. The administration must be sure that enough revenue is collected to pay all the costs and to leave enough of a profit margin to reward investors and attract new players.

A general business manager plus a team manager and several coaches direct the team toward accomplishing the two objectives. The manager coordinates the coaches' activities and consults with them when making decisions. The coaches work on improving the team's batting, pitching, and fielding, as well as advising the manager on field operations. The manager is responsible for coordinating the field operations as efficiently as possible.

Although the players are directed by the manager, they are the ones who perform. They are specialists in a specific activity, such as pitching, fielding, or hitting. They are expected to excel in their specialty and to contribute to the team's offense. Support services are also necessary to produce a winning team. These services include trainers, equipment managers, concession operators, ticket sellers and takers, ushers, announcers, scoreboard operators, musicians, and office personnel.

Transportation management requires the same kind of organization to accomplish its objectives of efficiency, service, and low cost. Transportation executives ensure that the company's objectives are being achieved and that resources are not being wasted. Managers concentrate on particular functions to be certain that they coincide with overall objectives. The managers must coordinate the efforts of those responsible for performing necessary duties. The specialists—just as the baseball players—perform specific tasks for the organization. Support services such as legal, accounting, and clerical staff assist in achieving the transportation objectives. In business, as in sports, management provides organization and control.

There are two forms of transportation management: industrial management and carrier management. Industrial management, commonly referred to as traffic management, is concerned with providing the transportation service desired by a firm during regular business operations. Industrial traffic management involves the transportation users, either shippers or receivers. Carrier management, on the other hand, involves the actual providers of transportation service, such as railroads and motor carriers. This chapter examines industrial traffic management, and carrier management will be discussed in Chapter 16.

Three benefits should be gained from your study of this chapter. First, it provides an understanding of the role and functions of an industrial traffic department. Second, it develops an awareness and appreciation of the significance of industrial traffic management's impact on the total integrated nature of this function with physical distribution, materials management, and logistics, three terms often used synonymously and described briefly later in this chapter. Third, this chapter illustrates the variety of career opportunities that are available in industrial traffic departments, as well as other departments involved in commodity movement. Although Chapter 17 is devoted to transportation careers, this chapter provides specific information detailing the elaborate structure of the industrial traffic department and the related careers possible.

Role of Traffic Management

During the early years of commercial development in the United States, traffic managers were rewarded and recognized for the special services they could obtain. Their ability to gain preferences in service, equipment supply, and low rates placed their firms in better competitive positions and made larger profits possible. Once governmental regulations were imposed on railroads, however, the ability to attract special advantages dwindled. Thus, opportunities did not exist for traffic managers to obtain special considerations. Traffic management began to be considered by corporate management as a necessary evil to keep a company operating, but not as an area that could offer real profit contributions. After all, each shipper enjoyed the same rates and services, and rebates were not possible.

Respectability began to return to traffic management once the motor carriers emerged as a major freight transportation mode. Users then had a choice between modes. Motor carriers could provide different services and arrangements than the railroads could. Analysis, change, and innovation in transportation became paramount. By the 1940s, traffic managers gained a level of respect as individuals who could provide positive benefits and competitive advantages by selecting an efficient, low-cost transportation system. The need for their expertise became apparent when transportation savings increased their firms' profit.

Transportation's role in other functional areas also became more evident as an interrelated activity. For instance, transportation costs influenced both the total cost of purchases and the selling price. Production costs were affected because of interplant movements, and inventory levels and costs were affected by the quantities carried in transporting vehicles. As the interfaces between transportation and other operating areas became evident to management, the need to elevate transportation to its proper stature surfaced. The impact of

297

transportation on a firm's profitability and survival demanded an organized traffic function, well managed by experts, to produce the lowest transportation cost consistent with the desired service. The transportation function could then interact with other departments to coordinate efforts and accomplish the firm's objectives.

Traffic management's role became more important as firms established separate departments to perform distinct functions. Because transportation affects so many areas of business operations, transportation decisions could not be left to each functional manager. Large firms established centralized traffic departments, staffed with many specialists. Smaller companies attempted to assign transportation responsibility to one or more individuals with the necessary background and experience.

Unfortunately, to this day, many firms still do not appreciate the role that transportation plays in successful operations. It is not unusual to find transportation decisions being made by purchasing agents, sales personnel, or inventory control managers in some firms. As a result, possible savings are lost, because the advantages of a coordinated, planned transportation program are lacking.

Scope and Functions of Traffic Management

Transportation's importance to a firm's survival should be evident to you by now. You may even have a better appreciation than many business executives who are involved in so many daily activities that they have little time left for transportation analysis and improvement. Fortunately, larger firms have passed that stage and usually enjoy the benefits of efficient traffic management. The extent of benefits depends on the volume of business conducted and the firm's operating complexity. Multiplant and multiproduct firms will probably realize greater benefits than single-plant companies with a limited number of products and markets. Industrial traffic management involves both internal and external functions and responsibilities.

Internal Traffic Management

The traffic department's basic function is to provide the transportation service necessary at the lowest possible total cost. Of course, many activities are required to accomplish that function. Some clerical activities are performed strictly within the traffic department, whereas others involve contact with other firms and carriers. Another group of activities entails contact with other departments within the same firm. All of these activities are considered internal functions. Those functions referred to as internal are required to bring about effective day-to-day transportation operations.

INTERNAL CLERICAL FUNCTIONS

Many daily operations in a traffic department are routine. The number of clerks necessary to perform daily duties depends on the volume of transportation handled by that department. Some firms have adopted electronic data processing equipment to handle repetitive tasks. These routine activities, classified as internal clerical functions, can be divided into five categories.

RATE QUOTATIONS
Many departments are interested in actual transportation rates. For example, the sales department needs rate information to determine the final selling price of a product, and purchasing agents need rate information to determine the final buying price on a potential purchase. The existing transportation rates must be available and accessible to these other departments. Most traffic departments maintain all rates and can provide this information. In most firms, individuals who can read tariffs and quote them accurately are referred to as *rate analysts*. They respond to day-to-day rate requests.

ROUTING
For many reasons, a traffic department may wish to specify a particular routing on a shipment. One route may be faster than another, or the firm may want to ensure that the shipment can be diverted, if necessary, to another destination. Specific routes are usually established by the traffic manager. The clerical staff sees that these routes are followed on all inbound and outbound shipments by appropriate notation on the bill of lading.

DOCUMENT PREPARATION
Chapter 14 discussed some transportation documents. The traffic department is responsible for preparing bills of lading and any other documents required. In some cases, this includes preparation of documents that are placed on each package, with shipping and delivery instructions as well as identifying marks.

FREIGHT CHARGES
Freight bills are received regularly by the traffic department. Each bill is compared with the department's records and, if correct, is approved for payment. If it is incorrect, the bill is paid, but an overcharge claim is presented to the carrier. Some firms employ outside agencies to audit their freight bills. These audit firms may conduct prepayment or postpayment audits. In postpayment audits, the typical practice is to pay the auditors a percentage of the savings that result from the incorrect carrier charges they uncover. Firms that

conduct prepayment audits usually are paid on a per-bill audited basis. Bills for accessorial charges such as demurrage, stop-offs, or icing also must be processed through the traffic department. The department verifies these charges before they are paid.

CLAIMS

Chapter 14 also discussed the documents necessary to file claims against carriers. The traffic department gathers the necessary documentation, prepares the freight claim, and presents it to the carrier. Generally, claim records are kept within the department until the matter is closed.

INTERNAL OPERATIONAL FUNCTIONS

Another group of routine internal traffic management functions is required to manage freight movements. These activities are called internal operating functions and are reviewed here briefly.

PRIVATE TRANSPORTATION

A firm that operates all or part of its own transportation service needs personnel to manage the service. Generally, policies exist for the use of private transportation, such as locations to be covered, commodities to be carried, and priorities. These policies are implemented in the traffic department. Vehicles are dispatched, records are kept, and any waiting lists are maintained. Often the traffic department creates a special subdivision to handle private transportation.

EQUIPMENT SUPPLY

In a producing company, vehicles must be available when products are ready for outbound shipment. The traffic department is responsible for having vehicles of the necessary size available when they are needed. The equipment supply function is usually a routine matter handled with carrier personnel. However, if the desired equipment is not available upon request, a higher-ranking traffic department official may have to become involved.

TRACING AND EXPEDITING

Unfortunately, transportation does not always proceed as planned. Firms may place orders for inbound materials and then discover that the shipment will be needed sooner than expected. Or carriers may take longer to transport a shipment than was anticipated by either the buyer or the seller. In either case, rush shipment becomes necessary. The shipment must first be located through tracing, and then rushed through to its destination, sometimes by rerouting. This procedure is called expediting. These procedures are routine in both the industrial traffic department and the carrier's operations department and are usually handled at the clerical level.

DIVERTING

As discussed earlier, a shipment's destination may have to be changed after the shipment has left its point of origin. The shipment must be traced and its destination changed. This is known as diversion, which is handled routinely.

IN-TRANSIT ARRANGING

In firms that can take advantage of the in-transit privileges described earlier, a regular routine must be established. The arrangements deal with either stop-off provisions or in-transit mixing. Records must be maintained for the shipments involved, the quantities affected, and the various locations. Again, these matters are fairly routine.

PERSONNEL ARRANGEMENTS

Traffic departments often arrange transportation for company personnel. The most common arrangements involve moving the personal possessions of transferred employees. In large firms, transfers occur regularly, and the traffic manager has an established procedure with household goods movers. Also, when personnel travel on company business, travel and lodging arrangements are usually made by the traffic department. In some firms, private aircraft are used to transport top-level managers.

INTERNAL INTERDEPARTMENTAL FUNCTIONS

An organized industrial traffic department is responsible for many operational activities. Many activities require contact between the traffic department and other departments within the firm. These are known as interdepartmental functions and are necessary for coordination, support services, or advice.

COORDINATION FUNCTIONS

A major purpose of an industrial traffic department is coordinating other departments' transportation requirements. Thus, a great deal of interaction takes place among the various departments. For example, the purchasing department should be aware of the correct purchase quantities to achieve the best freight rates. Because lower rates are often possible with large purchases, it may be to the firm's advantage (but not necessarily so) to plan purchases in larger quantities. If the firm's sales department is planning a special sales campaign, frequent shipments of larger quantities may be necessary, and the additional transportation service must be coordinated between the two departments. In the distribution area, loaded vehicles must be coordinated to arrive when storage space is available in any of the firm's warehouses or distribution centers to avoid excessive detention or demurrage charges.

Traffic coordination is also necessary with those departments involved with production, such as manufacturing and engineering. Manufacturing departments depend on a regular transportation flow, with inbound materials arriving when expected and outbound materials moving out quickly to avoid congestion. Engineering departments work with traffic departments to determine the appropriate packaging restrictions and requirements for transportation. Also, the design and shape of manufactured products must conform to transportation requirements. If the shipping and receiving sections are within the control of the production department, then a great deal of interaction with the traffic department will be necessary. Coordination is required between the traffic department and the finance department if the firm has to invest in transportation facilities or equipment.

SUPPORT SERVICE FUNCTIONS

The traffic department also must interact with other departments for support services. The accounting department secures credit arrangements with carriers, pays freight bills, and keeps records on claims filed against carriers. For any shipment that requires additional insurance coverage, the traffic department must work with those individuals responsible for insurance arrangements. Advice from the firm's legal department may be necessary regarding arrangements made with contract carriers, claim matters, or interpretations of transportation law.

ADVICE FUNCTIONS

The traffic department is responsible for giving advice, whether or not solicited, on transportation matters that affect other departments. This advice can involve rate quotations on quantities and locations for purchasing agents, attractive rate possibilities in new territories for the sales department, and new packaging designs or changes in carrier packaging requirements for the production department.

The scope and volume of the internal activities of an industrial traffic department vary with the size of the firm, the nature of the industry, and manner of operation. However, the activities described here are typical of the responsibilities of an industrial traffic department. The department's activities also extend to external functions and responsibilities.

External Traffic Management

All traffic functions require contact with persons outside the firm. Many of these contacts are routine and can be performed at the clerical level. Other external situations demand the attention of top-level traffic managers. These external activities can be classified as purchasing, liaison, carrier relations, regulation, and research.

PURCHASING

A traffic department's management might be viewed as performing a purchasing function. If a firm is involved in private transportation, management is responsible for the purchase and maintenance of the necessary equipment. Also, transportation service is purchased from common and contract carriers. The firm's traffic management selects both the modes and the individual carriers to be used. If more than one mode or carrier is qualified to handle the desired shipments, various service alternatives must be compared and a choice made.

LIAISON

Inbound shipments are received from vendors who sell to the firm, and outbound shipments are made to customers who buy from the firm. In both cases, the industrial traffic department acts as a liaison between the external parties. The department may consult with customers to determine desired routings or equipment specifications. Or it may advise vendors of the firm's desired routing for inbound shipments. Customers and vendors alike may need assistance in tracing shipments or may need advice on the use of the firm's private transportation or other matters.

CARRIER RELATIONS

A large part of an industrial traffic department's external activities involves relations with transportation carriers. The carriers' sales department personnel regularly visit industrial traffic departments. During these visits, carrier representatives analyze the traffic department's needs and explain how their firm can best satisfy such requirements. Of course, the objective is to persuade the traffic department to use the services of that carrier. The traffic department management must make its choices, based on the firm's needs and the service characteristics of the various carriers.

External relationships also include carrier negotiations. Negotiations can take several forms. For instance, the traffic department may be contemplating the purchase of property owned by a carrier. The traffic department's familiarity with carrier personnel may be beneficial to the purchase negotiations. The traffic department also negotiates freight rates. A firm seeking a lower freight rate will find that rate-reduction requests are handled more expediently if they are supported by carriers. In the negotiation, the traffic department tries to convince carrier representatives of the request's feasibility. If these negotiations are successful, the carrier will sponsor the request and forward it through appropriate rate proposal channels.

Negotiation is required if a user's product is to be reclassified. Traffic departments must negotiate reclassifications with both carriers and carrier bureaus.

Reclassification leads to reduced transportation costs, and the carriers must be convinced to approve a reclassification of commodities. It is also not uncommon for traffic departments to negotiate with carriers for more frequent service, changed time schedules, or more transportation vehicles with the desired specifications.

REGULATION

To keep abreast of regulatory procedures and clarify any questionable requirements, the traffic department interacts frequently with various regulatory institutions. The firm's best interests will be protected at formal hearings conducted by the regulatory bodies if the industrial traffic department is actively participating in those hearings. The hearing issues may involve rates, rules, or services in which the firm may be involved. The firm's traffic department also communicates with regulatory bodies regarding the interpretation of regulations or the legality of certain practices. Finally, most progressive traffic departments are taking an active role, either directly or through associations, regarding the nature and substance of any deregulation proposals.

RESEARCH

Transportation research conducted by the traffic department can lead to improved service and lower costs. Internal research can use company records to analyze past shipments and compare the performance of various modes and specific carriers. Because the traffic department maintains records on the routes and times of each shipment, the carriers with the best overall performance can be identified and preferred for future service.

External research is conducted to identify ways in which transportation methods and costs can be improved. New packaging materials and methodologies can be evaluated through technical journals and periodicals or by examining the packaging practices of other users in the same line of business. Loading and unloading methods can be improved by adopting the new technologies viewed at trade shows and reported in various transportation publications. Rate and classification changes that may affect a firm's operations and costs are detailed in various transportation publications that list all changes in rates.

The importance of transportation research is not to be minimized. If an industrial traffic department is to provide the desired service at the lowest cost, it must be on the alert for any updated information and technology that will be useful. The firm's transportation research requirements should be assigned to a high-ranking traffic official. Let us now examine the organizational structure of the industrial traffic department.

Organization of an Industrial Traffic Department

Any organization must have a planned structure to assure that its objectives are achieved. The organizational structure, which defines areas of responsibility and authority, includes high-level executives who establish policies for a functional area, managers who direct the activities of that area, and personnel who perform the required tasks. An industrial traffic department receives its mission, or overall policies, from a high-level management authority, such as the president or vice president of a firm. The exact organizational positioning of the traffic department within the firm varies and will be discussed in the next section. Of immediate concern here is the internal organization of the industrial traffic department.

There are almost as many traffic department organization structures as there are traffic departments. The highest traffic official can have a wide range of duties and responsibilities. The wider the range, the more important the traffic official will be in the firm's overall organization. It is not uncommon for a firm that spends millions of dollars yearly in transportation to have a vice president of traffic. The most common titles assigned to the highest traffic official are director of traffic or traffic manager. In a multiplant or multidivision firm, these titles are often expanded to corporate director of traffic or corporate traffic manager. These corporate officials will be supported by regional traffic managers who receive their policy guidelines from the corporate office. Regional traffic managers are responsible for a geographic portion of the country and may have traffic managers at each company facility.

The extent of the traffic department's organization structure depends on the firm's traffic volume. In a company with many shipments that need constant attention, a separate operations group may be established. It is common for a group to be responsible for all freight rates. Figure 15–1 is a hypothetical organization chart for a multiplant corporation with corporate traffic management and decentralized regional and local operations. In this example, the corporate traffic manager provides policy guidelines, and most of the traffic responsibilities are performed at the branch level. Two regional traffic managers coordinate the activities of the branch offices under their jurisdiction.

The branch traffic managers are responsible for all traffic activities within their territory. Assuming that many shipments are involved and the company uses rail, truck, and water transportation, separate divisions are established for those areas, as shown in Figure 15–2. This subdivision allows the assistant traffic managers to specialize in particular areas. The clerical assistance provided to these managers depends on the volume of business transacted. In some cases, the managers may have several assistants, but in others, only one or two clerks may be necessary.

305

FIGURE 15–1. Decentralized Corporate Traffic Department

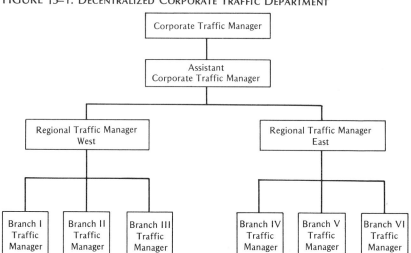

The traffic department's internal organization does not always follow the structure illustrated in Figures 15–1 and 15–2. The specific arrangement of a traffic department depends on the desires of the company. In the examples given, responsibilities were decentralized to each branch office. The corporate traffic manager and the regional traffic managers fulfilled a coordinating and advising function. This type of organization is *decentralized* because the primary responsibilities lie with the branch offices. The other extreme places the

FIGURE 15–2. Decentralized Branch Traffic Department

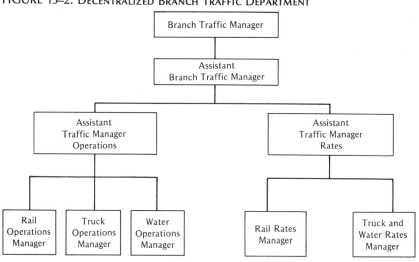

major management functions in the corporate office and restricts branch offices to day-to-day operations. Such an organizational arrangement is *centralized* because the major responsibilities are concentrated in one location.

A hypothetical, centralized organizational arrangement is shown in Figure 15–3. The corporate traffic manager directs the activities of two assistants who specialize in different functions—operations and rates. The assistant corporate traffic managers, in turn, have specialists who perform different functions. Direct reporting authority is shown by the solid line from the traffic managers to the corporate traffic manager. In addition, the corporate traffic manager is assisted by two regional traffic managers who are responsible for the day-to-day activities in the branch offices under their jursidiction. The branches may seek advice or assistance from the regional traffic managers. The regional traffic managers report directly to the corporate traffic manager, as shown by the solid lines. However, they may seek assistance from the specialist traffic managers or the assistant corporate traffic managers, depending on the matters involved. This relationship is indicated by dashed lines. The example in Figure 15–3 is hypothetical. Any number of different configurations could be developed, including assigning regional specialists to report to a regional traffic manager. Such an arrangement would be a blend of both a centralized and decentralized

FIGURE 15–3. Centralized Traffic Department

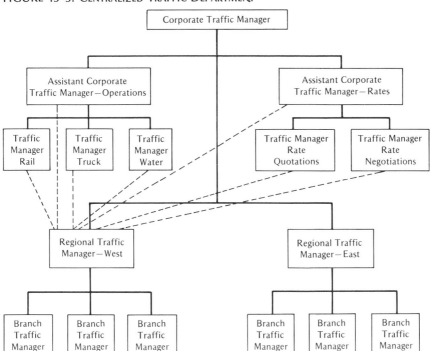

307

organization. The next section examines the positioning of a traffic department, whatever its internal structure, within the overall organizational structure of a firm.

The Traffic Department's Position in a Firm

The degree of importance of the traffic department can usually be determined by examining its organizational positioning within a firm. A company not heavily involved in transportation matters or a company that views traffic as a necessary evil, unable to contribute to profitable operations, will tend to situate the traffic department lower on the organization chart.

The traffic department's interrelationship with other departments in a firm has already been stressed. A firm's opinion of the traffic department's main role is reflected in the organizational reporting authority assigned. For example, a firm that emphasizes service to its customers may place the traffic department within the sales organization, with the traffic manager reporting to the sales manager. The sales manager uses the traffic department to provide the service necessary to assure a high sales level and to maintain good customer relations. A firm that emphasizes its manufacturing operations and wants continuous production may place the traffic manager in the production area. A firm that purchases large volumes of raw materials, components, and parts and is responsible for most inbound freight charges may have the traffic manager reporting directly to the purchasing agent. In other situations, it is not uncommon for the firm that spends millions of dollars yearly on transportation to place the traffic manager at a level equal to the sales manager, production officer, or purchasing agent. The most progressive firms consider transportation part of the total distribution network and place the traffic department under a physical distribution, materials management, or logistics executive. This type of structure has become more common during the last two decades. It is discussed in more detail in the next section.

The traffic department provides services for many departments and is not an end in itself. Therefore, the reporting relationship can be positioned within many departments. Figure 15–4 indicates only a few of the ways in which a traffic department could be placed in a firm that does not attach a high degree of importance to the traffic function. The dashed lines indicate the many possibilities for the department's placement. The traffic manager could report to the manufacturing manager, purchasing manager, or directly to the vice president in charge of production.

As noted earlier, a firm with complex transportation requirements, several operating locations, and a large annual expenditure will position the traffic department high in its organizational reporting structure. Firms with traffic

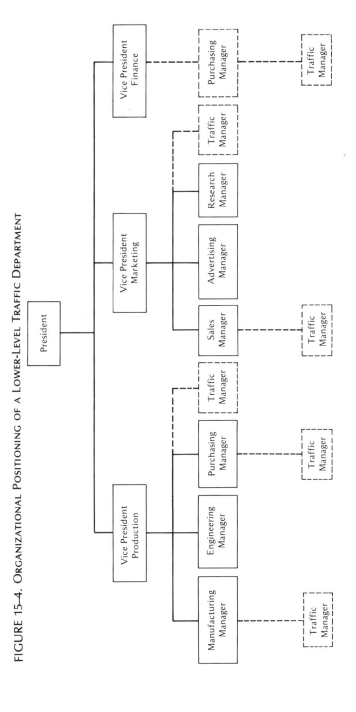

FIGURE 15–4. ORGANIZATIONAL POSITIONING OF A LOWER-LEVEL TRAFFIC DEPARTMENT

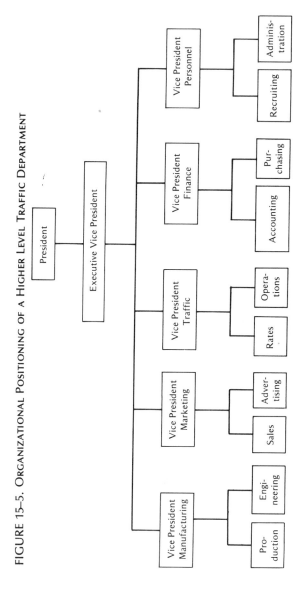

departments as extensive as those illustrated in Figures 15–1, 15–2, and 15–3 would be prime candidates for such a structure. Such firms would most likely have a vice president, traffic, reporting to one of the highest company officials, such as the executive vice president or the president. This arrangement, illustrated in Figure 15–5, shows the importance of the traffic function by its positioning with other vice presidential responsibilities. This arrangement is preferred, primarily because other functional areas cannot exercise influence over the traffic department to enhance themselves at the expense of efficient traffic management. As noted earlier, the firm may select to facilitate coordination of traffic with related activities by the establishment of a physical distribution, materials management, or logistics department. This form of organization and its supporting logic are now discussed.

The Development of Physical Distribution, Materials Management, and Logistics Departments

The terms *physical distribution, materials management,* and *logistics* are used to describe a trend over the past two decades to coordinate all managerial activities included in warehousing, order processing, inventory control, material handling, and transportation into a single organizational structure. The exact functions proposed for such integrated organizations also include, in some situations, purchasing, production scheduling, and customer service. In all cases, the primary emphasis in these integrated organizations is to provide greater overall management control over activities that are closely related in day-to-day operations. This section will briefly examine the main forces that have encouraged the development of these structures and will evaluate the impact on professional traffic management by reviewing a hypothetical organizational arrangement.

FORCES LEADING TO INTEGRATED ORGANIZATIONS

Over the past two decades, top managers have become increasingly aware of two factors that have a significant influence on profits. These are the total cost of operations and the quality of operations in terms of customer requirements and expectations. Operation of all aspects of transportation and storage has a great impact on both cost and quality of service.

From the viewpoint of the total economy, the cost of providing all aspects of movement and storage exceeds 20 per cent of the total gross national product

(GNP). For every trillion dollars of GNP, the national logistical bill exceeds $200 billion annually.[1] In comparison, the total national transportation bill for 1976 was $145.8 billion. Although transportation represents a significant portion of the overall cost of movement and storage, in most situations, it represents less than 50 per cent of the total cost of logistics.

During the 1950s, management became aware of the potential of *total cost analysis* of transportation/storage arrangements.[2] In 1956, a study of air freight pointed out that high freight rates characteristic of air transport could, in some situations, be more than offset by reductions in inventory holding and warehouse operation costs. Thus, it would be possible to spend more on transportation and reduce the total cost of the movement. Total cost analysis pointed out the potential in effective management of cost-to-cost trade-offs. The basic principle is that parts of a total movement system operating in a coordinated manner can produce greater end results than are possible through individual functional performance.

The quality of service aspect of integrated performance stresses that all forms of transportation and distribution exist only to assist a firm to make profitable transactions. Thus, at times it may be necessary to spend more dollars to improve the quality of service if it will result in more profitability. The lowest-cost way of performing a transportation movement may not be the most profitable. To illustrate, the lowest-cost method of movement may be to ship directly from a plant to a customer. However, if inventories are held in a warehouse close to the customer, shipments can be made faster but usually at a greater cost. In such a situation, the higher-cost method of delivery may be justified if it results in higher profits. Thus, in addition to cost trade-offs, it is important to consider cost/service trade-offs when designing customer distribution systems.

The desire to achieve a high quality of customer service while maintaining the lowest possible total cost has encouraged the development of integrated control organizations. The term *physical distribution management* is often used to describe integrated operations concerned with the movement and storage of finished products. In contrast, *materials management* is used to describe integrated operations that are concerned primarily with procurement and movement of materials, parts, and/or finished inventory to manufacturing and assembly plants. When both physical distribution and materials management are included in the same organization, the term *logistical management* is used to describe the combined operation.[3]

---

[1] Donald J. Bowersox, *Logistical Management*, 2nd ed. (New York: Macmillan Publishing Co., Inc., 1978), p. 4.

[2] Howard T. Lewis, James W. Culleton, and Jack D. Steel, *The Role of Air Freight in Physical Distribution* (Boston Division of Research, Graduate School of Business Administration, Harvard University, 1956).

[3] For expanded treatment, see Bowersox, op. cit., pp. 12–17.

TRAFFIC MANAGEMENT IN AN INTEGRATED ORGANIZATION

Regardless of the number of functions included in an integrated logistical organization, it will not operate up to expectations if it fails to incorporate professional traffic management. Within the broader management context offered in an integrated organization, many of the interdepartmental contacts noted earlier in this chapter fall within a single department. For example, contacts with purchasing may fall within the department. When traffic reports within an integrated organization, the potential for coordination is facilitated by the fact that many of the functional responsibility managers will report to the same executive.

In Figure 15–6, the reporting relationship of transportation and traffic is identified as part of the systems support services group. Reporting at this level, transportation is part of an organization concerned with the total integration of logistical performance. This group, support services, is not a staff organization. It is involved in day-to-day functional management within materials management, physical distribution, and inventory transfer operations. These groups may be viewed as either centralized or decentralized, depending on the nature of the operations performed by the organization.

The significant point in the integration of transportation into a logistical organization is that it facilitates coordination of quality performance at the lowest possible total cost. Unlike the organization arrangements of Figure 15–4, traffic management as illustrated in Figure 15–6 is part of a group that includes responsibility for a wide variety of closely related functions. In terms of modern organization concepts, the integrated structure shown in Figure 15–6 is becoming preferable to the highly specialized arrangement shown in Figure 15–5. Even though traffic is at a peer level with other functional executives in Figure 15–5, it is not part of an integrated structure as illustrated in Figure 15–6.

Summary

Transportation service requirements are not satisfied by accident. A firm must assure that it will receive the transportation service level necessary to maintain its competitive position through organized effort. Industrial traffic management exists for this purpose. Internal traffic management encompasses clerical, operational, and interdepartmental functions. Internal clerical functions involve rate quotations, routing, document preparation, freight charges, and claims. These functions are usually routine, once procedures are established. Operational functions, also routine, involve managing private trans-

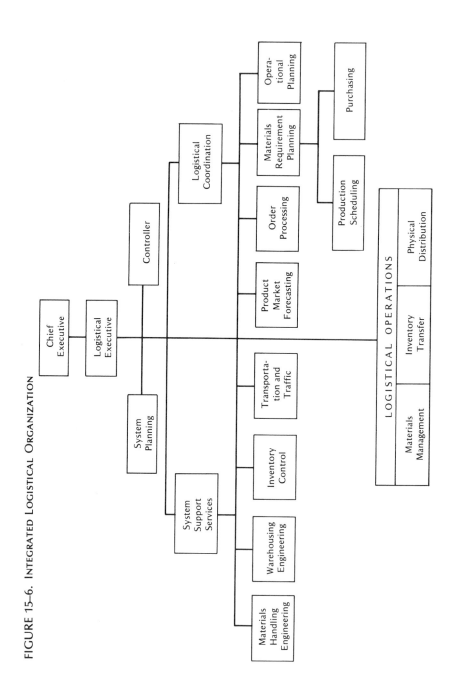

FIGURE 15–6. Integrated Logistical Organization

Chief Executive

Logistical Executive

Controller

System Planning

Logistical Coordination

System Support Services

Product Market Forecasting

Order Processing

Materials Requirement Planning

Opera-tional Planning

Transporta-tion and Traffic

Inventory Control

Warehousing Engineering

Materials Handling Engineering

Production Scheduling

Purchasing

LOGISTICAL OPERATIONS

Materials Management

Inventory Transfer

Physical Distribution

314

portation, equipment supply, tracing, expediting, diverting, in-transit procedures, and employee transportation requirements. Internal industrial traffic management also involves interaction with other departments in the firm to coordinate transportation requirements, provide support services, and give advice.

The industrial traffic department also has several external responsibilities. These responsibilities include purchasing equipment and supplies for private transportation and buying transportation service from modes and carriers. The traffic department acts as a liaison with the firm's vendors and customers and maintains carrier relations. Also, the traffic department stays informed of government regulatory matters and protects its company's interests in regulation hearings. The importance of traffic research should not be minimized. By keeping current on technological developments and updated methodologies, a traffic department can ensure that its company will provide the best available service.

Organizational structures for traffic departments vary. A traffic department can be decentralized, with most activities conducted at branch offices by branch traffic managers, or centralized, with the major functions performed at the corporate office. Combination arrangements conduct major activities at the regional level. The traffic department's position within a company's organizational structure varies. It may be given a low status with reporting responsibility to another functional manager. Or it may be given greater status with reporting responsibility directly to one of the firm's highest executives. Over the past two decades, more attention has been devoted to the formulation of integrated logistics departments that include the traffic management function.

Most of the traffic department's external activities involve representatives of transportation carriers. The department's effectiveness is often enhanced by this interaction with carrier management. Chapter 16 examines carrier management.

Questions for Chapter 15

1. Why was traffic management viewed more highly by industrial business management before regulation than afterwards?
2. Detail the internal clerical functions performed in industrial traffic departments.
3. Describe the internal operational functions that may be required in various industrial traffic departments.
4. Why should a close liaison exist between the traffic and purchasing departments of an industrial firm?
5. What benefits can accrue to a firm from research conducted by its traffic department?
6. Briefly differentiate between centralized and decentralized traffic departments.
7. What are the purchasing functions performed by industrial traffic management?
8. What is the role of a corporate traffic department in a decentralized traffic organizational arrangement?

9. How can the degree of importance attached to traffic management be determined in any given firm?
10. To which company executive does a traffic manager report?
11. What profit-influencing factors have led to increased attention to development of physical distribution, materials management, and logistics departments?
12. Describe the operational relationship of traffic management to physical distribution, materials management, and logistics departments.

16

Transportation Carrier Management

As noted in Chapter 15, industrial traffic management departments work closely with common or contract carriers. Even when a firm operates its own private trucking, it typically requires extensive use of common carriers to handle all transportation requirements.

To facilitate dealing with carriers, a familiarity with transportation carrier management, its organization, scope of operation, and responsibilities is useful.

317

In addition, anyone interested in a possible career in carrier management should be aware of all the activities that form a transportation company.

This chapter, therefore, seeks to develop an understanding of transportation carrier management for those who may find it necessary to use carriers for service and assistance and for those considering careers in carrier management and operations. Although transportation careers will be discussed in detail in Chapter 17, the major areas of carrier management and its organizational structure discussed in this chapter provide useful insights.

Carrier Management Development

The earliest carriers were privately owned. Railroads were owned by individuals who used the system to move their own products. For instance, rails were used to carry coal from privately owned mines to nearby ports for further transport by water. Anyone else wishing to use the rails was assessed a toll. These small-scale rail operations were usually managed by a single person. Other transportation modes developed in a similar manner. Motor freight transportation, for example, began with local shipments. The truck owner was the driver, and all shipments were arranged personally with local businesses. Thus, the owner was both manager and operator.

Because of these beginnings, transportation management developed from an operations orientation. As management evolved from single ownerships to partnerships to corporations, the operations focus remained. With a successful history based on the operating philosophy of providing freight transportation between two points, sophisticated management arrangements did not evolve for some time. The operations approach to management persisted even as the scope of transportation grew. Users sought out carriers who could fill their basic operational needs. The railroad industry, formed into large corporations as early as the mid-1800s, was the first mode to experience growing pains.

Problems were solved as they occurred, and most, if not all, involved providing the transportation service desired between two locations. An in-depth analysis of the broad transportation spectrum was beyond the ability and interest of operations-oriented managers. Thus, problem-solving methods reacted to symptoms, rather than to basic transportation problems. There was no attempt to adjust the service offered to specific shipper requirements. Even with tremendous industrial expansion, the basic orientation of emphasis upon moving commodities between two locations continued to prevail. As railroads grew, management persisted in stressing operations, and those employees who demonstrated operational expertise filled top management positions.

The marketing concept, which stresses a company orientation based on an analysis of consumer needs with development of service offerings to meet identified needs, was not, and sometimes still is not, considered important. During the railroad industry's early development, little need existed for a sales effort, because users sought out the carrier capable of providing the desired service. As competition grew and more than one carrier was capable of providing service between two locations, carriers began to encourage shippers to use their railroads instead of those of their competitors. But rather than providing the most appropriate service, carriers tried to convince shippers to "buy" the service offered. Many contemporary railroad critics cite such an excessive operations orientation as the railroads' basic problem during the 1960s and 1970s.

The trucking industry's growth closely follows that of the railroads. Service expanded from local shipments to regional service to national trucking companies. Trucking management, similar to railroad management, retained an operations orientation. There were exceptions in both railroad and motor freight management, but an operations orientation was characteristic of carriers during their development.

The carrier management discussions in this chapter will focus on the railroad industry because it has the most complex organizational structures. Railroads offer a greater number of services and have developed over a longer period of time than any other mode. When significant differences exist, motor freight carrier management will be examined.

Water carrier management, although not nearly as complex as rail or motor freight, also reflects an operations orientation. In fact, marketing activities have not been emphasized because of the lack of significant competition and the limited amount of special services offered. Pipeline operations are unique in that the extremely limited number of commodities and the almost total absence of competition eliminate the need for extensive management. Air freight transportation organizations will most likely expand as the mode develops from its current infancy stage. Until now, airlines have concentrated on passenger transportation and, at best, a separate division or department handles freight transportation. Thus, an examination of rail and some motor freight management should provide a good overview of the functions and activities involved in transportation organizations.

Carrier Management Functions

Every business firm has a reason for being, which provides the foundation for its organizational structure. The purpose of a business firm is not solely the accumulation of profit, because profit is a reward for providing a satisfactory service or making a desired product. For instance, oil companies exist to provide energy for automobiles and other vehicles. A specific product is involved—gasoline. On the other hand, the product offered by banks is financial service, such as checking, savings, and loan accounts.

Every business firm performs at least three separate functions. First, it must generate a demand for its product or service because few, if any, companies enjoy automatic customer demand. This is known as the *marketing* function. As the competitive level increases, the marketing function becomes more important. Oil companies try to persuade buyers to buy a certain brand of gasoline, and banking institutions emphasize interest rates, savings benefits, and lending services.

Second, firms provide services or products for buyers who do not, or cannot, obtain those services or products for themselves. This is known as the *operational* function. For automobile manufacturers, the operational function involves assembly and distribution of automobiles. A physician performs an operational function by examining patients, diagnosing problems, and performing surgery.

The third functional area involves the support services necessary to complete the firm's offering apart from the commercial or operational functions. This is known as the *administrative* function. For example, an appliance manufacturer needs research, accounting, and customer complaint departments as well as other internal operations that are incidental to the marketing and production of refrigerators, toasters, blenders, and food processors. Advertising agencies perform a promotional service and require support from such areas as billing, research, and general clerical staff.

The business firm also needs planning and direction to achieve its goals, which is the responsibility of high-level management. The marketing, operational, and administrative functions are not necessarily separate divisions within a firm, especially in smaller companies. Administrative responsibilities could be carried out by the same person who performs marketing functions, such as a firm's president making regular sales calls. Nevertheless, the functions must be performed, regardless of who is responsible for them.

Transportation carrier management is no different than any other business firm in this respect. In fact, it exemplifies the separation of the three business functions. A distinct marketing function is assigned to those individuals who are responsible for encouraging shippers to select their carrier to perform transportation requirements. These individuals also ascertain shippers' specific needs and attempt to modify the carrier's service and price to satisfy those needs. Different levels of management perform the marketing function. Operationally, carriers employ many people to perform the actual transportation service, such as truck drivers and train crews, and other personnel maintain facilities such as terminals, yards, and docks. Administrative management must ensure that the desired service is provided and properly documented. It must be attuned to the current and future demands of all shippers in order to continue in business. In day-to-day operations, management must be certain that shipper requests for information are satisfied, proper documents are maintained, rate tariffs and quotations are correct, claims are handled quickly, and all other requirements are handled satisfactorily.

Transportation carrier management extends in many directions. Carriers interact with both shippers and receivers on a wide variety of needs and demands. Efficient communication over wide territories is mandatory. Freight rates are continually negotiated and revised. Equipment must be supplied as required. Regulatory procedures require constant monitoring. Interchanges of equipment involve contact with other transportation carriers. Terminal operations require maintenance of a constant flow of inbound and outbound shipments and schedules. Obviously, carrier management is complex. It requires a structured organization with defined authority and responsibility and capable personnel for the carrier to be efficient and effective. Organizational types may vary, but a systematic management approach is mandatory for a carrier's survival. Before discussing organizational patterns, let us examine some basic issues that must be resolved before organizational structure can be identified.

Organization Issues

Unlike most service activities that are usually performed at a single location, the service that carriers provide involves moving products between two locations that may be separated by thousands of miles. Therefore, some basic decisions must be resolved before specific responsibilities can be assigned to individuals and departments. The issues to be addressed are those that concern a centralized or decentralized management structure, line versus staff personnel, organization types, and accountability.

CENTRALIZATION OR DECENTRALIZATION

Early transportation carriers operated in a limited geographic territory. Usually, management was concentrated in one location, and transportation facilities were limited in number. As territorial coverage expanded, additional facilities, personnel, and offices were added. With many employees situated away from the main office, management had to decide on the level of authority to be delegated to field management.

If management wants to retain decision-making authority at its main location, it adopts a *centralized* form of organization. Centralized authority is more feasible with fewer locations and limited geographic coverage. Decision making is consistent because the same individuals make all the decisions. However, centralization relies on efficient communications and a thorough knowledge of all circumstances in all territories.

As geographic coverage expands and more offices, facilities, and services are added, decision making becomes more complicated. Top management must then decide upon the amount of authority that will be delegated to field management. If decision-making authority is delegated, the firm adopts a *decentralized* form of organization. In such cases, the field managers are held accountable for successful operation and protection of the company's interests at their facilities. Top management must have confidence in the ability of field managers to achieve objectives and must develop adequate training to develop a managerial pool. The main benefit of decentralization is that decisions made locally can take into consideration characteristics peculiar to that geographic area.

The centralization versus decentralization issue is a critical one for transportation carriers because of the scope of operations involved. Each location has specific marketing, operational, and administrative responsibilities, but the adequate level of authority to administer these functions must be resolved. For example, specialized equipment may be necessary to provide transportation service for a shipper in one area. Should the management at the location from which this shipper is served be delegated the right to purchase the equipment and be held responsible for its profitable operation, or should the central office make the decision? Should movement schedules be established at each location, or should a line-haul plan be established at the central office to provide a more coordinated vehicle flow? These are just two of the questions that arise when a carrier attempts to decide on centralization or decentralization.

LINE AND STAFF ORGANIZATIONS

Personnel in small firms are directly involved in all the activities concerned with transportation service. Both managers and employees have specific duties in directing or performing each activity, such as vehicle maintenance, freight bill preparation and auditing, dispatching, dock loading and unloading, and rate quotations. Both can be considered *line personnel* because of their direct involvement in the flow of transportation service. As volume grows and each functional area becomes more specialized, however, there is a tendency to lose perspective of the firm's overall operation. In such situations, many companies have found it necessary to employ personnel to oversee the interactions between functional departments and to look for possible improvements. These individuals have no direct authority over line activities and are known as *staff personnel*. They usually report and make recommendations to a manager at a higher level than line managers. Acceptable recommendations are then passed down to the line managers for implementation.

If staff personnel are employed, the carrier must decide the reporting structure, extent of authority, and the areas the staff personnel will oversee. Without staff personnel, managers may become too involved in their own areas to consider the improvements possible through interdepartmental cooperation. With staff personnel, friction may develop between line and staff employees, which discourages individual initiative. Many large firms employ both line and staff employees successfully if care is taken to choose the proper individuals for those positions.

ORGANIZATION TYPES

The basic managerial structure can be developed using several different approaches. A carrier may desire to organize on the basis of different functions. For example, separate departments may be established for (1) rate analysis and quotation, (2) tracing, expediting, reconsigning, and diverting, (3) marketing, and (4) research. These departments would have separate managers and would apply their specialties to any product line carried by the transportation company. This is known as a *functional organization structure.*

Several carriers prefer to organize their managers by geographic region, with all activities under the direction of one individual, such as a general manager. Regardless of the activities involved, the general manager is ultimately responsible for their performance. All related activities are handled in the office established to service that region. A general manager is given overall responsibility, and supervisors direct specific performance. This is known as a *territorial organization structure.*

Under certain circumstances, a carrier may decide to organize by major product lines handled. For example, several railroads have separate divisions that deal exclusively with coal shipments. All marketing, operational, and administrative management areas related to coal shipments are contained within one department. Similar departments may exist for agricultural products, automobile products, and so forth. This is known as a *product line organization structure.*

The organizational types just described are not mutually exclusive. Carriers often use combinations of all three types. For example, the marketing and administrative areas could follow a product line pattern, and the operational area, a functional pattern. Similarly, the marketing area could be based on the functional pattern, whereas the operational and administrative areas follow the product line organization. This might be the case with unit train shipments of new automobiles or mined coal. Generally, the volume of business, the concentration of movements, and the complexities of the overall operation will dictate the organization type or combination pattern.

ACCOUNTABILITY

Business firms want to be assured that all of their operations contribute to profit. When all activities are in one location under the direction of a single management team, it is not difficult to identify accountability. However, when many locations are involved, it becomes more difficult to measure a specific location's profit contribution. Thus, management must address this issue, commonly known as *accountability*.

Should each location be held accountable for costs relative to the revenue generated? On the surface, the answer appears easy. If a location is not contributing to company profit at some predetermined level, it should be removed from the organizational structure. Unfortunately, the answer is not so simple in transportation carrier management. Several reasons account for the difficulty in arriving at an analysis of each location's contribution to profitability. For example, if centralized authority exists, locations are not in the position to make decisions that affect profitability. In a decentralized structure, an operations manager could decide to adjust the service level offered to a particular user or group of users to increase volume and revenues. But centralized organizational patterns place that decision at headquarters. If the decision is made not to increase the service level, the location's profitability will be affected.

If a location is simply an interchange point where products or vehicles are transferred, little revenue may be generated. Traffic flow is another reason that a location cannot be judged solely on revenue generated versus costs of operation. For example, trucking companies commonly use a decentralized organization pattern. Each terminal is judged on the basis of costs incurred and revenue generated. The terminal may be in a city that has more inbound shipments than outbound. The terminal manager is expected to generate enough outbound shipments to reduce the empty trucks leaving the terminal. However, if traffic to the location is unbalanced, then few outbound shipments may be available. A prime example is Detroit, Michigan. Numerous inbound shipments are required to assemble a single automobile. In such cases, the terminal must be retained or inbound shipments will be lost to a competitor. The terminal contributes to company profitability, but the revenue may be credited to the terminal from which the shipment originated. On a strict cost/revenue basis, the unloading terminal could be judged nonprofitable.

Government regulations have had a considerable impact on the organizational patterns of transportation carriers in the past. In many cases, carriers have been forced to serve less profitable locations in order to receive authority to serve areas that had greater volume and profit potential. The less profitable locations cannot be held accountable on a cost/revenue basis.

For these reasons and many others, the accountability issue must be addressed by top management when it establishes or revises the organizational pattern. A firm policy on location accountability cannot be stated without considering many other issues such as activities, specialties, territories, and other external variables.

Carrier Management Activities

Carrier management activities cover a broad spectrum. A great deal of interaction takes place with groups external to the firm, such as shippers and receivers, labor organizations, governmental regulatory bodies, and other transportation carriers. But the internal activities of the carriers are important because they assure that efficient transportation service will be provided. As discussed previously, the many activities performed can be classified into three broad groups: marketing, operational, and administrative.

MARKETING ACTIVITIES

Marketing activities generate revenue for carriers. Regular contacts are required between shippers and carriers on routine matters, problems, and future needs. To conduct these activities, carriers maintain three major marketing departments: sales, traffic, and pricing.

SALES DEPARTMENT

The sales department, as in all other industries, is responsible for generating revenue. Most carriers respect the importance of sales activities by assigning a vice president of sales to head the department. Large carriers subdivide the sales activity into regions and then districts within regions. The sales force calls upon traffic managers who have the authority to select carriers. The sales activity is extremely important when two or more carriers provide comparable service. Sales personnel encourage a shipper to select their carrier over all other carriers and should have a number of benefits to offer, such as efficient schedules, better special equipment, or improved communications.

Generally, the carrier's sales force and industrial traffic managers develop a quasipersonal relationship. The sales force maintains this good relationship with such extra activities as luncheon and dinner engagements, or participation in transportation organizations and associations. When a good relationship exists, business can sometimes be conducted informally by telephone, rather than requiring a personal visit each time. Nevertheless, personal visits by carrier sales personnel are scheduled frequently to discuss service problems, equipment supply, and future planning. The carrier's sales force is one of the most important and effective inputs to research activities.

The responsibilities of the sales force are greater than those of most other departments. Each salesperson must be familiar with the carrier's entire network and commodities handled. The sales force must be aware of the internal organization and operations, claim matters, and rate issues. Because the sales force is the primary contact between shippers and the carrier and conveys the company image, it is easy to understand the importance given to the marketing function.

TRAFFIC DEPARTMENT

Transportation companies maintain traffic departments that handle customer-related activities. The traffic department concerns itself primarily with the day-to-day activities required to provide customer service. Tracing and expediting services, diversion and reconsignment instructions, rate quotations, and accessorial charges are provided by traffic department personnel. This department also assists shippers in determining appropriate freight classifications and routings.

Traffic departments prepare required shipping documents, such as freight bills. Freight claim settlements are made through this department, and steps are taken to prevent future loss and damage claims. The department's interactions with shippers often involve operational matters. Therefore, just as the sales force is the commercial liaison between the carriers and shippers, the traffic department is the operations liaison.

PRICING DEPARTMENT

The marketing function is intended to increase the volume handled by a carrier. This can sometimes be accomplished through freight rate changes that encourage users to switch transportation modes or to increase their shipment volume. Thus, carriers maintain pricing departments to negotiate rate reductions on certain commodities. These departments investigate user requests for reduced rates.

Usually, the department is staffed with pricing specialists who are aware of the rate-making process and understand the reasoning behind all freight rates. These specialists often accompany sales personnel on calls to discuss rate matters. They objectively evaluate rate reduction requests and point out the ramifications of each request. In effect, they act as salespeople who must tactfully convince users why certain rate reduction requests cannot be accepted.

The pricing department is also responsible for evaluating freight rate increases. The personnel of this department must therefore be familiar with the economics of transportation in order to determine when a rate modification is justified. Here again, the pricing department interacts with shippers to explain the increase. Because of the potential impact of rate reductions based on volume increases handled by a carrier, the importance of the pricing department should not be underestimated.

OPERATIONAL ACTIVITIES

The product of transportation carriers is service. The marketing activities generate the volume to be handled, and the administration provides support. But the operational activities are responsible for the actual movement of commodities. The operations function includes four major departments: transportation, maintenance of way and structures, maintenance of equipment, and terminals.

TRANSPORTATION DEPARTMENT

The transportation department is responsible for moving commodities from one location to another. Whether they be railcars, trucks, barges, or airplanes, vehicles are used for movements. The transportation department develops and maintains operational schedules. Crews or drivers are dispatched and may have to be changed enroute, depending on the length and time of the journey. The location of each shipment must be known at all times so that the department can advise shippers and receivers regularly of the shipment's whereabouts. Vehicles must be stopped enroute, either to unload or to pick up additional shipments. In rail transportation, this would involve dropping off loaded cars at interchange or destination points and picking up other loaded cars to continue the journey. With trucks shipments, full or partial loads are dropped off at terminals and others are picked up. All of these activities are the responsibility of the transportation department. Performing them efficiently and effectively is necessary for carrier survival and profitability.

MAINTENANCE OF WAY AND STRUCTURES DEPARTMENT

Primarily among rail carriers, a maintenance of way department is established to provide safe and adequate ways for the vehicles. The way for railroads includes the tracks, ties, and ballast over which the trains operate. Railroad bridges and tunnels are also the responsibility of this department.

Governmental regulations establish the minimum requirements for safe transportation. The department oversees the rail carrier's adherence to those specifications and replaces tracks, ties, spikes, and ballast as required. Bridges and tunnels must be checked regularly to meet governmental standards.

For other modes, maintenance of ways is not a critical area. Motor freight carriers use public roads and highways, water carriers use public waterways, and air carriers have no structural ways to maintain. Pipelines are involved in way maintenance only to the extent of monitoring for blockages or leaks. Thus, rail carriers have the most extensive maintenance requirements of all modes.

MAINTENANCE OF EQUIPMENT DEPARTMENT

Pipeline equipment is stationary and products flow through it. All other modes have moving vehicles that must be in good operating condition. Transportation equipment is in continuous movement and requires routine maintenance to keep it serviceable. Rail, motor, water, and air freight carriers regularly maintain both line-haul and terminal equipment. The maintenance of equipment department assumes the responsibility of maintaining operational capability.

TERMINAL OPERATIONS DEPARTMENT

Other than local motor freight, carrier shipments originate at one terminal and terminate at another. Motor freight terminals are the nucleus of the carrier's operation. In addition to local pickup and delivery service, line-haul shipments are consolidated for movements to other terminals. A sales force and office staff are also situated at terminals. Weighing, equipment inspection, claim investigations, and document preparation are performed at rail terminals. Although an office is maintained at the terminal to handle these matters, both sales and overall administrative activities usually are performed at other locations.

ADMINISTRATIVE ACTIVITIES

The final major function of carrier management concerns the administrative activities that guide and support the marketing and operational functions. Administrative activities are usually centralized at the carrier's headquarters. Administrative activities can be subdivided broadly into three classifications: financial, labor, and general.

FINANCIAL ACTIVITIES

Many carrier departments or divisions are involved with financial matters. The accounting department pays all costs incurred by the carrier, such as materials and supplies, payroll, and rent. Incoming revenues from freight bills issued by the carrier are also processed in the central financial department.

A separate department deals exclusively with taxes. Taxes are assessed by federal, state, and local governments on properties owned, inventories carried, and payrolls. Large carriers own properties in many communities and states, and a great deal of record keeping is required to determine tax liabilities and to approve assessments.

Insurance departments are responsible for property, liability, and cargo insurance, as well as employee insurance plans, such as hospital, disability, retirement, and unemployment. Large carriers that own vast properties, haul large quantities, and employ many personnel maintain a separate insurance department.

The finance department supervises capital needs for equipment, property, and payroll and oversees the carrier's stock on the financial exchanges. The department borrows or lends money on a short-term basis and ensures the carrier's overall financial condition. Without a competent finance department, a carrier could find itself without the necessary cash flow to remain solvent.

LABOR ACTIVITIES

The labor activities concern two major areas: human resource development and labor relations.

HUMAN RESOURCE DEVELOPMENT. Transportation requires personnel with a wide range of expertise and education. The human resource development department screens, hires, and trains carrier personnel. Personnel needs range from dock or terminal laborers to high-level administrative personnel, marketing representatives, and operations managers. The department is responsible for filling management-level positions at various locations and regularly evaluates current employees for promotion. The success of any business firm depends on the calibre of its personnel. Therefore, the human resource development department plays an important role in successful carrier operations.

LABOR RELATIONS. A difficult issue in carrier management is labor relations. Most transportation operations activities involve intensive labor at the front-line staff level. Each transportation mode has a department responsible for dealing regularly with labor unions. Routine grievances are forwarded through union representatives to the labor union and then to the labor relations department. Wage negotiations with unions are often extensive and time-consuming. Work stoppages or strikes, which could shut down operations completely, can seriously affect a carrier's profitability. Labor relations is a delicate area of carrier management that deserves serious and constant attention.

GENERAL ACTIVITIES

General administration activities are those that do not fall under the financial or labor responsibilities. Each carrier has its own organizational pattern, and some of the activities described here could conceivably be placed within one of the departments already discussed. This broad grouping of activities includes legal, purchasing, claim prevention, public relations and advertising, and real estate.

LEGAL. Transportation activities require expert legal counsel. Carriers need legal representation on loss and damage claims and rate or service discrimination charges. Because carrier vehicles travel through many communities and are exposed to pedestrian and motor traffic, accidents can occur. In addition, employees may charge violations of employment practices. Legal counsel represents the carrier in all law suits. Some attorneys specialize in transportation and establish a private practice to serve many small carriers. Others are employed directly by large carriers in their own legal departments.

PURCHASING. Carrier purchases range from large locomotives and truck trailers to pencils and paper clips. Materials are purchased to maintain ways, service equipment, and furnish offices. Thousands of railcars, truck trailers, and tractors are purchased each year. Terminal, dock, and handling equipment, such as forklifts, must be purchased. A separate department supervises these many activities. Specialists in the department are familiar with different supplier offerings and can plan large purchases to obtain volume discounts. They are also aware of current market prices and supervise the sale of used carrier equipment.

CLAIM PREVENTION. Loss and damage claims occur regularly. Larger carriers receive a greater number of claims and plan preventive programs to eliminate the causes of these claims. The programs are conducted by a freight claim prevention department. Reports on all claims are filtered through this department and an investigation is conducted. If the cause can be determined, steps are taken to prevent future occurrences. If an immediate cause cannot be detected, a record is made of the claim and future claims are monitored. If a pattern can be determined, probable causes are assumed and preventive measures taken to reduce similar claims in the future. Although this might appear to be an expensive undertaking, the money saved on loss and damage claims can usually offset the expenditure for a freight claim prevention department.

PUBLIC RELATIONS AND ADVERTISING. Carriers are visible to the public, and negative attitudes sometimes develop. People may believe that too many trucks are on the roads or that traffic is stopped too long at rail crossings. Carrier public relations efforts are needed to improve the public's attitude toward the carriers. The carriers also advertise their services, especially in trade journals read by industrial traffic managers and purchasing agents. These promotional activities are performed by the public relations and advertising department. Public relations activities include carrier representation in fund-raising drives for foundations or charities, participation in community civic affairs, and favorable news articles on carrier activities. Advertising includes paid advertisements in trade journals, as well as distribution of promotional items such as imprinted scratch pads, pens, playing cards, and calendars.

More and more carriers are beginning to adopt a marketing philosophy by revamping their organization patterns and establishing a marketing department to coordinate sales, traffic, and pricing activities. However, public relations and advertising continues to be placed under the direction of various other carrier management officials. Although the advertising function commonly is associated with a marketing department in many firms, public relations administration generally is kept apart by most companies in the organizational scheme and cooperates with marketing departments or any other aspect of operations when required or advisable.

REAL ESTATE. Carriers are involved in three types of real estate: income-producing, industrial development, and operational properties. Income-producing real estate is a financial investment. The New York Central Railroad, no longer in existence, once had extensive real estate holdings, such as office buildings in New York City, from which large rental revenues were collected.

Industrial development is a prime concern of real estate departments. Carriers often purchase property along their rights-of-way and, as new industrial firms are established or existing firms expand, the real estate department encourages those organizations to purchase or lease the carrier's property. This procedure assures the transportation company of receiving the traffic volume that will move into or out of the new facilities. Many times, the property will be sold or leased below its market value because additional revenue will be gained by the carrier from freight charges. An efficient real estate department can assure the carrier a larger number of users, which results in greater operating revenues.

The final type of real estate is the purchase and development of operational property for terminals. In essence, this form of development concerns the location of terminals and their economic feasibility.

The foregoing summarizes the major marketing, operational, and administrative activities of a carrier on a departmental level. Not all modes or carriers perform these activities exactly as described, nor do they assign titles identical to those used here. The activities and titles described are those most commonly identified among carriers. The next section examines common organizational patterns found among transportation carriers.

Transportation Carrier Organization Patterns

Transportation is no different than any other industry in the diversity of its organizational patterns. The arrangement of activities and reporting authority depends on top management preferences. It is difficult to generalize about carrier management organization patterns because no definite rules apply. Therefore, this discussion is based on patterns that seem to occur most often among transportation carriers. Again, emphasis is placed on the rail and motor freight modes because they have the most elaborate organization structures.

EXECUTIVE DEPARTMENTS

Generally, small carriers have little difficulty in establishing an organization pattern. Major functional areas are well defined, and one individual is assigned total responsibility for each one. The arrangement shown in Figure 16–1 is typical of a small carrier's organization chart. Functional directors may have several employees reporting to them, depending on the volume of business and the range of activities performed. In contrast, large carriers need a much more elaborate organizational arrangement because of greater traffic volume. Vice presidents direct functional areas, which are subdivided even further. The top-level official of each area is a member of what is commonly known as an executive department. The executive department holds regular meetings to discuss problems and plans. Because each activity area is represented, these discussions can assess the impact any decision will have on all other activities. Figure 16–2 is based on a review of some major rail carrier executive departments and illustrates a comprehensive executive department.

Major carrier activities are represented in the executive department, and other officials report directly to those representatives. The reporting authority in Figure 16–2 would resemble the arrangement shown in Figure 16–3, with the

FIGURE 16–1. SMALL CARRIER ORGANIZATION PATTERN

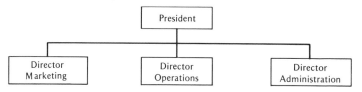

FIGURE 16–2. COMPREHENSIVE RAIL CARRIER EXECUTIVE DEPARTMENT

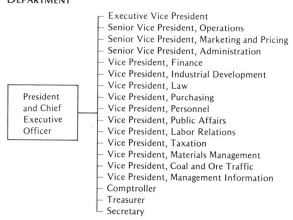

other vice presidents slots filled according to the preferences of the chief executive officer and perhaps the senior vice presidents.

The major functional areas can be further subdivided by vice presidents, as shown in Figure 16–3, or with directors assigned to each activity area within a functional division. The method of subdivision can take any pattern.

FIGURE 16–3. POSSIBLE REPORTING LINE OF EXECUTIVE DEPARTMENT

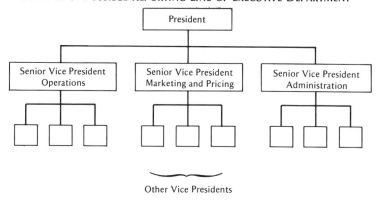

Other Vice Presidents

SUBDIVISION ORGANIZATION PATTERNS

As discussed previously, organizational patterns can tend toward any configuration, such as functional, territorial, or product line types. This discussion will use combinations to illustrate possible alternative arrangements.

MARKETING ORGANIZATION PATTERNS

The marketing function, which can include any number of activities, usually places the sales, traffic, and pricing departments under the authority of a senior official. Generally, the sales and traffic departments are decentralized and the pricing department is centralized. A typical pattern is shown in Figure 16–4. The regional arrangements shown in Figure 16–4 can be further subdivided into districts, depending on the number of carrier offices and traffic volume in each region. A possible arrangement for the western regional sales function is shown in Figure 16–5.

The same kind of subdivision is possible in the traffic department. The extent of commercial subdivision usually depends on the region involved. The carrier is likely to have a greater degree of subdivision in a region if it actually serves that region rather than merely maintains a sales office there. For example, the Norfolk and Western Railway Company maintains a sales office in Dallas, Texas, even though it does not serve any of the southwestern states,

FIGURE 16–4. COMBINATION MARKETING ORGANIZATION PATTERN

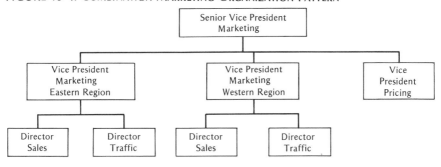

FIGURE 16–5. REGIONAL SALES ACTIVITY SUBDIVISION ORGANIZATION

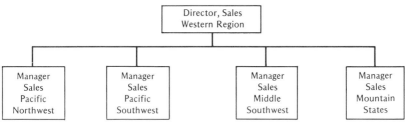

including Texas. However, the sales office calls upon industrial traffic managers in that region because N&W can participate in interchanges on shipments that originate in the Southwest and terminate in the Northeast. The sales office thus encourages users to include the N&W in routing instructions for the transportation service.

On the other hand, the carriers that actually service the southwestern region will likely have sales offices in every major southwestern city. In the trade, the carriers designate the offices located in areas the carrier does not serve as *off-line*, and those where transportation is provided as *on-line*. Off-line offices usually cover a wider territory than on-line offices. Thus, regional subdivisions will be more extensive where a greater number of on-line offices exist. The pattern of traffic department subdivision is similar to the sales department format.

OPERATIONS ORGANIZATION PATTERNS
Operations activities exist only in those areas served by the carrier. Generally, the organization pattern is more extensive than the marketing arrangement because centralization is much more difficult. Operations management must be closer to the areas served, and, in particular, terminal operation management is required at all locations. Transportation operations can be centralized to a degree. Maintenance can be centralized by scheduling major maintenance overhauls at only a few locations, whereas regular minor maintenance is performed at all locations. Maintenance of ways is better suited to centralization.

For a large carrier, the operations organization pattern for high-level officials might resemble that shown in Figure 16–6. The degree of further subdivision, again, depends on the extent of activities performed.

Of all operations activities, terminals are the most likely to have the highest degree of decentralization. This is particularly true with motor freight transportation in which the terminals are the nucleus of activity and the terminal manager has more responsibility and authority. Generally, motor carriers maintain one facility in a city, but rail carriers may have several facilities. The rail carriers then must add another management layer to coordinate local operations.

Figure 16–7 isolates the terminal operations area. Other operations activities can be either sectionalized along the same pattern or somewhat centralized at

FIGURE 16–6. HIGHER LEVEL OPERATIONS ORGANIZATION PATTERN

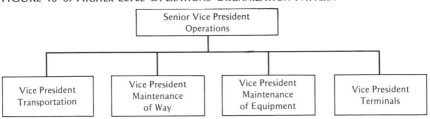

FIGURE 16–7. Regional Terminal Activity Subdivision Organization Pattern

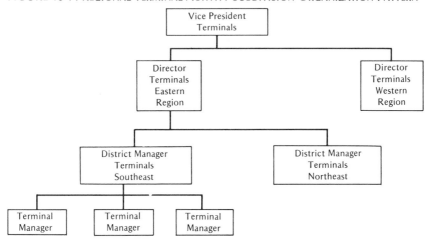

the district or regional level. In Figure 16–7, the two regions are subdivided into districts, and the districts are subdivided to include all terminals maintained by the carrier.

As stated earlier, motor freight terminal managers are often given more authority and responsibility than their rail counterparts. It would not be unusual for a motor freight terminal manager to be responsible for the firm's marketing, operations, and administration functions. Then, the organization pattern might resemble that shown in Figure 16–8, although the extent of authority and responsibility would be less than that possessed by corporate officials.

Administrative Organization Patterns

The variety of administrative activities makes it difficult to present a common organization pattern. However, administrative activities are most likely to be centralized. Most often, the highest-ranking administrative executive maintains

FIGURE 16–8. Motor Freight Terminal Organization Pattern

FIGURE 16–9. COMPANY ADMINISTRATIVE ORGANIZATION PATTERN

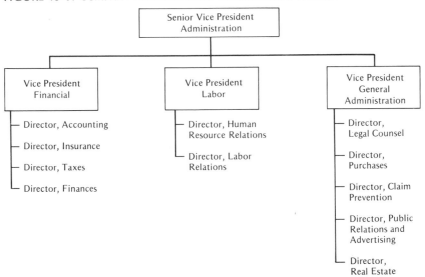

an office in the company headquarters, and fewer personnel are required to complete each activity. Based on the earlier discussion of administrative activities, a possible organization pattern is illustrated in Figure 16–9. The extent of subdivision within each activity area depends on carrier volume. Each activity area can be subdivided at the company headquarters or delegated to regions, districts, or local facilities.

This discussion on organization patterns has taken a general approach to the functional and activity areas of carrier management. However, circumstances change, and new organization patterns develop. Improved communications and more sophisticated carrier management will lead to new organization and management techniques that encourage greater efficiency and effectiveness. In the near future, a more unified and integrated approach to freight transportation management may develop.

Summary

Industrial traffic management's responsibilities involve a great deal of interaction with freight transportation carriers. A knowledge of transportation carrier management, therefore, is important not only for anyone dealing with carriers, but also for anyone considering a career in transportation.

Carrier firms developed from privately owned operations to partnerships to large corporations. Historically, an operations focus rather than a marketing orientation has characterized carrier management. Business firms, including carriers, perform three separate functions—marketing, operational, and administrative—which are not necessarily separate departments within a firm. Nevertheless, these functions must be performed regardless of who is responsible for them.

Some issues must be addressed before a carrier can determine an appropriate organization structure. These issues include centralization versus decentralization, line and staff organization, organization types, and accountability.

The internal activities performed by the carriers are classified according to marketing, operational, and administrative functions. The marketing activities are performed in the sales, traffic, and pricing departments. Operational activities are concentrated in the transportation, maintenance of way and structures, maintenance of equipment, and terminal operations departments. Administrative activities include financial, human and labor relations, and general activities, which include legal, purchasing, claim prevention, public relations and advertising, and real estate activities.

Organizational patterns among transportation carriers are diverse, and specific arrangements usually depend on the preferences of top management. Common organizational patterns are often based on the marketing, operational, and administrative activity areas, with various degrees of centralization or decentralization.

Industrial traffic management and carrier management offer attractive career opportunities. Both groups interact regularly and provide efficient and effective transportation service for the country. The final part of the text will examine career opportunities and future patterns of transportation in the United States.

Questions for Chapter 16

1. For what reasons do you expect carriers have developed an operations orientation as opposed to a marketing orientation?
2. Differentiate among the marketing, operational, and administrative functions performed by carrier management.
3. What is the major difference between line and staff personnel in carrier management?
4. What are the differences between functional and product line types of carrier management?
5. Discuss the issue of accountability in carrier management.
6. Describe the marketing activities performed in carrier management.
7. List the activities that may be classified within a carrier's administrative function.
8. Diagram an executive department organizational pattern for a large rail carrier.
9. In what way can the marketing function be further subdivided on a carrier organization chart?

10. What is the difference between a carrier's on-line and off-line office?
11. What motor carrier operational area is most likely to have the highest degree of decentralization?
12. Diagram the organizational pattern most likely to be found in motor freight terminal operations.

five

Transportation in a Contemporary Setting

Transportation's depth, breadth, and significance have been reviewed, and its many activities have been explored. The expertise of many individuals is required to keep transportation functioning and to plan its future development.

The wide variety of transportation careers is discussed in Chapter 17, which examines carrier, government, and industry positions. Individuals involved in transportation careers interact with each other, not only during their daily routines, but also through transportation-related organizations and associations, which also are reviewed in Chapter 17.

The development of transportation in the future will be guided by both internal efforts and external influences. Chapter 18 examines current attitudes and events that appear to be molding the future and offers some predictions regarding the nature of tomorrow's transportation system. The concluding comment calls for perpetuation of an efficient and effective transportation system that will continue to add to the growth and development of the economy and a higher standard of living for society.

17

Transportation Careers and Organizations

TRANSPORTATION CAREERS
  Carrier Employment Data
  Transportation Occupations
    Marketing Careers
    Operations Careers
    Administrative Careers
    Government Occupations
    Industrial Traffic Management Occupations

TRANSPORTATION ORGANIZATIONS
  Education-Oriented Organizations
  Modal-Oriented Organizations
  Industrial-Oriented Organizations
  General Organizations

SUMMARY

Career planning is not an easy task. It is perhaps the most important decision facing young adults. One's career choice is not, and should not be, based solely on the financial rewards possible. The decision should also consider an individual's interests and aptitude, the working environment, kinds of people involved, and the extent of education necessary to enter a particular field. Ideally, a career choice is made only after one has thoroughly investigated many possible career options.

This text has described the many facets of the United States transportation network. As you think back over this coverage, you can appreciate the variety of careers possible in the transportation industry. This chapter will examine some of those careers. The second part of the chapter reviews some transportation associations and organizations that offer opportunities for professional involvement if you choose a career in transportation.

Transportation Careers

It is difficult to imagine a vocation that could not be pursued within the field of transportation. Much like the federal government, the transportation industry offers a wide diversity of occupations. Professionals—attorneys, physicians, and accountants—are well represented. Career types range from company presidents to mail room clerks. A wide variety of specialists, such as computer technicians, engineers, and communication experts, pursue their careers within the transportation industry. It is almost impossible to determine the exact number of persons employed or the total compensation earned in the industry because of a lack of data. A brief explanation of this statement is necessary, particularly for anyone who might be involved in future transportation research.

Available government data are too broad to determine actual employment in freight transportation. Generally, government data report on all aspects of transportation, including automobile manufacturing and passenger transportation, subjects not included in this text. Including that information in a discussion of freight transportation career opportunities would be misleading.

Other available data are too restrictive. Figures are often compiled from reports submitted to the government, as required by the regulatory agencies. The railroad and pipeline industries are completely regulated, so information on those modes more likely is accurate. But any data reported on truck, water, and air, which are not completely regulated, describe employment only in operations under regulatory control. Data reported by various associations representing unregulated carriers may be exaggerated and are often only estimated. Thus, when you read that one out of every eight workers in the United States is employed in transportation, remember that those figures are based on all aspects of transportation and transportation-related industries, not only those covered in this text.

By no means is this intended to minimize the importance or size of the freight transportation work force. Millions of people are employed in the daily transportation activities discussed in this text. This should not be surprising because more than 400 railroads and tens of thousands of truck companies exist in the United States. The following review of some modal employment information is revealing.

CARRIER EMPLOYMENT DATA

Railroad employment data provide a good base to illustrate the number of people working in freight transportation. All railroads are regulated and are required to provide total operating information. Table 17–1 lists railroad em-

TABLE 17–1. Class I Railroad Company Employment and Average Earnings: Select Years

Year	Number of Employees	Compensation (Thousands)	Average Yearly Earnings Per Employee
1929	1,660,850	$2,896,566	$ 1,743
1939	987,943	1,863,503	1,886
1949	1,191,444	4,419,433	3,709
1959	815,474	4,986,253	6,115
1969	578,277	5,362,754	9,274
1970	566,282	5,711,280	10,086
1971	544,333	5,999,968	11,023
1972	526,061	6,424,920	12,213
1973	520,153	7,088,383	13,627
1974	525,177	7,475,834	14,235
1975	487,789	7,474,750	15,324
1976	482,882	8,278,413	17,144

Source: *Yearbook of Railroad Facts* (Washington, D.C.: Association of American Railroads, 1977), p. 57; and *Yearbook of Railroad Information* (Jersey City, N.J.: Eastern Railroad Presidents Conference, 1962), p. 83.

ployment data for selected years from 1929 to 1976. As you can see, almost one half million people with a total payroll in excess of $8 billion were "working on the railroad" in 1976. In reviewing Table 17–1, it is obvious that railroad employment has been declining for the past three decades. There are primarily two reasons: (1) advanced technology has reduced the demand for human labor, and (2) society's traveling habits have changed, with more emphasis placed on auto and air travel than on railroad passenger travel. The information recorded in Table 17–1 applies only to Class I railroads, which employ approximately 94 per cent of all railroad personnel. The *Defense Transportation Journal* breaks down 1976 railroad data into the general occupation groups and employment information shown in Table 17–2.

The other major mode employing a large number of people is the motor freight industry. The average number of employees and the total compensation paid in 1974, 1975, and 1976 are shown in Table 17–3. Again, the figures pertain only to Class I motor carriers. Because only about one third of all motor freight transportation is regulated, the data shown here should at least be doubled to approximate reality.

According to other sources, it might be safe to assume that the regulated carriers in pipeline, domestic and offshore water, and air freight would add another 50,000 employees to the information shown in Tables 17–1 and 17–3. Again, the information shown here does not include employees of nonregulated carriers or companies providing private transportation services.

TABLE 17–2. Class I Railroad Employment Data, by Groups, 1976

Employee Group	Average Number of Employees	Total Payroll (Thousands)	Average Annual Earnings
Executives, officials, and staff	16,105	$ 416,838	$25,883
Professionals, clerical, and general	99,312	1,519,490	15,300
Maintenance of way and structures	86,901	1,274,366	14,665
Maintenance of equipment and stores	102,996	1,600,895	15,543
Transportation, other than train, engine, and yard	25,591	415,612	16,241
Yardmasters, switch tenders, and hostlers	8,539	158,380	18,548
Train and engine service	143,438	2,892,832	20,168
Totals	482,882	$8,278,413	$17,144 (Avg)

Source: H. Stephen Dewhurst, "Career Opportunities in the Railroad Industry," *Defense Transportation Journal* (October 1977), p. 72.

TABLE 17–3. Class I Motor Freight Carriers Employment and Compensation Data

	1974	1975	1976*
Number of carriers reporting	755	770	852
Average number of employees	499,457	409,174	444,955
Compensation (thousands)	$6,622,213	$6,991,015	$7,564,246

* Estimates
Source: Compiled from *91st Annual Report of the Interstate Commerce Commission* (Washington, D.C.: U.S. Government Printing Office, 1977), p. 144.

TRANSPORTATION OCCUPATIONS

The discussion so far has reviewed overall employment in transportation with no specifics on the types of occupations available. The chapters on industrial traffic management and carrier management have given you a good perspective on various careers and levels of occupations. This section will examine further the many career options possible in any of the transportation modes. Each mode needs different occupational groups with varying levels of expertise; therefore, the discussion centers on specific occupational categories, rather than specific modal requirements. In addition, various organizations and associations that represent the modes need employees to fill positions on their staffs. Usually, these association positions require a full knowledge of the mode and related work experience.

Transportation careers can take almost any direction and can be obtained at any level. All transportation companies have a hierarchy, starting with highest-level executives. Careers are available in top management for the fields discussed in Chapters 15 and 16. For example, larger carriers assign senior vice presidents or vice presidents to individual functional areas, such as operations, marketing, finance, legal, personnel, and administration. Each of these officers has assistants. The term *assistant* is used in two ways. For example, an assistant vice president of marketing is the second-ranking position in the marketing area. However, an assistant to the vice president of marketing is an administrative position in which the individual usually is responsible for liaison and other administrative details assigned by the vice president. Several directors or managers, responsible for particular regions or product lines, usually report to vice presidents. Directors or managers, in turn, have assistants and supervisors assigned to specific activities. First-line supervisors are responsible for the performance of the personnel carrying out the functional area's assignments. In describing the types of transportation careers, the marketing, operations, and administrative subdivisions are once again useful.

MARKETING CAREERS

Marketing activities are geared toward generating revenue for the carriers. The marketing function from the pricing, marketing, and sales standpoints has been described. Each of these areas offer career possibilities. Regional sales managers are usually responsible for a number of sales managers in different sales offices of a region. District sales managers coordinate all sales activities in a territory. The company's sales policies and procedures are passed down from the top sales executive, usually a vice president, through the regions and to the district offices. District sales managers implement the policies and procedures through sales representatives who are responsible for reporting all sales data. Sales representatives call upon shippers and receivers and provide them with any desired information, inform them of the various transportation services available, and attempt to persuade the users to utilize the carrier's facilities. Usually, carrier sales representatives develop informal relationships with traffic managers through regular visits, luncheons, and association meetings.

A variety of marketing careers exist in transportation. Industrial traffic departments interact with their firms' marketing departments regularly but perform few actual marketing activities. In contrast, carrier marketing departments interact with shipper traffic departments regularly. In the marketing area, carrier personnel determine shipper needs and implement efforts to fill those needs. These efforts involve determining the number of vehicles that will be required over a future period, or specialized equipment requirements. Marketing personnel evaluate carrier services and schedules and plan operational changes. They also become involved with the shippers' requests for freight rate changes that might encourage additional traffic flow. In essence, marketing personnel become involved in a shipper's entire operations and may suggest changes in product volumes and scheduling, as well as uncover possibilities for additional sources or selling markets. In their regular routine, carrier marketing personnel interact with their own firm's sales, pricing, operations, or engineering departments, depending on the nature of the assignment.

Careers in pricing departments require an understanding of cost and revenue relationships, as well as of all components that make up the freight rates and accessorial fees charged by the carrier. As discussed in Chapter 13, each freight rate affects, and is affected by, other freight rates. Pricing personnel must be familiar with and able to understand these relationships. Pricing personnel also deal with people outside the firm. They discuss current or proposed freight charges with shippers, examine rate matters with their counterparts on other carrier staffs, and participate in rate bureau activities.

The marketing careers described are not totally separate. In smaller transportation firms, one individual might handle all marketing activities with the assistance of one or more specialists. In fact, all marketing personnel should be familiar with issues in other areas. For instance, sales representatives should know the marketing and pricing considerations involved between their firm and shippers. Performance effectiveness depends on this awareness. A sales representative should not expect to be treated warmly if the pricing specialists and the industrial traffic manager have had serious disagreements on freight rate matters. Thus, marketing transportation careers require individuals who have an understanding of each functional area, the personality to deal with many outsiders, and an ability to interact efficiently with other people within the firm.

OPERATIONS CAREERS

To most people, transportation operations center on the truck driver, the airline pilot, and the train conductor. Needless to say, transportation operations careers extend far beyond these visible positions. Operations careers offer the satisfaction of performing the efficient and needed service that makes a carrier successful. As with each major functional area, transportation operations careers exist at all management levels. Many carrier presidents began in operations. The operations area is usually headed by a senior vice president or a vice president, with assistants, regional managers, district managers, terminal managers, and supervisors. To many, operations careers are not considered as prestigious as commercial or administrative positions but, without operations, carriers would have a shoddy product to offer to shippers.

Beyond the higher-echelon operations executives, a wide variety of occupations are available, requiring varying degrees of specialization and expertise. Maintenance sections need civil, mechanical, and electrical engineers for each mode. Specialists in building crafts are needed for carrier facilities; mechanics service transportation vehicles; and shop supervisors, parts clerks, and machinists are needed in maintenance. Railroad carriers employ people to work on rights-of-way, such as track workers to keep the roadbeds in serviceable condition. In railroad and water operations, crews are necessary for each train or ship. Train dispatchers direct the movement of inbound or outbound trains and signallers assure safe access to the rights-of-way.

Terminal operations are extensive, regardless of the mode. Freight handlers and dock workers keep commodities flowing, vehicle dispatchers direct the flow of equipment over the highways, weighmasters weigh or reweigh shipments, and tower workers oversee yard operations. Each facility has a terminal manager, yardmaster, and/or superintendent, as well as computer specialists responsible for data processing for the firm's communication system.

Administrative Careers

Both the marketing and operations functions need the support of many other individuals. The organizational arrangement of the administrative function in carrier management was discussed in Chapter 16. Administration has the widest variety of careers of any of the three major functional areas. Each component in the administrative function needs a ranking executive. These executives may be senior vice presidents, vice presidents, directors, or managers. Each will have staffs, the size of which will depend on the amount and complexity of daily activities. Transportation real estate careers are pursued in industrial development departments, and financial careers are pursued in the comptroller's office, finance section, and accounting department.

The traffic department branch is a good entry point for careers in carrier management. Line workers are involved in expediting, tracing, and diversion activities. Larger carriers assign individuals to handle each of these activities separately, whereas smaller carriers assign combined responsibilities to fewer individuals. The traffic department section responsible for these accessorial services is commonly known as the customer service section.

Rate specialists are valuable to transportation companies. The complex nature of freight rates requires a special kind of person to leaf through volumes of tariffs to locate applicable classifications and freight rates. Several years of experience are necessary before an individual is considered proficient as a rate analyst. Computer specialists are now becoming involved in rate matters, and freight rate data are being computerized at a rapid rate.

Claims sections offer a number of career opportunities. Some individuals investigate and process claims made against the carriers. Others are involved in claim prevention methodologies, including better packaging and transportation vehicle redesigns. Often, legal services are necessary for claim settlements. The carrier's legal staff works on claims, regulatory matters, and any other issues requiring legal expertise.

Personnel managers recruit the necessary personnel for most of a carrier's total operations and administer the firm's total benefit package. Labor relations experts handle the company's labor matters, particularly with the many unions representing transportation employees. They become involved in contract negotiations and renegotiations, economic benefit packages, and all grievance matters filed by unionized personnel.

Purchasing agents and buyers in transportation companies fill daily needs for materials and supplies up to and including transportation vehicles such as trucks, tractors, trailers, freight locomotives, and terminal material handling equipment. Carriers also offer career opportunities for public relations and promotion personnel who work with company executives, the media, and transportation organizations and associations to maintain a favorable corporate image and to upgrade society's image of the industry.

As you can see, a wide variety of transportation careers are possible. The diversity of any particular carrier's career opportunities depends on the firm's size and number of activities performed, but almost any conceivable vocation can be pursued in transportation. Career opportunities also exist in government regulatory institutions.

GOVERNMENT OCCUPATIONS

Chapter 12 described the three major federal government regulatory bodies. Various bureaus and offices were detailed. From that description, it is evident that a great number of career opportunities exist within the federal government for both transportation specialists and generalists. In addition, a tremendous number of clerical positions are available to process the volumes of documents and data reported to and maintained by these regulatory bodies. Often, these clerical positions are starting points for careers in transportation regulation administration.

The regulatory institutions' employment data reported in Chapter 12 indicate more than 3,200 employees. In addition, the Department of Transportation reportedly employs more than 65,000 individuals (excluding the United States Coast Guard), with various transportation interests and educational backgrounds. Governmental transportation careers also extend to state governments, each of which has intrastate transportation regulation responsibilities. Estimates on total transportation regulation employment in state commissions are misleading, because those careers often involve regulatory responsibilities over other industries or utilities. It is safe to say, however, that tens of thousands of transportation careers exist in governmental regulation activities and represent a wide variety of interests and disciplines. Also to be considered are careers available within industrial firms.

INDUSTRIAL TRAFFIC MANAGEMENT
OCCUPATIONS

Chapter 15 described industrial traffic management activities. Each of these activities offers career possibilities. Many are similar to those within a carrier's organization, but others are distinctly different. For instance, the top industrial traffic management executive coordinates all traffic-related matters—interdepartmental, intradepartmental, and extraorganizational. Positions are available for traffic managers or supervisors at all company facilities, with the degree of responsibility determined by upper management. Larger corporations generally have more extensive traffic departments with many specialists handling research, rate negotiations, private transport operations, and carrier relations.

Beyond careers in transportation, many firms have adopted integrated logistics organizations that offer employment opportunities. It is common practice to provide cross-assignments for middle managers to broaden their scope of understanding of all facets of physical distribution and materials management operations. Thus, many people who enter the job market in transportation end up in other related management positions.

Although industrial traffic management personnel interact with carrier personnel regularly, a large network of associations and organizations exists to facilitate the interaction of these executives on a professional and social basis. The next section of this chapter discusses some of these organizations which, incidentally, offer additional career opportunities.

Transportation Organizations

Almost every industry in the United States is represented by some type of organization. Most companies affiliate with industry organizations, and membership has many benefits. For instance, organization meetings provide information on new technologies, exchanges of educational materials, and knowledgeable guest speakers. These meetings give representatives the opportunity to interact with their counterparts in other firms of the same industry.

Other organizations represent functional areas and not particular industries. The National Council of Physical Distribution Management (NCPDM) and the Society of Logistical Engineers (SOLE) consist of logistics and distribution executives, regardless of the industry or firm by which they are employed. The American Marketing Association (AMA) is another example. Its members are involved in marketing activities such as sales, research, and advertising.

These organizations, whether industry- or function-oriented, usually have annual meetings where all members have an opportunity to meet other members, exchange ideas, attend programs, hold elections, and enjoy social activities. Many organizations also hold monthly or quarterly meetings on a local or regional basis.

The transportation industry has hundreds of such organizations. The fact that such a large number exists should be no surprise, in view of the many occupations in transportation. Some organizations are function-oriented, and others are oriented to the transportation industry in general. Still others organize for specific modes. Although it is not possible to describe every transporta-

349

tion-related organization, the following illustrates the kinds of organizations that exist.

EDUCATION-ORIENTED ORGANIZATIONS

Every organization, no matter the industry, offers educational benefits to its membership. Therefore, it is somewhat misleading to classify transportation organizations as education-oriented. Yet, the industry does have organizations dedicated solely to the education of transportation personnel, regardless of the type of firm in which they are employed, specialization, or executive level. One of these is the American Society of Traffic and Transportation (AST&T), headquartered in Louisville. As stated in its constitution:

> The objects and purposes of the Society are to establish, promote, and maintain high standards of knowledge and professional training; to formulate a code of ethics for the profession; to advance the professional interests of members of the organization; to serve as a source of information and guidance for the fields of traffic, transportation, logistics, and physical distribution management; and to serve the industry as a whole by fostering professional accomplishments.[1]

The AST&T chapters across the United States hold frequent meetings on contemporary education topics and transportation issues. Membership is possible only after an individual has satisfactorily completed a series of examinations and written an original paper on a transportation topic. Members are exposed to updated transportation educational information and have the opportunity to interact with people of similar interests.

This organization allows associate membership to those individuals who have not completed all requirements so that those persons can enjoy the many benefits involved until becoming full members. A listing of the chapters is shown in Appendix A. Further information regarding AST&T and its chapters can be obtained from its national headquarters in Louisville, Kentucky.

Another education-oriented organization is Delta Nu Alpha Transportation Fraternity, Inc., (DNA), headquartered in Orlando, Florida. As with AST&T, DNA's membership is open to any individual in a transportation-related occupation, regardless of firm or industry. As stated in one of DNA's publications:

> Delta Nu Alpha (DNA) is a transportation organization and its primary purpose is education. The educational concentration is threefold: First, [they] are interested in dealing with grade school and high school students in terms of advising them of what transportation is all about and that it is an interesting field for career development. The second area that [they] concentrate on in education is the college and university. There, [they] work with the university to develop curriculums, as well as assist in advising in the development of their transportation-related programs. In addition to this, [they] are very much interested in continuing the development and education of those individuals that are working in transportation or related fields; therefore, [they]

---

[1] Taken from the 1978 membership roster, Constitution and Bylaws, American Society of Traffic and Transportation, Louisville, Kentucky, p. 3.

conduct seminars and educational training programs at the local chapter and regional level. Also, DNA has an annual meeting which is also geared toward continued education.[2]

DNA has approximately 180 business and university chapters across the United States. The chapters hold monthly meetings with an educational program. The annual meeting consists of two or three days of educational sessions with guest speakers from transportation firms and universities. Membership requirements are not as rigid as those of AST&T. DNA attempts to upgrade transportation education, and AST&T strives to maintain a high educational level among transportation personnel.

A listing of those cities and colleges maintaining local DNA chapters affiliated with its national headquarters can be found in Appendix B. Further information regarding the organization or its local chapters can be obtained by corresponding with its national headquarters in Orlando, Florida.

The third major education-oriented organization is involved in a number of physical distribution activities, including transportation matters. The purpose of the National Council of Physical Distribution Management (NCPDM), headquartered in Oak Brook, Illinois, is as follows:

> To develop the theory and understanding of the physical distribution process, promote the art and science of managing physical distribution systems, and to foster professional dialogue and development in the field of physical distribution management, operating exclusively without profit and in cooperation with other organizations and institutions.[3]

Instead of formal chapters, the NCPDM has roundtables operating in major United States industrial centers. Periodic meetings feature programs geared toward contemporary physical distribution and transportation matters. The annual national meeting, similar to those of AST&T and DNA, consists of a series of educational sessions and business meetings.

A listing of the locations of NCPDM roundtables can be found in Appendix C. Further information regarding NCPDM and its roundtable activities can be obtained by contacting the headquarters in Oak Brook, Illinois.

The three organizations described here have education as their prime purpose and are not restricted to any particular transportation mode or occupation. The organizations described in the next section are more specific as to industry type or occupation.

MODAL-ORIENTED ORGANIZATIONS

All transportation modes have a stake in the industry. Users of the mode are also concerned about the industry's well-being. The Transportation Association

[2] *Creative Approaches to the Transportation Management Job* (Orlando, Florida: Institute for Management Development, National Education Committee, Delta Nu Alpha Transportation Fraternity, undated), p. 1.
[3] *NCPDM: What It's All About* (Chicago, National Council of Physical Distribution Management, undated), p. 1.

of America (TAA) represents a variety of interests in transportation, including suppliers, shippers, or financiers. Any firm with an interest in transportation can affiliate with TAA. The association provides a forum where separate interests and issues can be aired and any differences resolved without governmental interference. The association's major thrust is its role as a unified voice in major transportation issues facing the country. It does not represent specific carrier or shipper interests. It lobbies on overall transportation matters and maintains a favorable image for the entire industry. TAA also conducts studies for overall transportation improvements.

Separate organizations also exist for each mode. And still other organizations focus on particular activities involved in providing transportation service. It is impossible to describe the wide variety of transportation organizations.[4] The kinds of organizations that exist within each mode will be described. Generally, each mode has a major carrier organization. These major organizations lobby to protect the mode's interests; perform research studies; and formulate, revise, and promote rules and regulations that pertain to all carriers within that mode. The success of these associations tends to inform federal and state governments of the interests of each mode.

Two examples of modal organizations are the Association of American Railroads (AAR) and the American Trucking Associations (ATA). Membership is not mandatory for all carriers, but affiliation provides services, such as newsletters and industry information, not to mention the benefits derived from a unified approach to industry accomplishments and resolution of mutual problems. The ATA is structured in specific councils to allow special interest groups to organize. For example, a separate council exists for private carriers, regular route common carriers, and numerous other groups.

Within each mode, other associations are directed to particular interests. Examples of particular interest organizations are the Interstate Towing Association, representing towing companies involved in water transportation; the National Automobile Transporters Association, representing carriers of motor vehicles such as trucks and new cars; and the American Railway Engineering Association, representing professional railroad engineers.

Membership in modal transportation organizations encourages the personal development of those employed in transportation occupations. In almost all cases, modal transportation organizations hold annual meetings where members across the country can meet and interact with others of similar interests. In addition, these organizations provide a regular flow of updated information to members on the most current events in the field.

---

[4] For a detailed list of transportation organizations, the reader is referred to directories, such as the periodic publication of *National Trade and Professional Associations of the United States and Canada and Labor Unions* (Washington, D.C.: Columbia Books, Inc.).

INDUSTRIAL-ORIENTED ORGANIZATIONS

Transportation users also have the opportunity to interact with other freight shippers and receivers. Some organizations are restricted to users. Policies are formulated that protect shipper interests and present a united front to carriers and to national transportation policy officials. An example is the National Industrial Traffic League (NIT League), consisting of industrial traffic managers dedicated to preserving free enterprise in the transportation industry and to protecting users' interests with carriers and governments. Another example is the National Association of Shippers Advisory Boards, a regional federation of industrial traffic managers, mainly in rail freight, who are interested in maintaining a sound railroad network.

The industrial-oriented organizations interact on a regular basis with transportation carriers and various levels of government. They are usually represented at annual meetings of modal organizations and participate in local meetings to keep informed on transportation activities. At annual meetings, policy issues are resolved and resolutions proposed that will have an impact on the entire United States transportation network. These organizations represent the demand half of the demand/supply equation of transportation economies.

GENERAL ORGANIZATIONS

The TAA was described earlier as a general transportation organization. Its major thrust is coordination of all transportation interests, and it is a strong political force. Few local activities are conducted by the TAA. Each major city, however, has local transportation or traffic clubs that conduct monthly meetings. These organizations provide all carrier, industrial, and governmental personnel involved in transportation with a common meeting place in a social atmosphere. Whereas the education-oriented organizations restrict themselves to educational matters, the local clubs present a variety of programs and special events. Programs may deal with civic or transportation matters or may be strictly entertainment. The local organizations affiliate with Traffic Clubs International (TCI), a federation of all local transportation and traffic clubs. Its annual meeting consists of educational or national transportation policy matters.

A listing of those cities that have transportation and traffic clubs affiliated with TCI is shown in Appendix D. Further information regarding their meetings and other activities can be obtained by contacting TCI's headquarters in Orlando, Florida.

Transportation organizations exist for many reasons and purposes. They may focus on marketing, operating, or administrative matters. They may be concerned only with education, or they may combine interests. They may be involved only in specific interests, such as track maintenance or oil-hauling by motor freight. An individual can usually find a transportation organization dedicated to any area. It is not surprising to find transportation personnel affiliated with several organizations and taking advantage of the benefits of each. These memberships afford a well-rounded knowledge of the field and expose an individual to a wider variety of transportation matters. Daily performance, as well as career development, is enhanced through such organizations. The effectiveness of these associations, and all organizations in total, can mean a great deal to the future of the transportation industry, as well as its participants.

Summary

Career planning should consider not only the financial rewards possible, but also interests and aptitude, working environment, kinds of people involved, and the extent of education necessary for a particular occupation. The transportation industry offers a wide variety of career options.

The railroad industry employed more than one half million people with a total payroll of more than $8 billion in 1976. The portion of the motor carrier industry that is regulated employed an estimated 444,955 persons in 1976, and that figure should be more than doubled to account for nonregulated carrier employment. The pipeline, water, and air industries might add another 50,000 employees to these figures.

Careers with transportation carriers are extremely varied and can be subdivided into the marketing, operations, and administrative categories. Several careers representing varied interests also are available in the federal and state regulatory institutions, which currently employ tens of thousands of transportation-related personnel. Career opportunities also exist within industrial traffic departments, where the division of responsibility may not be as great as in the carrier modes.

Transportation organizations and associations may be oriented toward an industry in general, or toward a functional area, or toward a particular mode. Organizations may focus on education, modal concerns, or industrial interests. Other organizations open their membership to anyone interested in transportation matters. These organizations can contribute a great deal to the future of the transportation industry as well as to its participants.

Questions for Chapter 17

1. Name a variety of professional careers available in the transportation industry.
2. What are the functional transportation areas in which higher-level executive positions exist?
3. Describe the different types of commercial careers possible in transportation.
4. Suggest the kind of education that would be required for a transportation pricing career in carrier management.

5. List at least five kinds of career positions possible in transportation operations.
6. What kinds of clerical activities provide a good background for higher-level administrative careers in carrier management?
7. At which governmental levels and in which agencies can an individual pursue a transportation career?
8. In which industrial departments can transportation positions be found?
9. What is the difference between an industry-related and a function-related transportation organization or association?
10. Name the three main organizations primarily dedicated to transportation education.
11. Describe the difference between modal-oriented and industry-oriented transportation organizations.
12. What benefits can accrue to individuals who participate in transportation organizations and associations?

18

Future of Transportation

Future projections are at the same time both difficult and easy. Difficulties arise because the impact of actions that can mold the future is uncertain. Laws, by themselves, do not ensure future compliance. For example, despite 55-mile-per-hour speed limits, some people continue to ignore the law. Future projections can be based upon sophisticated statistical techniques, but such procedures are usually based on history. There is no assurance that the facts of a highly regulated transportation industry will continue in the future.

Predicting transportation's future is an intriguing challenge. In past decades, the transportation industry's structure remained relatively consistent. The common carrier concept was accepted and the regulatory process, although criticized at times, appeared to be a foregone conclusion. Thus, the future could be

356

predicted with some certainty because the regulatory process provided specific guidelines. All of that changed during the 1970s. Regulatory body decisions became more liberal and rigidity disappeared. The Carter administration, living up to its promise to reduce federal bureaucracy, focused on transportation and restructured the industry's future direction. Some carriers suffered financially and others prospered. A basic question developed regarding the extent of competition that was ultimately desirable, both within and among modes. Energy, from both a cost and supply standpoint, became a major issue during the early 1970s and a serious problem later in the decade. The rising cost of living became everyone's concern. Firms were forced to take a more active approach toward increasing transportation productivity in an effort to slow the overall rate of inflation. This discussion of transportation's future will look at the regulatory process, environmental concerns, each mode's role in the total transportation network, and, finally, the challenge to industrial traffic management in a restructured business climate.

Transportation Regulation

Transportation regulation first came about because the industry was considered a utility that affected the public interest and an economic activity that is indispensable to the progress of the standard of living. Problems that developed during the formative years of large transportation companies could not be resolved without imposing state and federal restrictions on business operations. The regulation system expanded in degree and extent as industrial activity grew. As regulations increased, so did their cost, with major agencies employing tens of thousands of people at a cost of several million dollars. The agencies' regulatory decisions were often conflicting, and many people believed that transportation efficiency was inhibited by the regulatory process.

Consumer and government attitudes during the 1970s went a long way toward changing the entire concept of transportation regulation. Popular sentiment supported a less constrained transportation system, with competition within and among modes determining the industry's behavior, similar to that of most other industries. Air passenger and freight transportation was deregulated and the CAB, the overseeing agency, was scheduled to be phased out. The new mood in Washington encouraged requests from selected railroads that they be deregulated and allowed to compete on a free enterprise basis. Motor freight carriers, on the other hand, generally opposed the deregulatory attention aimed at them by federal authorities. Nevertheless, several studies that indicated the potential cost savings and service improvements possible from trucking industry

357

deregulation led the Nixon and Carter administrations to propose that deregulation be implemented. Several formal plans were presented during the late 1970s that became the center of controversy among politicians and lobbying groups. These plans resulted in far-reaching legislative enactments regarding trucking regulation and proposals regarding the extent of railroad control in 1980, with implications that the thrust would not subside in this new decade.

Pipeline regulation has not been a major problem from the government's standpoint because of the lack of competition and the relatively limited network. Pipeline regulation, now the responsibility of the Department of Energy, is closely tied to energy planning. Similarly, water transportation regulation has not been an issue because only a small portion of freight tonnage is regulated. However, this situation may change if water carriers begin to lose business to the deregulated railroad industry.

DEREGULATION DIRECTION

Washington policy makers will confront many issues during deregulation attempts. If all of these issues are confronted and altered, the result will be a completely different transportation system than has been characteristic during the twentieth century. Selected major areas that are being examined for modification or elimination are entry/exit provisions, certification, rate setting, and contract, multimodal, and private carriage.

Entry/Exit

Under the regulated system, prospective carriers could not enter a mode without approval from a regulatory body. CPCNs were required, and usually the carrier had to prove that a need existed for the proposed service. This requirement was equivalent to proving that the existing competition was inadequate for shipper needs. The process was difficult and was opposed by existing carriers. The regulatory bodies protected those carriers from intensive competition and brought relative stability to the mode. In some cases, a carrier that wanted to discontinue authorized service had to seek regulatory permission to withdraw from an area. Thus, the regulatory process ensured that no community would be left without transportation.

These procedures will be modified or eliminated entirely by further re-regulation and deregulation legislation. The re-regulation effort relieved the requirement to prove necessity for the applicant's permission to obtain certification, but applied only under given circumstances. All carriers are not free to participate in any desired shipments they may choose, even under the 1980 legislation. Total constraints may disappear in the future and carriers will have to prove only that they are "fit, willing, and able" to provide transportation service on any shipments they desire. If too much competition exists in a particular area, economic supply and demand and the quality of service provided by each carrier would determine the survivors. Exit would be permitted any time a carrier believed the volume was insufficient to provide a satisfactory profit. In theory, another carrier or another mode would enter to pick up the void.

The major concern expressed regarding exit provisions is that geographic areas might be left without service because carriers would not want to handle small volumes to and from remote communities. Responses to solve this problem range from government subsidy to a government-run carrier operation. In any case, it appears the government would not be totally removed from transportation, even under a completely deregulated system.

CERTIFICATION

Since 1935, motor carriers had been required to specify in their CPCNs all commodities hauled between two locations. The 1980 trucking legislation allowed carriers to haul commodities in product groupings, or general categories. Trucking companies, therefore, no longer are limited in authority to haul specified commodities. This, soon, may give way to any carrier being allowed to haul any commodity. This action, coupled with freedom of entry, would create a situation of total and unrestrained competition from a service standpoint. No longer could carriers depend on the restrictions that protected any movements from open competition. With each potential haul subject to more intense competition, long-range planning by carriers will be affected.

RATE SETTING

One of the most complicated issues in deregulation is the method by which the modes set freight rates. Rate agreements are reached through the bureau or conference systems, a practice protected from antitrust laws by the Reed-Bulwinkle Act of 1948. The entire procedure has been modified on a phase-in basis in the 1980 re-regulation thrust. Carriers will be required to set local rates individually without other lines' concurrence or voting privileges. Carriers will be allowed to raise or lower rates within a stated zone of reasonableness without regulatory body approval.

Many people fear that rate wars will cause chaos in the industry, with price cuts elminiating competiton and rate increases to follow. Supporters of deregulation point to the Federal Trade Commission and the Department of Justice as arbiters in such situations.

Carriers under a free pricing atmosphere would most likely pay more attention to the actual cost of providing service and relate it to the rates charged. It would no longer be necessary to charge higher rates in some areas to offset below-cost rates to other communities. This, similar to certification, could leave some communities without healthy carrier competition or without service altogether.

CONTRACT CARRIERS

Rules pertaining to contract carriers have changed considerably in 1980 and may change further in the years ahead. Contract carriers now can haul the stipulated commodities between any points in the United States, once the application is supported by a shipper and approval by the ICC. However, contracts can be protested by existing carriers. A further relaxation of these rules may prohibit current carriers from protesting contract applications and open the trucking industry to a further intensity of competition. Thus, contract carriers may be allowed to haul any commodity for any shipper between any points on a contract basis.

In addition, regulations pertaining to contract carriage by common carriers have been loosened. The ICC relaxed its position during the late 1970s to permit contracts between rail carriers and shippers. The 1980 trucking re-regulation legislation allowed common carriers to act in a contract-carrier capacity when possible, even to the extent that one vehicle may contain commodities hauled under both a contract and a common-carrier basis. It is possible that future re-regulation thrusts will allow private carriers to haul for unrelated companies on a contract or common-carrier basis.

MULTIMODAL

Under regulatory restrictions, carriers within a mode had been prevented from owning or controlling a carrier in another mode. Power, influence, and strength in one mode were believed to affect the manner in which a carrier would perform in another mode and therefore endanger competitive stability. In many cases, this restriction inhibited multimodal activities. In a deregulated system, multimodal ownership would be permitted in an effort to encourage innovation and efficiency. Transportation costs might well be reduced and service improved if multimodal ownership and freedom of operation is allowed.

In the past, multimodal service such as TOFC and COFC had been a cooperative effort between rail and motor carriers. With deregulation, rail carriers could be able to expand operations into trucking to provide multimodal service. In the past, railroad trucking was limited to freight that had a prior or future movement by rail.

PRIVATE CARRIAGE

Private carriage would take on new dimensions in a deregulated transportation system. Past regulations have restricted companies operating their own transportation vehicles to hauling products owned exclusively by that company, with few exceptions. In fact, private trucks have not been allowed to legally haul freight for separate companies under the same corporate control. Many companies have been discouraged from providing their own transportation service because of the high costs involved. Under the currently-revised system, private carriers are allowed to haul products owned by all subsidiary companies, as long as the subsidiaries are owned in their entirety by the parent organization. In addition, the rules regarding hauling for nonaffiliated firms may be relaxed considerably. Early in 1978, selected private carriers were granted common carrier operating authority by the ICC.

These actions will encourage more firms to enter private carriage because of the reduced costs possible from efficient equipment utilization and additional backhaul opportunities. Motor freight carriers thus would face competition from private carriers who do not necessarily have to show a profit from transportation operations.

The issues discussed are by no means comprehensive. They have been introduced to familiarize you with the scope of changes that could result from a deregulated system. Without doubt, deregulation or reregulation will substantially affect the future of the total transportation network. The remainder of this chapter assumes that a significant degree of deregulation will occur during the 1980s.

Transportation Environmental Concerns

No business enterprise can afford to make long-range plans or decisions without considering the environment. Environmental interest groups influence the operations of all industries, and transportation is no exception. Each transportation mode alters the environment in some way, whether through pollution, energy, or aesthetics. An expanded highway system to accommodate more trucks or additions to the pipeline network will affect the physical environment. More trucks and planes will increase noise and air pollution.

A future transportation network with more companies competing among the several modes could easily lead to a greater number of vehicles. Technological advances in environmental controls undoubtedly will accelerate, especially in the modes successful in increasing their proportion of total freight movements. Disregard of the environment would antagonize environmentalists and give federal authorities new causes for concern. Thus, it can be expected that transportation managers will take environmental issues seriously.

A major factor affecting transportation's future is the growing energy problem. The largest energy consumers are truck and air carriers, which also hold the greatest promise for improved transportation service. The overall speed of transportation service will be improved with greater participation by these carriers, but scarce energy supplies and continuing fuel cost increases may offset this benefit. The choice will be between low-cost transportation using slower, more energy-efficient modes, such as rail and water, or high-cost transportation offering speed and lower total distribution costs, but severely draining energy supplies. The increased ability of motor freight carriers to fill backhauls may increase fuel efficiency and reduce the impact of higher energy costs. Similarly, advances in material-handling technology for air freight can reduce the impact of higher fuel costs in that mode.

In the long run, fewer highway motor vehicles will haul commodities a greater percentage of time, thereby increasing fuel efficiency. From a competitive standpoint, the manner in which the industry is restructured will determine the amount of fuel waste or conservation that can be expected in the future. The additional volumes handled by air freight companies, with increased containerized handling and lower overall distribution costs, may offset fuel costs, but greater fuel usage remains an obstacle in air freight transportation's future.

The next section will explore the future of each mode, based on current developments and under the assumption of substantial deregulation or additional re-regulation.

Modal Considerations

All of the freight transportation modes will develop a different image as the twentieth century progresses and attitudes change. Although unprecedented freight volumes will enter the transportation stream, the role played by each mode in the future distribution network may change drastically.

RAILROAD

The railroad industry holds the promise of regaining the prominence it enjoyed in the early decades of the twentieth century, although its manner of operation must change significantly. It remains to be seen, however, if the industry will take advantage of the opportunities. Fuel conservation measures will make more shipments available to the railroads, which are more efficient energy users compared to other modes. Railroads are able to move large quantities for long distances at adequate speeds and low cost. However, slow terminal operations hinder the railroads' overall service performance. Also, a marketing approach—determining customers' needs and offering a service package to satisfy those needs—has been lacking.

A many-faceted challenge faces the railroads and their future role in the transportation network. First, service improvements must receive priority attention. As a potential response to the fuel dilemma, railroads must prove they are capable of offering the types of service demanded by the shippers. Otherwise, shippers will continue to use more costly, fuel-consuming modes to avoid long transit delays. Failure to improve service standards will limit the railroad industry to low-value, bulk items almost exclusively. The industry will then experience continued declining volumes and will be unable to take its place as a viable alternative in the transportation network.

Second, the industry needs large amounts of capital to update facilities. Profits should accrue from the shipments regained from other modes. Additional capital must be attracted from investors, and the federal government will undoubtedly add subsidies to improve rail facilities. Roadbeds must be modernized to accommodate the increased activity. Rolling stock improvements will be required so that a complete fleet of vehicles can be available on demand. Multipurpose standardized railcars should be developed to improve asset utilization. Multimodal services will have to be expanded by additional equipment purchases. Freedom from regulation will enable rail carriers to take advantage of TOFC and COFC services. Increasingly mechanized terminal operations and improved communications through electronic data processing will improve service. Unquestionably, these improvements will help the railroads survive in a free enterprise economic structure.

Third, the rail carriers collectively must examine the competitive situation and attempt mergers that would offer continuous routes and faster service. Carriers with small volumes in communities where many rail carriers compete should consider withdrawing and concentrating in those areas where efforts can be put to better use and with greater profitability potential. In the past, duplicate facilities have resulted in underutilization and higher costs. Greater volumes handled by fewer competitors should reduce total costs.

Fourth, from a competitive standpoint, rail carriers should attempt to recapture long-haul movements that have been lost to motor carriers. The energy situation will favor rail on transcontinental hauls. However, it will be necessary for the railroads to improve the quality of service if they are to become competitive with trucks.

Finally, rail carriers will have to intensify marketing efforts by identifying shipper needs and designing service and equipment packages to satisfy those requirements. Suggestions for multimodal movement, for instance, will attract shippers and develop goodwill in the long run. Pricing decisions more closely related to the cost of providing service, rather than the long-standing value-of-service concept, will attract additional customers.

Rail transportation's future is bright with opportunities. However, the responsibility remains with the industry to capitalize on those opportunities.

TRUCK

In contrast to the potentially bright future facing the railroad industry, motor carriers face serious problems. The motor industry's energy needs are a limitation to continued growth. If freedom of entry and liberalization of commodity restrictions continue, common carriers will face many new competitors. The industry has the advantage of being able to haul smaller quantities of high-value commodities in a short period of time. Because of rail failures, many trucks run long distances and require backhauls to remain economically viable. The combination of increased competition and fuel conservation may place such operations in jeopardy.

Deregulation will bring competition from private, contract, and independent, owner-operator carriers. Also, other common carriers that could not compete before because of lack of operating authority will enter once protected markets. Every trucking firm will be subject to a greater degree of competition from similar firms with similar equipment serving many different routes. In addition, rail deregulation will allow railroads to reduce their long-haul rates. Private carriers will be able to offer lower rates on for-hire service because they will need only to cover the variable costs of returning vehicles to loading points. Likewise, contract carriers will be permitted to serve more customers at more locations with more commodities and will have greater freedom to seek backhauls.

All of these factors will put a great deal of pressure on what now represents the backbone of the trucking industry—the regular route common carriers. The successful companies will be those that are quick to respond to these conditions. Many experts predict a wave of mergers that will result in a concentration of approximately ten major carriers dominating the industry. Under such conditions, empty miles will be minimized, fuel efficiency increased, and operating costs reduced to keep rates low. Shipments without backhaul opportunities may have to be sacrificed. The concentration is expected to reduce the number and, consequently, the frequency of service offered by regional carriers.

On the positive side, more opportunities will arise for motor carriers to add business by attracting users on those routes where the carrier is now running empty. Any added business will reduce overall costs and allow lower rates. Another positive aspect is the possible standardization of maximum weight requirements and authorization to haul double trailers across the United States. Individual vehicles no longer would have to be loaded with the lowest maximum weight, and the increase in total weight limitations and the use of double trailers will allow greater payloads to offset higher driver wages.

Chapter 11 introduced a new deregulation thrust of the motor carrier industry, known as *master certification*. The ICC had proposed that motor carriers may apply for operating authority to haul products in twelve different industry segments in one application, to be granted in one certificate. The industry segments were as follows:

1. Heavy and specialized haulers.
2. Temperature-control services.
3. Lumber and building materials.
4. Metals.
5. Bulk materials.

6. Household goods.
7. Armored car and related services.
8. Haul-a-way vehicles.
9. Wrecker services.
10. Boats.
11. Courier services.
12. Film carriers.

In this proposal, entry controls would have been eliminated. Rather than prove that a particular carrier's request for permission to haul commodities in any of these industry segments is necessary from a competitive standpoint or to handle the large volumes available to be moved, the carrier would have had to prove only that it is "fit, willing, and able" to participate in providing transportation service. The restraints placed on the carriers involve the issue of rates. Freight rates still would be subject to the ICC's approval. However, a *zone of reasonableness* would be allowed. The zone of reasonableness allows each carrier to increase or reduce its rates on particular shipments a certain percentage without prior approval of the ICC. In addition, each carrier must publish its own tariffs, and the bureau pricing method could not be used.

Although master certification was not approved by the Motor Carrier Act of 1980, carriers are allowed to haul commodities in general groupings, which total 51 separate classifications. The mood of the ICC was reflected in the master certification proposal and may emerge again during the 1980s with authority for any carrier to haul any commodity, as long as it is "fit, willing, and able."

A greater cooperative effort between motor carriers and the airlines and railroads is expected to increase the volume of multimodal shipments. In the future, the motor carrier industry will more often serve as a feeder to rail, water, and air terminals where containers or trailers will be transferred for line-haul shipment. In fact, the 1980 trucking legislation allows motor carriers to participate in the transportation of commodities at any point along a railroad line if the trucking firm has certification to haul between the locations involved in the rail shipment. Failure to provide this service could cause motor carriers to lose this business to the other modes that will be free to expand their service offerings to include final pickup and delivery of containerized shipments.

The overall motor common carrier industry appears to be at somewhat of a disadvantage given the regulatory and energy outlook. However, the industry has demonstrated a capability to adjust to change and maintain a prominent role. The industry may have to adjust to many environmental problems and to the nature of shipments hauled, but its potential is by no means diminished. Concentration appears to be a logical reaction to deregulation.

WATER

Not as volatile as the other modes, water transportation has played a relatively stable role in the overall transportation network. Because only a small part of water freight transportation is regulated, deregulation does not present as many problems to water as it does to other modes. The prospects for water transportation's future appear to be on the upswing. The increased use of containers will continue to reduce overall handling costs and improve shipment speed. Advanced technology in container handling will make water transportation more attractive to potential users.

The water freight industry will face more price competition from a deregulated railroad industry. However, the economics favor water in any attempt by rail to penetrate on the basis of price. In fact, the early 1980s may see water carriers enjoying opportunities to haul tonnages previously handled by rail carriers, if the railroads, given more alternatives, decide not to compete for low-profit movements. The rail industry may not be in a position to take advantage of all its opportunities. Thus, water carriers may find a more prominent shipping role along the coasts, the Great Lakes, and the major inland rivers. The desire to reduce shipping costs will lead many users to look to water transportation's ability to haul large quantities at low rates as a solution to the problem.

PIPELINE

Historically, pipeline shipments have centered on oil products, but the slurry concept continues to offer potential. Environmentalists generally oppose the expansion of pipeline transportation, but its low energy use and low operating cost make it too attractive to be ignored. Additional commodities, such as agricultural products, may be added to pipeline traffic, and expanded networks are expected to serve larger territories by the end of the twentieth century.

Successful pipe slurry transportation may attract freight from rail and water. In the past, rail and water mode proponents have been somewhat successful in forestalling advancements in pipeline transportation. In the future, however, separate interests will give way to the greater need for low-energy, low-cost, continuous freight transportation. The future of pipelines is limited only by the rate of technological advances in slurry applications. It has been predicted that finished products enclosed in minicontainers floated in water will become a future pipeline reality. The pipeline industry may very well emerge as a major transportation force before the end of the twentieth century.

AIR

Air freight transportation, a weak contender in the first half of the twentieth century, began to realize its potential in industrial distribution during the 1970s. Regularly scheduled cargo flights became commonplace. A number of major airports throughout the United States built separate terminal facilities solely for air freight shipments. To attract traffic, some airlines established separate sales and marketing departments to solicit freight shipments and to identify shipper needs. In Chapter 15, the concept of integrated logistics was introduced as an effort to increase overall efficiency and reduce costs. With the realization that higher transportation costs may result in lower total distribution costs, users are more likely to turn to the speed provided by air transport. Lower inventory, warehousing, and communication costs may offset high air freight rates. The future potential of air freight expansion beyond emerging shipments rests with the total cost concept.

Container improvements make handling easier and less costly. Vehicle modifications to permit more and larger containers to be hauled may reduce air carriers' operating costs and permit rate reductions. In short, air freight holds significant potential for increased participation in the transportation network.

This potential is hampered somewhat by energy availability. Air freight is the greatest energy consumer on a per-unit basis among all the transportation modes. As fuel costs and shortages increase, the variable costs of moving freight by air will increase more rapidly than those for other modes. Although the economic benefit of faster shipments in distribution is valid, implementation may be hindered by the unavailability or extremely high cost of fuel. Minimal offsetting factors will be larger aircraft that do not use proportionately larger quantities of fuel and products made from lighter synthetic materials.

Each mode has the potential to increase the absolute volume carried as well as its proportionate share of total transportation tonnage. In all cases, however, adaptation to a changing environment and technological advances are necessary to realize the potential. The carrier management within each mode will be responsible for ensuring that its firm remains competitive and takes advantage of every available opportunity. The future of transportation has similar implications for industrial traffic management.

Managerial Implications

The industrial traffic manager was an integral force in business firms until the advent of transportation regulation. Only in recent decades has top management again looked to the traffic department as a possible avenue for cost reduction. Given re-regulation and deregulation thrusts, transportation's future will be dynamic. Future industrial traffic managers will have to be astute and able to adapt to the changing transportation environment. They will be required to have the ability to view the entire transportation network, constantly improve a firm's transportation service, and at the same time maintain low costs. In particular, industrial traffic managers can seek changes in the areas of freight rates, service offering, multimodal operation, contract carriers, private transportation, and communication. In addition, increased effort and money must be required for transportation research. The extent of change experienced in each area will be directly related to the degree of future deregulation.

FREIGHT RATES

The rate bureau method of establishing freight rates was a convenience to traffic management because prices between two points on any given commodity were usually the same, regardless of the carrier used within a mode. In the future, this method will not exist, and rates will vary by individual carriers. Company tariff files will be more expansive because each carrier will publish individual price lists.

Rate negotiation, an important element in traffic management, will receive greater emphasis. The long process of freight rate approval through regional bureaus may be abolished. Under these conditions, traffic managers will be expected to negotiate rates directly with carriers. The carriers' methodology of costing must be understood and applied for successful rate negotiation. These rate negotiations will be of utmost importance in keeping a firm competitive as others negotiate reduced rates to gain market advantages. Traffic managers in the future will be held more accountable for the freight rates confronted by the firm.

SERVICE OFFERING

The potential loss of the traditional common carrier concept that may accompany deregulation will place a greater responsibility on industrial traffic managers to ensure regular and continued service for the firm's distribution system. In larger commercial areas, more alternatives will be available from which to choose. In smaller communities, where less competition exists, the traffic manager's relationship with carriers must be such as to ensure that the firm has viable transportation.

Equipment supply is another matter that will demand the traffic manager's attention. With less long-range certainty, carriers most likely will not maintain transportation vehicles to satisfy every conceivable shipment opportunity. Thus, the traffic department will need to assess the carrier's equipment situation and ensure that needs are fulfilled. Equipment shortages, as in the past, can affect a firm's relationship with its customers as well as the inventory levels maintained throughout the system.

MULTIMODAL OPERATION

Traditional shipping patterns will give way to new distribution methods. More attention will be given to consolidated shipments and mixtures of products transported in containers. With a more cooperative effort between modes and with the possibility of carriers being permitted to own multimodal operations, more consolidated and container shipments will develop. Traffic managers will be called upon to devise shipping arrangements that take advantage of these possibilities. They will need to gather data on markets, quantities shipped, and usage rates in order to suggest alternative shipment patterns.

With multimodal operations, the traffic manager will be responsible for negotiating specialized equipment and applicable rates. Carriers that seek new opportunities but are less constrained by rigid regulations will be more responsive to shipper requests if they have the potential for regular and profitable shipments. However, the responsibility for initiating these actions will lie with traffic management.

CONTRACT CARRIAGE

As noted earlier, contract carriage has been restricted regarding the number of customers, commodities, and locations that could be served. Particularly in motor freight carriage, contract carriers often experienced empty backhauls because of regulatory restrictions. Now that restrictions are relaxed, many possibilities will exist for a firm's transportation requirements to be filled by contract carriers. Traffic managers will need to be alert to greater opportunities in contract carriage. Capable carriers with reliable, regular service and the proper equipment must be located and arrangements made for the desired service. The end result could be energy conservation, lower transportation costs, and more dependable service.

PRIVATE TRANSPORTATION

Private transportation has received much attention in recent years. Many firms have purchased trucks out of dissatisfaction with common carrier service and rising freight costs. Others have found they could earn a higher return on investment by providing their own transportation. The future, however, could go either way. With a free competitive environment, carriers may pay more attention to service requirements to reduce the trend toward private carriage. On the other hand, with relaxed regulatory restrictions on private transportation movements, more firms may be attracted to this type of operation. With greater possibilities existing for full deployment of contract carriers, it appears, at least philosophically, that private carriage will not continue its accelerated pace.

COMMUNICATION

Efficient business operations depend on current information provided by an accurate communication system. More than ever before, the dynamic nature of future transportation will demand speedy and accurate information transmittal.

369

With more shipments and more carriers, status reports will require current information. Information must also be received from vendors or transmitted to customers. Obtaining and maintaining shipment information will be easier than in the past because of computer advances in information processing. During the 1970s, carriers and users cooperated in implementing communication systems whereby carriers computerized all movements. Shippers were provided a code and allowed entry directly into the carrier's computer to receive immediate information regarding shipment status. Advances in communication systems of this type will continue to enhance the relationship between carriers and shippers. It will provide the instant information necessary for traffic departments to operate efficiently.

From a procurement standpoint, continually changing freight rates will affect the buying function. Purchasing agents will need to be apprised of all changes that may affect source decisions. On the marketing side, sales personnel will require information regarding rate changes that will enable them to expand market territories or revise selling prices in existing areas.

Traffic departments will continue to be responsible for providing current shipment information so that the desired inventory levels are maintained or corrective actions taken, both by the firm and its customers. With more and more attention being paid to inventories because of high carrying costs, traffic departments can be expected to have more responsibility and accountability in this area.

More information is being demanded by top management, and computer technology has made it possible to provide this information. Progressive traffic departments have already computerized rate, route, and movement information. They will be capitalizing on computerized information maintenance and processing as the advantages of doing so become more evident in the years ahead.

TRANSPORTATION RESEARCH

Research is an important and necessary aspect of any management position. Future transportation needs will call for more extensive and regular research activity than ever before. Regular communication channels will be unable to process the changes in transportation as fast as they will occur. New rates will be implemented almost immediately. Technological advances will appear as fast as carriers and other users can implement them. Multimodal improvements will appear in various combinations. Traffic managers will be required to maintain regular contact with people working in these areas. They will also require more constant contact with individuals external to the firm to assess traffic flows and examine possible contract or private carriage possibilities. Improved communication methodologies will be devised and put into use. Traffic managers will need to search for possible applications within their own firms. Material handling systems will be devised that will be adaptable to loading and unloading at manufacturing and inventory/storage locations. Traffic managers will need to assess their applicability.

Failure to perform transportation-related research will seriously affect a firm's competitive posture. Traffic managers who do not perform adequate research will find other individuals assuming those responsibilities. More than ever before, sophisticated traffic management will be required to seek out ways for the firm to gain a competitive advantage. Traffic managers will be expected not only to adapt to the many changes, but to instigate activities to help direct the changes.

Concluding Comment

The major part of this text has described transportation as it now exists. This final chapter has examined some of the events that are likely to occur during the 1980s and has assessed their potential impact on transportation. Predicting the future is more difficult than examining conditions as they are or were. Yet, some certainties are evident. Transportation is indispensable to commerce and it is certain that it will always exist. Transportation is a major cost item in the nation's economy and will not lose its importance in that regard. In the past, transportation has been subject to rigid regulations that served to insulate the industry. In the past, transportation has been subject to rigid regulations that served to insulate the industry. As the events in 1980 have demonstrated, this is changing. The regulatory procedure has undergone material changes and the deregulation effort is expected to produce more change. Carriers will be responsible for providing efficient transportation at the lowest possible cost. Shippers will be responsible for cooperating with carriers and avoiding abuses to keep the system financially stable. The government will be responsible for allowing both carriers and shippers to interact with as little interference as possible. Should any of these groups fail in their responsibilities, major problems in transportation will continue. Such failure will result in higher and higher distribution costs. The challenge is clear.

Questions for Chapter 18

1. Why would you expect transportation to be more dynamic in the future than it has been in the past?
2. For what reasons would you expect motor carriers to oppose deregulation efforts?
3. What impact would reducing the rigid CPCN requirements have on the level of competition in motor freight?
4. How would carrier long-range planning be affected by less government regulation?

5. Discuss the impact on freight rates if rate bureaus no longer were exempt from anti-trust violation.
6. What is the overall competitive effect of reducing regulations on contract carriers?
7. Under relaxed private carriage restrictions, what is the likely effect on the number of firms providing their own transportation service?
8. Which modes most likely will be affected adversely by fuel shortages?
9. What factors will contribute to a rejuvenation of the railroad industry?
10. Why should greater concentration in the motor freight industry lead to transportation cost reductions?
11. What overall distribution cost savings result from a greater number of air freight shipments?
12. How will an industrial traffic manager be able to improve a company's profit position in a deregulated transportation environment?

Appendix A
American Society
of Traffic and
Transportation, Inc.,
Chapter Locations

HEADQUARTERS

P.O. Box 33095
Louisville, Kentucky 40232

CHAPTER LOCATIONS

Alabama
District of Columbia (D.C., Virginia, and Maryland)
Florida
Georgia
Greater Delaware Valley (Philadelphia)
Illinois
Indiana
Kentucky
Louisiana/Mississippi
Michigan
Minneapolis/North Central
Missouri
New England
New York (Metro, Rhode Island)
New York (Rochester)
North California (Bay Area)
North and South Carolinas
Ohio/Western Reserve
Oklahoma
Pacific Northwest (Oregon)
Pennsylvania (West Pittsburgh)
Puget Sound (Seattle)
South California (Los Angeles)
Tennessee

Texas
Wisconsin

REGIONS

Central

Illinois
Indiana
Iowa
Kansas
Michigan
Minnesota
Missouri
Nebraska
North Dakota
Ohio
South Dakota
Wisconsin

Eastern

Connecticut
Delaware
Maine
Massachusetts
New Hampshire
New Jersey
New York/Metro
New York/Rochester
Pennsylvania
Rhode Island
Vermont
West Virginia

Southern

Alabama
Florida
Georgia
Kentucky
Maryland
North Carolina
South Carolina
Tennessee
Virginia
Washington, D.C.

Western

California
Colorado
Idaho
Montana
Nevada
Oregon
Utah
Washington
Wyoming

Southwestern

Arizona
Arkansas
Mississippi
New Mexico
Oklahoma
Texas

Canadian, Foreign, and Non-Contiguous States

Alaska
Canada
Hawaii
All other foreign countries

Appendix B
Delta Nu Alpha
Transportation
Fraternity, Inc.,
Chapter Locations

HEADQUARTERS

1040 Woodcock Road
Suite 201
Orlando, Florida 32803
(305) 894-0384

CHAPTER LOCATIONS

Akron, Ohio
Alamo Chapter (San Antonio, Texas)
Albuquerque, New Mexico
Alavti (Albert Lea, Minnesota)
Aloha (Honolulu, Hawaii)
Antietam (Hagerstown, Maryland)
Arizona Alpha (Phoenix, Arizona)
Atlanta, Georgia
Auburn University
Augusta, Georgia
Austin (Austin, Texas)

Beta Upsilon (Indianapolis, Indiana)
Big Sky (Butte, Montana)
Birmingham, Alabama
Bloomington, Illinois
Blue Ridge (Hickory, N.C.)
Boston, Massachusetts
Brazosport (Freeport, Texas)
Brazos Valley (College Station, Texas)
Bristol County (Fall River, Mass.)
Broward County (Ft. Lauderdale, Florida)

Buffalo Alpha (New York)
Bux-Mont (Willow Grove, Pa.)

Cape Fear (Fayetteville, N.C.)
Capital (Harrisburg, Pa.)
Cascade Chapter (Bend, Oregon)
Central Connecticut (Hartford, Conn.)
Central Iowa (Des Moines)
Central Michigan (Lansing, Michigan)
Central New Jersey (New Brunswick)
Central Ohio (Columbus, Ohio)
Centralia (Illinois)
Channel Islands (Oxnard, California)
Chapter-of-the-Redwoods (Santa Rosa)
Charlotte, North Carolina
Charleston, South Carolina
Chautauqua (Jamestown, N.Y.)
Cha-ver (Champaign, Illinois)
Chesapeake (Baltimore, Maryland)
Chester County (Chester, Pennsylvania)
Chicago, Illinois
Cincinnati, Ohio
Cleveland, Ohio
C.M.D. (Los Angeles, California)
Connecticut Alpha (New Haven, Connecticut)
Cowboy State (Casper, Wyoming)
Crossroads (Cheyenne, Wyoming)

Dallas, Texas
Dayton, Ohio
Decatur, Illinois
Delaware (Muncie, Indiana)
Delaware Valley (Bristol, Pennsylvania)
Denver, Colorado
Derbytown (Louisville, Kentucky)
Detroit, Michigan

Eastern Montana College (Billings, Mont.)
Easton, Pennsylvania
E-Cen-Ill. (Mattoon, Illinois)
El-Co-Wa (Elmira, New York)
Elkhart, Indiana
Evansville, Indiana

Fairfield County (Bridgeport, Connecticut)
Fort Smith, Arkansas
Fort Wayne, Indiana

Fort Worth, Texas
Fresno, California

Gateway Chapter (Pocatello, Idaho)
Gateway City (Jacksonville, Florida)
Gem (Boise, Idaho)
Golden West (Garden Grove, California)
Greater Aurora (Illinois)
Greater Chico, California
Greater Hazleton, Pennsylvania
Greater Milwaukee
Greater Peninsula (Newport News, Virginia)
Greater Valley Forge (Pennsylvania)
Green River Comm College

Hampton Roads (Norfolk, Virginia)
Harbor Alpha (Long Beach, California)
Head-of-Lakes (Duluth, Minnesota)
Highline College
Houston, Texas
Huron Valley (Ypsilanti, Michigan)

Illowa (Illinois-Iowa)
Inland Empire (Spokane, Washington)
International (Port Huron-Sarnia, Ontario)

Johnstown, Pennsylvania

Kingsport, Tennessee
Knoxville, Tennessee
Kent State University

Lake County (Waukegan, Illinois)
Lake Michigan (Muskegon, Michigan)
Lancaster, Pennsylvania
Lehigh Valley (Allentown, Pennsylvania)
Lewis & Clark (Portland, Oregon)
Lexington, Kentucky
Little Rock, Arkansas
Lookout (Chattanooga, Tennessee)
Los Angeles Alpha
Lubbock, Texas

Madison, Wisconsin
Marina West (Englewood, California)
Marion, Ohio
Matro (Ft. Worth, Texas)
Memphis, Tennessee

Miami, Florida
Michiana (South Bend, Indiana)
Mid Kansas Alpha (Abilene, Kansas)
Midway (Huntington, West Virginia)
Mississinewa (Marion, Indiana)
Mohawk Valley (Rome, New York)
Monroe, Louisiana
Monterey Peninsula (Salinas, California)
Moraine Valley (Palos Hills, Illinois)
Mountain State (Parkersburg, West Virginia)

Nassau-Suffolk (Long Island, New York)
Naugatuck Valley (Waterbury, Connecticut)
Newark, New Jersey
New York, New York
Nola (New Orleans, Louisiana)
Northeast Michigan (Saginaw, Michigan)
Northeast Wisconsin (Green Bay, Wisconsin)
Niagara University
Northern Colorado (Ft. Collins, Colorado)
Northwest Ohio (Lima, Ohio)
Northwest Suburban (Des Plaines, Illinois)

Oakland, California
Oil Capital (Tulsa, Oklahoma)
Oklahoma City, Oklahoma
Old Dominion (Richmond, Virginia)
Omaha, Nebraska
Omicron (New York)
Orange County (Fullerton, California)
Oregon University (Eugene, Oregon)
Owensboro (Kentucky)

Parks College (Cahokie, Illinois)
Palmetto (Greenville/Spartanburg, S.C.)
Penn State University (University Park, Pa.)
Peoria, Illinois
Philadelphia, Pennsylvania
Phoenix, Arizona
Piedmont (Winston-Salem, N.C.)
Pioneer Valley (Springfield, Massachusetts)
Pittsburgh, Pennsylvania
Power City (Massena, New York)
Presque Isle (Erie, Pennsylvania)
Profile (Manchester, New Hampshire)

Quaker City #4 (Philadelphia, Pa.)

Racine, Wisconsin
Ramapo Valley, New Jersey
Rappahannock Area (Fredericksburg, Va.)
Reading, Pennsylvania
Rhode Island (Providence)
Roanoke, Virginia
Robert Morris College (Corapolis, Pa.)
Rochester Alpha (New York)
Rockford, Illinois

Sacramento, California
Salt Lake City, Utah
San Bernardino, California
San Diego, California
San Fernando, California
San Francisco, California
San Gabriel Valley, California
San Jacinto (Deer Park, Texas)
Santa Barbara/Goleta, California
Santa Clara Valley, California
Seafair (Seattle, Washington)
Sequoia (Redwood City, California)
Shawnee (Shawnee, Oklahoma)
Shreveport (Shreveport, La.)
Sierra Cascade (Redding, California)
Sierra Nevada (Reno, Nevada)
Siouxland (Sioux City, Iowa)
Skokie Valley, Illinois
Southern Maine (Portland, Maine)
Southern Nevada (Las Vegas, Nevada)
South Shore Alpha (Quincy, Massachusetts)
Southwest Chicago (Chicago, Illinois)
Southwestern Michigan (Kalamazoo, Michigan)
St. John's University (Staten Island, N.Y.)
St. Louis, Missouri
Staten Island, New York
Stockton, California
Syracuse Alpha (New York)
Syracuse Beta (University of Syracuse)

Tar Heel (Raleigh-Durham, N.C.)
Tau Alpha Sigma (Albany, New York)
Tennessee Alpha (Univ. of Tennessee-Knoxville)
Toledo, Ohio
Trenton, New Jersey
Tri-Cities (Binghamton, New York)
Tri-County (Camden, New Jersey)
Triton College (Palos Hill, Illinois)

Tri-State College (Angola, Indiana)
Tucson, Arizona
Tulsa, Oklahoma
Twin City (Minneapolis-St.Paul)

University of Akron
University of Alabama
University of Arkansas
University of Maryland

Volunteer (Nashville, Tennessee)

Wabash Valley (Terre Haute, Indiana)
Washington, D.C.
Watatic (Fitchburg, Mass.)
West Michigan (Grand Rapids, Michigan)
Western Kentucky (Bowling Green, Kentucky)
West Mississippi (Vicksburg, Mississippi)
White River Valley (Columbus, Indiana)
White Rose (York, Pennsylvania)
Wilkes Barre-Scranton, Pennsylvania
Wilmington, Delaware
Wisconsin Valley (Wisconsin Rapids, Wisconsin)
Worcester, Massachusetts

Youngstown, Ohio
Youngstown University (Youngstown, Ohio)

UNIVERSITY/COLLEGE CHAPTERS *

Syracuse Beta University
University of Tennessee
University of Oregon
Penn State University
University of Maryland
Youngstown University
Tri-State College
University of Alabama
Auburn University
Green River Community College
Alavti (Albert Lea Area Voc. Tech)
Highline College
University of Arkansas
Matro (Tarrant County Jr. College)
Parks College
Kent State University

* Also included in alphabetical listing

Triton College
Golden West College
Texas A & M University
Niagara University
Robert Morris College
Eastern Montana College
University of Akron
St. John's University

Appendix C
National Council of Physical Distribution Management Roundtable Locations

HEADQUARTERS

2803 Butterfield Road
Oak Brook, Illinois 60521
(312) 655-0985

ROUNDTABLE LOCATIONS

Atlanta, Georgia
Baltimore/Washington
Boston, Massachusetts
Chicago, Illinois
Cincinnati, Ohio
Cleveland, Ohio
Columbus, Ohio
Dallas, Texas
Houston, Texas
Indianapolis, Indiana
Kansas City, Missouri
Michigan
Milwaukee, Wisconsin
New York, New York
Northern New Jersey
Philadelphia, Pennsylvania
Pittsburgh, Pennsylvania
St. Louis, Missouri
San Francisco, California
Southern California
Twin Cities, Minnesota
Western New York
Westchester County/Lower Connecticut

Appendix D
Traffic Clubs
International
Affiliations

HEADQUARTERS

1040 Woodcock Road
Orlando, Florida 32803
(395) 894-8312

AFFILIATIONS

Alabama

Northeast Traffic and Transportation Club

Arizona

Phoenix Traffic Club
Tucson Transportation Club

Arkansas

Central Arkansas Transportation Club

California

Citrus Belt Traffic Club
Women's Transportation Club of Fresno
Harbor Transportation Club
Women's Transportation Club of Long Beach
Los Angeles Transportation Club
Women's Traffic Club of Los Angeles
Oakland Traffic Club
Women's Traffic Club of Oakland
Progressive Traffic Club
Women's Traffic Club of San Francisco
San Jose Women's Traffic Club
Transportation Club of Southern Alameda County

Valley Transportation Club
North Bay Women's Transportation Club

Canada

Durham Region Transportation Club
Lakeshore Industrial Transportation Club
Traffic Club of Hamilton
Le Club de Trafic de Montreal, Inc.
Montreal Women's Traffic Club
Club de Trafic du Quebec, Inc.
Niagara District Transportation Club
Transportation Club of Toronto
Vancouver Women's Transportation Club

Colorado

Traffic Club of Denver, Inc.

Connecticut

Bridgeport Traffic Association
Bridgeport Women's Transportation Association
Housatonic Valley Transportation Association
Traffic Club of Eastern Connecticut
Central Connecticut Transportation Association
Women's Traffic Association of New Haven County
Women's Travel and Transportation Club of Hartford
Connecticut International Trade Association

Washington, D.C.

The Traffic Club of Washington, D.C.

Delaware

Traffic Club of Wilmington

Florida

Traffic Club of Jacksonville
Women's Traffic Association of Jacksonville
Polk County Traffic Club
Traffic Club of Greater Miami
Traffic and Transportation Club of Panama City
Traffic Club of Tampa

Georgia

Southwest Georgia Traffic Club
Atlanta Women's Traffic Club

Transportation Club of Atlanta
Augusta Traffic and Transportation Club
Northwest Georgia Traffic Club
Columbus Traffic Club
Savannah Women's Transportation Club

Idaho

Treasure Valley Traffic Club
Magic Valley Traffic Club

Illinois

Fox Valley Traffic Club
The Chicago Transportation Club
Traffic Club of Chicago
Women's Traffic Club of Chicago
The Greater Will County Transportation Club
Transportation Club of Little Egypt, Inc.
Transportation Club of Central Illinois

Indiana

Indianapolis Women's Traffic Club
Women's Calumet Traffic Association

Iowa

Professional Women in Transportation
Transportation Club of Des Moines, Inc.
Transportation Club of Sioux City
Women's Transportation Club of Sioux City

Kansas

Mid-Kansas Traffic Club
Traffic Club of Wichita
Wichita Women's Transportation Club

Kentucky

Ky-O-Va Traffic Club
Women's Traffic Club of Louisville
K.I.T.M. Traffic Club

Louisiana

Central Louisiana Traffic and Transportation Club, Inc.
The Traffic and Transportation Club of Greater New Orleans
Women's Traffic and Transportation Club of New Orleans
Traffic and Transportation Club of Shreveport
Women's Traffic Club of Shreveport

Maine

Maine Traffic Club

Maryland

Traffic Club of Baltimore, Inc.
Women's Traffic and Transportation Club of Baltimore
Delmarva Traffic Club, Inc.

Massachusetts

The Transportation Club of New England
Women's Traffic Club of New England
Traffic Clubs of Southeastern Massachusetts, Inc.

Mexico

Club de Trafico de Guadalajara, A.C.
Club de Trafico de Mexico, A.C.
Club de Trafico de Monterrey, A.C.

Michigan

Eastern Michigan Traffic Association
Metropolitan Traffic Clubs
Traffic Club of Detroit
Women's Traffic Club of Detroit
The Motor City Traffic Club of Detroit
Pontiac Traffic Club
Women's Traffic Guild of Detroit
Transportation Association of Michigan

Minnesota

Twin Cities Women's Traffic Club
Transportation Club of Minneapolis and St. Paul

Mississippi

Gulf Coast Traffic Club
Central Mississippi Traffic and Transportation Club, Inc.

Missouri

Traffic and Transportation Club of Kansas City, Inc.
Women's Traffic Club of Greater Kansas City, Inc.
Women's Traffic Club of St. Joseph
Traffic Club of St. Louis, Inc.
Women's Traffic Club of Metropolitan St. Louis

Nebraska

Lincoln Transportation Club
Omaha Transportation Club, Inc.
Women's Transportation Club of Omaha

New Jersey

New Jersey Women's Traffic Club

New Mexico

Albuquerque Transportation Club

New York

Women's Transportation Club of Broome County
Women's Transportation Club of Buffalo
The Traffic Club of New York, Inc.
Women's Traffic Club of New York, Inc.
Transportation Club of Rochester
Women's Transportation Club of Rochester
Transportation Club of Syracuse, Inc.
Women's Traffic Club of Syracuse
Northern New York Transportation Club

North Carolina

Western North Carolina Traffic Club
The Charlotte Traffic and Transportation Club
Charlotte Women's Traffic Club
Central Piedmont Traffic Club
Catawba Valley Traffic Club
High Point Traffic and Transportation Club
Eastern North Carolina Traffic Club
Women's Traffic Club of Winston-Salem
Winston-Salem Traffic Club

Ohio

Cincinnati Traffic Club
Cincinnati Women's Traffic Club
Women's Traffic Club of Cleveland
Columbus Transportation Club
Miami Valley Traffic Club
Toledo Transportation Club

Oklahoma

Women's Transportation Club of Tulsa

Oregon

Portland Traffic Club
Transportation Club of Portland

Pennsylvania

Traffic Club of the Lehigh Valley, Inc.
The Traffic Club of Erie
Women's Traffic Club of Harrisburg
Lancaster Traffic Club, Inc.
Traffic Club of Philadelphia
Women's Traffic Club of Philadelphia
Women's Traffic Club of Pittsburgh
Reading Traffic Club, Inc.
Women's Traffic Club of Reading
Wyoming Valley Traffic Club
Women's Traffic Club of York

South Carolina

Charleston Traffic Club
Women's Transportation Club of Charleston
Columbia Traffic and Transportation Club
Midlands Women's Transportation Club
Piedmont Traffic Club

Tennessee

Chattanooga Transportation Club
Knoxville Traffic and Transportation Club
The Traffic Club of Memphis
Women's Traffic Club of Memphis

Texas

Amarillo Traffic Club
Sabine District Transportation Club
Women's Transportation Club of Golden Triangle
Corpus Christi Traffic Association
Transportation Club of Dallas
Women's Transportation Club of Dallas
Pineywood Transportation Club
Traffic Club of El Paso
The Transportation Club of Ft. Worth
Women's Traffic Club of Ft. Worth
Galveston Texas City Traffic Club
Houston Freight Carriers Association
Houston Traffic Clerks Association
Transportation Club of Houston

Women's Traffic Club of Houston
Traffic Club of East Texas
Transportation Club of Lubbock
San Antonio Traffic Club
Women's Transportation Club of San Antonio
Four States Traffic Club, Inc.

Utah

Transportation Club of Salt Lake City

Vermont

Green Mountain Transportation Club

Virginia

Appalachian Traffic Club
Lynchburg Traffic and Transportation Club
Norfolk-Portsmouth Traffic Club
Women's Traffic Club of Norfolk-Portsmouth
Richmond Traffic Club
Women's Traffic Club of Richmond

Washington

Women's Traffic and Transportation Club of Seattle
The Transportation Club of Tacoma
Women's Traffic Club of Tacoma

West Virginia

Kanawha Valley Transportation Club

Wisconsin

Green Bay Traffic Club
Fox River Valley Traffic Club
Milwaukee Traffic Club
Transportation Club of Milwaukee, Inc.
Women's Traffic Club of Milwaukee
Traffic Club of Racine, Inc.

Selected Bibliography

BENSON, LEE. *Merchants, Farmers, and Railroads: Railroad Regulation and New York Politics, 1850–1887*. Cambridge, Mass.: Harvard University Press, 1955.

BOWERSOX, DONALD J. *Logistical Management*. 2nd Ed. New York: Macmillan Publishing Co., Inc., 1978.

BUCK, SOLON JUSTUS. *The Granger Movement*. Lincoln, Neb.: University of Nebraska Press, copyright by Harvard University Press, 1913.

DAVIS, GRANT M., MARTIN T. FARRIS, and JACK J. HOLDER. *Management of Transportation Carriers*. New York: Praeger Publishers, 1975.

DEARING, CHARLES L., and WILFRED OWEN. *National Transportation Policy*. Washington, D.C.: The Brookings Institution, 1949.

FAIR, MARVIN L., and ERNEST W. WILLIAMS, JR. *Economics of Transportation and Logistics*. Dallas: Business Publications, Inc., 1975.

FERGUSON, MAXWELL. *State Regulation of Railroads in the South*. New York: AMS Press, 1968.

FLOOD, KENNETH U. *Traffic Management*. 3rd Ed. Dubuque, Iowa: Wm. C. Brown Publishers, 1975.

GERMANE, GAYTON E., NICHOLAS A. GLASKOWSKY, and J. J. HESKETT. *Highway Transportation Management*. New York: McGraw-Hill Book Company, Inc., 1963.

GUANDOLO, JOHN. *Transportation Law*. 2nd Ed. Dubuque, Iowa: Wm. C. Brown Company, Publishers, 1965.

HAEFELE, EDWIN T. *Transport and National Goals*. Washington, D.C.: The Brookings Institution, 1969.

HARPER, DONALD V. *Transportation in America: Users, Carriers, Government*. Englewood Cliffs, N.J.: Prentice-Hall, Inc., 1978.

HAZARD, JOHN L. *Transportation: Management, Economics, Policy*. Cambridge, Maryland: Cornell Maritime Press, 1977.

HUDSON, WILLIAM J., and JAMES A. CONSTANTIN. *Motor Transportation: Principles and Practices*. New York: The Ronald Press Company, 1958.

KIRKLAND, EDWARD CHASE. *Men, Cities, and Transportation: A Study in New England History, 1820–1900*. Cambridge, Mass.: Harvard University Press, 1948.

KNORST, WILLIAM J. *Transportation and Traffic Management*. Vol. I. 11th Ed. Chicago: College of Advanced Traffic, 1968.

KOLKO, GABRIEL. *Railroads and Regulation*. Princeton, N.J. Princeton University Press, 1965.

LOCKLIN, D. PHILIP. *Economics of Transportation*. 7th Ed. Homewood, Ill.: Richard D. Irwin, Inc., 1972.

LIEB, ROBERT C. *Transportation: The Domestic System*. Reston, Va.: Reston Publishing Co., Inc., 1978.

NORTON, HUGH S. *National Transportation Policy: Formulation and Implementation*. Berkeley, Calif.: McCutchan Publishing Corp., 1966.

PEGRUM, DUDLEY F. *Transportation Economics and Public Policy.* 3rd Ed. Homewood, Ill.: Richard D. Irwin, Inc., 1973.

RINGWALT, J. L. *Development of Transportation Systems in the United States.* New York: Johnson Reprint Corporation, 1888.

SAMPSON, ROY J., and MARTIN T. FARRIS. *Domestic Transportation: Practice, Theory, and Policy.* 4th Ed. Boston: Houghton Mifflin Company, 1979.

TAFF, CHARLES A. *Commercial Motor Transportation.* Cambridge, Md.: Cornell Maritime Press, Inc., 1975.

———. *Management of Physical Distribution and Transportation.* 6th Ed. Homewood, Ill.: Richard D. Irwin, Inc., 1978.

WILSON, G. LLOYD. *Interstate Commerce and Traffic Law.* New York: Prentice-Hall, Inc., 1947.

WOOD, DONALD F., and JAMES C. JOHNSON. *Contemporary Transportation.* Tulsa, Oklahoma: PPC Books, 1980.

WYCKOFF, D. DARYL. *Railroad Management.* Lexington, Mass.: D. C. Heath and Company, 1976.

Name Index

393

Subject Index